The Banjo of the Bush

OTHER BOOKS BY CLEMENT SEMMLER

For the Uncanny Man: Essays, Mainly Literary
Barcroft Boake: Poet of the Stockwhip
A.B. "Banjo" Paterson
Kenneth Slessor
A.B. Paterson — Great Australian
The Art of Brian James and Other Essays on Australian Literature
Douglas Stewart
The A.B.C.: Aunt Sally and Sacred Cow

Edited

Stories of the Riverina
Literary Australia
Coast to Coast 1965–66
The World of Banjo Paterson
Twentieth Century Australian Literary Criticism
A Frank Hardy Swag

The Banjo of the Bush

The Life and Times
of A.B. "Banjo" Paterson

by

CLEMENT SEMMLER

UNIVERSITY OF QUEENSLAND PRESS

First edition 1966 (reprinted 1967)

Second edition 1974 (reprinted 1984)

University of Queensland Press
Box 42, St Lucia, Queensland, Australia

Typeset by University of Queensland Press
Printed by The Dominion Press-Hedges & Bell,
Maryborough, 3465

Distributed in the UK, Europe, the Middle East, Africa, and the
Caribbean by Prentice Hall International, International Book
Distributors Ltd, 66 Wood Lane End, Hemel Hempstead, Herts.,
England

Distributed in the USA and Canada by Technical Impex
Corporation, 5 South Union Street, Lawrence, Mass. 01843 USA

Cataloguing in Publication Data

National Library of Australia

Semmler, Clement, 1914-   .
   The Banjo of the bush.

   Previously published: St. Lucia, Qld.: University
   of Queensland Press, 1974.
   Bibliography.
   Includes index.

   1. Paterson, A.B. (Andrew Barton), 1864-1941.
   2. Poets, Australian — Biography. I. Title.

A821'.2

Library of Congress

Semmler, Clement.
   The Banjo of the bush.

   Bibliography: p.
   Includes index.
   1. Paterson, A.B. (Andrew Barton), 1864-1941 — Biography.
2. Poets, Australian — 19th century — Biography.
I. Paterson, A.B. (Andrew Barton), 1864-1941. II. Title.
PR9619.3.P28Z88   1984   821 [B]   84-3550
ISBN 0-7022-1756-5

To those bush pioneers,
including my forbears in the Murray Mallee,
who farmed the marginal lands of the Australian outback
and, in the face of drought, heat and dust,
achieved in the end a kind of subsistence.

And the bush has friends to meet him, and their kindly voices greet him
    In the murmur of the breezes and the river on its bars,
And he sees the vision splendid of the sunlit plains extended,
    And at night the wondrous glory of the everlasting stars.
— A. B. PATERSON, "Clancy of the Overflow"

Contents

Illustrations

Preface to Second Edition

I suppose the most significant happening in the Banjo Paterson story since the first edition of this book appeared in 1966 was the publication in 1973 of Richard Magoffin's *Fair Dinkum Matilda*. In writing of the controversy about the origins of "Waltzing Matilda" I had concluded: "[It] is of all bush songs, the best remembered. And while there may be reason for doubt about its musical origins, there need be none about the words and their writer — A. B. "Banjo" Paterson."

Magoffin, Queenslander and "bushie", bush balladist and scholar, has earned his particular place in our literary history with an absorbing piece of splendidly documented research which proves once and for all that, as he simply and finally puts it, "A. B. Paterson wrote the words of 'Waltzing Matilda' at Dagworth Station, near Winton, Queensland, in 1895, to a memorized version of 'Craigielea' played by Christina Macpherson".

I must record, too, my gratitude to my friend and literary colleague Colin Roderick, Professor of English at James Cook University, Townsville, and Australia's foremost Henry Lawson authority, who, in a review of *The Banjo of the Bush* in *Australian Book Review* in February 1967, brought to light some fascinating additional information on Paterson's boyhood and later life which most valuably supplemented the rather limited biographical information to which I had access.

This included a biographical note in the Melbourne *Review of Reviews,* when *The Man From Snowy River and Other Verses* first appeared in 1895. It was written by "a well-informed correspondent" who, Professor Roderick suspects, was Paterson's publisher, George Robertson. It revealed that in his boyhood Paterson used to visit his father's property in Queensland, delighting

> to turn out along with the station "hands" and take a
> share in the mustering, drafting, branding, washing, and
> shearing during the day, and at night steal off to the men's
> huts to hear them tell regal lies of "back-block"
> adventures, of desperate rides and wonderful feats on road
> and racecourse, until he became imbued with the very
> spirit of the bush and thoroughly acquainted with what
> may be termed the "back-block vernacular".

But much more interesting and illuminating was an account by Bernard Espinasse in *Table Talk* (31 January 1896) of an interview with Paterson — then a practising lawyer in Sydney — which Professor

Roderick also discovered, and which told much of Paterson the man, the origins of his verse, and his attitudes to bush life. Espinasse wrote:

> I found Mr. Paterson surrounded by legal weapons. Sheaves of blue foolscap, folded lengthwise and tied with red tape, lay at his elbow, and on the desk, opened at the 252nd page, lay a volume of Max Nordau's *Degeneration*. The Australian Joachim Millar is a hater of shams and conventional hypocrisies, and an admirer of Nordau, whom he is reading studiously. (Again the irreconcilable — poetry and Max Nordau!) On learning the purport of my visit, Mr. Paterson very courteously consented to be interviewed on the spot, a considerable violation of a rule to which he invariably adheres, that of keeping his professional (i.e., legal) position strictly apart from his literary duality . . .
>
> In appearance, Mr. Paterson gives but little clue to his identity for the average and uninformed observer to "gush" over. About the middle height, loosely built, with the legs of a horseman — at the first glance — and the long arm and prehensile hand that is nature's gift "out back", he is, perhaps, the last man whose forte — meeting him for the first time — you would be likely to say lay in the pen. That is, till you looked at his face. And then possibly the first thing to strike you in the dark-complexioned, mobile countenance would be the abundant evidences of humour. But the eyes are once more the windows of the soul. Quick moving, large and bright, they carry in their depths a light which promises well for the future of another and still better *Clancy of the Overflow* . . .

Paterson then discussed his literary beginnings and attitudes:

> "I began to write for the *Sydney Bulletin* about eight years ago. My first contribution was an account of a glove fight! After that I sent in some sentimental verses, which were printed, somewhat to my surprise. After that I began to pay more attention to writing, but always as a pastime. In 1888 I wrote *Clancy of the Overflow* and *Pardon, the Son of Reprieve,* and woke up to the fact that I was becoming known as a writer of verse, and from that time forth I seem to have 'caught on' with Australian readers everywhere. I often receive letters of congratulation from men out back who have read my pieces. You see, I *understand* them and their lives, and they know it. I've got a number of presents too from perfectly unknown donors, probably bushmen, who simply address 'The Banjo, Sydney', and it finds me . . .
>
> I went in a great deal for athletics when I was younger. I've won a number of steeple-chases as an amateur rider. And I really think I was prouder of those triumphs than

I've been of anything I've written. Polo is another sport I'm very fond of, which, as you say, accounts for the 'Geebung Polo Club' . . .

I am very particular about my work. It is not enough for me that a line scans correctly, or that it even contains a thought, it must satisfy me. And sometimes a verse takes a lot of re-arranging before it does satisfy me. No I can't say I'm an 'inspired pen-pusher', but my lines come easily enough. Though I take a lot of pains over them before I think them good enough for print. I don't know that I'm wholly satisfied with any of my work. I always think I can do better. My bush pieces I think are the best I've done. Though I know a good deal about riding, and at one time was hardly ever off a horse I haven't done much in the way of racing stuff. In that kind of verse you can't get away from a likeness to Lindsay Gordon. I attach most value to pieces like *The Wind's Message,* at least I hope they're new."

He explained the origin of his pen-name and talked about his books.

"It has nothing to do with my second initial — B. — as some people seem to think. By the way, my first name has been misprinted. It is not Arthur, but Andrew. 'Banjo' was the name of a horse I once rode. I was at a loss for a signature for my first contribution, not wishing to put my own name, and Banjo being in my mind at the time, I just slapped that down, and, somehow, it stuck to me.

Eh! my book? Oh! well, it was the *Bulletin* made me publish, and I've done very well out of it. I owe a great deal to Archibald. If it hadn't been for him I should never have come before the public as an author at all. My second book is in the press now, but I've not quite finished my part of the work. It will deal with the rough aspects of Queensland cattle life. I'm going to spend my vacation in the North to study types and brush up my bush know-ledge. You can't write about a thing unless you know it thoroughly, or at least, you shouldn't."

Finally Espinasse got from Paterson his reactions to contemporary literature — and, indeed, to Australian painting.

As to the effect upon him of contemporary literature, Mr. Paterson frankly acknowledges that he seldom reads verse, and that when he does he prefers the simplest forms of poetry. Involved phrases and obscure ideas, however finely expressed, do not commend themselves to him. It is there-fore hardly surprising to hear that his favourites are Tenny-son and Longfellow. In the way of prose his library com-prises a miscellaneous collection which would delight the heart of a bibliophile. Some of the books on its shelves are over 150 years old. Darwin's *Origin of Species* is cheek by jowl with Sterne's *Sentimental Journey,* in the rare old binding and quaint black letter of a bygone age. A very rare copy of *The History of an Atom* (long out of print, and a veritable book-hunter's treasure-trove), is wedged between two volumes of *A Golden Shanty!* . . .

Mr. Paterson (who, by-the-bye, is just into the thirties), is a moderate smoker, almost a non-drinker, and owns to a fancy for dogs. He has already spent a good deal of money on paintings by local artists, and intends to add very considerably to his present art gallery. One fine water-colour sketch of a mob of wild horses by Mahony occupies the pride of place on his walls . . .

Professor Roderick also confirms that the date of publication of *The Man From Snowy River and Other Verses* was, in fact, 19 October 1895 (setting right a contradiction in my book between "October 1895", p. 68 and "early in that year", p. 88) and has established, too, that rather than acting as a legal adviser for Lawson only in 1899 (as I implied) Paterson had drafted agreements for him with his publishers, Angus and Robertson, as early as 1895.

For the rest, I take the welcome opportunity to thank the many hundreds of readers who wrote to me from all parts of Australia with corrections and pieces of information as well as appreciations — thus testifying to the extraordinary affection in which Banjo Paterson is still obviously held by his fellow-countrymen. "Mrs. B. MacSmith", referred to in my Foreword should, correctly, read "Mrs. L. Mac Smith". Edward Fisher of Surrey Hills, Victoria (formerly No. 1878 of the 6th Light Horse Regiment in World War I) supplied me with details (most valuable to a future biographer or anthologist) of hitherto undiscovered verses and prose articles Paterson wrote for the regimental magazine *The Kia Ora Cooee* which was written and edited by troops of the Australian and New Zealand Light Horse units on desert duty. These included "The Army Mules", a ballad which his fellow soldiers rated as up to the standard of "The Man from Snowy River"; indeed, one of them commented: "Someone must have sent Banjo a niner laced with water from the Snowy River." And I was especially delighted to receive from A. B. Paterson's son, Hugh, a most graceful letter in which he commented inter alia: "He did not talk very much about himself and I think it fair to say that you told me a lot about him which I did not know." I am very grateful to Hugh Paterson for allowing me to use several hitherto unpublished photographs of his father, which are included in this second edition.

Finally, I thank my dear friend Maie Casey (so doughty a champion of Australian literature and art and a notable contributor herself) for allowing me to reprint her original Introduction, and Lloyd O'Neil, my 1966 Lansdowne publisher, for so generously ceding me the paperback rights of my book. This second edition of

The Banjo of the Bush remains basically unchanged, except for additional illustrations and the inclusion of this Preface.

March 1974   CLEMENT SEMMLER

Foreword to First Edition

IT ALWAYS SEEMED to me a regrettable lack in our literature that a detailed biographical study of A. B. Paterson had not hitherto been attempted. What has happened in our time, as H. P. Heseltine remarked in an essay in *Meanjin* during 1964 on the occasion of the centenary of Paterson's birth, is that we have retained from his literary career a number of well-loved poems, but not an image of the man who wrote them. Paterson made little effort, apart from his published work, to ensure that his memory was perpetuated — a mark, of course, of his monumental modesty. Nor does biographical material come easily from family sources, and while one respects the reservations thus involved, the task of doing homage to a man who was a truly great Australian in character, deed, and achievement is hardly thereby made the easier.

I am the more indebted therefore to those who assisted me over a period of some three years of collecting and noting biographical and personal details. There were those who remembered Paterson and gave freely of their recollections — C. H. Bateson, Vince Kelly, M. H. Ellis, the late Sir Norman Kater, Sir Edward Knox, Sir Daryl Lindsay, Peter Macgregor, Mrs Sylvia Palmer and especially Miss Florence Earle Hooper who, some twenty years ago, in the columns of the Yass *Tribune Courier* attempted the first biographical assessment of Paterson and whose material help and encouragement during the time I was writing this book I most gratefully acknowledge.

For help with references and in numerous aspects of my research, I gratefully record my thanks to the National Library and the Australian War Memorial in Canberra, and to the *Sydney Morning Herald* Library. Angus and Robertson, Paterson's publishers, gave me willingly the freedom of their house, making available out-of-print texts, letters, records, and through the memory of Miss Grace Harvey, the unpublished ms. of *Racehorses and Racing in Australia*. It is a particular pleasure to me therefore that the "old firm's" imprint appears on the overseas editions of this book. But most of all, in this category of institutions and their staffs, I thank the Mitchell Library in Sydney; I do not believe this book could have been written without its resources and the unfailing and courteous help of its people. The riches of this truly magnificent store-house of Australiana are freely available — I was not the first and assuredly will not be the last of those who, hoping to make some contribution to Australian literature, have profited from the foresight of its founder, David Scott Mitchell.

Oscar Mendelsohn generously let me read and quote from the manuscript of his *A Waltz with Matilda* and corresponded with me on certain points arising; Sir Charles Moses after he retired from the General

Managership of the Australian Broadcasting Commission gave me several letters from Paterson he found in his files; the reminiscences of Mrs B. MacSmith of the Orange district about Paterson's forbears and early life came to me through an interview recorded by Athol and Margaret Emerton, through whose efforts also I was able to read a play by Elizabeth Stanford Thomas based on these reminiscences.

Not least, there were my colleagues of the A.B.C. who helped me in many ways — in turning up books, scripts, correspondence and documents, making available the results of their own research, and contributing various anecdotes gleaned and remembered. There are too many to list but I thank them most sincerely. From the A.B.C. archives, by the way, came to the light the most interesting series of Paterson's radio scripts, *The Land of Adventure* from which quotations are made in this book.

Finally I was greatly assisted by the books, essays and studies listed in the Bibliography at the end of this book, quotations from which, where they occur, are acknowledged in the text. Particular acknowledgement is gratefully made to Angus and Robertson Ltd. for permission to quote from Paterson's verse and prose; to the *Sydney Morning Herald* whose columns carried so much valuable Paterson writing and forged a memorable link between a great Australian and a great newspaper; and to Mirror Newspapers Ltd. for quotations from the *Evening News*. I must mention too that there was a group of books I found to be essential texts to a study of Paterson in his times — and I list especially Russel Ward's *The Australian Legend*, John Manifold's *Who Wrote the Ballads*, Vance Palmer's *The Legend of the Nineties*, A. W. Jose's *The Romantic Nineties*, Norman Lindsay's *Bohemians of the Bulletin* and H. M. Green's superbly detailed *History of Australian Literature*. And always at my back, that most splendid of repositories of the literature of the period, the files of the *Bulletin*.

CLEMENT SEMMLER

Introduction

As MANY other Australians will be, I am most grateful to Clement Semmler for his comprehensive and penetrating book — The Work, Life and Times of A. B. Paterson. I have been glued to it in its least acceptable form, galley sheets, coiling and uncoiling myself through it with excitement and close attention.

My father, who was a Melbourne surgeon brought up at Longwood in Victoria, gave me the first taste of Banjo Paterson. I grew up in that period of childhood when men sang to us when we wandered in and out of their rooms while they dressed; if they did not sing they recited, or perhaps spoke, poetry and verse. The sounds brought a sense of action and rhythm: the lines were simple racy statements that evoked a life we understood and sometimes shared. Many men then sang, as they still do in the open country, and they quoted verse to bring them pleasure, to keep themselves awake, or sometimes to send themselves to sleep.

Most Australians are aware of Banjo Paterson. He is the great link between the Australia of the eighteen nineties — a period forgotten, unknown, in detail though not in essence — and now. He was masculine, robust, a writer for men, one of the first writers of ballads to emerge as someone who belonged to this country, one of the first Australian coins out of the mint. He was no longer the man transplanted from the Old Country trying not to feel homesick and alien in a subtle and often hostile land. Australia was the home of Paterson and he loved the bush and knew it, as he knew the kind of men he encountered there.

For the great armies of city dwellers that we now have I cannot resist quoting from his ballad "In Defence of the Bush":

> For the rain and drought and sunshine
>   Make no changes in the street,
> In the sullen line of buildings
>   And the ceaseless tramp of feet.

We are nationally bound together by Paterson's ballad of "Waltzing Matilda" where the music and the verses, polished and slightly altered from his original words by common usage, come together into a kind of vigorous perfection. I first heard it, myself, consciously, in Canberra in 1932, sung from the top of our Duntroon house by a builder from Quean-beyan, Jimmy Beecher, who was mending the roof. He altered the words a bit, as many have done, to suit his own taste and the words floated down to me, clear and rich: "Waltzing Matilda, Matilda, my *Darling!* You'll come a-waltzing Matilda, with me!"

Some of the value of this book lies in Paterson's descriptions of the life and persons he met in the Boer war where he had gone as war correspondent; and later in Egypt in the First World War where he was in charge of horses. His passport to both countries was his knowledge of horses, and from South Africa he revealed the same ability to pick young men as potential winners (Allenby, Haig, Churchill) as he did colts and fillies.

In Bloemfontein in 1900 he asked Rudyard Kipling, whom he had come to know, how he as an author obtained his material. Kipling replied: "Some of it I saw; some of it I was. As for the rest, I asked questions." This might have been said by Paterson. Through the extracts quoted from him while away from Australia he emerges in perspective as a man of exceptional character and perception, and as a superb writer. Much that he wrote in those years is of first class importance and fits into history. One can scarcely wait to read the expected edition of A. B. Paterson's prose writings which are to include material as yet uncollected and unpublished.

I had the pleasure of meeting Paterson once myself in the Hotel Canberra in the 1930's. This meeting was to me of great interest, of course, since my father was a fan of his and so was I. But I was also interested because one of his nieces, Ruth Whiting (née Lumsdaine and a daughter of his sister Florence) was a much admired friend of mine and I looked at him therefore with special visual attention, hoping to find in him some trace of the noble qualities I admired in her — which I did find. Niece and uncle were dark-complexioned with sad brilliant eyes, fine aristocratic bones and elegant carriage. They had personality without too much emphasis; the strength was there but it was contained.

Clement Semmler's book is a much needed extension of the character of a man admired and loved by many Australians. Banjo Paterson was a great writer of ballads, at his best a true poet, and a prose writer of exceptional ability. This book gives us also a picture of the Australian times in which he lived with his intelligent, lively and dinkum friends, without bunk. It reveals their staying power, energy, directness and dry laconic wit — qualities we like to think we still possess.

Canberra 1966   MAIE CASEY

CHAPTER I

Paterson and the Bush Ballad

> *All human beings not utterly savage long for some infor-*
> *mation about past times and are delighted by narratives*
> *which present pictures to the eye of the mind. But it is*
> *only in very enlightened countries that books are readily*
> *accessible. Metrical composition which in a highly civilized*
> *nation is a mere luxury is, in nations imperfectly civilized,*
> *almost a necessity of life, and is valued less on account*
> *of the pleasure which it gives to the ear than on account*
> *of the help which it gives to the memory. A man who can*
> *invent or embellish an interesting story and put it into a*
> *form which others very easily retain in their recollection*
> *will always be highly esteemed by a people eager for amuse-*
> *ment and information, but destitute of libraries. Such is*
> *the origin of ballad poetry, a species of composition which*
> *scarcely ever fails to spring up and flourish in every society*
> *at a certain point in the progress towards refinement.*
>
> —LORD MACAULAY: quoted by A. B. Paterson in
> the Introduction to his *Old Bush Songs*.[1]

> *. . . While living in the bush I used to hear a great lot of*
> *bush songs. "The Wild Colonial Boy", "Dunn, Gilbert*
> *and Ben Hall", "The Squatter's Man", "The Old Bark*
> *Hut", and so forth — I would like to find out something*
> *about these and get the words . . .*
>
> —A. B. PATERSON.[2]

A. B. PATERSON AND the Australian bush ballad crossed at many points
during his life, and the involvement seems so complete over this distance
of years that the ballad and Paterson have, in the minds of most,
coalesced. But there is a cardinal intersection where we can, as it were,
dissociate the two parties — where we can see the distinction more clearly
between the ballad as anonymous bush song and the ballad as literary
composition; where we appreciate the better Paterson's activities as
balladist *and* student of the ballad; and, above all, where we can discover,
if we are to understand properly Paterson's contribution to our poetry
and, more important, do it justice, some of the historical significance
and the development of the only form of traditional literature — the
first authentic voice of song — that Australia can claim in its brief two
hundred years as a civilized, or at least settled, country. This point of
intersection was the publication in 1905 of *Old Bush Songs*, collected

and edited by A. B. Paterson, then forty-one years of age.

The balladist who owed so much of the enthusiastic readership of his verses to the forms and appetites already established, who had found abundant nourishment for his talent in the virgin outback soil of plain and bushland and had thereby cropped richly for some twenty years, now put back that which enabled this very soil to produce other notable and distinctively Australian harvests of literature in the years to follow. For none can deny the influence on our poetry of this century of the balladic undercurrent of the 1880s and the 1890s. "I hope," wrote Paterson in the introduction to his collection, "to rescue these rough bush ballads from oblivion." He was the first to attempt this, and even had he written nothing himself that endured, he would occupy an honoured place in the history of our literature for that achievement alone. In what has become a modern renaissance, he was our first folk-song collector. Fifty years later Nancy Keesing and Douglas Stewart in their anthology *Old Bush Songs* wrote, "It would not have been possible to complete this book without the collection of A. B. Paterson," which "was the nucleus of this book and his method has served as a model for us."

But as well as collecting and writing ballads, Paterson made yet another memorable contribution to our folk-music, as will be examined in more detail later in this book. Some of his ballads went *back* into folk-lore; he reversed the process, even in his lifetime, whereby usually ballads as sung or recited are eventually collected and put into print. His ballads, printed first, went into circulation by word of mouth, and with music composed to them, or to existing airs, finished up as songs of the outback in the hands of people who had never read a line of them in print.

Paterson, in considering the bush songs he collected, took the view that sixty or seventy years in Australian history were equivalent in density of action, turbulence and development to three hundred years in the life of an older and settled nation. He saw a parallel between the Australian hinterland practically bereft of communications, and England, Scotland and Ireland before printing was in common use. Above all, he remarked a progression in the subject matter of the bush songs having a chronological relevance and related, especially in the latter stages, to the changing economic circumstances of the times, and the position of the bush workers and small farmers as against the wealthy squatters.

In the "crude, early days" as Paterson called them, land was cheap and to spare, and labour in keen demand. As for this workforce, before the gold rushes of the 1850s at least half the population of Australia was of Irish extraction, and this proportion extended to the settlers and nomads of the bush. The bush songs thus showed the influence of Irish street ballads, and Irish names frequently appeared. Paterson noted that "the mixture of Irish wit and pathos" lent itself to the effective singing of the songs, and his own ballads consciously reflected this, in spirit and substance, with titles like "Tommy Corrigan", "Gilhooley's Estate", "Mulligan's Mare" and "Father Riley's Horse" (" . . . the folks were mostly Irish round about . . . ").* Names like Clancy, Kiley, Regan and Murphy recur.

Among the bush songs he collected Paterson was especially fond of "Paddy Malone in Australia" — an Irish immigrant's account of his adventures in the Australian outback —

> Wid a man called a squatter I soon got a place, sure,
> He'd a beard like a goat, and such whiskers, Ohone!
> And he said — as he peeped through the hair on his faitures —
> That he liked the appearance of Paddy Malone.
> Wid him I agreed to go up to his station,
> Saying abroad in the bush you'll find yourself at home.
> I liked his proposal, and 'out hesitation
> Signed my name wid a X that spelt Paddy Malone.
>   Oh, Paddy Malone, you're no scholard, Ohone!
>   Sure, I made a criss-cross that spelt Paddy Malone.
>
> A-herding my sheep in the bush, as they call it —
> It was no bush at all, but a mighty great wood,
> Wid all the big trees that were small bushes one time,
> A long time ago, faith! I s'pose 'fore the flood.
> To find out this big bush one day I went further,
> The trees grew so thick that I couldn't, Ohone!
> I tried to go back then, but that I found harder,
> And bothered and lost was poor Paddy Malone.
> Oh, Paddy Malone, through the bush he did roam!
> What a Babe in the Wood was poor Paddy Malone.

— and of "Paddy's Letter, 1857" with a similar theme:

> 'Tis a beautiful country to practise economy.
> Though the houses out here are not quite waterproof,
> But they're illigant houses for studying astronomy —
> You can lie on your back and read stars through the roof.

Paterson noted that the latter was sung to an old tune called "Barney O'Keefe, 1848".

The date is interesting because it is doubtful if any of these surviving bush songs were written much before the beginning of the 1800s. The earliest of these were the convict songs, and here we see the emergence of the first Australian ballad-heroes — a logical outcome in this case of the hatred of authority — among the *currency* lads, the community of common folk comprising emancipated convicts and Australian-born colonists to whom Australia, and no other country, was "home".

The most widely known of this group of songs was "Bold Jack Donahoe". The version which Paterson set down began:

---

* In this connection one recalls the tribes of Doyles and Donahoes who constituted a type of lawless bush element in Paterson's novel *An Outback Marriage*.

'Twas of a valiant highwayman and outlaw of disdain
Who'd scorn to live in slavery or wear a convict's chain;
His name it was Jack Donahoe of courage and renown —
He'd scorn to live in slavery or humble to the Crown.

Paterson noted that "The Wild Colonial Boy", which he also included
in his collection, had a common chorus with "Bold Jack Donahoe". But
he did not include many others of this type, and it was left to collectors in
much more recent years[3] to bring to light other convict and bushranger
songs. It is an interesting sidelight on Paterson that he wrote only two
or three ballads (one of them "In the Stable", most unsympathetic in
tone) about bushrangers. This is not because he was without first-hand
knowledge of bushrangers and their ways. Apart from his study of the
bush songs he collected, he relates that as a small boy he went to school
at Binalong with the young descendants of the bushranger Gilbert and
thus learnt much of the lore (although John Manifold has subsequently
pointed out[4] that Gilbert died unmarried, and that it is more likely that
Paterson sat alongside the "young Dunns"). Dunn, a bushranger scarcely
less notorious, is canonized jointly in the song "Dunn, Gilbert and Ben
Hall". Again, in compiling his bush songs, Paterson had undoubtedly
drawn on a number of ballads written down by one Jack Bradshaw,* self-
styled "the last of the bushrangers", who used to proclaim his deeds to
sceptical Sunday afternoon audiences in the Sydney Domain during the
1890s; it is quite probable that Paterson had contact with him personally.

But there was a strong streak of propriety in Paterson's make-up, and
he would not have been disposed to have given that same adulation to the
exploits of lawbreakers which the anonymous composers and singers of
these bush songs did, and which, in our own time, is extended by cinema
addicts, television-viewers, and readers of pulp magazines to the bushranger equivalents of our modern society — gangsters and crime czars,
and mysterious agents who operate just beyond the pale of legality. It is
interesting to recall the views of one Cunningham, a Royal Naval
surgeon, who conducted four shiploads of convicts to New South Wales
in the early 1820s. He came to the conclusion later on that ballad-singing
was an important cause of bushranging: ". . . the vanity of being talked
of, I verily believe," he wrote, "leads many foolish fellows to join in this
kind of life — songs being often made about their exploits by their
sympathising brethren". Certainly Paterson in all his ballads was more
concerned with the action, colour, courage and humour emerging from
bush life than with what one might call the questionable element.

But it remains true that the old bush songs championed the underdog;
it was a natural transition to the anti-social hero, the bushranger, who

---

* Bradshaw, Dublin born, died in 1937 at the age of ninety-one. He wrote two books
(in fact collections of pamphlets) : *The True History of the Australian Bushrangers,
by Jack Bradshaw who was Personally Acquainted with them All* and *Highway Robbery
under Arms without Shedding Blood* together with *Twenty Years of Prison Life in the
Gaols of N.S.W. by Jack Bradshaw the last of the Australian Bushrangers.* His chief
claim to fame was to have devised an idea of holding up a bank with a tiger snake
tied to a broomstick, so that no charge could ultimately be laid for "robbery under
arms"!

would, in the words of "The Wild Colonial Boy", "never rob a hearty chap that acted on the square". H. M. Green noted in his *History of Australian Literature* the parallel with Robin Hood and the English outlaw ballads, the paradox that, with all the implied contempt for law and order (and the depiction of police as stupid, cowardly and only successful by force of numbers), the profession of bushranging was regarded as compatible with genuine loyalty to the British crown (a theme, indeed, that Sir Walter Scott developed in *Ivanhoe*). Thus we have artless lines like:

> . . . we'll sit and sing Long Live the Queen,
> Dunn, Gilbert and Ben Hall!

Here there is mateship as well as loyalty — and enough has by now been written about the mateship tradition in the development of Australian egalitarianism. But a corollary of these general tendencies in the subject matter of our early bush songs was the hostility (in an anticapitalistic sense) of the poor to the rich, the latter being the squatter class.

Paterson noted this as the second stage in the progression referred to. With the squatters firmly established as a class, the bush-workers found it harder to live on the wages offered; moreover, what was expected of them made life a drudgery. "The Squatter's Man", included in his collection (with the note that "ten–ten" connoted the weekly ration of ten pounds of flour and meat supplied) is as good an example as any:

> " 'Tis now I want a useful cove
> To stop at home and not to rove.
> The scamps go about — a regular drove —
> I s'pose you're one of the clan?
> But I'll give ten–ten, sugar an' tea;
> Ten bob a week, if you'll suit me,
> And very soon I hope you'll be
> A handy squatter's man.

> "At daylight you must milk the cows,
> Make butter, cheese, an' feed the sows,
> Put on the kettle, the cook arouse,
> And clean the family shoes.
> The stable an' sheep yard clean out,
> And always answer when we shout,
> With 'Yes, ma'am', and 'No, sir', mind your mouth;
> And my youngsters don't abuse."

> He sent me to an old bark hut,
> Inhabited by a greyhound slut,
> Who put her fangs through my poor fut,
> And, snarling, off she ran.
> So once more I'm looking for a job,
> Without a copper in my fob.
> With Ben Hall or Gardiner I'd rather rob,
> Than be a squatter's man.

Then came the ballads which, according to Paterson, commemorated the days of the free selectors — when the large holdings and runs of the squatters were thrown open to purchase. Now it might be thought strange that Paterson could comment on this without bitterness. When he was a small boy his father, with a bank loan, had bought Illalong Station in the Yass district not far from the Lambing Flat (now Young) diggings. But trouble with drought, and especially with free selectors (the Free Selection Act had just been passed and droves of selectors converged on the better-watered parts of the property), caused the bank to foreclose and the Patersons had to give up the property. Yet Banjo Paterson had much sympathy for the selectors and small farmers, which led him as a young man in Sydney to write a polemical tract (in Henry George vein) on the iniquities of the existing systems of land ownership, and especially the "cruel mistake" of land being granted away in fee simple. Therefore, when he wrote about the bush songs that dealt with the free selectors, he described some of them as "paeans of victory" and seemed to applaud this fact. So he set down for the first time songs which have become classics in our folk-lore: "The Free Selector — A Song of 1861", "The Eumerella Shore"—an idyll of honest Australian roguery—and "The Broken Down Squatter" — which gave the other side of the story:

> When the country was cursed with the drought at its worst
> And the cattle were dying in scores,
> Though down on my luck I kept up my pluck,
> Thinking justice might temper the laws.
> But the farce had been played, and the Government aid
> Ain't extended to squatters, old son;
> When my dollars were spent they doubled the rent,
> And resumed the best half of the run.
> Chorus: For the banks are all broken, they say,
>   And the merchants are all up a tree.
>   When the bigwigs are brought to the Bankruptcy Court,
>   What chance for a squatter like me?

Paterson also collected many songs which might be regarded as of this vintage, reflecting the novelty of bush life and which John Manifold classifies as "Jackaroo Songs" — obviously written by these "usually educated young men studying the art and mystery of station management"[5] who liked to think of themselves as fully fledged stockmen or bushmen. These included "The Stockmen of Australia", "The Australian Stockman", "The Dying Stockman" and others. Then there are those that might be termed occupational songs since they cover the whole range of the emerging class of bush-workers: shearers, drovers, teamsters and the like ("Mustering Song", "The Overlanders", "The Murrumbidgee Shearer"), even unto the humble swagman, forever fixed in another treasure which Paterson unearthed, "The Old Bark Hut":

> If you should leave it open, and the flies should find your meat,
> They'll scarcely leave a single piece that's fit for man to eat.
> But you mustn't curse, nor grumble—what won't fatten will fill up—

For what's out of sight is out of mind in an old bark hut.
Chorus: In an old bark hut, in an old bark hut.
For what's out of sight is out of mind in an old bark hut.

In most of this latter group of songs the characteristic Australian humour stemming from physical hardship realistically observed — ranging from the lighthearted to the wry and sardonic — inevitably makes its appearance. This is especially noticeable in the final phase of this bush-song cycle to which Paterson drew attention in his collection — the free selector as employer of labour (a rather droll situation since now the wheel had come full circle). This gave plenty of scope to the bush humorists among the anonymous composers of these songs, especially when they sang of the "cockies" (the small settlers or cockatoos, scratching out an existence). "The Stringybark Cockatoo" (the stringybark tree, Paterson explained, was an unfailing sign of poor land) is a gem of its kind. A miner, down on his luck "took a job of reaping off a stringybark cockatoo":

Ten bob an acre was his price — with promise of fairish board.
He said his crops were very light, 'twas all he could afford.
He drove me out in a bullock dray, and his piggery met my view.
Oh, the pigs and geese were in the wheat of the stringybark cockatoo.

The hut was made of the surface mud, the roof of a reedy thatch,
The doors and windows open flew without a bolt or latch.
The pigs and geese were in the hut, the hen on the table flew,
And she laid an egg in the old tin plate for the stringybark cockatoo.

For breakfast we had pollard, boys, it tasted like cobbler's paste,
To help it down we had to eat brown bread with vinegar taste.
The tea was made of the native hops which out on the ranges grew;
'Twas sweetened with honey bees and wax for the stringybark
                                                              cockatoo.

For dinner we had goanna hash, we thought it mighty hard;
They wouldn't give us butter, so we forced down bread and lard.
Quondong duff, paddymelon pie, and wallaby Irish stew
We used to eat while reaping for the stringybark cockatoo.

Paterson also transcribed "The New England Cocky", "The Old Bullock Dray", "To-morrow I'm Losing my Darling" and "River Bend" — all in this vein.

With a modesty characteristic of his whole life Paterson took no credit for his work in collecting these songs. He merely hoped, he said, "to rescue these rough bush-ballads from oblivion". Yet the rewards were sure. It was as if some of their patina rubbed on to his own ballads. His boyhood love of the outback was intensified by the continuing nostalgia he felt for it while having to earn his living in the city; all this was enriched in him by the genuine feeling for the Australian earth implicit in these old songs. They helped him towards a truer perspective of the life and thought of the bush pioneers, reinforcing his own observations of the values they accepted, if sardonically, in their everyday lives. Drought and death were inevitabilities always at their back; friendship or mateship was not so much a nicety of living as a necessity for survival even more valuable than love between man and woman, the applications of which were largely practical:

> Oh Willie, dearest Willie,
> I'll go along with you,
> I'll cut off all my auburn fringe
> And be a shearer, too,
> I'll cook and count your tally, love,
> While ringer-o you shine,
> And I'll wash your greasy moleskins
> On the banks of the Condamine.

All this passed into Paterson's verse, and while it is a problem sometimes to work out where he drew from the songs and where he and they shared common sources, at least we can agree with H. M. Green that he was "the first verse-maker . . . to breathe the same air as the old bush song-makers".[6]

So it is that at least the characteristics common to Paterson's verse and the old bush songs can be easily distinguished. Both mirrored what Russel Ward has called the "popular Australian stance". There was the rather ironical acceptance of the rough with the smooth; a happy-go-lucky mood and a spirit of independence and careless adventure balanced by plain-spoken directness; and an absence of sentiment (there were few references to women since the bush was first of all a challenge to the men who ventured into it). Naturally, since Paterson developed the literary ballad (as distinguished from the bush song), he introduced many variants and refinements, and, indeed, an essential poetry largely lacking in the songs. Thus he was, for A. G. Stephens for instance, "the ordinary bush bard sublimated".[7]

On the other hand, it is important to stress that the songs were meant to be sung, not read. This is intrinsic, even in their composition. "No doubt," wrote Paterson, "some of the songs were begun by one man and finished or improved by another or several others."[8] The subsequent researches of scholars and folk-song collectors have confirmed that Paterson was close to the mark. There is little evidence of group-composition, but group *encouragement* undoubtedly fired the inspiration of those trying to work stories out of their unlettered systems. Russel Ward quotes "Duke" Tritton on the writing of "Shearing at the Bar":

> Well, that came to me by being up at the pub one afternoon, one Saturday, and I suppose there'd be thirty or forty shearers there from various sheds, and everyone of them was talking about his shearing . . . shearing, nothing else. And the point that struck me, nobody seemed to gash them, no matter how rough they were. Well, I got

stuck into that, and I thought: "Well, that's an idea", . . . and I made up a story about it in rhyme. At that time I had no intention of it being sung, but my cobber, Dutchy Bishop, he suggested we put a tune to it, and we tried several, and the one we tried it on was of all things in the world When Irish Eyes Are Smiling. . . . Well, it started on that but it got a bit difficult to hit those high notes, and so we chopped it down a bit. . . . I take the credit for making it up myself — but when I look back, I had a hell of a lot of offsiders! Everybody was putting in a verse or a line here and there: 'Try this', and 'Try that'. One would have one version and then another would add something else, and so we came to the one that finally developed. . . . There were quite a few learnt this song, you know, and they spread it around the country. One time we were having a bit of a session; there was one bloke sang three verses of it and claimed it as his own. And I took exception to that. And there were a few blows exchanged, and he apologized after; and he admitted it wasn't when I sung the other verses to him.[9]

It was a situation duplicated hundreds of times wherever, in the lonely places of the early days, nomadic bush workers came together: shearers, teamsters, stockmen, boundary riders. "There was no place to go," wrote James Devaney, a bush veteran, to H. M. Green,

> . . . no ready-made entertainments, no newspapers even; no dances, no womenfolk, no pubs. But there was good fellowship and mateship, and so they entertained themselves around the camp-fire. The recitation was popular; the song was more popular. . . . I think that a bushman with a "turn" for that sort of thing would originate one of these crude camp-fire ballads, about some event or person in vogue at the time; others would hear it and would sing it themselves later on, at other places; and they would put in a word here and a line there, when they couldn't remember the original, or when they thought of something better than the original. Someone adds a verse here and there, and so, as the ballad travels the length and breadth of the country it becomes altered, and I should say improved.[10]

Sometimes, it should be noted, the tune was forgotten on the way and the words set to another, so that two or three versions of a ballad circulated simultaneously. It is an appropriate coincidence that the same experience was to befall Paterson's "Waltzing Matilda"; of all his ballads, this comes closest to the bush songs (indeed there are those who argue that it *did* originate from an old bush song) in the sense that its appeal is as a ballad to be sung. And as Paterson emphasized, the bush songs

> should be heard to an accompaniment of clashing shears when the voice of a shearer rises through the din caused by the rush and bustle of a shearing shed, the scrambling of the sheep in their pens, and the hurry of the pickers-up; or when, on the roads, the cattle are restless on their camp at night and the man on watch, riding round them, strikes up "Bold Jack Donahoe" to steady their nerves a little

. . . The true bushman never hurries his songs. They are designed
expressly to pass the time on long journeys or slow, wearisome rides
after sheep or tired cattle; so the songs are sung conscientiously
through — chorus and all — and the last three words of the song
are always spoken, never sung.[11]

Between the bush songs and Paterson, as the doyen of our literary
balladists (one cannot argue this strictly chronologically, but allowing
for some overlapping, the general periods are successive), we find a small
group of Australian poets essaying the ballad form to greater or less
extent — and it is thus that the literary ballad, as against the bush song,
emerges. It is doubtful if Paterson was influenced by any of these, even
by Adam Lindsay Gordon (1833-70) who was the best known and probably the most accomplished of the group — though Paterson undoubtedly
took some of Gordon's verses as a model early in the piece. Gordon did
have an influence, certainly in their formative periods, on some of Paterson's contemporaries, but Paterson's style and approach, his empathy with
the outback, his inspiration drawn from the bush and its people, meant
that he outstripped Gordon as a balladist with ridiculous ease, even if
Gordon was occasionally capable of writing verse in this medium of
greater poetic power.

It can be accepted, however, that the literary ballad depended primarily
on several elements. There was excitement, preferably with a touch of the
ironic or cynical; a genuine feeling for and love of the land, with the
inner certainty that the land healed itself and that inevitably, with
patience and courage to await it, rebirth followed after drought —
death; as a corollary of this, some elements of gloom and melancholy
brought on by environment; and interwoven in it all, the dominant
Australian characteristic to "give it a go" and take a risk. This being the
case, it must be said that these motifs occur continually in Paterson's verse,
only sporadically in Gordon's. Paterson's "The Man from Snowy River"
completely eclipses "The Sick Stockrider" because Paterson replaces
soliloquy with action; his bushranger ballads have the feeling and
atmosphere (based on his own knowledge of the bush people concerned)
which Gordon lacks in such a "literary" ballad as "Wolf and Hound";
and with a certain amount of intentional parody, we may be sure,
Paterson packs more of the characteristic Australian attitudes into two
verses of "How the Favourite Beat Us" than Gordon was able to
accomplish in the whole of "How We Beat the Favourite" (even apart
from considerations of language and topical interest):

I said to the jockey, "Now listen, my cockey,
You watch as you're cantering down by the stand;
I'll wait where that toff is and give you the office;
You're only to win if I lift up my hand."

I then tried to back her — What price is The Cracker?
"Our books are all full, sir," each bookie did swear;
My mind, then, I made up, my fortune I played up,
I bet every shilling against my own mare.

Nevertheless, Gordon is significant as a turning-point in the growth of Australian poetry: he was the bridge between folk-songs and formal literature; if he was not so important as a poet, as a national figure, even a legend,* he was the catalyst for much of the inspiration and articulation among the popular poets who began to appear in print.

Henry Kendall (1839-82) attempted the ballad, but even "Jim the Splitter", the best known of those he wrote, is artificial and unconvincing; on the other hand, James Brunton Stephens (1835-1902) the Scottish schoolmaster who settled in Queensland and eventually extinguished his poetic genius at a desk in the Queensland Public Service, wrote several ballads that were as racy and idiomatic as any, and deserve much wider currency than they have:

> Oh, where the deuce is the track, the track?
> Round an' round an' forward, an' back?
> "Keep the sun on yer right," they said —
> But hang it, he's gone an' got over my head!

> "Keep clear o' the timber-getters' tracks,"
> But wich is wich, I'd beg to ax?
> They forks and jines, the deuce knows how —
> I wish I'd a sight o' either now!
>
> ("Off the Track")

One of Stephens's contemporaries, fellow-Queenslander George Essex Evans (1836-1909), who was also a school teacher before finding employment in the Queensland Public Service, and was at best a minor poet of the period, wrote at least one ballad "A Drought Idyll" that is Patersonian in a robustly humorous way:

> McGinty left his pumpkin-pie and gazed upon the scene:
> His cows stood propped 'gainst tree and fence wherever they could lean;
> The horse he'd fixed with sapling-forks had fallen down once more;
> The fleas were hopping joyfully on stockyard, path, and floor;
> The flies in thousands buzzed about before his waving hand;
> The hungry pigs squealed as he said, "Me own, me native land!"

> "Queensland, me Mother! Ain't yer well?" he asked. "Come tell me how's —"
> "Dry up! Dry up!" yelled Mrs Mac, "Go out and feed the cows."
> "But where's the feed? McGinty cried, "The sugar-cane's all done —
> It wasn't worth the bally freight we paid for it per ton.
> I'll get me little axe and go with Possum and the mare
> For 'arf-a-ton of apple-tree or a load of prickly-pear."

---

* Even in November 1889, Barcroft Boake from an outback station wrote to his father in Sydney: ". . . there is not a bushman or drover who does not know a verse or two of 'How We Beat the Favourite' or 'The Sick Stockrider'. I call this fame. Gordon is the favourite — may I say only poet of the back-blocker."
        — in my monograph *Barcroft Boake* (1965)

But Paterson, whose first verses (in the sense that they can be definitely ascribed to him) appeared in the *Bulletin* in 1886 when he was twenty-two, when Kendall and Gordon had already passed on and Stephens and Evans were past their prime as creative writers, was now to spark off an interest in Australian ballads (and for that matter, in Australian poetry) unprecedented in his time, and indeed in any period of Australian literary history, including our own. Paterson, of course, was not to know this, then. In the preface to his *Old Bush Songs* he was pessimistic about the future of the bush ballad. He mentioned a bushranger song that had within thirty years disappeared in the very area where it was most sung:

The diggings are all deep sinking now, the shearing is done by contract, and the cattle are sent by rail to market, while newspapers travel all over Australia, so there will be no more bush ballads composed and sung, as these were composed and sung, as records of the early days of the nation.

Even fifty years later H. M. Green was no more optimistic: he saw, in retrospect, "The Wild Colonial Boy" give way to "The Man from Snowy River" and that, in turn (over almost the whole of outback Australia), to "the cheap, cosmopolitan rubbish of the crooner".[12] And, indeed, as the boundary-rider gave way to the jeep and even the light aeroplane; and the long week's ride, with the stars and the dingoes for company, to the daily sweep from the homestead; and the drover, loping along beside his straggling flock and the clouds of dust to the semi-trailer juggernauting along the highways belching petrol fumes; and the old guitar round the campfire to the transistor set — it would seem that Green was right, and the ballad certain of extinction. And so it might have been but for two reasons. Banjo Paterson, the personification of the Australian overland, has persisted because of the continuing interest in his verse, so that we have the phenomenon of a ballad-writer, most of whose work was published before this century was much under way, having year after year more copies of his work sold than any contemporary poet. And again, since the Second World War, and after some fifty years during which no one (except for an odd enthusiast indulging what seemed to be an eccentricity) seemed to be interested in collecting Australian folk-songs, suddenly individual collectors, societies, researchers and scholars[13] appeared on the scene and the folk-song renaissance (admittedly part of a world-wide trend) was upon us.

This has manifested itself both in publication and performance. Now it is true, as John Manifold has reminded us,[14] that mere publication does a doubtful service to folk-songs: "it preserves them, but it preserves them dead like stuffed animals in a museum". Yet publication has made Australian bush songs and ballads just as accessible and appreciated as they were at the beginning of this century. Folk-songs are heard these days in concert halls, on radio and television broadcasts, in clubs, hotels and folk-cellars, and, just as they were a hundred years ago, in homes, around campfires, in pubs and along roads and beaches. And, together with imported songs in this idiom, "The Wild Colonial Boy" and "Eumerella Shore", as well as Paterson's "Waltzing Matilda" and "The Billygoat Overland", are a cherished part of the repertoire.

NOTES

[1] Published Angus & Robertson, Sydney, 1905. Later editions were published, the seventh in 1930.

[2] In a letter to Mr Thomas Whitely of Blackheath, 27 July 1896. This extract is quoted by H. P. Heseltine in "'Banjo' Paterson: A Poet Nearly Anonymous", *Meanjin*, No. 4, 1964.

[3] In this field Russel Ward, Geoffrey Ingleton and John Meredith have been especially active.

[4] In *Who Wrote the Ballads* (1964).

[5] Op. cit.

[6] In *A History of Australian Literature* (1961).

[7] In the *Bulletin*, 26 October 1895.

[8] In his Introduction to *Old Bush Songs*.

[9] In his Introduction to *The Penguin Book of Australian Ballads*.

[10] Op. cit.

[11] Op. cit.

[12] Op. cit.

[13] Including Russel Ward, Percy Jones, Douglas Stewart, Nancy Keesing, John Manifold and many others.

[14] In the Preface to his *Penguin Australian Song Book* (1962).

CHAPTER II

Paterson, the Literary Ballad and the 1890s

*The bush ballad was born when its folk and literary pro-
genitors had come together and produced Paterson.*

— H. M. GREEN: *A History of Australian
Literature:* 1961.

*Talk of "a nest of singing birds"? Everyone sang. Everything
was worth writing about, in verse, if possible. The diggings
and the seaports, the slums and the Outback, the selections,
and the stock-routes and the wheatfields and the artesian
bores, all found their poet, and usually found him in high
spirits.*

— A. W. JOSE: *The Romantic Nineties:*
1933.

PATERSON WILL ALWAYS be identified with the 1890s, a period round which there has been much writing[1] and discussion; which has, rather arbitrarily, been made to fit any number of theories about Australian nationalism; but which was indeed a period of considerable ferment and crisis — a storm-centre of Australian historiography — equally remarkable for the spate of its literary output. No less, is Paterson held in our time to be the archetype of the Australian bushman. An elaboration of both these circumstances is essential to a proper appreciation of Paterson's life and writing.

From 1860 to 1890 Australia rapidly progressed towards self-sufficiency and prosperity, supported mainly, then as now, by the wool trade. The rough socialism of the outback, the beginnings of secondary industries in the cities, were pointing ahead to unionism, and ultimately to a sense of nationhood. Railways and the telegraph were webbing the eastern seaboard especially, into a network of communications and breaking down the barriers between the colonies. But financial and economic disaster came with the turn of the 1890s. The gold-fields had petered out; wool prices fell; banks and pastoral companies, which had so liberally for many years underwritten the pastoral and mining industries, suddenly dried up their funds. Along with this came a series of droughts spreading over seven years; it is difficult not to be moved at the record of outback children, born during these years, terrified by the unknown sound of rain clattering on the galvanized-iron roofs of homesteads. As the depression worsened, nearly a dozen major trading banks closed: unemployment spread like a rash as manufacturing industries ceased as rapidly as they had boomed, and thousands of city workers joined the nomadic dispossessed and jobless bush folk (for many Illalongs and Kiley's Runs were foreclosed upon and amalgamated into larger holdings). There were fires along the tracks. M. H. Ellis recalls:

> Literally thousands of Australians lived on the road or in "humpies" in the last decade of the nineteenth century. Their fires blazed along the tracks, their concertinas and accordions made music. They were far from being all of what is called "the working classes" and though many of them had never heard of mateship, class disappeared in the face of adversity.[2]

Miseries were intensified by black years of strikes and lockouts; in the 1880s mass unions of unskilled workers had been formed to take advantage of the shortage of labour — but now, with depression on their doorsteps, the employers resisted, and there was trouble which almost came to civil conflict, especially with the shearers' and miners' unions.[*] The great strikes ended in inevitable defeat for the workers since most of the State governments threw in with the employers — but out of defeat came victory, in a sense, with the consequent resolve of labour to enter politics and win the States back. Unionism after all was the organized manifestation of mateship.

The move towards Federation was a concomitant of these happenings; the shattering nature of many of these experiences prompted more and more Australians to look into themselves and their country and their relationship with the rest of the world. There was another thing, too. Once a population of three million, homogeneous in texture (for in no other country had there been such a blending of British national stock with so little foreign admixture), began to assume a common outlook, the steps to nationhood were the more certain. By 1890 about three-quarters of Australia's population was Australian-born; it knew no other country, climate or customs than those it had been born to. There was discernible a growing distrust of foreigners, centred at this time mainly against the Chinese who stayed on after the gold rush immigration; and this local xenophobia was the seed of the White Australia policy to come. But all this surging nationalistic growth throughout the 1890s was to lead inevitably to the Convention Bill of 1898 — that there be established under the Crown "a Federal Union of the Australian Colonies".

[*] "On Dagworth, Robert MacPherson with his brother and the station-hand sheared and guarded the woolshed against unionists for six weeks. Then on a very dark night with a high wind blowing, while the overseer was on guard, the unionists poured a bush rifle fire into the hut where his wife and children were, and a match was struck in the shed, starting a blaze from what appeared to be kerosene. The overseer and the brother fired at the rifle flashes, and one of the brothers rushed to the shed to let out 140 lambs penned for the next day's shearing, but a fusillade from the unionists made it impossible to get near the pen or put out the fire. Soon shed and lambs were burning. Then the wind dropped and a soft rain began to fall, obliterating the tracks of the unionists who got clear away."
— from *Christison of Lammermoor* by Mrs M. M. Bennett (1927), which was one of Paterson's favourite books about the Australian outback. It was at Dagworth station that Paterson wrote "Waltzing Matilda".

Yet this was a cultural no less than a nationalist awakening, and while, as we will see, the scene as set was most favourable to a literary resurgence, there were other cultural elements playing their part too. The theatre, for instance, was very much alive on three levels. In legitimate drama, George Rignold, an English actor turned director-entrepreneur, developed an increasingly sophisticated appreciation especially with Shakespearian presentations. Another entrepreneur, Alfred Dampier, also offered a diet of Shakespeare, but found much more popular success with his stage versions of *For the Term of His Natural Life* and *Robbery Under Arms*. It is recorded that "the public's taste for melodrama exceeded its appetite for Shakespeare, and Dampier was obliged to play five nights of the former to support one night of the Bard".[3] On a second plane J. C. Williamson had formed his Comic Opera Company, and having with considerable acumen acquired the sole rights of the Gilbert and Sullivan repertoire, surfeited the middlebrows then as now. And Harry Rickards took an eight-year lease of the Garrick Theatre in Sydney, gave it the new name of the Tivoli and began to build up his famous vaudeville circuit. Altogether, as Paul Maguire has commented, "The Australian stage of the eighties and nineties was rich in plays and players. It reflected the upsurge of vigour in Australia at large."[4]

The Sydney Town Hall was opened in 1890, with the celebrated English organist T. H. Best invited to Australia for recitals to mark the occasion. This followed the Melbourne Exhibition of 1888, for which a music festival was organized, with a specially recruited orchestra of seventy players under the English music director Frederick H. Cowen. The concerts given on this occasion were said to have been the most polished in Australian music history to that time. The University of Melbourne had just been endowed with a Chair of Music by Francis Ormond; to this was appointed Marshall Hall, a most energetic and vigorous personality, who soon organized a symphony orchestra. The memory of Hall's Bohemianism and eccentricity has perhaps outweighed his musical achievements — he wrote poetry and named one collection "Hymns Ancient and Modern", and was given to walking around his garden in pyjamas — but the example of his musical enthusiasm saw a similar endowment by Sir Thomas Elder of a Chair of Music at the University of Adelaide in 1897. All this, and Italian opera too — because J. C. Williamson had teamed up about that time with fellow-entrepreneur George Musgrove so that Australian audiences for the first time heard *Cavalleria Rusticana*, *I Pagliacci* and *L'Amico Fritz*.

Closer perhaps to literature in this renaissance of the 1890s was the emergence of an Australian school of art. Tom Roberts, Arthur Streeton and Charles Conder were achieving that feeling of light and heat so typical of the outback scene. Hitherto Australian artists seemed to have been unwilling to accept the beauty of their landscapes — the poets, even as far back as Harpur and Kendall, had responded much more willingly. But Australian art seemed obsessed with the subdued tones and cloudy skies inherited from England — Australian forests, like Marcus Clarke's were "funereal, secret, stern". Now, however, came the heroic pastorals of Roberts — "Shearing the Ram" and "The Breakaway" having the same dramatic effect as "The Man from Snowy River" and "Clancy of the Overflow" — and the landscape themes of Streeton: the dangers of pioneering, heat and dust, bushrangers, drought, desert and thirst. Here were in art the themes of the bush ballads. The Heidelberg School, in the spirit of the 1890s, sought to convey the actual appearance of Australia, and found its subject matter, enthusiastically, in the bush and the desert no less than in the near-city environs.

Above all, the ideal of a free, compulsory and secular education was now a reality. Victoria had led the way in 1872; by 1890 all colonies had followed suit; what was more, each had its public library (and there were even libraries in some country districts) and its university — graduates were passing out into public life.

So here was a cultural upheaval, and a nation thirsting for its own literature. Everything Australian suddenly became worth writing about: the slums, the outback, the diggings, the seaports, the selections, the stock-routes, the wheatfields. It was naissance* rather than renaissance, permeated with two characteristic Australian virtues: a good-tempered humour and inviolable mateship. Jose wrote:

> A good deal of my time just then was spent up-country and I found everywhere men's — especially young men's — minds working as if some superbaker had permeated them with spiritual yeast. Young men brought me manuscripts or sketched for me their notions of a pan-Australian romance. With them it was simple to deal, by refering them to the omnivorous *Bulletin*. But what was one to do with a bank-manager — I met him in a southern township — who had submerged himself in Diderot and the Encyclopaedists as thoroughly as Brennan submerged himself in Mallarmé? . . . Never since Elizabeth's days had a whole nation so unanimously clamoured for mind food."[5]

But how did this cut across the outback, and the typical figure of the outback, the bushman, the Clancy who wrote with his "thumbnail dipped in tar" (and "Clancy of the Overflow" was written in 1889)? This very fact of a universal education allied to an improvement in communications, as Russel Ward, with a nice irony, has put it, "brought Sydney nearer to the bush . . ." so that the bushman "became the natural culture hero on whose supposed characteristics many Australians tend, consciously or unconsciously, to model their attitude to life".[6] Yet it is unfair to call this a "stereotype". Francis Adams, a young Englishman who had spent five years in Australia from 1884 to 1889, returned to London and wrote in *The Australians: A Social Sketch* (1893):

---

* But Norman Lindsay in his *Bohemians of the Bulletin* (1965) has given a completely different view. ". . . If ever there was a moribund limbo in all cultured values, it was this country in that era. It was given over to the skulduggery of politicians, to bucolics plucking the wool off sheep, to a press with an intellectual status little above that of the *Bogwallah Banner*, edited mainly by parsons, and to the domination of all moral, social, aesthetic, and intellectual values by a virulent mob of wowsers, extracted from English Nonconformists, Scotch Presbyterians and Irish Catholics — all this plus a lingering flavour of the convict system . . ."

The gulf between colony and colony is small and traversable compared to that great fixture that lies between the people of the Slope and of the Interior. Where the marine rainfall flags out and is lost, a new climate, and in a certain sense, a new race begin to unfold themselves . . .

It is not one hundred, but three and four and five hundred miles that you must go back from the sea if you would find yourself face to face with the one powerful and unique national type yet produced in the new land . . . Frankly I find not only all that is genuinely characteristic in Australia and the Australian springing from this heart of the land but also all that is noblest, kindliest and best . . .

Adams is, in so far as our literature is concerned, an almost unknown voice. But here, with a flash of extraordinary insight, he had glimpsed and fixed for posterity an Australian idea, a spirit, as Henry Lawson had written, "that is roused beyond the Range",[7] a stimulus for popular and literary imagination which twenty years later Dr C. E. W. Bean memorably re-affirmed:

The Australian, one hundred to two hundred years hence, will still live with the consciousness that, if he only goes far enough back over the hills and across the plains he comes in the end to the mysterious half desert country where men have to live the lives of strong men. And the life of that mysterious country will affect the Australian imagination much as the life of the sea has affected that of the English . . .[8]

No one saw this more clearly than Andrew Barton Paterson. The words of Adams and Bean are near enough to a statement of his creed — for Paterson was the chronicler and poet of these outback people, of the western plains, of the illimitable spaces of the interior. Norman Lindsay, reminiscing of Paterson, recalled that "he believed isolation in the Bush made individuals of men".[9] And Paterson's verse and prose abound with these individuals, named or anonymous, through whose agency the legend of the Australian plainsman, the overlander, the mountain rider has been perpetuated (and even the "Digger" is an off-shoot from this legend) — "The Man from Snowy River", Clancy, Saltbush Bill, Old Kiley.

But Paterson, like his contemporaries among the balladists, needed a means of communication since there was now a literate community sparsely scattered in thousands of small settlements throughout the hinterland and interior: in stations, townships, shearing-sheds, mining-camps, and wherever else its nomadic elements congregated. The need of this community for an organ to reflect its idiom, aspirations and sense of unity was no less acute — and J. F. Archibald in 1880 had met this by founding the *Bulletin*. Now, as Russel Ward observes, the undoubted success of this journal was more because of the demand for bush material than of any particular policy exercised by Archibald. At the beginning there was little sign of outback writing: but some verses of Gordon and one or two attempts at bush balladry started a movement of correspondence, prose contributions and verse which soon saw the *Bulletin* well established as "the most important single medium by which the bush 'aethos' was popularized".[10]

Paterson at twenty-two made his first signed contribution to the *Bulletin*, on 12 June 1886, with a ballad "The Bush Fire", although he probably wrote some anonymous verses in the previous year about the Soudan contingent. Like the older *Bulletin* writers with whom he was to be associated in the years to follow he owed much to Archibald's personal advice. Archibald had a journalistic instinct for the public taste and for what new writers could contribute to it that was uncanny. Sir Frank Fox, editor of the *Lone Hand*, recalls that Archibald once boasted jokingly that he had only once put a good thing into the waste-paper basket, and that was a bull pup. Even a novice writer could be sure of an acknowledgement and advice if his contribution showed promise for the journal. In the early years of the *Bulletin* many of the writers did not differ from their readers except that they had more reading and the ability to write verse.

Archibald was always on the watch for talent. So he encouraged Barcroft Boake; he heard of a man with an inexhaustible flow of island stories, working in a Manly quarry, and so discovered Louis Becke; he was convinced that Lawson, a young coach-painter whose verses and pieces of prose came sporadically into his office, had the mark of genius; he advised Brady against reading Kipling, telling him rather to "write his sea stuff in his own way". His advice to the young Paterson was on the same lines. On the second and third ballads Paterson had submitted in 1886 — "A Dream of the Melbourne Cup" and "The Mylora Elopement" — Archibald had scribbled on the respective MSS: "Doggerel. Fun in the idea. Might be remodelled", and "Rough but humorous".[11] However, he called Paterson up to see him.

> Off I went [wrote Paterson] . . . and climbed a grimy flight of stairs at 24 Pitt Street, until I stood before a door marked "Mr. Archibald, Editor". On the door was pinned a spirited drawing of a gentleman lying quite loose on the strand with a dagger through him, and on the drawing was written: "Archie, this is what will happen to you if you don't use my drawing about the policeman!" It cheered me up a lot. Evidently this was a free and easy place. Anyone who wants to know what Archibald looks like should see his portrait by Florence Rodway in the Sydney Art Gallery. It is a marvellous likeness of the bearded and bespectacled Archibald, peering at a world which was all wrong. Not that he ever put forward any concrete scheme for setting it right; he diagnosed the diseases and left others to find the cure.
>
> In an interview of ten minutes he said he would like me to try some more verse. Did I know anything about the bush? I told him that I had been reared there. "All right," he said, "have a go at the bush. Have a go at anything that strikes you. Don't write anything like other people if you can help it. Let's see what you can do."[12]

So Paterson joined that easy-going and much-reminisced-about sodality of *Bulletin* writers, although there is no evidence that he was ever an active member of the cliques which grew up around the various celebrities. There was a group which clustered around Lawson of which Le Gay Brereton was the presiding genius, and another around Victor Daley — the Dawn and Dusk Club, whose president was called the Symposiarch, with several Heptarchs beneath him and the club rules printed in Chinese.* Paterson is remembered often outside the *Bulletin* office with groups of writers including Lawson, Roderic Quinn, Randolph Bedford, E. J. Brady, Edward Dyson and others. He also met at this time William Goodge, just back from carrying his swag through the shearers' camps, full of the love of the outback and shortly to take over the editorship of the Orange *Leader*, where he wrote his rather ironical bush ballads.

But Paterson does not seem to have formed any particular friendships with his fellow-writers; on the other hand, he greatly admired and began close associations with the *Bulletin* artists, the American Livingston Hopkins and the Englishman Phil May, who had been brought out in 1883 and 1886 respectively as staff artists, since illustrations were now becoming an important part of the *Bulletin*. "Hop" was a grave and dignified man with a sense of his own importance; he had strong principles, and more than a touch of the puritan. May, on the other hand, was irresponsible, erratic and the despair of his more sober-minded colleagues, a born story-teller with an unfailing sense of humour, a good companion, with hosts of friends, hangers-on and parasites. Hopkins was a painstaking and careful craftsman who drew the weekly political cartoon. "Give him an idea for a comic picture," Paterson wrote, "and he would make three jokes grow where one only grew before."[13]

At the other extreme, May, who was responsible for cartoons on the passing scene and its oddities, drew in a hurry, often in the early hours after late parties. He told Paterson he had learned his drawing by practising on costermongers and street arabs in London. On one occasion according to Julian Ashton,[14] Traill, the *Bulletin* editor, reprimanded him, saying, "We are paying you very liberally for the small amount of work you are putting into your drawings." May answered, "Mr Traill, when I can do them with half as much work I shall charge you twice as much." Ashton recalls of May: ". . . he had a very observant eye, slightly hooked nose and an expressive and mobile mouth. His manner was courteous and nearly always deferential, and he could 'suffer fools gladly' to a degree that I do not remember to have seen equalled. . . ."

Paterson and Hopkins were attracted to each other because "Hop" too was a country boy: he had been brought up on an Ohio farm; later he had taken a job as a conductor on a sleeping-car, travelling all over the U.S.A., and sketching as many passengers as he could. Paterson on one

* The motto of the club was "Roost High and Crow Low". There was no subscription fee, and according to George Taylor in *Those Were the Days* (1948) its objects included those ". . . to establish a society for the erection of ancient ruins in Australia . . . to form a fund for the establishment of Australian Old Masters . . . to form a branch society for being tired of the newer poets . . . and to obtain cash offers for conferring the patronage of the Club upon tradesmen with the right to use the name of the Club in their advertisements . . ."

occasion took Hopkins on a buggy-ride down through the rough bush to
the head of the Murrumbidgee River. Paterson wrote that

> . . . he compared everything unfavourably with Ohio until down on
> the river flats, I showed him a crop of maize which reduced him to
> civility. He had to get out of the buggy and handle the maize before
> he would believe that it was real. And he said there was nothing to
> draw in this unspeakable stringybark wilderness until we passed an
> old deserted woolshed built of slabs and bark, with a big beam
> sticking out through the top as a lever to press the bales. He said that
> this in itself was worth the trip, and he spent an hour drawing it, and
> made an etching which I wish I had now.[15]

Paterson always hoped that someone would one day collect Hopkins'
"little etchings" — he felt sure they would "come into their own".

Hopkins remained with the *Bulletin* till 1928: undoubtedly his influence in raising cartooning to an artistic level prompted the opportunities
which led to such brilliant artists working for the *Bulletin* and other
newspapers and journals as David Souter, Norman and Lionel Lindsay,
E. W. Lambert, Frank Mahony, Will Dyson and David Low.

Phil May returned to London early in the 1890s — he was unable by
temperament and ability to adapt himself completely to life in Australia.
On the urban side he was superb — his Woolloomooloo and city types
were sketched in the full spirit of the 1890s. But, as Vance Palmer recalls,
the bush baffled him — "even a trip to the Blue Mountains was a wild
adventure in strange territory,not to be repeated too often".[16]

Nevertheless, Paterson had a deep affection for May and on his first
visit to London in 1901 renewed his friendship with May, now living in
St John's Wood, one of the leading cartoonists for *Punch*, and the un-
crowned king of Bohemia:

> There are Bohemians of the beer and backbiting variety, but Phil
> was the genuine article. He earned about two thousand a year and
> spent three thousand. An extraordinarily skinny man, with a face
> like a gargoyle, he was a self-taught artist, a self-taught actor; could
> give a Shakespearian reading as well as most dramatic artists, and
> could dance a bit if required. He knew everybody in the artistic,
> literary and theatrical world, and his Sunday evenings at St John's
> Wood gathered together the brightest and best of the Bohemians.[17]

But Paterson's literary bond was with his fellow-writers about the
Australian bush — balladists as well as those writers of sketches and
short stories (and it is opportune at this point to say that Paterson as a
prose writer has been consistently under-rated). Apart from the quicken-
ing pulse of nationalism which was apparent to greater or less extent in
these writers (unconsciously democratic in form, "offensively" so in
Furphy or Lawson), they shared other characteristics and emotions.
There was a consciousness of the Australian landscape — manifested in
the greyness and brownness and redness of the outback with its occasional

bursts of colour, whether the golden mist of a wattle-tree or the rose-pink flush of a babble of grey galahs turning against the sky; and the environmental influence of the irregular, unpredictable rhythms of drought and fertility, of flooded streams and dry creek-beds, of dust and of greenness, with always the vivid-blue skies offering day after day a benediction of winter sunshine or a curse of dry burning heat. These writers were entirely self-sufficient and relied not in the slightest on old-world examples; they shared a good-natured fatalistic humour, an ironic acceptance of reverses (even death), a laconic understatement of their troubles, optimism never defeatism, and the willingness to gamble on something being "bound to turn up". They believed in mateship and the doctrine of a helping hand; they accepted at face-value a stranger or new chum (as long as he was an Australian). They wrote from horse, from on foot, from down the mines, from back-breaking selections, from shearing-sheds and overland camp-fires — "tranquillizing their own loneliness, rejoicing in their own heroic exploits, grinning with a certain pride at their own hard-bitten reflections".[18] Their most characteristic mode of expression was the bush ballad, a simple versification, usually in primitive metre, often in ragged rhyme, of outback life: incidents, characters, anecdotes, and especially, adventures. The old bush songs had pointed the way; the dramatic surge into literacy even in the isolated townships and stations gave the audience; the *Bulletin* was largely the medium. The result was a combination of nascence and eager fulfilment by an astonishing variety and medley of writers, never to occur again. Out of it came vigour, space, freedom and humanity — the qualities of the ballad at its best. And Paterson was king. No more appropriate and memorable assessment of our literary balladists exists, than H. M. Green's:

The Australian ballad falls into a number of sub-groups. The most characteristic, and on the whole the most important, if only on account of its leader, is the equestrian: here Paterson canters down the centre, dreaming of the wide plains; with Ogilvie out on one flank, waving at a girl in the distance and Boake on the other, smoking himself into a deeper gloom: and, not far off, "The Breaker" taking a tricky colt over a high fence. Then there are the swagmen led by Henry Lawson, who humps a heavy drum along the dusty road. Dyson leans over the windlass of a mine, and, near him, a party of prospectors strings off into the far west. Farther ahead and later in time, Souter is talking to a mallee farmer beside his stump-jump plough; and "John O'Brien" waits for his Sunday flock, who are gathering round the little church. Over the eastern horizon, on a Port Jackson wharf, Brady listens to a half-drunken sailor's story of seas and mermaids and strange cargoes. though occasionally he wanders inland; Will Lawson is not far from him, and Souter leaves his mallee farmers to make a sea voyage now and then . . .[19]

Of Lawson and his associations with Paterson there is detail to come; "Breaker" Morant, as we shall see, pointed up a blind spot in Paterson. Barcroft Boake, the ill-starred youth who lived a few glorious years of happiness in the bush before he returned to the city and in depression hanged himself at the age of twenty-six, came closest in the excitement and tempo of his ballads of horsemanship ("Stride for stride, lengthened wide, for the green timber belt / The fastest half mile ever done on the plain") to those of Paterson. His entire output of bush verses almost all in the *Bulletin* was concentrated in his last years, 1889-91; yet the opinion of those qualified to judge is that had he lived his span he would have excelled Paterson. Certainly, the ballad by which he is best known, "Where the Dead Men Lie" —

> Where brown Summer and Death have mated —
>   That's where the dead men lie!
> Loving with fiery lust unsated —
>   That's where the dead men lie!
> Out where the grinning skulls bleach whitely
> Under the saltbush sparkling brightly;
> Out where the wild dogs chorus nightly —
>   That's where the dead men lie!
>
> Deep in the yellow, flowing river —
>   That's where the dead men lie!
> Under the banks where the shadows quiver —
>   That's where the dead men lie!
> Where the platypus twists and doubles,
> Leaving a train of tiny bubbles;
> Rid at last of their earthly troubles —
>   That's where the dead men lie!

— is one of the classic bush ballads of our literature, and evoked from Paterson a most genuine, understanding, and felicitously-expressed tribute:

> . . . Most bushmen feel the influence of the intense stillness of a night out on the plains when the tropical stars blaze overhead and the dimly seen clumps of saltbush and low scrub look like the encampment of a mighty army; but to very few of us is it given to express their feelings in such words as came with the poetic inspiration of Barcroft Boake . . .[20]

Will Ogilvie, a young Scot (so were Gordon and Paterson Scots; hence Douglas Stewart's playfully ingenious if untenable theory about the Australian balladists as a reincarnation of the old Border rhymers), came to Australia in 1889 at the age of twenty and in this exciting and surging period stayed for twelve years, falling in love with Australian horses and girls and the verses of A. L. Gordon.* He roamed through the back country working as a drover, horse-breaker and rouseabout; his stamping grounds were especially the south-east of South Australia, along the

---

* One of his two volumes of verse was called *Fair Girls and Gray Horses.*

Warrego, and the western plains of New South Wales, which he loved as
deeply as Paterson: "I loved the wide gold glitter of the plains / Spread
out before us like a silent sea . . .". Like Paterson he had a natural feeling
for the bush and its sights and sounds, and for the colour of the words
that described them. He is best remembered in his ballads of horse and
saddle; his rhythms leap and sing:

> The station lads had heard the sneer that travelled far and wide
> And flung the answering challenge: "Come and teach us how to ride!
> Roll up ye merry riders all, whose honour is to guard!
> We've mustered up the ranges and The Rebel's in the yard;
> His open mouth and stamping foot and keen eye flashing fire
> Repeat the temper of his dam, the mettle of his sire.
>
> ("The Riding of the Rebel")

And even if, as can be seen by these lines, he lacked the intensity of image
and the more convincing familiarity with his subject that made the horseback ballads of Paterson and Boake superior, he was probably at times a
better craftsmen than either, and when it came to movement and action
allied to natural rhythmic control, some of his ballads in this idiom rank
with Paterson's:

> Store cattle from Nelanjie! By half-a-hundred towns,
> By northern ranges rough and red, by rolling open downs,
> By stock-routes brown and burnt and bare, by flood-wrapped river-
>   bends,
> They've hunted them from gate to gate — the drover has no friends!
> But idly they may ride today beneath the scorching sun
> And let the hungry bullocks try the grass on Wonga run;
> No overseer will dog them here to "see the cattle through",
> But they may spread their thousand head — for we've been droving
>   too!
>
> ("We've Been Droving Too")

Edward Dyson, who was twenty-five years old in 1890, was associated
with Paterson and Lawson in the phrase coined in the *Bulletin* "Paterdylaw and Son"* — their first books of verse appeared within a year of each
other in the 1890s. He spent his boyhood near Ballarat in Victoria, where
he was born, and he wrote many of his ballads about the mines. But his
horizons were the bush and the plains of the outback too, and if he is
correctly regarded as a lesser balladist, one finds oddly recurring similari-
ties with Paterson's verses, in form, mood and technique. Like Paterson
he had that constant blend of humour ranging from the sardonic to the
boisterous (his "A Friendly Game of Football" is the nearest of our
ballads to Paterson's more famous, but hardly more lively, "The Geebung
Polo Club") and his lapses into sentiment, if more frequent than Paterson's, are often strangely parallel both in the direction of this sentiment
and the poetic result.

---

* "At the midpoint of the nineties . . . almost everybody swore 'Paterdylaw and Son'."
— H. M. Green in "Roderic Quinn", *Southerly*, Vol. XI, No. 1, 1950

Paterson's "In the Droving Days" (his reverie of an old grey horse at an auction sale — "only a pound for the drover's horse?") — reminds one very much of Dyson's "The Old Whim Horse", but the latter, if anything, is much nearer to lyric poetry than to ballad:

> . . . In a gully green, where a dam lies gleaming,
> And the bush creeps back on a worked-out claim,
> And the sleepy crows in the sun sit dreaming
> On the timbers grey and a charred hut frame,
> Where the legs slant down, and the hare is squatting
> In the high rank grass by the dried-up course,
> Nigh a shattered drum and a king-post rotting
> Are the bleaching bones of the old grey horse.

The remaining balladist and contemporary of Paterson who deserves mention in this context was E. J. Brady. He was five years younger than Paterson, but they were often in each other's company during their *Bulletin* days. Brady worked as a tally-clerk on the wharves at Woolloomooloo; these were the sailing days; he fraternized with the sailors and acquired the nautical jargon. The chanty became to him what the old bush song was to Paterson. Yet if it seems strange, therefore, to yoke him with the bush balladists, the fact is that Brady was not a sailor but he did travel in the bush, alternately as bush worker and itinerant journalist, and for a while he farmed there. And as Douglas Stewart has noted,[21] Brady's bush rhymes and ballads are more vital and understandably authentic than his salt-water ballads, and in one or two of them he has caught even more tellingly than Paterson or Boake (and perhaps this was his journalistic sense) the romance of the Australian bush; he seems to be aware looking forward as well as back of the history that was being made around him, that was being written in men's memory and of which he would in fullness of time be a part:

> My camp was by the Western Road — so new and yet so old —
> The track the bearded diggers trod in roaring days of old;
> The road Macquarie and his wife, a hundred years ago,
> With warlike guard and retinue, went down in regal show.
>
> The moon had silvered all the Bush; now, like an arc-light high,
> She flickered in a scattered scud that dimmed the lower sky;
> And, dreaming by my dying fire, whose embers fainter glowed,
> I saw their shadows flitting by — the People of the Road.
>
> ("The Western Road")

These, then, were Paterson's fellow-writers and friends, the contemporaries who, with him, were the chief makers of these bush ballads which grew out of the people of the time, and which embodied those simple outback qualities still a part of our national temperament and collectively a part of our democratic ethos, no matter how urban and centralized our life has become. Yet of them all Paterson was predominant, and this was the judgement of his readers, in his time no less than in the present, for since his first collection *The Man from Snowy River and Other Verses* appeared in 1895, it has outsold, down all these years, the work of any other Australian poet. As a bush balladist he is, in the words of one of our most distinguished literary critics, "widest in range, most fertile in the creation of national types, whether humorous or heroic, as deft as any in versification . . . , most typical of the proud, robust and sardonic spirit of his age, surest in his instinctive understanding that the first thing a balladist should do is tell a story".[22] He is, too, because of this, or as part of it Australia's best-loved poet.

NOTES

1. In addition to A. W. Jose's book, Vance Palmer's *The Legend of the Nineties* (1954) enjoys a high reputation.
2. In the *Bulletin*, 9 January 1965.
3. A. L. McLeod in *The Pattern of Australian Culture* (1963).
4. In his *The Australian Theatre* (1948).
5. A. W. Jose in *The Romantic Nineties*.
6. In his *The Australian Legend* (1958).
7. In his ballad "The Natives of the Range", the *Bulletin*, 27 August 1892.
8. In his *The Dreadnought of the Darling* (1911).
9. In an A.B.C. radio documentary broadcast on 17 April 1964.
10. Russel Ward, op. cit.
11. MSS. in Mitchell Library, Sydney.
12. In his reminiscences in the *Sydney Morning Herald*, February/March, 1939.
13. Ibid.
14. In *Now Came Still Evening On* (1941).
15. Op. cit.
16. In his *The Legend of the Nineties*.
17. In *Happy Dispatches* (1934).
18. Douglas Stewart, in his Preface to *Australian Bush Ballads* (1955).
19. In his *A History of Australian Literature*.
20. In a review of Boake's *Where the Dead Men Lie, and Other Poems*.
21. Op. cit.
22. Douglas Stewart, ibid.

CHAPTER III

The Pioneers

But now the times are dull and slow, the brave old days are dead
When hardy bushmen started out, and forced their way ahead
By tangled scrub and forests grim towards the unknown west,
And spied at last the promised land from off the range's crest.

A. B. PATERSON.

This is the place where they all were bred;
Some of the rafters are standing still;
Now they are scattered and lost and dead,
Every one from the old nest fled,
Out of the shadow of Kiley's Hill.

A. B. PATERSON.

ANDREW BARTON PATERSON was born on 17 February 1864 at Narambla, near Orange in New South Wales. His father Andrew Paterson was a lowland Scot, son of a captain in the East India Company, whose family before him had for generations been farmers in Lanarkshire. A forbear, William Paterson, had been one of the founders of the Bank of England in 1794, had financed William III and had floated a sort of Scottish East India Company at Darien on the Isthmus of Panama into which thousands of his fellow Scots had poured (and lost) their money. In his reminiscences Banjo Paterson recalled that, instead of upbraiding William when he returned to Scotland, the luckless investors subscribed £10,000 to put him on his feet again, but Paterson added drily that William was an ancestor "whose talents I, unfortunately, failed to inherit".

Andrew Paterson at the age of sixteen, his brother John and a sister — "of bold and roving stock that would not fixed abide . . ." — emigrated to Australia in the 1850s; after gaining some station experience in the Riverina, the brothers took up a station called Buckenbah (also spelled Buckinbar) at Obley, near Yeoval in the western district of New South Wales. Held on lease from the Crown, at a few pence an acre, the land was poor and dingo-infested — there were no fences and the sheep had to be shepherded; the cattle roamed at large and were quite easily mustered and driven away by anyone who wanted to stock up cheaply. "In these surroundings," Paterson wrote, "I, the immature verse writer, son of Andrew Paterson, had my first taste of bush life."[1]

Andrew Paterson had married Rose Barton daughter of Robert and Emily Barton of Boree Nyrang station near Cudal, which is situated at a point roughly fifteen miles equidistant from Molong and Orange, and some forty miles south of Andrew Paterson's Buckenbah station. Emily

Barton, A. B. Paterson's grandmother, was a remarkable woman who was to have a very great influence on him: on his development as a poet and writer and on his love for the Australian bush. She was the daughter of Major Darvall; one of her brothers was Sir John Bayley Darvall a prominent Sydney lawyer and a member of the New South Wales Legislative Assembly; the Bartons and the Darvalls had come to the colony in the same ship the *Alfred* in 1834, and a shipboard friendship led to their marriage in 1835, when Robert Barton with his young bride of twenty-two journeyed west to the Molong district and their Boree Nyrang station.

Emily Darvall, unusually well-educated in London and Paris, was a writer of verse all her life; none of it was ever more than minor verse, but in later life she had it privately sheet-printed for her friends. It was, however, an indication of her sensibility and literary inclinations. Even on the *Alfred* coming to Australia she kept a diary,[2] which, apart from her references to a slowly ripening friendship with "Mr Barton", shows an eager observation and a direct and unaffected writing style:

Thursday, 19th September.
. . . The sun set in beauty, the moon arose and danced upon the waters, the band played, the whole of the inhabitants of our floating home came out on deck and the whole scene became a mass of movement.

Hornpipes and reels were performed on all sides and the straw-bonnets of the little emigrant children gleaming in the moonbeams showed that they were not left out in the jubilee. . . .

Saturday, 28th September.
. . . We have got 260 emigrants on board and are very much crowded. Papa has taken great pains to make the maids as comfortable as possible, but Sarah has done nothing but grumble and cry till this morning when, having been appointed stewardess, she began to bustle about cheerfully enough. It is just the best thing they could have done with her. . . .

Sunday, 29th September.
Morning again, and through the opened port
Darts the first crimson ray: waking, I bless
The first return of light: and rising, hail
The glistening waters and the lovely shore,
The wooded hill and mast-concealed isle,
The shining page which Nature to our eyes
From her vast book of beauty here presents.
Does the bright sun sprinkle one watery path
With yellow spangles but to lure us on
From England, home and friends?" . . .

Monday, 7th October.   Lat. 34.58.   Long. 15.38.
Wind still fair, weather delightful. A great deal of the romance of

the sea is destroyed by the smell of the potatoes which are getting rotten, and are being sorted on the quarter deck. A rainy evening. I beat Mr. Stewart at chess. He is my first victim.

Tuesday, 8th October.   Lat. 32.41.   Long. 17.44.
. . . The Captain sits exactly in the centre of one side of the table. He is an elderly man with very short white hair, a red face, a large mouth and a broad Scotch accent. He appears to be very vigilant for his voice is terrific in the night when he generally scolds incessantly as if he had no need of sleep himself, and did not imagine that other people could wish for any. . . .

Monday, 15th October.   Lat. 18.30.   Long. 25.8.
. . . On Mr. Eastmuir's right hand are Mr. & Mrs. Sillitoe, quite respectable shop-keepers of the best class. She suffers still from sea-sickness and consequently remains a good deal below. . . . On Mr. Eastmuir's left hand and opposite to Mama and Papa are Frederick and Rose. Then a vacant place for Mr. Barton, who is still sick, and then Mr. Stewart, a silly good-humoured Scotchman with very little to say but quite inoffensive. . . .

Sunday, 20th October.   Lat. 7.0.   Long. 24.17.
. . . A practical joke was played last night, which might have had serious consequences. Mr Hamilton and some others tied a rope to the port which they thought was Mr Stewart's and amused them-selves with making it dance up and down. Mr Mould was passing by Mr Barton's door at about midnight when he heard him implor-ing someone to come in and fasten his port as it was making a dread-ful noise. Mr Mould knew of the trick, explained it to Mr Barton, who was much amused at the notion, and hastened to get the mistake rectified. It was rather a disagreeable thing for poor Mr Barton who is stretched on his back and unable to move, but he seemed to enjoy it as much as anyone. . . .

Tuesday, 22nd October.   Lat. 5.24.   Long. 25.37.
Nothing extraordinary except an entire day of rain so that we could not go on the poop for one moment all day. Mr Barton made his first appearance but not having spoken to me I cannot give anything like a description of him. In the evening we played at the American game, at which Mr Docker shone pre-eminently. We had some very good answers.

Friday, 25th October.   Lat. 2.36.   Long. 27.21
. . . Mr Barton seems to be a pleasing gentlemanly person . . .
Tuesday, 29th October.   Lat. 5.21.   Long. 31.33.
Yesterday afternoon, while we were all at dinner there was a cry of "Man Overboard!" and a general rush to the poop. They first said it was a child which alarmed Mama very much. . . . I met Mr Barton who kindly stopped me to say that it was a sailor and that he had

got hold of the lifebuoy which Mr Pierman, an intermediate passenger, had cut down with much presence of mind, just as the man
floated past. The boat was lowered and he was soon picked up, as
we were not going more than five knots an hour. He was found to be
so tipsy that they could hardly keep him in the boat, and when
brought back he was put into irons for the remainder of the day.
This morning he was quite unconscious that he had ever been in the
water.

It is quite wonderful that he should have been able to catch the
lifebuoy in such a state of intoxication.

Boree Nyrang took its name from the tribe of Boree aboriginals that
lived in the Molong district. Emily's home was a hut to begin with, but as
over the twenty-five years she lived there her nine children were born and
brought up, it became a rambling homestead. The single-mindedness with
which this talented and cultured woman threw herself into the task of
being a pioneer's wife in an unfamiliar, arduous, indeed hostile, environment and turned her hut into a home can best be shown by the reminiscences of one John Hood,* of Stone Ridge, Barwickshire, who visited
Australia in the years 1841-42:

On the 10th November, 1841 I accompanied my eldest son to Boree
Nyrang, the station of Robert Barton, Esq. This gentleman is in
several ways connected with Scotland, and knowing that my son was
only lately settled in the neighbourhood, and that his accommoda-
tion was not what he wished it to be, hospitably and kindly requested
him to bring me to spend some time at his house. . . . Mr Barton
received us very kindly, with a warm welcome — a point of first-rate
importance in a visit, and good cheer of every kind, including
delicious sauterne and excellent porter. (No man can, prior to
experience, duly estimate a glass of London porter on a hot day
16,000 miles from the Thames.) The first day, which is sometimes a
little stiff and formal, passed agreeably away, amid general conversation. This is also a very large station, not quite so well situated perhaps as Captain R.'s, but possessed of a better cottage. Many thousand
sheep bleat on the ranges, and the wool harvest, in all its shapes, was
going on. . . . In this station everything seemed to go on like clock-
work. Regularly every morning Mr Barton starts for the washing pool
by nine o'clock, and there overlooks the shearers, until the dinner
hour; whilst I, after accompanying him the first day to see the process
and the difficulties his scientific skill had overcome in obtaining a
level for a proper fall, amused myself in the house, talking to the
blacks — of whom there is a tribe in the district; or in reading, as
the library contained an excellent — though small — collection of
books — a possession invaluable at so great a distance from Pater-
noster Row. . . .

* In *Australia and the East* (1843). The author presented a copy of this book to Mrs
Barton.

I have now passed three days here, and have been most hospitably entertained. The forenoon I have always to myself, and the evenings flit away quickly with my talented host, whose conversational powers are aided by his extensive wanderings in most of the countries of Europe, and in many Eastern lands. We saw last night a pastime of a description I have long desired to see — a corroboree. . . .

John Hood passed through Boree Nyrang again on Christmas Day 1841 and wrote:

. . . I called at the door to ask for our friends. We were urged to eat our Christmas dinner with this most hospitable family, and on my declining, my kind host brought me the most delightful draught I ever drank under a broiling sun, a large tumbler of claret, and heartily do I wish that I, some day or other, may see him at Stoneridge, that I — in my turn — might try my hand at hospitality. . . .

He recorded his goodbye to Boree Nyrang on 10 January 1842:

I called to-day at Boree to take farewells of my kind friends. . . . May grass grow, and water run speedily at Boree, and may my excellent and hospitable acquaintance long live to show kindness to the stranger, and to enjoy the greatest blessing this world can offer to man — domestic happiness.

His reference to the travels of Robert Barton is an interesting one. Mr Barton had been a sea-captain; and though one is inclined to wonder at this from the evidence of his long period of seasickness aboard the *Alfred*, it explains his travels in Europe (i.e., around the Mediterranean) and in the East. It is worth mentioning too that Mr Hood travelled down the River Lachlan to the "Buckinbar" country and recorded that it was "extremely bad"; the plains "as level as if a roller had passed over, but no verdure. All was arid red earth, and sand, and interminable wooden flats" — all of which accords with Paterson's own recollections[3] of the country as "worth no more" than the "few pence per acre" to the Crown.

Emily's courage and patience must have been monumental. Prowling aboriginals were always a threat to the homestead; on one occasion the Boree tribe, pursued by a tribe from the Yass country, turned at bay and waged a pitched battle in the homestead itself; many were slaughtered in the garden until jackaroos came to the rescue, flourishing guns. The aboriginals had, however, ransacked the house, taking all the food and tobacco; Emily Barton with her children found safety in a back room. Her lot was made harder because her husband broke his leg when thrown from a horse; it never properly set, and he was lame thereafter; he became irritable and morose. Nor did he ever adapt successfully to the life of a squatter; he had an indifferent head for business and in her later life Emily Barton recalled that he had brought £20,000 to Australia (a considerable sum for those days) and had used it mainly to stock his holding with sheep, cattle and horses. He paid 22/6 a head for sheep; yet within

two years their price fell to 2/6d. Undaunted by droughts and failing
crops and all the discomforts so engendered, Emily Barton, who did not
leave the station for twenty-five years, clothed and fed her large family,
looked after their every need (there was no doctor within nearly a
hundred miles) and, above all, educated them. It was told of her that, if
the governess of the moment could not teach Latin, she would be sent to
help in the kitchen while Mrs Barton took the lesson; if there were no
governess, she would have the boys stand round the kitchen table reciting
their French and Latin verbs while she made the bread and puddings.

Yet still she found time to jot down her odd verses: not good verse,
admittedly, and heavily influenced by the literary traditions she had
inherited, but full of a genuine sincerity and almost passionate feeling.
Here are some lines she wrote in 1843, part of a poem "Our First Little
Home on the Plains of Boree":

> O, proud are the halls of our own British land,
>   And fair are the cottages round them that rise;
> And oft, in my dreams, on the green hills I stand,
>   Whence in childhood I gazed on the pale northern skies.
> I was blest, I was blest! yet I would not retrace
>   Even youth's buoyant step on the steep mountain side.
> No, my husband, I gaze on thy bright, honest face,
>   And I love the wild land that has made me thy bride.
>
> And O, should kind Heaven our barque ever steer
>   O'er the wide rolling waves to our home in the West,
> To dwell in the mansions to memory dear,
>   Or sleep by the graves where our forefathers rest,
> My pray'r shall be still to the Ruler above,
>   That wherever in future our dwelling shall be,
> It may be the abode of Content, Peace and Love,
>   Like our first little home on the plains of Boree.

The Bartons' best friends were the Smiths; Mr John Smith was the
overseer of a large adjacent property known as The Molong Run. Two
of his daughters married Barton boys, and the eldest daughter subsequently became godmother to A. B. Paterson. Andrew Paterson made
several visits to Gamboola, one of the Smith properties on The Molong
Run, to buy sheep. Here on one occasion he met Rose Barton, one of
Emily's daughters, fell in love with her and later married her at Boree
Nyrang. (Weddings and christenings were homestead affairs in those
days.) Very soon after this, in 1860, Robert Barton died; droughts, labour
shortages because of the gold-rushes, and depressions had taken their toll
both of him and of his property — and Boree Nyrang was sold. Emily
Barton, as elegantly buoyant and intellectually alert as ever, having
discharged the responsibilities of a pioneer's wife with classic fortitude
and optimism, left the district for Sydney and a new life in a charming
old home at Gladesville, where she could pursue for the rest of her life
in the charm and tranquillity of her advancing age, her literary and

cultural interests and where she was to exert a strong and shaping influence on the schoolboy and youth Andrew Barton Paterson when he was sent to live with her and continue his education in Sydney.

Narambla, where Banjo Paterson was born, nestles beside Summer Hill Creek; about twelve miles further on, this stream joins with Lewis Ponds Creek at Ophir, where Australia's first payable gold was discovered in 1851. At Narambla a miller named Templer had built, in the 1840s, a flour mill, first worked by wind-power, but later by steam. It served the colonists for many miles around. Templer met and married Emily Barton's sister, who had come out to Australia with her in the *Alfred*, and when, many years later, the young Mrs Rose Paterson was about to have her first baby, it was decided that the rough home at Buckenbah, far in the bush country, was no place for the event and that she should go to Narambla which was near Orange (on the Orange-Ophir road about two and a half miles north-east of the town) and suitable medical help.

Those who remember Narambla — a smallish station home built of weatherboard, with not many rooms but wide verandas back and front — recall especially its beautiful front flower-garden, the very particular joy of Mrs Templer, in which she sought to create a pocket of the English countryside still so dear to her. For this was an English garden with an array of highly-scented flowers: roses predominant, stocks, lilacs, wallflower, lavender, bordered by violets. The wide front veranda was covered in jasmine, honeysuckle and climbing roses. The boy Paterson, paying frequent visits to his great-aunt's home, never lost his memories of it, and many years later, in his poem "On Kiley's Run" recalled the old Narambla home:

> The roving breezes come and go
> On Kiley's Run,
> The sleepy river murmurs low,
> And far away one dimly sees
> Beyond the stretch of forest trees —
> Beyond the foothills dusk and dun —
> The ranges steeping in the sun
> On Kiley's Run.
>
> 'Tis many years since first I came
> To Kiley's Run,
> More years than I would care to name
> Since I, a stripling, used to ride
> For miles and miles at Kiley's side,
> The while in stirring tones he told
> The stories of the days of old
> On Kiley's Run.
>
> I see the old bush homestead now
> On Kiley's Run,
> Just nestled down beneath the brow
> Of one small ridge above the sweep

Of river-flat, where willows weep
And jasmine flowers and roses bloom.
The air was laden with perfume
On Kiley's Run.

The ruin of the old mill can still be seen on the hillside; there is no trace
of the homestead: nothing but a few of the ornamental trees that once
surrounded it.

Gone is the garden they kept with care;
Left to decay at its own sweet will,
Fruit-trees and flower-beds eaten bare,
Cattle and sheep where the roses were,
Under the shadow of Kiley's Hill.

Until he reached the age of five, "Barty", as he came to be called,
lived at Buckenbah, in the wilds of the bush. Only stray childhood
memories remain; he saw little of his father who in an effort to balance
the continuing difficulties with droughts and poor prices on the Buckenbah property, spent a good deal of time away from home pioneering in
Queensland. In fact he took up some land there, and on one occasion
undertook the arduous project of droving sheep from the poor country of
Buckenbah to the richer land he had taken up in Queensland. But he
was caught in flooded country between two rivers for so long that he had
to shear his sheep on a sandhill and much of the wool was lost or
damaged. There were open skirmishes with aborigines which added to the
danger of his journeys. A. B. Paterson himself did not remember the name
of his father's property in Queensland, but understood that it adjoined
Lammermoor, the station described in *Christison of Lammermoor*,[4] which
he regarded as "probably the second-best tale ever told of bush life;
Jeannie Gunn's *We of the Never Never* being the best".[5]

There were plenty of reasons why A. B. Paterson should have held this
opinion of *Christison of Lammermoor*. Robert Christison, a young Scot,
the son of a Berwickshire parson, had emigrated in 1852 to Victoria at
the age of fifteen, penniless and owing his second-class fare, but, within
a few years of work on Victorian sheep stations, had become an expert
bushman, horseman and horsebreaker. He won many amateur races,
including a Geelong Steeplechase on Camel in 1857, which would have
impressed Paterson. Christison headed north to Queensland in the 1860s,
took out an occupation licence for virgin country in the Tower Hill
district, which he christened Lammermoor, and, with only his Victorian
savings, his horses and the clothes he wore, set about stocking and building his station. Within thirty years, after enduring every possible priva-
tion of drought, depression and conflict with aborigines (whom he
eventually won over by his own friendship and kindness), he was master
at the end of the century of a huge property with forty thousand cattle,
including one of the finest stud herds in the country, five hundred of the
best stockhorses, a homestead every slab of which he had split and placed
himself, as he had every log in his great stockyards. He had surveyed every

mile of the hundreds of miles of fencing, and planned every one of the dozen pumping plants on the property. He was up every morning of the year at daylight to ride long distances supervising the work; he sat in his office till midnight working on his station papers. *Christison of Lammermoor*, one feels, could well have been an important source-book for Brian Penton's *Landtakers*. At any rate Christison himself embodied all those qualities of bushman, pioneer and horseman which A. B. Paterson esteemed — qualities which in some part, he undoubtedly considered, were shared by his own father, who, with much less success had vainly tried to wrest such a fortune too from the hostile Australian outback.

For eventually Andrew Paterson's losses in Queensland were so great that, along with the difficulties of running Buckenbah, both properties had to be sold, the latter to a Thomas MacCulloch. With a bank loan, Andrew Paterson then bought a station called Illalong, further south in the more fertile Yass district. But ill-luck followed him again, and for reasons already given,[6] the bank foreclosed and Illalong too had to be sold. But luckily the buyer of Illalong, Henry Browne, also had the adjoining properties of Bendemire and Dandaraligo and he made Andrew Paterson manager of all his properties. The Illalong homestead was built on Illalong Creek, in the Parish of Binalong, in the County of Harden, about four miles from Binalong township and rather more than two hundred miles from Sydney. Binalong is a corruption of Benelong, who was the chief of an aboriginal tribe belonging to another part of the State. The townspeople changed the name to Binalong.

Young Barty's home therefore remained at Illalong, and here, in bush surroundings in many ways idyllic for a growing boy, he spent his childhood.

NOTES

[1] In his *Sydney Morning Herald* reminiscences.
[2] A copy was made available to me by Florence Earle Hooper.
[3] Op. cit.
[4] By Mrs M. M. Bennett (Robert Christison's daughter) : published 1927.
[5] Reminiscences, op. cit.
[6] See p. 6.

CHAPTER IV

A Bush Boyhood

*I think Australian boys who have never been at school in
the bush have lost something for which town life can never
compensate . . .*

— A. B. PATERSON.[1]

ALTOGETHER THERE WERE seven children in the Paterson family: Andrew
Barton ("Barty"), Hamilton, Florence, Jessie, Edith, Grace and Gwen.
But Barty was by his own later admission a lonely child (he was twelve
years older than his brother), and in a way this was the genesis of his
great and abiding love of the bush. For, like many a lonely bush child
before him, he found constant and unlimited pleasure in the sights and
sounds about him. The rather barren district of Yeoval in which Buckenbah lay did not offer many attractions; but since Paterson was only five
when his father moved south to Illalong it was natural enough that his
consciousness of what the bush could offer stemmed from this point of
time. Apart from the more fertile and hence scenic environment of the
Yass district, it offered highly romantic possibilities to a growing boy. The
station at Illalong, to begin with, was on the main route between Sydney
and Melbourne, so that the exciting traffic of horsemen, bullock teams,
drovers and especially coaches became a familiar sight. Indeed Cobb and
Company's coaching system was by 1870 at the peak of its efficiency.
Using relays of horses — sometimes urged along at breakneck speeds of up
to ten miles an hour — the coaches made the 600-mile journey between
Sydney and Melbourne in five days.

It was even more stirring to a young imagination that the gold diggings
at Lambing Flat (now called Young) were only a day's ride away, and that
the gold escort came past twice a week with an armed trooper, rifle at
the ready, riding in front and another on the box with the coachman.
Like a city boy well nourished on television who hopes he may some day
or other see a bank robbery take place before his eyes, young Barty Paterson, since the daydreams of small boys hardly vary with the times, "used
to hope that the escort would be 'stuck up' outside our place so that I
might see something worthwhile, but what with the new settlers and the
scores of bullock teams taking loads out to the back country no bushranger stood half a chance of making a getaway unseen. . . ."[2]

The bullockies with their teams fascinated the lad. Here, for a start
was his introduction to the great "characters" of the bush. His parents
warned him not to talk to nor become friendly with the teamsters, who
were suspected among other enormities of conduct, of horse-stealing, but

young Barty found them well worth getting to know. They were compassionate people: they travelled with their families, dogs, sometimes even their fowls which hopped down from the wagons as soon as camp was made to scratch for food. Like "The Road to Hogan's Gap", the roads were unmade:

> . . . if you should miss the slope
> And get below the track,
> You haven't got the slightest hope
> Of ever getting back . . .

In wet weather the tracks, once they were cut up, became quagmires; wagons sank down to their axles, and the bullockies had to try a new track. As Paterson recalls from his boyhood memories:

> Thus the highway became a labyrinth of tracks half a mile wide, with here and there an excavation where a wagon had been dug out; and when, as often happened, a wagon got stuck in the bed of a creek, they would hitch two teams of bullocks to it, and then (as one of the bullockies said) either the wagon or the bed of the creek had to come.[3]

The boy Paterson, during his lonely vigils on the track, made friends with many of the bullockies; they yarned with him, and were pleased on occasions to give him demonstrations with their great whips — cutting deep furrows in the bark of nearby trees. When he said it was no wonder the bullocks pulled, a bullocky replied:

> Sonny, if I done that to them bullocks I'd want shooting. Every bullock knows his name and when I speak to him he's into the yoke. I'd look well knockin' 'em about with a hundred miles to go and them not gettin' a full feed once a week. Many a night I've dug up a panel of a squatter's paddock and slipped 'em in, and I've been back there before daylight, to slip 'em out and put the panel up agen. So long as they'll stick to me I'll stick to them.[4]

Shades of the "Eumerella Shore" and the free selectors who helped themselves to a few cattle occasionally! Paterson made reference to this type of stock free-loading practice in his novel *An Outback Marriage*, but it is surprising how few of his childhood experiences are projected into his verse, although undoubtedly these bush types that he met helped him to create such identities as Salt Bush Bill and Mulga Bill. But one of his best-known ballads stemmed from his first visit to a race-meeting, and probably his passion for the sport of horse-racing may have begun at this point too.

One New Year's Day the station rouseabout (a youth of eighteen) took the eight-year-old Paterson to the Bogolong picnic races nearby. (Bogolong is now Bookham on the Hume Highway between Sydney and Melbourne.) Bookham, as Paterson recalls, was made up of two pubs with a half a mile of road between; ". . : one pub," said the knowledgeable rouseabout, "to ketch the coves coming from Yass and the other to ketch the coves from Jugiong". The racecourse was some distance from the town, laid out through a gum and stringybark scrub; there was no grandstand; and the racehorses were tied to trees here and there. The men from Snowy River were there, wild, reckless riders; others, just as accomplished horsemen, from the rough Murrumbidgee country; aboriginals; half-castes and a few townspeople from Yass and nearby centres. The young Barty had ridden over on a pony with a light saddle; just before the main race, the Bogolong Town Plate, was run, he saw a tall Murrumbidgee horseman removing the saddle and putting it on his racehorse. The mountain man told him not to worry; the race was "ketch weights"; he therefore wanted to borrow the lightest saddle he could, and he promised the boy a ginger beer if his horse, Pardon, won. As Paterson recalls

> . . . Imagine then the excitement with which I watched Pardon's progress — watched him lying behind the leaders as they went out of sight behind the stringybark scrub; watched them come into sight again, with Pardon still lying third; and then the crowning moment as he drew away in the straight to win comfortably . . .[5]

When the Murrumbidgee man assured him — as he gave him his ginger beer ". . . bitter, lukewarm stuff with hops in it . . ." — that Pardon could not have won without his saddle, the boy's joy was complete. Many years later Paterson admitted* that this boyhood experience was the origin of his ballad "Old Pardon, the Son of Reprieve":

> Then loud rose the war-cry for Pardon;
>   He swept like the wind down the dip,
> And over the rise by the garden
>   The jockey was done with the whip.
> The field was at sixes and sevens —
>   The pace at the first had been fast —
> And hope seemed to drop from the heavens,
>   For Pardon was coming at last.
>
> And how he did come! It was splendid;
>   He gained on them yards every bound,
> Stretching out like a greyhound extended,
>   His girth laid right down on the ground.
> A shimmer of silk in the cedars
>   As into the running they wheeled,
> And out flashed the whips on the leaders,
>   For Pardon had collared the field.

* With characteristic modesty he wrote in his *Sydney Morning Herald* reminiscences in 1939: . . ."Years afterwards I worked the incident into a sort of ballad called 'Old Pardon, the Son of Reprieve'." But only a year before, in an article headed "Looking Backward" (*Sydney Mail*, 28 December 1938) he had given a different version: "My father's cousin owned a bush horse called Pardon in the days when they ran mile races in three heats. Pardon was left in a stable at a bush pub on a very rigid diet awaiting his race on the morrow; but being gifted with brains and resource Mr Pardon managed to knock down the rails of his stall and to get at a bale of lucerne. Tradition goes that by the time daylight came he had eaten most of it . . . he seemed in no shape for racing. In these circumstances his victory was, to say the least of it, creditable, and earned the tribute of a set of verses."

Schooldays were now at hand. The boy Paterson, however, did not need to go to school for his rudiments of learning; the Paterson household was, despite its isolation from more populous centres, never lacking in an appreciation of the things of culture. Rose Paterson had inherited from her mother, Emily Barton, a love for music — and the Paterson children had this passed on to them. Books were plentiful: Andrew, the father, was a keen reader, and on one occasion when he brought home for his children a complete set of Scott and Dickens and was upbraided by his wife for "such extravagance", he replied, "My dear, I have given them an education".[6] A governess had been employed to teach Barty to read and write; and when he had also been taught the other educational necessity of being able to catch and saddle a horse, it was decided that he should ride bareback (the beginnings no doubt of his subsequent prowess as a horseman) the four miles to the little bush school at Bina-long — "a two-pub town", Paterson recalled, "famous for the fact that the bushranger Gilbert was buried in the police paddock".[7] Whether in fact he sat in school, as he claims, with the young boys and girls who were the descendants of Gilbert is open to doubt, since as John Manifold has subsequently pointed out,[8] Gilbert died unmarried. Of course they may have been Gilbert's descendants notwithstanding, but they are more likely to have been the young Dunns, descendants of another local bush-ranger and member of that celebrated triumvirate, "Dunn, Gilbert and Ben Hall". Since Paterson did not stay in the district long, it is obvious that the confusions of childhood clouded his recollections; in any case had he stayed longer he would have learned more than a verse or two of "The Ballad of Ben Hall's Gang" and would not have had, some thirty years later, to advertise for it for his collection of old bush songs.

But out of these early days did come one of his very few bushranger ballads, "How Gilbert Died". Now since Paterson was never very pro-bushranger in all his life and writings and, as in his novel *An Outback Marriage*, classed bushrangers with the less desirable elements of bush life and saw little that was heroic or redeemable in their lives and actions, it is the more surprising that this ballad, written incidentally in his best literary ballad style, is pro-bushranger to a remarkable degree.

> Then he dropped the piece with a bitter oath,
>   And he turned to his comrade Dunn:
> "We are sold," he said, "we are dead men both! —
>   Still, there may be a chance for one;
> I'll stop and I'll fight with the pistol here,
>   You take to your heels and run."

> So Dunn crept out on his hands and knees
>   In the dim, half-dawning light,
> And he made his way to a patch of trees,
>   And was lost in the black of night;
> And the trackers hunted his tracks all day,
>   But they never could trace his flight.

But Gilbert walked from the open door
  In a confident style and rash;
He heard at his side the rifles roar,
  And he heard the bullets crash.
But he laughed as he lifted his pistol-hand,
  And he fired at the rifle flash.

Then out of the shadows the troopers aimed
  At his voice and the pistol sound.
With rifle flashes the darkness flamed —
  He staggered and spun around,
And they riddled his body with rifle balls
  As it lay on the blood-soaked ground.

There's never a stone at the sleeper's head,
  There's never a fence beside,
And the wandering stock on the grave may tread
  Unnoticed and undenied;
But the smallest child on the Watershed
  Can tell you how Gilbert died.

This is in marked contrast by the way to his other bushranger ballad about the same gang, "In the Stable", where the members of it were depicted as most unpleasant characters indeed:

Robbing the coach and the escort, stealing our horses at night,
Calling sometimes at the homesteads and giving the women a fright.

In addition to two of the most despicable crimes in the bush calendar — molesting women and stealing horses — Paterson had them in this ballad commit the equally black deed of wantonly killing a horse, so that when at the end they were all captured and killed, justice seemed to have been well served: "none of 'em lived to be hung."

But reverting to "How Gilbert Died", the clue is surely in the last couplet: that Paterson wrote this ballad with sentimental and nostalgic memories of his days at the little bush school at Binalong. For these were halcyon days to him — as his later reminiscences and recollections in various publications showed. (Since he wrote "In the Stable" much later, no doubt by then he was looking at things more with the squatter's jaundiced eye.) Paterson remembered especially his gaunt Irish schoolmaster, who, in his spare time, was devoted to the pastime of raising and training kangaroo dogs and gamecocks. Sometimes the children were taken out in a group into the paddocks to watch a kangaroo dog run down a hare; sometimes

... the elite of the school, the poundkeeper's son and the blacksmith's boy, would be allowed as a favour to stop after school and watch a "go-in" between two cocks without the steel spurs, as part of their training for more serious business . . .⁹

The youngsters who sat in the schoolroom with him came from huts, selections, and homesteads far and near; from them Paterson learned even at the juvenile level concerned, a good deal of bushcraft and bush-lore; but he always marvelled, even in later life, at their lack of sophistication and common sense in more worldly things. Such as, for instance, excuses for being late for school: inevitably the standard reply was: "Father sent me after 'orses." With the dry humour that characterizes many a Paterson prose piece in the *Bulletin*, Paterson recollected that, "as their parents were largely engaged in looking after horses, mostly other people's . . .", this was more than probable, but became very thin as an excuse with constant repetition. So the more astute young Paterson took his schoolmates in hand and drilled into them a series of more convincing excuses, such as books forgotten and the return to get them, no clock in the house, an errand to the storekeeper and so on. But when the time came and one, Ryan, was late and challenged by the schoolteacher his eyes rolled, his jaw dropped and he gasped out the old familiar "Father sent me after 'orses".

There were the usual highlights in Paterson's two years or so of bush schooling. The arrival of the school inspector, supposedly unheralded, was in fact well taken care of by bush-telegraph, so that the minute the inspector arrived in town a schoolboy was posted as a "cockatoo" on a distant fence to signal a warning of the inspector's approach, and when he finally entered the schoolroom, there was a scene of admirable industry.

When the railway came to town, so did the navvies, and their many children — tough, cunning and completely uninhibited. When the school teacher, in desperation, used the cane more frequently, the mothers, often "fierce, snorting Irishwomen", decended on the schoolroom, and the school teacher, to the great delight of his pupils, cowered before their shrill and threatening abuse. Not that they needed to have done this: the children in question were quite capable of fending for themselves; they had travelled and drifted with their parents all over the colony and had a "fluency in excuse and fertility in falsehood" that their awed school-mates could admire but never emulate.

As for the navvies themselves, their drinking bouts were frequent and prolonged, in many cases ending in what was colloquially known as "the horrors" or "the jumps"; in fact the townspeople evolved an even briefer description: they would simply say that so-and-so "had 'em" or had "got 'em". "Well I remember," Paterson recalled,

> . . . the policeman, a little spitfire of a man about five feet nothing, coming to the school and stating that a huge navvy named Cornish Jack had "got 'em" and was wandering about the town with them, and he called upon the schoolmaster in the Queen's name to come and assist him to arrest Cornish Jack. The teacher did not like the job at all and his wife abused the policeman heartily, but it ended in the whole school going, and we marched through the town till we discovered the quarry seated on a log pawing the air with his hands. The sergeant and the teacher surrounded him so to speak, but to our

disgust he submitted very quickly and was bundled in a cart and
driven off to the lockup. Such incidents as these formed breaks in the
monotony of school life and helped to enlarge our knowledge of
human nature.[10]

Certainly Paterson stored these and other bush experiences, and the tales
of the early days told him by his father and grandmother, so that he had
a rich variety of subject matter to hand for his ballads and prose sketches;
these latter, often little more than bush anecdotes, gained much colour
from this sort of remembered incident. The rough bush folk, many living
just within the law, who are described in *An Outback Marriage*, stemmed
directly from such a community as that at Binalong. But these bush
schooldays were all too soon ended.

In 1874, Barty's parents decided he should go to school in Sydney, as
a day-boy, living with his grandmother at Gladesville. He was enrolled
at Sydney Grammar School, but had first of all to attend for a few months
a private preparatory school — "where we were all young gentlemen", he
drily recalls, "and had to wear good clothes instead of hob-nailed boots
and moleskins in which my late schoolmates invariably appeared. . . .
nobody ever 'had em', and nobody was sent after 'orses, nobody wore
spurs in school."[11] To his horror there was the ultimate indignity for a
bush-bred boy: he had to learn dancing.

Soon, however, he went over to Sydney Grammar School, one of
Sydney's "Great Public Schools", which since its foundation in 1857 has
numbered among its alumni such eminent Australians as Sir Edmund
Barton, Sir Hubert Murray and Sir Robert Garran. There is not much
record of Paterson's six years' stay at this school. We do know that he
looked forward perhaps with even more eagerness than his companions to
the school vacations, so that he could return to his much-loved haunts at
Illalong. There was throughout his life a strong bond between him and
his five younger sisters; certainly his visits home were the events of the
year for them. But as he was growing older, he was also absorbing with
more understanding and sensibility the scenes and characters which were
to become the stuff of his verse and prose. Sometimes on these vacations
he went camping with some of his cousins along the Murrumbidgee, on
its upper reaches and in the Snowy country: here especially, he found
material for his future verses. He was now, too, developing his remarkable
skill in riding, shooting and bushcraft — and this in spite of a shortened
and weakened right hand, which was an affliction carried throughout his
life. Indeed, Sir Edward Knox who knew him later recalls that even in
middle age, Banjo had a characteristic pose when, with his stiff right arm,
he developed a queer, cramped action in stuffing tobacco in his pipe. The
cause of this had been an undetected break in the arm when he was an
infant and his aboriginal nurse-girl had let him fall to the ground. The
boy determined that this should be no handicap; he learned to ride and
play tennis with his left hand; he was a keen cricketer, playing for his
school team and also for the Illalong team when he was home on holidays;
he believed too that the skill in riding he developed was because the
weakness of the right arm gave him a more sensitive bridle hand. At one

stage doctors thought it necessary to remove his whole thumb down to the wrist, but a later operation, though severe, saved the thumb.

Paterson in later years when asked about his years at Sydney Grammar School was usually non-committal, remembering or preferring to remember, the usual physical manifestations rather than the scholastic progress of this period. He recalled, for instance, a fight between two doctors' sons which lasted a whole lunch-time, for a couple of hours after school, began early next morning and finished just before school started, mainly because one of the boys' hands gave way. The moral, said Paterson, was that it was better to let boys have boxing-gloves and encourage them to use them: it was the surest way of keeping fights down.

He also recalled a practice called "wallarooing" — a favourite winter pastime. Boys would wander round the playgrounds casually, the ringleaders singling out some quiet and inoffensive youth, whereupon, at the cry "wallaroo him", the unsuspecting boy was grabbed and pushed to the ground. His mouth was stuffed with grass, his hat stamped as flat as a plate, his boots taken off and hurled away; then his persecutors went off in search of the next victim. *Sic tempora, sic mores.*

But Paterson's innate modesty always prevented him from admitting that he had in fact been a good, conscientious student, and if his school career could not be described as brilliant, it was not far removed, since he shared the Junior Knox Prize with George Rich, later Mr Justice Rich of the High Court. He matriculated at the age of sixteen, and sat for a university scholarship; years later he said characteristically that he missed it "by a mile and a half", but the fact was that his failure was very much narrower than that. At any rate, he then was entered in a solicitor's office to take articles. It is strange how the biographical error has persisted so frequently that he studied at the University of Sydney. Vance Palmer in *The Legend of the Nineties*, Denton Prout in *Henry Lawson — The Grey Dreamer*, even Percival Serle in his *Dictionary of Australian Biography* are among a number of quite distinguished writers who seem not to have taken the trouble to check their facts.

As for Paterson, his laconic and characteristic comment, many years on, was: "If I had paid as much attention to my lessons as to fish and rabbits, I, too, might have been a Judge of the High Court. There is a lot of luck in these things."[12]

NOTES

[1] In "My Various Schools" (*Sydneian*, May 1890).
[2] In his *Sydney Morning Herald* reminiscences.
[3] Ibid.
[4] Ibid.
[5] Ibid.
[6] Quoted by Florence Earle Hooper in *Andrew Barton Paterson: A Memoir* (Pt. 1), *Yass Tribune-Courier*, 6 June 1949.
[7] In his *Sydney Morning Herald* reminiscences.
[8] In *Who Wrote the Ballads* (1964).
[9] In his *Sydney Morning Herald* reminiscences.
[10] In "My Various Schools" (*Sydneian*, May 1890).
[11] Ibid.
[12] In his *Sydney Morning Herald* reminiscences.

CHAPTER V

Growing Up in Sydney

And lo, a miracle! the land
But yesterday was all unknown
The wild man's boomerang was thrown
Where now great busy cities stand . . .

— A. B. PATERSON.

. . . whereas the country around Melbourne for miles is
mostly as flat as a pancake, the suburbs of Sydney literally
revel in beautiful building sites. For choice, there are the
water frontages below the town or up the Parramatta River,
which is lined with pretty houses, whose inhabitants come
up to Sydney every morning in small river steamers . . .

— R. E. N. TWOPENNY: *Town Life in Australia*: 1883.

EMILY BARTON had, early in the 1860s, settled in Gladesville, a waterside suburb of Sydney on the Parramatta River near Hunters Hill. There were, and are, few prettier spots in Sydney than some of these river suburbs; Gladesville in present-day Sydney has surrendered a good deal of its charm to the pressure of working-class housing, and is not as fashionable, nor has it maintained its natural riverscapes as effectively, as adjacent suburbs like Longueville, Northwood and Hunters Hill. But in the 1870s it was indeed a "village of gardens and flowers". Even twenty-five years later it could be noted that "the . . . fashionable suburbs are Elizabeth Bay, Potts Point, Rushcutters Bay, Gladesville, Point Piper . . . At all the above places the houses are mostly large, and are surrounded by beautifully laid-out grounds."[1]

Gladesville was originally settled by the building of inns to give rest and food to wayfarers — the drivers and passengers of teams, drays and coaches — for the section of the Great North Road (now Victoria Road) to Maitland via Wiseman's Ferry had been built in 1832 to connect with a punt or ferry service established across the river at Gladesville, from Bedlam Point to Abbotsford on the western-suburbs bank of the Parramatta. The suburb took its name from one John Glade who, at about this time, had a grant of fifty acres in this vicinity; he built a stone cottage overlooking what is now Glade's Bay. At Bedlam Point, just above the punt terminal, Rockend Stone Cottage had been built — originally as an inn. But it failed to get a licence — an inn had already been licensed on the other side of the river at Abbotsford — and Rockend became a home, with a delightful garden running down to the water's edge. This was where Emily Barton eventually came to live; the punt berthed at the bottom of the garden and she kept her carriage in the driveway for her journeys to the city.

Here, with the hard days spent, she made her home a centre of cheerful culture and an attraction to her neighbours and friends, including, incidentally, some of the "best" families of Sydney: the Blaxlands, Murray-Priors, Betts, le Gay Breretons, Fitzgeralds and Windeyers. Edward Marsden ("Teddy") Betts was a celebrity throughout the colony. He was Assistant Superintendent of the Gladesville Mental Hospital (his mother was the youngest daughter of the Reverend Samuel Marsden, famous in early colonial history), and became Mayor of Ryde and later of Hunters Hill; but he was best known as an outstanding amateur rider in race meetings all over the country. He was a member of the Australian Jockey Club, serving for many years on its various committees — and he took a personal interest in the boy Paterson and encouraged him to become a first-class horseman.

For Barty Paterson had come to live with his grandmother at Rockend in 1874. The effect this intelligent and cultured environment had on his adolescent development in the next ten years or so is incalculable. It was not only a matter of his formal education — Mrs Barton, for instance, gave him a fluency in French, as well as a love for Carlyle, Ruskin and Swinburne — but also that she told him endless stories of her pioneering days in the bush, linking him with the outback of the 1840s and 1850s and instilling even more deeply into him an Australianism that was to colour his writing for the rest of his life. Beyond this, the graces of living which so characterized the daily round at Rockend saw Paterson gradually change from the rather shy and awkward boy into a young man whose polished wit, elegance of manner and athletic gamesmanship, allied with saturnine good looks, made him one of the most gay and sought after young men of the 1890s. All this was to come to the boy who now, in the company of Emily Barton's son, Frank (a well-known Sydney solicitor who later on became Master-in-Lunacy), made his daily journey by steamer ferry along one of the most beautiful waterways in the world to his school in the city.

To a boy growing up in Sydney in these years — and a country boy to boot — the city was a surging, stimulating metropolis, bustling with growth, kaleidoscopic with attractions. The citizens were still ingenuously proud of their fine new Post Office with its high granite-pillared front and of their "Tow Nall" (as a visiting writer heard it colloquially referred to) : "a good deal of confectionery ornament about it, and no massiveness, but it is possessed of great beauty."[2] Even in those days the traffic appeared greater than it was because of the narrowness of the streets; soon after the young Paterson arrived in the city, the steam trams appeared, exciting contraptions with upper-decked passenger cars in tow. Although their introduction brought about the gradual elimination of the horse omnibus, these still played an important rôle in public transport for many years — with their two carpet-cushioned seats facing each other along the length of the bus, and straw-covered floor. Supplementing these larger vehicles were hundreds of hansom cabs plying up and down the main streets, their most frequent rendezvous in George and Pitt Streets.

Some Saturday nights Barty Paterson was taken into the city as a special treat; for then Sydney was in its glory as thousands of its citizens promenaded the main streets, thronging about the shops and the open air markets. Gas-lamps flared fitfully in the shops; outside cheapjacks shouted their wares; so did barrel organists and dozens of itinerant street musicians. Larrikins in "pushes", young women then as now in small groups doubtfully eyeing their pursuers, housewives carrying loaded baskets of fruit and groceries, solid burghers with their families — until nine or ten o'clock it seemed the entire population was out of doors, and the slow-moving crowds took up the whole width of the streets. Then as now unsightly structures jutted out into the thoroughfares, especially in George and Pitt Streets often with three or four different styles of colouring and lettering according to the greater or less inartistic abilities of the shopkeepers attempting these decorations.

As for Sydney itself, the years between 1875 and 1885 saw a suburban population and development explosion paralleled only by that which has taken place since World War II. Because adequate vehicular and water transport, the construction of roads and bridges, thriving industry and trade had paved the way for it, building activity boomed. Suburban estates were sub-divided, and building lots were auctioned in their tens of thousands — from Botany and Alexandria in the south, to the cow-paddocks of Ashfield and Burwood in the west, to the Harbour's north-side, where pockets of suburban dwellings — at North Sydney, Wollstone-craft, St. Leonards and Chatswood — gradually coalesced in a rash of house-building. As an English observer wrote:

> The overflow of bricks and mortar has spread like a lava-flood, over the adjacent slopes, heights, and valleys, till the houses now lie, pile on pile, tier on tier, and succeed each other row after row, street after street, far into the surrounding country; and the eruption is still in active play, and everywhere the work of building and city extension proceeds at a rapid pace. The invasion of construction has bridged the harbour, and laid out streets innumerable on the North Shore; masonry crowns every island in the spacious basin — every projecting buttress of rock maintains a pedestal of wall and gable and roof. Verandahs overrun the heights, and chimney-stacks peep out from the hollows. The sand drives are covered with cottages, the very marshes have a crop of dwellings, that are constantly springing up, like mushrooms . . .[8]

The 1870s were significant years in the city's history; for it was during this time that the suburban population outstripped that of the city proper. At the beginning of the decade the proportion was of the order of 63,000 to 75,000; by 1891 the figures were 125,000 against 100,000. Much of this population concentrated around those waterways down which Barty Paterson's steamer carried him each morning; in truth, the "bastard Venice of the Antipodes", as Sir James Martin had described the colonial capital in the 1860s, had flamboyantly come into its own.

The society of Sydney still rotated around Government House. In the

1870s Sir Hercules Robinson was a most popular Governor; a genial administrator and an immaculate gentleman with all the mannerisms of the late Victorian aristocratic circle, his entourage was cultivated by the new and old families of Sydney. "His fondness for field sports and the manly character of his utterances," recorded the *Australian Handbook* of 1878, "makes him much liked by a large proportion of the community." During his régime Australia's first International Exhibition, with its Garden Palace in the Botanical Gardens, was held in 1879, to which the eager fifteen-year-old Paterson was taken; he shared in the city's dismay when, a few years later, the Palace was burned to the ground in Sydney's most spectacular fire up to that time. His uncle Frank Barton also took him to the Royal Agricultural Society's Shows, in those years held at Prince Alfred Park (the venue was changed to Moore Park in 1880). For the rest of his life, indeed, Paterson was enthusiastically interested in Agricultural Shows (city or country), which in their organization and presentation are institutions peculiar to Australia. In his latter years he seldom missed a Sydney Show, and he was a familiar figure in the official pavilions. One of his best short stories, "Sitting in Judgement", concerns a country show where Paterson from his many years of experience painted a picture faithful in every detail —

> . . . Crowds of sightseers wandered past the cattle stalls to gape at the fat bullocks; side-shows flourished, a blasé goose drew marbles out of a tin canister, and a boxing showman displayed his muscles outside his tent, while his partner urged the youth of the district to come in and be thumped for the edification of the spectators.
>
> Suddenly a gate opened at the end of the show ring, and horses, cattle, dogs, vehicles, motor-cars, and bicyclists crowded into the arena. This was the general parade, but it would have been better described as a general chaos . . .

— and wove his plot about the judging of the jumping horses by a trio of bush characters incredibly true to life:

> From the official stand came a brisk, dark-faced, wiry little man. He had been a steeplechase rider and a trainer in his time. Long experience of that tricky animal, the horse, had made him reserved and slow to express an opinion. He mounted the table, and produced a notebook. From the bar of the booth came a large, hairy, red-faced man whose face showed fatuous self-complacency. He was a noted show-judge because he refused, on principle, to listen to others' opinions; or in those rare cases when he did, only to eject a scornful contradiction. The third judge was a local squatter, who was overwhelmed with a sense of his own importance.

During this period of Paterson's boyhood in Sydney there was also an event which excited all those who thought seriously about the economic future of the colony (and to Emily Barton as Mrs Robert Barton of Boree Nyrang it was especially significant) : the arrival from London in October

1879 of the first ship fitted with refrigerating chambers, the s.s. *Strath-leven*. It was to take the first shipment of frozen meat back to London, and so mark the beginnings of a staple export for the colony. Paterson remembered, too, his grandmother's delight at another less spectacular but no less notable event, when the University of Sydney, after years of stubborn resistance in its Senate, in 1881 granted admission to women on equal terms with men.

These were but a few of the colours that limned the background of A. B. Paterson's adolescent years in Sydney. But where Paterson's good fortune lay was that he was living in a family circle, and thus an environment, which could hardly be regarded as typical of the city's times. If J. A. Froude, after his visit to the colony in the early 1880s, rather exaggerated the intellectual state of the young nation, it was indeed true that the average Sydneyite did not have a great deal of time for literature and the arts:

> . . . they have no severe intellectual interests. They aim at little except what money will buy; and to make money and buy enjoyment with it is the be-all and the end-all of their existence. They are courteous and polite, as well to one another as to strangers, in a degree not common in democracies. They are energetic in bringing out the material wealth of the soil. They have churches and schools and a university, and they talk and think much of education, etc. They study sanitary questions, and work hard to improve the health of their city, and to keep their bay unpolluted. They are tunnelling out a gigantic sewer through several miles of rock and clay, to carry the refuse of the town to the open ocean. But it is only to conquer the enemies of material comfort, that their own lives may be bright and pleasant. . . . with the exception of two or three leading lawyers and the more eminent statesmen, there were no persons that I met with who showed much concern about the deeper spiritual problems, in the resolution of which alone man's life rises into greatness. They have had one poet — Gordon — something too much of the Guy Livingstone type, an inferior Byron, a wild rider, desperate, dissipated, but with gleams of a most noble nature shining through the turbid atmosphere. He, poor fellow, hungering after what Australia could not give him — what perhaps no country on earth at present could give him — had nothing to do but to shoot himself, which he accordingly did . . .*

Not that Paterson was an intellectual. Far from it. Like most Australian youths, he loved the outdoors — indeed, it had been his cradle. And in his teens he became fascinated by the Parramatta River and its environs. He noted that the colonists had bestowed names on the settlements along

---

* In *Oceana or England and Her Colonies*; cf. some seventy-five years later, John Douglas Pringle: "If their culture is to be judged by the general standard of education and the arts among the population, once again it must be said that Australia has little or none. Indeed, there is a terrifying crudity in the manners and pursuits of the masses." (*Australian Accent*, 1958.)

its banks in affectionate remembrance of their old country: Putney, Chiswick, Mortlake and so on. He watched after school the wood-boats and fruit-boats (for the river was then one of the great producers of firewood and fruit for the city), with mainsails and jibs hoisted, bowling along the river with the westerly wind behind them. As he wrote nostalgically many years later:

> ... If the wind died away and they were left in the doldrums — well, they didn't worry. They anchored and caught themselves feeds of fish which they cooked on their little galley fires, the scent of frying red-bream mixing not unhappily with the aroma of guavas, grapes, and the big hautboy strawberries which now seem to have gone out of fashion. Then, when the tide turned, they would up with the anchor and drift down till they opened up the harbour where there was always some sort of a breeze. They would strike Sydney some time or other, and would deliver their cargo into horse-drawn carts and would then point the boat's nose up river again, back to the gardens and the splitting of firewood with wedges and American axes ...[4]

He spent, with his young friends of the district, as many of his leisure hours as he could on the river. They bought an old boat which they scrubbed and painted till it was reasonably shipshape: it was a fine fishing boat, he drily recalled, for there was usually as much water inside it as out, which kept the fish fresh till they got home. But fishing was only part of their river interests. Across the water from Rockend was the headquarters, at Abbotsford, of the Sydney Rowing Club; here came the great scullers, as long as the sculling boom lasted. The championship course was on this very stretch of water:

> Beginning with Hickey and Rush [Paterson recorded],[5] on down through Ned Trickett and Elias Laycock, to Beach and Hanlan, Stanbury and Maclean, and last and greatest of them all, Harry Searle* — we knew every man of them, and could tell them by their styles at three quarters of a mile distance. Walking with their trainers through the little town of Gladesville they were like Kingsley's gladiators stalking through the degenerate Romans ...

The craze had begun in earnest when Ned Trickett, a long-armed quarryman, of Greenwich, one of Sydney's nearer riverside suburbs, who had gained his proficiency by rowing every day to his work, had been sent to England where he had defeated the English champion. He in turn was beaten by the Canadian champion Hanlan. "Then it was that the old river came into its own," Paterson wrote, in an enthusiastic, graphic and hitherto unpublished account of the events that followed:

* Henry Ernest Searle ("The Clarence Comet") was born in Grafton in 1866. In 1889, after his Australian successes, he went to England and defeated W. J. O'Connor, champion oarsman of America, on the Thames Championship course. He contacted enteric fever on the way back to Australia, and died in Melbourne in the same year at the age of twenty-three.

... From far and wide came the scullers, English, Australians, Canadians, and New Zealanders. Like the oysters in Lewis Carroll's verses

"Thick and fast they came at last
    and more and more and more,
All hopping through the frothy waves
    and scrambling to the shore."

It became a matter of national importance that we should find a man to beat this Canadian. The river scullers were tried, also the men from the North Coast but none stood the test. Then Dr Fortescue, a leading surgeon in Sydney, was asked to examine a blacksmith named Beach who hailed from the South Coast. This Beach — sometimes known as Gipsy Beach — was an Englishman by birth, but had come out here at an early age. His face was the face of Bismarck, the man of blood and iron; his frame was knotted with muscles built up by years of swinging the sledge hammer; but he knew next to nothing about wager-boat rowing. Consider the colossal confidence of trying to beat the champion of the world with this novice sculler! Except that Dr Fortescue lived on the Parramatta River, he had little or no claim to know anything about race rowing; but he said that of all the thousands of men whom he had examined in his life, none could compare with Beach, and he was prepared to back him against Hanlan or any other small man. Friends argued with him and expostulated with him, but he said: "No, there never was a man like this. He'll beat Hanlan."

So now they had the man and the money and it is a matter of history how Beach beat him, not once only, but every time that they met — and these matches started such an orgy of sculling as never was seen in the world before.

From twenty-five to thirty men could be seen on any fine morning swinging along in their sculls at practice — and such men! From riverside farms, from axemen's camps in the North Coast timber country, from shipyards and fishing fleets, they flocked to the old river as the gladiators flocked to Rome in the last days of the Empire. Hanlan, who had toughened himself by work as a fisherman, Maclean, an axeman, who could fell any tree, using an axe in either hand, and never resting till the tree came down; Searle who, as a youngster rowed a boat about the Clarence River, taking orders for and delivering meat on account of a local butcher — he too was caught up in the renaissance of rowing, and found himself translated from the butcher's boat to the championship of the world. Catching the prevailing epidemic, the Clarence River people staged a huge handicap for professional scullers and Searle was handicapped somewhere near the limit. Hanlan went up to row at it, and was put on the scratch mark. During a practice row one day, he found himself alongside a flaxen-haired giant rowing a heavy old-fashioned wager-boat. They paddled alongside each other for a while, chatting, and then Hanlan said: "Well, goodbye, son, I must be going on." As he quickened up, the flaxen-haired youngster went with him, and, try as he would, Hanlan could not shake him off.

"Who's that fellow?" said Hanlan when he came in; and he was told that he had been rowing alongside the local ex-butcher-boy.

"Well," said Hanlan, "I don't want any butcher-boy in mine. He'll win this handicap by half-a-mile."

Not only did Searle win the handicap and the world's championship, but he proved himself probably the best sculler the world ever saw. He had such chest development that the scullers said, and implicitly believed, that he had one rib more than any other man.[6]

Meanwhile, the sixteen-year-old Paterson settled down to his work in a solicitor's office; it would seem clear from his attitudes and conversations in much later life, that he found it irksome and looked for his escape in his annual holidays in the bush and in making the most of his leisure hours with his Gladesville friends. Mrs Sylvia Palmer, daughter of Frank Barton, remembers being told as a small girl that Barty and his friends lived in a shack of their own along the river for a time; they also owned a battered horse-drawn vehicle (the equivalent of a modern jalopy or hot rod) in which, in the evenings and at week-ends, they thundered along the Gladesville streets with horses in tandem.

But at least, as he admits, his law training began to teach him about the world. His firm did a good deal of shipping business, and he remembered the occasion of one of his first jobs: to gather evidence for the defence of a sea-captain summonsed for not showing a riding-light over the stern while at anchor. It seemed too easy. The captain had seen the boatswain fix the light; the boatswain remembered fixing it; the chief officer remembered its reflection in the water. But the Bench found the captain guilty in double-quick time and fined him £5. The flabbergasted young Paterson began to console the captain. "Oh, well," said the latter, "I didn't know you had to have a riding light. They'd drive a man mad with their regulations in these —— places!" So the budding lawyer learned his first lesson: a case at law was something like a battle — if you listened to the accounts of each side, you could never believe they were talking about the same fight.

Later he became managing clerk for a firm which handled the business of several banks; it was here that he began to see and understand the plight of the smaller property-holders, and he relished less and less the task of trying "to screw money out of people who had not got it". He thought it was time he should put the world right. Accordingly he began to read seriously history and economics — and undoubtedly he was influenced by the theories of Henry George, because he produced a pamphlet, "Australia for the Australians — a Political Pamphlet Showing the Necessity for Land Reform Combined with Protection". Nor did he make any bones about his views, and since he was barely out of his teens when he wrote it, one can only admire, in a political and social climate far more conservative than now, the courage of his words. "It is of the greatest importance to every man amongst us," he began, "that he should have some clear idea of what position he occupies in relation to other people and that he should understand what it is that fixes his prospects and circumstances in life." He deplored the necessity for unemployment in the colony, the absurdity of country people crowding into the towns, the overcrowding of the professions. This indignation soon spilled over:

> Let those who do not see the necessity for any change or questioning of the present arrangement of affairs, take a night walk around the poorer quarters of our large colonial cities and they will see such things as they will never forget. They will see vice and sin and misery in full development. They will see poor people herding in wretched little shanties, the tiny stuffy rooms fairly reeking like ovens with the heat of our tropical summer. I, the writer of this book, at one time proposed, in search of novelty, to go and live for a space in one of the lower-class lodging houses in Sydney, to see what life was like under that aspect. I had "roughed it" in the bush a great deal. I had camped out with little shelter and very little food. I had lived with the stockmen in their huts, on their fare, so I was not likely to be dainty, but after one night's experience of that lodging I dared not try a second. To the frightful discomfort was added the serious danger of disease from the filthy surroundings and the unhealthy atmostphere. I fled. And yet what I, a strong man, dared not undertake for a week, women and children have to go through from year's end to year's end. And there were places compared with which the one I tried was a paradise . . . Do you, reader, believe that it is an inevitable law that in a wealthy country like this we must have so much poverty?
>
> It is difficult to imagine a number of people so great that our country could not carry them. When we think of the great rolling fertile plains of this continent, the wonderfully rich river flats, and the miles of and thousands of miles of agricultural land, spreading all over the country and hardly yet trodden by man, it is very evident that pressure of population on subsistence has nothing whatever to do with our difficulties . . .
>
> If it is the dream of a visionary that in such a country every man might be comfortably off, and might get a living easily, certainly, and with a large amount of leisure, then God help the people of such a country. They deserve to have it taken from them and given back to the blacks. . . .

He then went on to urge decentralization, a back-to-the-land movement, but argued bitterly, as he did strongly, that first of all the present system of granting land away in fee simple should be abolished:

> When the land was granted away in fee simple a cruel mistake was made which has early shown its effects on us and our prosperity. The present system is absurd and unjust, in that it enables some people to get a lot of benefit from the community to which they have no right, and it discourages industry and prevents production.

If, said Paterson, it could be argued that he was a "Henry George, etc." —
and he agreed with George's arguments against fee simple tenures but not
with his remedy — he (Paterson) had read Mill and Adam Smith too
and found there was "no other side". Every economist had supported
these arguments; they were old before George was born.

> To whom [continued Paterson] does the finest house in Sydney
> belong? It belongs to a man who inherited a huge fortune made solely
> out of the rise and rents of real estate near Sydney: a man who counts
> his fortune by hundreds and thousands, and spends most of his time
> in England. He never did a day's work in his life, and yet can have
> every luxury while hundreds of his fellow countrymen have to toil
> and pinch and contrive to get a living.

Of course, the land-hungry could be told to go outback — where there
was plenty of land. But what sort of land?

> There is an almighty difference between such land as this and the
> rich lands on the coast rivers, down about Illawarra, and on the
> banks of the Hunter and Macleay. The injustice, the stupidity of the
> arrangement consists in the fact that our immediate predecessors
> granted away for ever and ever in fee simple, free of rent, the best
> lands we had, and left the present generation to wilderness.

Unless the evils of the absentee-owner situation were remedied ("we
are creating the largest landed proprietors yet known") , Paterson forecast
that Australia would become another Ireland of tenant farmers ("and
then the fun will begin . . . plenty of good landlord shooting then").
Indeed, he wove this interesting thought into a stanza of one of his earlier
ballads, "On Kiley's Run":

> I cannot guess what fate will bring
>   To Kiley's Run —
> For chances come and changes ring —
> I scarcely think 'twill always be
> Locked up to suit an absentee;
> And if he lets it out in farms
> His tenants soon will carry arms
>   On Kiley's Run.

As for the shape of the reform, he was less than certain: some means had
to be devised whereby "no-one can hold land idle and unproductive while
others are anxious to use it and whereby all value created by the State
will go to the State".

Paterson in his later years was clearly ashamed of his "first literary
effort" (which, he said, "fell as flat as a pancake") .[7] It is hard to understand why he should have been embarrassed to recall it, since both he and
his father had suffered as a result of the system he had attacked. Moreover, there would be many who agreed with him, including poets and

writers of his day (especially Boake and Lawson, Morant and Ogilvie)
who had seen the evils of the existing land-grant system too, and the bush-
workers who were the victims of the system, not to mention the selectors
struggling on marginal lands — the families whose privations were the
basis of the rather sardonic humour of the later writings of Steele Rudd.
Indeed, it has always been wrongly supposed of Paterson, as noted by
Gavin Long,[8] that he was an upholder of the established order, against
the image of Lawson as the angry young reformer; that Paterson was "the
spokesman of the squattocracy and the station owners". This was certainly
not true of Paterson the balladist and *Bulletin* sketch writer (even if
Paterson in his last years among the coteries of the Australian Club took
a less impassioned and more detached view of life around him.*) But in
his hey-day he wrote about the underdogs of bush and city life: the jockey
(in his day at any rate), the jailbird, the drover, the station-hand, even
the horse thief, Andy Regan, ". . . hunted like a dog — By the troopers of
the Upper Murray side". Especially too — and this is in a direct line from
his political pamphlet — one recalls his ballad "Reconstruction from a
Farmer's Point of View" (not subsequently included in his collections
after its original publication in the *Bulletin* of 17/6/'93) which reads in
part:

> So the bank has bust its boiler! And in six or seven years
> It will pay me all my money back — of course!
> But the horse will perish waiting, while the grass is germinating
> And I reckon I'll be something like the horse.
>
> There's the ploughing to be finished and the ploughmen want
> 　　　their pay,
> And I'd like to wire the fence and sink a tank;
> But I own I'm fairly beat how I'm going to make ends meet
> With my money in a reconstructed bank.
>
> And they say they've lent my money, and they can't get paid it
> 　　　back,
> I know their rates percent were tens and twelves.
> And if now they've made a blunder after scooping all this
> 　　　plunder,
> Why, they ought to fork the money out themselves.

---

*At the age of seventy-four, however, Paterson was still moved to write, in explaining
that "On Kiley's Run" was the story of a station or rather of many stations rolled into one:
". . . I am old enough to have seen the transition from cattle to sheep and to have seen
a station of 80,000 acres all taken up in 640-acre blocks with their attendant conditional
leases. Some of these blocks were taken up by bonafide settlers, and others by dummies
acting in the interests of station-owners. At the age of seventeen I held one of these
dummy blocks and duly transferred it when the time came. The bonafide settlers were
referred to in speeches as 'the sturdy yeomanry, the country's pride', but in course of
time almost all these bonafide settlers sold their blocks to the station-owners and moved
on to fresh fields and pastures new, leaving things exactly where they were when they
started — except that the station had become a vast freehold instead of a vast lease-
hold . . ."

("Looking Backward", *Sydney Mail*, 28 December 1938)

At any rate Paterson, now rising twenty-one, decided to try his hand at verse. This was hardly surprising. He was reading a great deal of verse at this time, and was, indeed, very much under the influence of Swinburne; what was more germane to his blossoming talent as a balladist and writer of narrative and light verse is that there seems little doubt that he was also reading Browning, Calverley, Praed and W. S. Gilbert. Then, too, his father had written verse as a hobby and, indeed, had some political verses published in early numbers of the *Bulletin*; his sister Jessie* and brother Hamilton had also tried their hand at verse-writing. It was natural enough, then, that Paterson should look to the *Bulletin* for publication: in his view it was "the most unsatisfied paper in Australia".

By the time Paterson came to submit his first verses (in 1885), the *Bulletin* was five years old and beginning, under the vigorous editorship of W. H. Traill, to make its mark in Australian journalism. Traill had not been in at the birth, as it were; on the other hand J. F. Archibald, whose name is more of a household word wherever the *Bulletin* is discussed, had begun with the magazine as a sub-editor in 1880, when it was founded by an Irish journalist, John Haynes, with Roman Catholic support, largely in opposition to the *Protestant Standard*. Apart from its vigorous denunciations of Orangemen, it was also used as a medium of Free Trade propaganda, since Haynes was a rabid anti-Protectionist. He had borrowed the name for the journal from the *San Francisco Bulletin*. He invited Traill to join the paper in 1881 as business manager; Traill took over the editorship when Haynes and his partner McLeod were jailed for failing to meet the costs of a libel action in 1882. Archibald had not yet taken over the editorship (he did so on Traill's retirement in 1887, from which date the *Bulletin* might be said to have begun its best years); but even in 1885 Archibald was clearly the power behind the throne, and was — certainly on the literary side, as I have already outlined in an earlier chapter — taking the initiative in the search for and encouragement of contributors.

At any rate, Paterson, who, by the way, by this time had been admitted to the Roll of Solicitors ("Now remember girls," his proud mother said to his equally proud sisters when they heard the news, "Barty's opinion is worth six and eightpence.") ,⁹ submitted his verses, and, as has already been described, was summoned by Archibald and given advice as to his future writing. It seems clear from the recollections of Emily Barton, confirmed by Paterson's own reminiscences, that he had "strung together four flamboyant verses about the expedition against the Mahdi", that he was the author of one of the poems in issues of the *Bulletin* of 1885, all

* One of Jessie's verses entitled "Ode: To the Southerly Buster" published in a Sydney newspaper in January 1897 began:
> Wind of the South, all hail!
> Oh wind that comest roaring from the sea
> That comest grand and glorious, fresh and free!
> All day we longed and listened for thy feet,
> We drooped and sickened in the stifling heat.
> Night came. The darkness came and still no breath
> No breeze to stir the air, and still as death . . .

unsigned and angry, about the Soudan Contingent.* Perhaps the most typical of Paterson's later style was the one beginning:

> So you're back from your baptism of glory
> And you bring a few spots on your hands,
> That our country may change her glad story,
> To the wail of the blood-guilty lands!

Paterson claimed that, since he was afraid to use his own name "lest the editor, identifying one with the author of the pamphlet, would dump my contribution, unread, into the waste-paper basket . . . ",[10] he adopted the pen-name of "The Banjo" after a "so-called racehorse" his family had owned at Illalong. This pseudonym was not used for the Soudan Contin-gent verses (if they were his) but first appeared under "The Bush Fire, an Allegory", a mediocre and rambling effusion of twenty-five six-line verses which appeared in the *Bulletin* on 12 June 1886. Then followed in October "A Dream of the Melbourne Cup", which, though it was modestly sub-titled "A Long Way After Gordon", showed the promise of high equestrian balladship to come:

> But one draws out from the beaten ruck
> And up on the rails by a piece of luck
>   He comes in a style that's clever;
> "It's Trident! Trident! Hurrah for Hales!"
> "Go at 'em now while their courage fails;"
> "Trident! Trident! for New South Wales"
>   "The blue and white for ever!"

> Under the whip! with the ears flat back,
> Under the whip! though the sinews crack,
>   No sign of the base white feather;
> Stick to it now for your breeding's sake,
> Stick to it now though your hearts should break,
> While the yells and roars make the grand-stand shake,
>   They come down the straight together.

After this came "The Mylora Elopement" — a little style-conscious, with its striving after alliterative effect in its opening lines —

*The news of General Gordon's death at Khartoum was received in Sydney on 11 February 1885. On the following day the *Sydney Morning Herald* published a letter from Sir Edward Strickland suggesting that Australia should follow the Canadian example and offer military assistance to Great Britain. A special Cabinet meeting decided on the same day to offer five hundred infantry, plus two batteries of field artillery and guns. Amid remarkable scenes of patriotism in March 1885, a hastily recruited contingent of 750 men from New South Wales left Sydney for the war in the Soudan against the Mahdi. Since all this was done without Parliamentary sanction, the legislature was called together to grant the Government an indemnity for its un-constitutional action. This was almost unanimously granted although there was oppo-sition from a number of quarters; Henry Parkes who was not in Parliament at the time stirred up opposition in the press and later won a by-election on the dispute. The contingent did very little fighting and suffered little loss (six deaths, mainly from fever), returning to Sydney on 23 June, when it was disbanded.

By the winding Wollondilly where the weeping willows weep,
And the shepherd, with his billy, half awake and half asleep,
Folds his fleecy flocks that linger homewards in the setting sun
Lived my hero, Jim the Ringer, "cocky" on Mylora Run.

— but with the Patersonian touch more surely emerging:

The sound of a whip comes faint and far,
A rattle of hoofs, and here they are . . .
Well ridden! well ridden! they wheel — whoa back!
And long and loud the stockwhips crack . . .

Next was "Only a Jockey", written about the death of one Richard
Bennison, a fourteen-year-old jockey, thrown and killed on a Melbourne
racecourse. The horse, according to the press report, was "luckily un-
injured". Perhaps by our more sophisticated standards it is over-
sentimental, but Paterson wrote with indignation and compassion:

Fourteen years old, and what was he taught of it?
What did he know of God's infinite Grace?
Draw the dark curtain of shame o'er the thought of it,
Draw the shroud over the jockey-boy's face.

In March 1887 the *Bulletin* published a poetical poem "The Deficit
Demon" (a not very successful attempt at lampooning: Sir Patrick Jen-
nings and Sir Henry Parkes appeared as "Sir Patrick the Portly" and "Sir
'Enry the Fishfag" — Paterson demonstrated later that he could write
political verse much more effectively), and in April "Our Mat", a
tritely phrased but no less deeply felt set of verses about an office doormat
made by prisoners at Darlinghurst Jail, beginning:

It came from the prison this morning
Close-twisted, neat-lettered, and flat;
It lies the hall doorway adorning
A very good style of a mat.

That T has a look of the gallows
That A's a triangle I guess;
Was it one of the Mount Rennie fellows
Who twisted the strands of the S ?

It is a fair assessment that neither of these two poems were thought worthy
to be printed in later collections.

Paterson had nothing further published in the *Bulletin* until the
Christmas issue of 1888, when "Old Pardon, the Son of Reprieve"
appeared. There are three good reasons why this date may be regarded
as the introduction to another period in Paterson's progress. First of all,
"Old Pardon" marks the beginning of the characteristic bush-ballads by
which Paterson was now to establish his reputation in the 1890s and

after; second, this blossoming forth coincided with the fat years of the *Bulletin* and the aggregation of the famous identities of the literary scene of the period; and third, Paterson, at twenty-four, now entered fully and enthusiastically into the life of Sydney and began to see the horizons of the Australia beyond New South Wales beckoning and challenging him.

NOTES

1 In *How to Know Sydney* (1895).
2 David Kennedy in *Kennedy's Colonial Travel* (1875).
3 James Inglis, in *Our Australian Cousins*.
4 In "On the River" — a script prepared for broadcasting on the A.B.C. by A. B. Paterson in 1933.
5 In his *Sydney Morning Herald* reminiscences.
6 In "On the River".
7 In his *Sydney Morning Herald* reminiscences.
8 In "Young Paterson and Young Lawson", *Meanjin*, 1964, No. 4.
9 Florence Earle Hooper in her *Biography of A. B. Paterson* (Part 3), *Yass Tribune-Courier*, 20 June 1949.
10 In his *Sydney Morning Herald* reminiscences.

CHAPTER VI

At Full Gallop

*... the strongest emotion felt by this vigorous young man
in his twenties was a nostalgic hankering for the way of life
he had known in his youth ...*

— VANCE PALMER.[1]

*So there is Paterson: the anonymous begetter of legendary
poems, the gifted amateur careless of his gifts, the protector
of the superficial integrity of our minds. These images of
the man must surely go some way in explaining his hold on
our popular culture.*

— H. P. HESELTINE.[2]

PATERSON'S RESPONSIBILITIES became greater as the 1890s approached. His
father died in June 1899 and his mother (with her sight failing badly)
and his sisters came to Gladesville to live. Grandmother Barton was now
in her seventies, and Paterson was the head of the household. Furthermore he was taken into partnership by J. W. Street (a brother of Philip
Street, who had been a fellow pupil with Paterson at Sydney Grammar
School and who later became Chief Justice of New South Wales), an
association he was to continue until 1900. Yet these circumstances in no
way inhibited his writing activities; he plunged even more enthusiastically into the life of the younger circle in Sydney, and indeed in the next
ten or twelve years tasted excitement and adventure on a scale that he
would hardly have envisaged a few years back as a lawyer's clerk in a
musty city office.

He found that life as a full-blown lawyer-in-partnership was not without its difficulties. These were hard times. "I saw bank booms," he wrote,
"land booms, silver booms, Northern Territory booms, and they all had
one thing in common — they always burst."[3] On the other hand, as a
balladist he went from success to success. In 1889, for instance, he had no
less than fourteen poems published in the *Bulletin*, culminating with
"Clancy of the Overflow"* in the Christmas issue (Paterson recalls that
he was paid 13/6d. for it), of which Rolfe Boldrewood, writing at the

---

* Among the George Robertson papers at the Mitchell Library is a note dated
18 January 1913 from Angus & Robertson to Paterson, explaining that the firm was
producing a volume of Australian poetry for schools; it wished to include some of
Paterson's poems including notes. Would he explain whether "Overflow" referred to an
old station of that name or just what did he have in mind? Paterson noted on the
letter: " 'Overflow' is not intended to refer to any particular run. It is just used as a
typical name."

time, said, " 'Clancy of the Overflow', quoted by a writer who signs himself 'Banjo', is in my opinion the best bush ballad since Gordon. It has
the true ring of the snaffle and spur combined with poetic treatment — a
combination not so easy to attain as might be supposed." J. F. Archibald,
in quoting this appreciation in the *Bulletin*, stated that the author
"The Banjo" was "a modest young man of Sydney". Certainly "Clancy"
has remained down the years the best known, along with "The Man from
Snowy River" and "Watzing Matilda", if not necessarily the best, of
Paterson's ballads. And its origin, Paterson wrote later, was in ". . . a
lawyer's letter which I had to write to a gentleman in the bush who had
not paid his debts. I got an answer from a friend of his who wrote the
exact words, 'Clancy's gone to Queensland droving and we don't know
where he are' . . .".[4]

But hindsight can discern certain tendencies in Paterson's verse even to
this point, which, as it turned out, were signs of things to come. First of
all, he was falling out of love with the law, an echo of which feeling we
see in one of his 1889 poems, "In re a Gentleman, One" —

> Alas for the gallant attorney,
>   Intent upon cutting a dash!
> He starts on life's perilous journey
>   With rather more cunning than cash.
> And fortune at first is inviting —
>   He struts his brief hour in the sun —
> But lo! on the wall is the writing
>   Of Nemesis, "Gentleman, One".
>
> For soon he runs short of the dollars,
>   He fears he must go to the wall;
> So Peter's trust-money he collars
>   To pay off his creditor, Paul;
> Then robs right and left — for he goes it
>   In earnest when once he's begun.
> *Descensus Averni* — he knows it;
>   It's easy for "Gentleman, One".

— and a less subtle confirmation in ballads he wrote in the following
year. In one of these, "Gilhooley's Estate", the lawyers call in "a barrister-
man with a wig on his head" despite the widow Gilhooley's entreaties to
"keep the expenses as low as you can". The Judge orders a suit to be
brought — "a nice friendly suit" with the costs to be borne by Gilhooley's
Estate:

> So Mrs Gilhooley says, "Jones, you'll appear!
>   Thim barristers' fees is too great;
> The suit is but friendly," "Attorneys, my dear,
>   Can't be heard in Gilhooley's Estate."
>
> From the barristers' quarters a mighty hurrah
>   Arises both early and late:
> It's only the whoop of the Junior Bar
>   Dividing Gilhooley's Estate.

Paterson's animus is more pointed in the other ballad, the little-known, because never re-printed, "The Hypnotist", where he pillories the doctor ("I certify that the cause of death / was something Latin and something long / And who is to say that the doctor's wrong"), the banker, the editor, but especially the lawyer:

> I saw a barrister wigged and gowned
> Of stately presence and looks profound —
>
> I take your brief and I look to see
> That the same is marked with a thumping fee,
> But just as your case is drawing near
> I bob serenely and disappear,
> And away in another court I lurk
> While a junior barrister does your work
>
> For the lawyer laughs in his cruel sport
> While his clients march to the Bankrupt Court.

But most of all Paterson was beginning to chafe at being cooped up in a city office; his heart was in the bush, and he poured his heart into "Clancy of the Overflow", where antithetically to the "kindly voices" and the "vision splendid" of the outback he wrote of the city:

> I am sitting in my dingy little office, where a stingy
>   Ray of sunlight struggles feebly down between the houses tall,
> And the foetid air and gritty of the dusty, dirty city,
>   Through the open window floating, spreads its foulness over all.
>
> And in place of lowing cattle, I can hear the fiendish rattle
>   Of the tramways and the buses making hurry down the street;
> And the language uninviting of the gutter children fighting
>   Comes fitfully and faintly through the ceaseless tramp of feet.
>
> And the hurrying people daunt me, and their pallid faces haunt me
>   As they shoulder one another in their rush and nervous haste,
> With their eager eyes and greedy, and their stunted forms and weedy,
>   For townsfolk have no time to grow, they have no time to waste.
>
> And I somehow rather fancy that I'd like to change with Clancy,
>   Like to take a turn at droving where the seasons come and go,
> While he faced the round eternal of the cash-book and the journal —
>   But I doubt he'd suit the office, Clancy, of The Overflow.

He took whatever opportunity he could — on vacation and at week-ends — to get back into the country, whether it was longer trips into the outback or short excursions into the Blue Mountains and the outer city areas. On one occasion he went as far west as the Darling, where he was fascinated to see for the first time a river steam-boat:

Tied up to a tree at the foot of a Chinaman's garden is the steamer "Wandering Jew", waiting for the river to rise. She is built of slabs nailed together and her builders seem to have determined to put into her as many different kinds of wood, and as many different lengths, colours and thicknesses of timber as possible. In shape, she is a good deal like the ace of diamonds, with paddle-wheels, sticking out on either side; her hold is floored with the odds and ends of slabs left over from her construction and grass is growing in her empty hold. But her Captain refuses to be down-hearted. He speaks in true nautical fashion of meeting "other vessels" on his voyage, and says that he has a chart of the river showing all the snags; but that trees are constantly falling into the river and forming new snags which make navigation dangerous.

He says that his boat can do three knots an hour against the current; but has made as much as fourteen knots when coming down with a flood. The deck-hand, who is also the fireman, says that he fires her with logs. "Sometimes they send the wrong lengths aboard," he says, "and then I have to cut 'em up myself. I'm a fireman," he says, "not a wood-and-water joey."[5]

But his sights were set beyond New South Wales, to other colonies and to the Northern Territory and the islands beyond. He has recorded that he was in correspondence at this time with a former schoolmate of Sydney Grammar School, who had rowed stroke in the school crew, had had a brief career as a journalist (his career ending when, assigned to report a pleasure trip on the Hawkesbury River where all the tourists were seasick, he headed his copy "Three hours' sorrow for three shillings") and had eventually gone "blackbirding" in the New Hebrides. He wrote Paterson vivid accounts of the perils and adventures of this doubtful calling, which made the latter more and more discontented with the life he was forced to lead.

This discontent was perhaps reflected, too, in a developing iconoclasm, a rebelliousness in some of his verse. Probably a cynical strain in his make-up was being developed by the intensity and scope of his reading at the time. He recalls, for instance, that he was especially influenced by Carlyle's *Past and Present*, where he thought he had found "a workable formula for saving the world". He found grounds for much reflection in Carlyle's thesis that men were quite unfit to govern themselves and was fond of quoting a Government contractor whom he had heard say that "if six hundred men were left leaderless on any job, two hundred of them would go off after women, two hundred after strong drink, while the spiritless remainder would go on with the job". It is difficult to imagine the tranquil and almost sardonically detached Paterson of his last years, as affectionately recalled by some of his contemporaries, as something of a young angry of the nineties. His penchant for writing about the underdog, the little people of the outback, has already been noted; the feeling of the dispossessed squatter's son was strong in him as a young man, and in any situation where absentee squatters, banks, pastoral companies and other such individuals or institutions were involved his sympathies were clear and unequivocal. "Moneygrub" as the generic term for the absentee landowner was freely used by Paterson as indeed it was by Boake. He also showed a surprising tendency (bearing in mind that the moral and religious conscience of the 1890s was vastly less flexible than of the 1960s) towards mocking conventions and institutions with varying degrees of irony — as, for instance, in a spring-time piece he wrote in 1898, "Now Is the Time When Song Birds Mate":

> Now Love so subtly stirs men's hearts
> To Hymen they've recourse,
> Just when last summer's wedded tarts
> Take action for divorce.

Again, in some light verses inspired by a news item about an Irish M.P. imprisoned for an offence against the police, he wrote:

> Immure him in the dungeon that rots beneath the moat,
> And load with chains his ankles, let sackcloth be his coat;
> Take from him vest and trousers — his inmost garments fleece,
> His crime is most atrocious — he spat at the perlice! ! !

And the culmination came in a hilarious but astonishingly irreligious and irreverent lengthy ballad called "The Scapegoat", which, no mattei how much Paterson may have written it with his tongue in his cheek, was the strongest of meat by 1890s standards — for Jews and Christians alike. It appeared in the same Christmas number of the *Bulletin* as "Clancy"; indeed, it was given pride of place over that ballad, as over "An Idyll of Dandaloo", also in this issue. It was displayed on a full page with comic sketches by "Hop". Incidentally, it demonstrated Paterson's rapidly developing skill in coping with complicated metrical and rhyming structures in his ballad-forms:

> We have all read how the Israelites fled
>   From Egypt with Pharaoh in eager pursuit of 'em
> And Pharaoh's fiery troops were all put in the soup
>   When the waters rolled softly o'er every galoot of 'em.
>
> The Israelite horde went soaring abroad
>   Like so many sundowners out on the wallaby.
> When Moses who led 'em and taught 'em and fed 'em
>   Was dying he murmured, "A rorty old hoss you are,
> I give you command of the whole of the band,"
>   And handed the Government over to Joshua. . . .

The ballad went on to describe how he ordered the ritual of the scape-goat, with Paterson indulging in satirical irreverences even more studied:

> By this means a Jew whate'er he might do
>   Though he bungled or murdered or cheated at loo

> Or meat on Good Friday (a sin most terrific) ate,
> Could get his discharge like a bankrupt's certificate.

After a farcical account of how the scapegoat got the better of his sacri
ficers, Paterson concluded with his "moral":

> The moral is patent to all the beholders —
> Don't shift your own sins on to other folks' shoulders;
> Be kind to dumb creatures and never abuse them,
> Nor curse them nor kick them, nor spitefully use them. . . .

> Remember, no matter how far you may roam
> That dogs, goats and chickens, it's simply the dickens,
> Their talent stupendous for 'getting back home'.

> Your sins, without doubt, will aye find you out,
> And so will the scapegoat, he's bound to achieve it.
> But die in the wilderness! Don't you believe it!

Not surprisingly, but a matter nevertheless for the greatest regret to the
student and admirer of Paterson, the ballad was never re-printed.

Meanwhile, Paterson was meeting and getting to know many of the
writers of the *Bulletin* school. He met, about 1890, Henry Lawson and
an easy relationship, if not quite a friendship, followed for many years.
He still, nevertheless, preserved his anonymity as far as the reading public
was concerned. It is interesting to note that when the *Bulletin* in 1890,
to celebrate its tenth anniversary, published *A Golden Shanty*, an anthology of prose and verse selected from its own columns, both Lawson and
Paterson were accorded junior rank only. Contributions from writers such
as John Farrell, Victor Daley, Francis Myers, Thomas Bracken and others
were given precedence in the contents list. Lawson was represented by
"His Father's Mate" and "Faces in the Street", and Paterson was the tail-
ender, with "Old Pardon" and "Clancy of The Overflow".

It is interesting to note the name of John Farrell in this anthology.
Paterson did not make many close friends even as a young writer and
man-about-town, but he became most attached to Farrell who was thirteen
years his senior: he was one of the very few people (A. W. Jose was
another) from whom Paterson occasionally sought advice on his own
writing. There was a further bond between them in that Farrell was an
ardent advocate of Henry George's economic theories. Farrell formed the
Single-Tax League of which Paterson was for a time a member, and
Farrell had a good deal to do with the visit of Henry George to Australia
about this time. Farrell was a minor poet — his best-remembered poem is
"How He Died", which was collected in a volume under that title, with
other poems — but he was primarily a journalist, and all the time Paterson knew him he was a leader-writer for the Sydney *Daily Telegraph*, and
remained in this occupation until his death in 1904. It is obvious that
Farrell sharpened Paterson's interest in journalism; and perhaps Farrell

is the only newspaperman in Australian history who at one time ran a brewery — in Goulburn in the 1880s.

It is probable that the stimulus of Lawson's success prompted Paterson to try his hand at writing prose sketches. From this point on Paterson wrote at regular intervals in the *Bulletin* for the next ten years or so, short stories, sketches and pieces of reportage which, obscured from general recognition by his greater reputation as a bush-balladist, nevertheless deserve comparison with any other writing about the outback. There is nearly always an underlying humour — but, as one follows the sequence of these prose pieces, the developing gifts of observation of character, an eye for detail, the graphic colouring-in of an event, clearly point the way to Paterson's later involvement with journalism.

His first prose piece appeared in the *Bulletin* of 4 January 1890. It was called "How I Shot the Policeman", and there is a curious parallel, which was probably not accidental, with a prose piece by Edward Dyson appearing a couple of weeks earlier *(Bulletin,* 21 December 1889). It also dealt with a policeman, "The Tiredest Man":

> The tiredest man I ever knew is dead. His name was Gideon Smith. He died in comparative oblivion at the early age of 52 years . . . Recognizing that chronic weariness was their son's strongest characteristic, his parents secured him a position in the police force at an early age and for 20-odd years he fluttered feebly about his beat, dragging his feet after him with a painful effort, lurking in the shadows hooked to convenient projections, sleeping in unfrequented places, leaning hopelessly in out of the way corners and hanging dejectedly over railings and horse-troughs, and growing more and more fatigued as the years rolled by . . .

Paterson's piece began:
> He was a short, fat, squat, baldheaded officer with a keen instinct for whisky, and an unlimited capacity for taking things easy. He would have been a tall man had Providence not turned round so much of his legs to make his feet. He used to mooch about the village at night . . .

Probably Paterson thought *he* could write about a policeman too, and this was the stimulus he needed. But even here Paterson's journalistic flair for getting into his subject quickly, and the quick, neat brush of the bit of detail here and there is noticeable; and, as it turned out, the sketch was much more effective than Dyson's, even though only half as long. Paterson had mistaken the constable rattling his door-handle for a stray horse for which he had set a booby trap of a two-pound dumb-bell; the policeman was knocked unconscious.

Paterson's ironical regard of contemporary institutions and customs was not to be denied even at this early stage in his development as a writer. As he frantically sought to revive the policeman,

I heard the jury bring in a verdict of guilty with a strong recommen-
dation for mercy and I knew *that* meant hanging for certain — as
people recommended to mercy always perish on the scaffold in
Australia . . .

But in the end all was well:

I loaded him up with whisky, gave him a substantial Christmas box
and sent him on his way as good as new. I believe you could shoot
him with dumb-bells every night in the week on the same terms.

Writing with increased assurance, Paterson produced some magnificently authentic pieces in the next year or so: "His Masterpiece" (about
the classic bush liar); "Victor Second"; "The Cast-Iron Canvasser"
(exploiting his larger-than-life, Mulga Bill technique); "The Downfall
of Mulligan", and especially his comically grim account in the epistolary manner ("The History of a Jackaroo in Five Letters") of an
English remittance man sent out to Australia as a jackaroo:

In India one generally goes into the Civil Service, nothing to do and
lots of niggers to wait on you, but the Australian Civil Service no
fellow can well go into — it is awful low business, I hear. I have been
going in for gun and revolver practice so as to be able to hold my
own against the savages and the serpents in the woods of Australia . . .

Paterson conveyed his disillusion and decay —

. . . The horses of course gave him the slip, and he got lost for two
days looking for them, and his meat was gone bad when he got
home. He killed a sheep for tucker, and how do you think he killed
it? He *shot* it! It was a ram, too, one of Moneygrub's best rams, and
there will be the deuce to pay when they find out. About the fourth
day a swagman turned up, and he gave the swaggy a gold watch
and chain to show him the way to the nearest town, and he is there
now — on the spree, I believe. He has a fine throat for whisky, anyhow, and the hot climate has started him in earnest . . .[6]

— and finally his death, in the words of the coroner's jury, ". . . by sun-
stroke and exposure during a fit of *delirium tremens*, caused by excessive
drinking". It would not be uncharitable, however, to note in Paterson's
attitude here a chauvinistic contempt for the new chum.

All these pieces appeared during a year or so; during this time too
Paterson wrote his most famous ballad "The Man from Snowy River".
In December 1892 what is generally regarded as his most humorous ballad
appeared, "The Man from Ironbark" — the *Bulletin* bestowed on it the
honour of an entire front page display with illustrations by Lionel
Lindsay.

The identity of the "modest young man of Sydney" was becoming more
and more intriguing to the *Bulletin*'s readers as the ballads and bush-

pieces signed by "The Banjo" were increasingly eagerly looked forward to in each issue. One set of verses, at least, could possibly have been missed. There is in the Mitchell Library, Sydney, a letter dated 12 December 1906 written by J. Brunton Stephens to A. G. Stephens:

Dear A. G. S.

I came across "The Lost Drink" in the *Bulletin* 1 Aug., 1891, p. 24. It is signed B. Thought you might like to know if you had not yet come across it.

Yours,
B. S.

The poem in question — a rather flippant trifle about a hangover and its consequences — was later established as being by Paterson, although it was never subsequently re-printed. Another ballad, invariably included in more recent collections of his verse, "How McGinnis went Missing", had appeared in September 1899 unsigned.

Paterson's mother had died in 1893; his sisters, to whom he was devoted and they to him (they were especially proud of his writing), became his special responsibility. Mrs Sylvia Palmer has told me that Paterson was a very handsome young man, very popular with the young ladies. His sister, later Mrs Guy Huntley, has left a striking pen-picture of him:[7]

. . . about five feet ten inches in height, of very athletic build. He was an expert horseman and played polo and was an outstanding tennis player, a fairly good boxer and rifle-shot. His hair was dark and his eyes were brown, but not very dark and were very keen and clear with a penetrating look. His nose was slightly aquiline and the darkness of his complexion depended on whether he was working outdoors or indoors. He had a moustache for a short time — rather short than drooping. As a rule he spoke quickly. He was not unduly spare, though muscular and quite well-covered. He danced beautifully.

It was said that Paterson at the time was engaged to a Gladesville girl and that he was on one occasion chided for not paying sufficient court to her and indeed for not going ahead with his marriage. He replied that he could not think of this when he had his young sisters and his polo ponies to look after. He had by this time achieved a local reputation as a horseman, riding at amateur race-meetings and at meetings of the Sydney Hunt Club; polo had become his particular passion and he kept his ponies stabled at Gladesville. Paterson's reminiscence of how he became interested in polo is shaded with his characteristic irony:

. . . a cavalry officer came out from England and started a polo club. . . . we took to it like ducks to water. This polo business brought us in touch with some of the upper circles — a great change after the little bush school, the game cocks, and the days when I looked upon the sergeant of police as the greatest man in the world . . .[8]

But Paterson and his favourite polo pony "Pegasus" were a skilful combination; he played as representative of New South Wales colony and

Sydney teams against the Victorian and other teams,* and from his polo-playing game came at least one of his better known ballads, "The Geebung Polo Club", commemorating the time when, as Paterson recalls, "we played a match against the Cooma team, real wild men with cabbage-tree hats and skin-tight pants, their hats held on by a strap under their noses". Paterson translated this experience into lines such as these:

> They were long and wiry natives from the rugged mountain side,
> And the horse was never saddled that the Geebungs couldn't ride;
> But their style of playing polo was irregular and rash —
> They had mighty little science, but a mighty lot of dash:
> And they played on mountain ponies that were muscular and strong,
> Though their coats were quite unpolished, and their manes and tails
>   were long.
> And they used to train those ponies wheeling cattle in the scrub;
> They were demons, were the members of the Geebung Polo Club.

He described the ballad, with his usual modesty, as "a jingle which has outlasted much better work".

In October 1895, whether by the initiative of Paterson himself or the publishers (although the story is that Paterson made the approach), Angus & Robertson published *The Man from Snowy River and Other Verses* by A. B. Paterson and the identity of "The Banjo" was thus revealed. The tall, quiet and handsome young solicitor, already well known in the best sporting and social circles, became the celebrity of the colony overnight. The book had a preface by Rolfe Boldrewood (no doubt on the strength of his praise in his literary column a few years earlier of "Clancy of The Overflow"), which added little and, as Florence Earle Hooper has remarked, was "very V˙ torian". It is worth recalling for its Gordonian overtones and the click ridden Romanticism from which Australian critical writing had not yet emerged:

> It is not so easy to write ballads descriptive of the bushland of Australia as on light consideration would appear. Reasonably good verse on the subject has been supplied in sufficient quantity. But the maker of folksongs for our new born nation requires a somewhat rare combination of gifts and experiences. Dowered with the poet's heart he must yet have passed his "wander-jahre" amid the stern solitude of the Austral waste — must have ridden the race in the backblock township, guided the restless stockhorse adown the mountain spur, and followed the night-long moving spectral-seeing herd "in the droving days". Amid such scarce congenial surroundings comes off that finer sense which renders visible bright gleams of humour,

---

* "He won a lot of amateur races here in Sydney in the 1890s and was recognized as one of the best amateur riders of his day. He also played polo for N.S.W. and in the first team that I think ever played in N.S.W."
— Norman Lindsay, in *Bohemians of the Bulletin*, 1965.

pathos and romance, which, like undiscovered gold, await the fortunate adventurer. That the author has touched this treasure trove, not less delicately than distinctly, no true Australian will deny. In my opinion this collection comprises the best bush ballads written since the death of Lindsay Gordon.

The collection itself comprised the best verses Paterson had written to date; odd political and humorous poems were not included; there were however some omissions thought worth while to be later re-printed, such as "Mulligan's Mare", "The Corner Man" and "In re a Gentleman, One". The contents of *The Man from Snowy River and Other Verses*, as a matter of bibliographical record, were: an introductory poem "I have gathered these stories afar . . .", "The Man from Snowy River", "Old Pardon, the Son of Reprieve", "Clancy of The Overflow", "Conroy's Gap", "Our New Horse", "An Idyll of Dandaloo", "The Geebung Polo Club", "The Travelling Post Office", "Saltbush Bill", "A Mountain Station", "Been There Before", "The Man who was Away", "The Man from Ironbark", "The Open Steeplechase", "The Amateur Rider", "On Kiley's Run", "Frying Pan's Theology", "The Two Devines", "In the Droving Days", "Lost", "Over the Range", "Only a Jockey", "How McGinnis went Missing", "A Voice from the Town", "A Bunch of Roses", "Black Swans", "The All Right 'Un", "The Boss of the Admiral Lynch", "A Bushman's Song", "How Gilbert Died", "The Flying Gang", "Shearing at Castlereagh", "The Wind's Message", "Johnson's Antidote", "Ambition and Art", "The Daylight is Dying", "In Defence of the Bush", "Last Week", "Those Names", "A Bush Christening", "How the Favourite Beat Us", "The Great Calamity", "Come by Chance", "Under the Shadow of Kiley's Hill", "Jim Carew", and "The Swagman's Rest". It is fair to say of Paterson's subsequent two collections that there is little in them superior to his best work in this first volume.

The reception given this book of Australian verse was remarkable. In the first place, as a literary occasion, its appearance met with spontaneous praise, by no means parochially inspired. A. G. Stephens, by this time firmly ensconced as a the grand panjandrum of the *Bulletin's* celebrated Red Page, wrote:

> . . . it is stirring manly stuff that one rejoices to read and remember: Mr Paterson indeed like the old Cavalier lyrists is able to combine the power to do and the power to write. Wolfe could only take Quebec, he couldn't write "Gray's Elegy" but "The Banjo" rides and wins his steeplechasing and then, one may believe, sits down with a still tingling pulse and conveys the tingling to the pulses of his readers . . .[9]

Another reviewer found Paterson's bushman ". . . an interesting cove, fond of bright sunsets and interesting in speech"; yet another, while making the usual comparisons with Gordon, and rather artificially with Edgar Allan Poe and Swinburne ("there is a touch of Mr Swinburne's

alliterative rhythm — especially his use of sibilants — in many lines"),
went on to say:

> . . . Mr Paterson finds inspiration for his songs in the phenomena of
> bush life; the humour that sparkles round campfires. . . . All this
> gives a true Australian atmosphere to his verse and explains its fast
> growing popularity. . . .[10]

The *Spectator* drew attention to "the true lyrical cry" of some of his
ballads, continuing that they

> . . . take hold of the mind from the passionate love they express of
> the Australian scenery and from the stimulating character of the wild
> and lonely life of the station or the drover on those silent hills and
> plains.[11]

Overseas, the London *Times* considered that Paterson at his best compared "not unfavourably with the author of *Barrack Room Ballads*",[12]
which seemed praise indeed. The *Glasgow Herald* described the ballads,
especially "the racing ones", as "full of such go that the mere reading
makes the blood tingle".[13] The Edinburgh *Scotsman* commented:

> . . . albeit Mr Paterson is not above vilifying the Scot by representing
> him to be fond of his whisky and by writing a villainously bad
> dialect of Scotch that is worse than the worst whisky ever fabricated
> for export to the colonies, his book will have a hearty welcome here
> from all who value poetry that is racy of the soil that produced it.[14]

Lord Rosebery in a letter[15] to Angus & Robertson dated 23 April 1896
wrote, *inter alia*, "I am delighted to see that young Australia is producing
literature of so striking a character"; Andrew Lang (20 January 1896)
from St Andrew's, Scotland[16] promised to review the poems, saying,
". . . pray convey my thanks to Mr Paterson whose work (as I think you
know) I have always admired much . . ."; Rudyard Kipling, in a much
lengthier and more critical assessment (from Vermont, U.S.A., dated
10 December 1895) [17] commented:

> . . . Some of Mr Paterson's verse I read (and enjoyed) in last year's
> Xmas *Bulletin* — "The Amateur Rider", "The Two Devines" and
> best of all, to my thinking, "Saltbush Bill". "The Travelling Post
> Office" is new and catching to me and I like it, as do I like all the
> descriptions of droving, shearing and tramping [*sic*] . . . I want Mr
> Paterson to write more and more about the man who is born and bred
> on the land — to say what he does and what he thinks of things and
> how he manages his affairs: all without any moral reflections run
> in. People will always do their own reflecting if you put a straight
> tale before them. "A Bushman's Song" to take an instance makes one
> think five times as much as "A Voice from the Town". "Till I drink
> artesian water from a thousand feet below" is good and real and

that is the kind of thing most folks want to know more about. I hope you will not be offended with this and will give my best salutations to Mr Paterson and tell him to do it again. . . . Wishing him good luck and you good sales,

Very sincerely yours . . .

Paterson, the young author, was concerned about his sales too. He wrote to the publishers in October 1895 sending a list of his friends who, he felt sure, would buy the book; if the second edition "hung fire", he felt sure he could "scare up a lot more purchases, I think". He had an idea for sales promotion — a card "stuck in booksellers' windows" with the title of the book, "Now on Sale" and a drawing of Mahony's sketch.

As it turned out he had little cause to worry. The sale of *The Man from Snowy River and Other Verses* is a lasting phenomenon of the Australian book trade. To date almost 110,000 copies have been sold, exclusive of his *Collected Verse*. The sales at the time of its first publication are remakable enough by present day figures; they were astounding by 1890s experience. The first edition sold out in the week of publication;* 2,350 copies were sold in six weeks, 7,000 within a year.

Here was, for the first time in Australia, the spectacle of a popular poet. One wonders if it was not for the first and last time; "Banjo" Paterson, despite the competition of all the forms of mass communication since invented and developed, surely dominates the national consciousness more than any other literary figure. He was, and is, a popular poet in a different way from John Betjeman or Robert Frost in their own countries; in the latter cases the title has been dubbed on to explain a type of plain-man's folksy verse; in Paterson's case his ballads forced the legend, and sustained it, and Betjeman is most unlikely in seventy years' time to have the same aura about his name in his own country as Paterson in Australia.

Paterson's success was, of course, directly related to the lack of other forms of communication competing with the printed word. It was assisted by the word-of-mouth as it were, once his identity was established, of his own sporting reputation; assisted again by the formidable influence throughout most of settled Australia of the *Bulletin*; and assisted finally by the fact that poetry in his day was spoken (or sung) as much as it was read, and it was much more than now an accepted means of entertainment for the ordinary literate population. Since Paterson's ballads were so obviously suited to recitation, his success was certain. The nearest parallel in his day was Kipling in England, and one can argue Kipling's enormous readership for reasons (for example, *Barrack Room Ballads*) that were broadly similar.

One of the direct influences of the predictable popularity of Paterson's published verse, not only in 1895, but in ensuing years, was that it helped materially to establish the bushman in the national admiration as a

* "The Banjo's book was issued by Angus & Robertson on October 19th. By the first week in November the publishers had sold the entire edition, handed the author his share of the profits, squared all accounts, and were lying low for another record-breaker."

— *Bulletin*, 22 November 1895.

romantic and archetypal figure. At the turn of the century, as Russel Ward notes, ". . . he had more influence on the manners and *mores* of the city-dweller than the latter had on his".[18] He was then, even if not now, the nearest to a "noble frontiersman" that we shall ever have in our history. Clancy is the symbol of all this.

The other achievement of Paterson through his ballads was as a myth-maker. Vance Palmer wrote that "men cannot feel really at home in any environment until they have transformed the natural shapes around them by infusing them with myth. . . ."[19] This myth-making in the nineteenth century was carried on by the ordinary bush-folk themselves: around campfires, in the shearing sheds, in the droving camps. Yarns and songs were crystallized in the ballads; and "The Man from Snowy River" is a case in point. It is said that Paterson with a companion, some time in 1890, on a visit to the Snowy Mountains area, camped at the hut of Jack Riley at his lonely outpost on a cattle station bordering Mount Kosciusko. Riley, whose reputation as a fearless rider and stockman was almost legendary in the district, is said to have told Paterson a story of a colt that "got away" in the mountains. In 1892 the ballad itself appeared; not un-naturally Riley's claims to be the original Man from Snowy River have been consistently argued,* so much so that when he died a headstone was erected on his grave giving him the title.† But the claims of other famous riders for the honour have been similarly put forward: Lachie Cochran of Adaminaby, Hell-Fire Jack Clarke, McEacharn of the Thredbo, Louder of Yass, George Hedger of Numbla Vale, Jim Spencer of Jindabyne‡ and Jim Troy. It is the same with Mulga Bill: even as recently as 1960, one William Henry Lewis, who died at the age of eighty and had spent most of his life as a bushman in western N.S.W., Queensland and the Northern Territory, was claimed to have been the original Mulga Bill. What has happened, of course, is that his characters are still believed by many people to have had as real a bodily existence as The Banjo himself.

Paterson a few years before his death left the matter in no doubt, when he wrote:[20]

> The Man from Snowy River . . . was written to describe the cleaning up of the wild horses in my own district. To make a job of it I had to create a character, to imagine a man who would ride better than anybody else, and where would he come from except from the Snowy?

* cf. interview in A.B.C. "Week-End Magazine" television programme, 31 May 1964, with Leo Byatt, aged seventy, who claimed he rode with Riley. ". . . But he was seen by a lot of people — a lot of people attested to when he chased this horse for a start and that . . . he came back leading it and they knew that he had to go through this rugged country to catch him. That gave him a great name as a bushman and . . . a rider too."

† In the Corryong (Victoria) Cemetery. He died on 16 July 1914.

‡ Jim Spencer's claims have been canvassed by Percy Harris, a Jindabyne identity, who, in a tape-recorded interview (part of a Jindabyne Oral History Project held in the National Library, Canberra), states that Paterson knew Spencer in the Snowy country. Harris discounts Riley's claim to the honour; he says Riley was a tailor by trade who "never seen a horse"!

And what sort of horse woud he ride except a half-thoroughbred mountain pony?

I felt sure there must have been a Man from Snowy River and I was right. They have turned up from all the mountain districts — men who did exactly the same ride and could give you chapter and verse for every mile they descended and every creek they crossed. It was no small satisfaction that there really had been a Man from Snowy River — more than one of them. . . .

Paterson's achievement as a myth-maker went far beyond his own expectations: the ride of "The Man from Snowy River", much more than being talked about only by the bush folk

> . . . down by Kosciusko where the pine-clad ridges raise
> Their torn and rugged battlements on high,
> Where the air is clear as crystal, and the white stars fairly blaze
> At midnight in the cold and frosty sky,
> And where around the Overflow the reedbeds sweep and sway
> To the breezes, and the rolling plains are wide,

has become a legend over the length and breadth of Australia and in a good many other parts of the world as well. The fact remains, as Elioth Gruner, who knew Paterson and admired his verse, once said, " 'The Man from Snowy River' is a ballad, not a newspaper report".[21]

Soon after his book had appeared, and because he found he was being lionized in Sydney to the point of embarrassment, Paterson took a holiday in Queensland, visiting a number of stations where he had friends. It was at one of these that he wrote "Waltzing Matilda". He returned to Sydney to an even busier social and writing life than before. While his interest in his law business was steadily diminishing, there was still work to be done in his office; with his dry, quiet wit and his handsome presence, as well as his now-established reputation as a writer, he was sought after for dinners and balls; he was *persona grata* at Government House, where he played polo with the Governor's aides. Florence Earle Hooper recalled that she had met "old ladies who in their girlhood were thrilled to be introduced to the famous young man".[22]

He became more involved than before with young writers and artists, some of whom were obsessed with the idea of founding Australian schools in art and literature. These included A. W. Lambert, Arthur Adams, Frank Fox, A. W. Jose (who wrote that he helped Paterson "with proof sheets and occasional suggestions that a phrase here and there needed polishing") ,[23] Andrew Soutar, George Essex Evans, the Lindsays (though Norman Lindsay mentions that he did not meet Paterson until after the latter's return from the Boer War) , Harry Stockdale and others. Journals and magazines of writing were started and failed. One of them, the *Antipodean*, however, ran for two years. Paterson was joint editor, with Essex Evans, of one issue (February 1898), to which he contributed "Saltbush Bill's Second Fight" (with illustrations by Frank Mahony) and "Ballad of the Calliope". The issue also included poems by J. Brunton Stephens and J. B. O'Hara, stories by Essex Evans, Roderic Quinn, Edward Dyson and Steele Rudd ("A Day at Shingle Hut"), a bush sketch by Rolfe Boldrewood, a children's story by Ethel Turner and several anonymous articles, one of which "Sport in Australia — a chatty article" was, by its style, more than likely by Paterson.

Jose recalls that another of these journals, the *Australian Magazine*, was born hopefully with a nominal capital of £3,000 and a real one of some £100. It ran six issues in six months during 1899 for a total loss of just over £100, dying "amid the hilarious laughter of its parents". These included Christopher Brennan and le Gay Brereton on the literary side and George Lambert and Sid Long on the artistic side. Lawson contributed poems and a story; other contributors included Will Beattie, Roderic Quinn and Brennan himself; ". . . from Paterson we could get only a casual discourse on polo".[24] This article[25] incidentally is worth passing mention. The Paterson drollery is apparent in one of his remarks that "those who have the money to purchase first-class horses cannot ride them, and those who can ride them have not the money". Nevertheless, he made it quite clear that he had become addicted to the game, not because of any social prestige that might come from it, but rather because he considered there was "no better training for riding, coolness and dash" — thus spoke Paterson the dedicated horseman.

Paterson continued to contribute his ballads and prose sketches to the *Bulletin*; he also ventured occasionally into literary criticism, and his good sense and practical approach, combined with the directness and succinctness of the best journalism, suggests that he could, with much advantage to his readers as well as himself, have ventured more into this kind of writing than he did. His splendid review of Barcroft Boake's *Where the Dead Men Lie and Other Poems* (1897) has already been mentioned; he was also commissioned by Angus & Robertson to write an introductory memoir for a new edition of Marcus Clarke's *For The Term of His Natural Life*. It was a nice combination of literary allusion —

> . . . as Rossetti says of Byron, "he underwent no training that could have elicited his finer and eliminated his more perilous qualities . . ."

— and of, one might say, horse-sense, as, when referring to Clarke's first novel *Long Odds*, he wrote:

> . . . one might as reasonably ask a great tragedian to give a good nigger-minstrel performance as expect the author of *For The Term of His Natural Life* to write a horse novel. Only one worse failure to get down to horse-novel level exists; Tolstoi in *Anna Karenina* gives us about the worst account of a horse race ever written.

His appreciation of *For The Term of His Natural Life* was perceptive and well argued:

> . . . The characters are all powerfully but vaguely drawn — titanic figures in a gloomy atmosphere; but it is not in skill of character-

drawing that the wonderful fascination of the book depends . . .
Almost every incident detailed in the book may be found in the
convict records; he neither added nor took away one single fact. He
simply by the magic of his telling converted a dull, sodden brutal
incident into a moving episode of his drama . . .

Towards the end of 1898 an opportunity came his way that he had been
for years eagerly seeking — to make a tour of the Northern Territory.
He was commissioned by the Eastern and Australian Steamship Company
to contribute an article to its Tourist Guide on the types of big-game
sport available in the Territory, including buffalo-shooting and alligator-
hunting. Paterson jumped at the chance, and spent several months there,
which he always regarded as among the most exciting in his life. Out of
this experience came one of his wittiest and neatest prose sketches — the
little known "The Cycloon, Paddy Cahill and the G.R." — which he sent
back to the *Bulletin*[26] soon after he had spent some time in Palmerston
(now Darwin). Paterson, the discerning and naturally gifted journalist,
was coming into his own. It is a brilliant piece of reporting by any
standards, old or new:

> . . . There is only one great land mark in Palmerston history — the
> cyclone which some years ago blew the town down. A lot of it isn't
> rebuilt yet. This atmospheric disturbance, locally known as 'the
> cycloon', is one of the three topics of conversation in Palmerston;
> the second is the Government Resident (the G.R.). He is an English
> barrister, and, in his own person, Supreme Court head of, the Mining
> Jurisdiction, Protector of Blacks, and Police Magistrate. No wonder
> they talk about him. Good man for the position too as he doesn't care
> a damn for anybody, and, starting from that safe basis, discharges
> his varied duties with a light heart. The third subject of discussion
> is Paddy Cahill, the buffalo shooter; he is popularly reported to
> pursue the infuriated buffalo at full gallop, standing on his saddle,
> and dressed in a towel and a diamond ring, and yelling like a wild
> Indian. The trinity of the N.T.: The cycloon, the G.R. and Paddy
> Cahill! The inhabitants sit about the shady verandahs and drink,
> and talk about one or all of the three. They start drinking square gin
> immediately after breakfast, and keep it up at intervals till midnight.
> They don't do anything else to speak of, yet they have a curious
> delusion that they are a very energetic and reckless set of people. But
> it's all talk and blasphemy. There is an Act compelling a publican
> to refuse drink to an habitual inebriate. This is locally known as the
> "Dog Act" and to be brought under the Dog Act is a glorious dis-
> tinction, a sort of V.C. of Northern Territory life.

Paterson was entranced by the new horizons of the Territory. The wild
game abounding was especially attractive to him since it allowed him to
indulge in one of his favourite pastimes. He wrote enthusiastically of
wild and pigmy geese, the Burdekin duck, brown quail and snipe. The

fish "with fine large mouths and big appetites" were there for the taking.
As for buffalo-shooting,

> . . . To my mind [it] is the best sport to be had in Australia. The
> excitement of the approach of the big mob, the desperate race over
> the plains, the grip of the carbine as the horse overhauls the mob and
> the shooter selects his animals, and drives home the spur for the final
> rush, the downward shot into the broad, blue back, and the exulta-
> tion as the huge beast topples over; all these make up a sport hard
> to match anywhere. After experience of most Australian sport from
> pig sticking to steeple chasing I give preference to this buffalo shoot-
> ing and an American who had been shooting big game on the Rocky
> Mountains informed me that he preferred this to any sport that he
> had in America. It is the combination of riding and shooting that
> makes it so fascinating.[27]

He used this particular episode as an exciting addition to a novel he was
writing at the time, *An Outback Marriage*. There were other experiences
which also gave him material for his writing. He went out sailing in a
Japanese pearling-lugger, donned a diving-suit and went down to the
sea floor. He met Billy Makalla, a Melanesian who, fresh from his native
island as a primitive savage, within a few years of shipping from the
Islands in a trading schooner commanded his own lugger "with the
confidence of an Admiral". He met a Lancashire girl who had come out

> . . . to teach the little black heathen. For a while she listened to their
> excuses for not attending school until she heard one urchin say to
> another that she was "plenty big fool". Then she left a pupil teacher
> in charge of the children and went around the native villages with
> a whip, routing out the little black truants and flogging them to
> school. A method of ensuring attendance not laid down in the
> curriculum, but it had most satisfactory results. Then she married
> an owner of a diving outfit, and lived happily ever afterwards.[28]

Paterson was amazed at the ability of the Japanese divers and Island
natives to find their way across trackless waters without knowing any
navigation. He came to the conclusion that as divers, compared with
Malays and Islanders "for sheer hard work on the open bottom, the
Japanese will outlast any of them". He also saw the tragic, but common
enough, death of a Japanese diver whose air-pipe had fouled. From this
incident came his ballad "The Pearl Diver". And out of the memory of
his visit to the Territory came his nostalgic ballad "By the Grey Gulf-
Water":

> Far to the Northward there lies a land,
>   A wonderful land that the wind blows over,
> And none may fathom or understand
>   The charm it holds for the restless rover . . .

When Paterson returned to Sydney the rover was restless indeed. His career as a lawyer hung by a thread, and it is probable that the lure of travel and free-lance journalism (not to mention a constant hankering to get back on the land) would have led him to cut the thread soon enough. But then the Boer War came to the rescue, and saved Paterson from having to make the decision for himself. He was one of a number of enthusiastically patriotic Australians who did not wait for the Government to move, but in the field of active journalism at last (as war correspondent for the *Sydney Morning Herald* and the Melbourne *Argus*) he set sail for Capetown with the volunteer New South Wales Lancers in October 1899.

NOTES

[1] In *The Legend of the Nineties* (1954).
[2] In "Banjo Paterson: A Poet Nearly Anonymous", *Meanjin*, No. 4, 1964.
[3] In his *Sydney Morning Herald* reminiscences.
[4] In "Looking Backward".
[5] In a script *Bush Life* written by Paterson for the A.B.C. in 1935, but hitherto unpublished.
[6] *Bulletin*, 5 September 1891.
[7] In the possession of Florence Earle Hooper.
[8] In his *Sydney Morning Herald* reminiscences.
[9] In the *Bulletin*, 26 October 1895.
[10] In *Review of Reviews*, 15 October 1895.
[11] In *The Spectator*, 30 May 1896.
[12] Quoted in a *Bulletin* article, 27 June 1896.
[13] As above.
[14] As above.
[15] In the Mitchell Library, Sydney.
[16] Ibid.
[17] Ibid.
[18] In *The Australian Legend* (1958).
[19] In *The Legend of the Nineties* (1954).
[20] In "Looking Backward".
[21] Quoted in the Jindabyne Oral History Project tapes held in the National Library, Canberra.
[22] In conversations with the author.
[23] In *The Romantic Nineties* (1933).
[24] Ibid.
[25] *Australian Magazine*, 6 July 1899.
[26] 31 December 1898.
[27] In *Eastern and Australian Steamship Co. Tourist Guide* (1899).
[28] In a script *Pearl Fishing*, written by Paterson for the A.B.C. in 1935, but hitherto unpublished.

CHAPTER VII

Paterson and Lawson

. . . the twin deities of Australian literature in the Nineties
. . . were Banjo Paterson and Henry Lawson . . .

— A. W. JOSE.[1]

IT IS NOT MY particular concern here to make a comparative assessment of Paterson's and Lawson's work in verse and prose: to the extent that it is necessary, this can be left to a later chapter. But in tracing the chronology of Paterson's life there should be a suitable pause to consider how and when the lines of their work and life crossed, as indeed they did in the early 1890s.

It seems that Paterson and Lawson met early in 1888 through their work for the *Bulletin*. Lawson had spent the previous few months in Melbourne doing odd jobs, but, inspired by reason of having had his first few poems published in the *Bulletin*, including "A Song of the Republic" and "Golden Gully", immediately haunted the *Bulletin* office. He had arrived back in Sydney practically penniless, and set to work composing more verses.

> I was in print. [he wrote] . . . I felt strong and proud enough to clean pig-styes if need be, for a living for the rest of my natural life — providing the *Bulletin* went on publishing the poetry.[2]

Paterson, whose verse, as "The Banjo", had begun to appear a year or two before Lawson, was just as keen to continue with his contributions, but, unlike Lawson, it was hardly a matter of dire necessity; as a managing law clerk his bread and butter was assured.

Gavin Long[3] has pointed out, however, that there is a curious similarity in vein, as well as in output, of these two as verse-writers, certainly up till the early 1890s. In a sense this culminated in the publication by Angus & Robertson of a book of collected verses by each writer, both with titles angled at a nationalistic awareness: *The Man from Snowy River and Other Verses* (1895) and *In the Days when the World was Wide and Other Verses* (1896), the latter with a Mahony drawing of a sun-downer on the title page.

Both had begun with verses of a quasi-patriotic type: at least it could be said that "The Soudan Contingent" with its references to the "spots on your hands" and "blood guilty lands" and "A Song of the Republic" —

Sons of the South, awake! Arise
Sons of the South, and do.
Banish from under your bonny skies
Those old-world errors and wrongs and lies,
Making a hell in a Paradise
That belongs to your sons and you.

— were the work of indignatories-in-verse.

By the end of 1888 each had published about the same amount of verse
with not much difference in quality. Although Paterson forged ahead
during 1889, it is a coincidence that each appeared in the Christmas 1889
Bulletin with a nostalgic, sentimental piece, each piece eminently quot-
able, of a period and a way of life that is past: Paterson's "Clancy of The
Overflow" and Lawson's "The Roving Days", which has the same singable
quality:

Oft, when the camps were dreaming,
    And stars began to pale,
Through rugged ranges gleaming,
    Swept on the Royal Mail.
Behind five foaming horses,
    And lit by flashing lamps,
Old Cobb and Co., in royal state,
    Went dashing past the camps.

Oh! who would paint a goldfield,
    And limn the picture right,
As old Adventure saw it
    In early morning's light?
The yellow mounds of mullock,
    With spots of red and white,
The scattered quartz that glistened,
    Like diamonds in light.

And even when "The Man from Snowy River" appeared in April 1890,
Lawson followed this, a month later, with "The Song of Old Joe Swallow", which immortalized the deeds of the bullock-teams and their drivers
in the "days o' long ago":

But in spite ov barren ridges an' in spite ov mud and heat,
An' dust that browned the bushes when it rose from bullicks' feet,
An' in spite ov cold an' chilblains when the bush was white with frost,
An' in spite ov muddy water where the burning plain was crossed,
An' in spite ov modern progress an' in spite ov all their blow,
'Twas better land to live in in the days o' long ago . . .

It was not long after this that Lawson took a job in Brisbane with the
Boomerang, a weekly newspaper founded a few years before by William
Lane. It was there that Lawson met A. G. Stephens, who also worked at

that time on the staff of this paper, and it was there that there began an association that was helpful to Lawson, since Stephens recognized and encouraged Lawson's talent, and did his best to infuse into him some sense of artistic discipline: ". . . no-one can know him or read his books," Stephens wrote some years later, "without seeing the sterling metal of the man — whatever the flaws in the casting . . .".[4] On the other hand, there is no evidence that Paterson, aloof from the necessity of writing as a daily grind, knew A. G. Stephens as more than a *Bulletin* acquaintance, and Paterson was never a member of Stephens' stable of young writers.

Lawson worked only for nine months on the *Boomerang* (he also contributed to Lane's Brisbane *Worker* during this period) and then came south again, passing through country bitter with the aftermath of the 1891 shearers' strike which had ended in triumph for the pastoralists. Lawson's mood —

> Crawling home with empty pockets
> Going back hard-up
> Oh it's then you learn the meaning of "humiliation's cup".

— matched the times.

Not long after he arrived back in Sydney the celebrated "*Bulletin* battle" between him and Paterson took place. Now, there are few writers on the period who have failed to comment on what is regarded as the contrasting ideologies of Lawson and Paterson. The extreme argument is that Paterson was the representative of the squattocracy, the educated sportsman and bush-dilettante; Lawson was the underdog, the union man, oppressed by the forces of bush-capitalism. This is a long way from the truth, since Paterson, as we have noted, was just as much concerned with the rights of the bush-worker, with the principles of mateship and unionism:

> ". . . We shear non-union here," says he. "I call it scab," says I.
> I looked along the shearing-shed before I turned to go.
> There was eight or ten dashed Chinamen a-shearing in a row.
> . . . . .

Paterson's radicalism was just as deep-seated as Lawson's, even if more intellectual and less emotional. His writings in the *Bulletin* in these years are proof enough of that.

But there is little doubt that their "rhyming-match" in the *Bulletin* of 1892 gave rise to some of these misconceptions: to the mistaken idea that there was antipathy, even hostility, between them, as contained in such a statement as ". . . the relations between the *Bulletin*'s two chief bards were usually on the edge of animosity . . .".[5] Far from it. Paterson was as friendly with Lawson and his family as his rather reticent and retiring disposition would allow him to be, a disposition which he used as a deliberate shield between himself and the somewhat excessive Bohemianism of his contemporaries with their cliques, circles and clubs, with their "beery good-fellowship and facile emotionalism".[6]

The fact was however that in June 1892 Lawson and Paterson concocted the idea of their bush-controversy; as Paterson recalls it:

> Henry Lawson was a man of remarkable insight in some things and of extraordinary simplicity in others. We were both looking for the same reef, if you get what I mean; but I had done my prospecting on horseback with my meals cooked for me, while Lawson had done his prospecting on foot and had had to cook for himself. Nobody realized this better than Lawson; and one day he suggested that we should write against each other, he putting the bush from his point of view, and I putting it from mine.
>
> "We ought to do pretty well out of it," he said, "we ought to be able to get in three or four sets of verses before they stop us."
>
> This suited me all right, for we were working on space, and the pay was very small . . . so we slam-banged away at each other for weeks and weeks; not until they stopped us, but until we ran out of material . . ."[7]

Lawson led off with "Borderland" in the *Bulletin* of 9 July 1892 (retitled "Up the Country" in his *Poetical Works*) and a polemical opening:

> I'm back from up the country — very sorry that I went
> Seeking out the Southern poets' land whereon to pitch my tent
> I have lost a lot of idols, which were broken on the track
> Burnt a lot of fancy verses, and I am glad that I am back.

Instead of the happy bush country of other poets, he found

> Treacherous tracks that trap the stranger, endless roads that gleam
>   and glare
> Dark and evil looking gullies — hiding secrets here and there!
> Dull dumb flats and stony "rises" where the bullocks sweat and bake
> And the sinister "gohanna", and the lizard and the snake
> . . . . .
> Land where gaunt and haggard women live alone and work like men,
> Till their husbands, gone a-droving, will return to them again

Lawson may have been referring in his opening lines to his recent trip through the country from Brisbane down to Sydney; on the other hand, certain lines suggest that he was writing of the middle west of New South Wales, and he perhaps had in mind a visit he had recently made to Eurunderee, one of the small townships of his boyhood.

Paterson retorted with a forty-line poem (23 July — the same issue that carried Lawson's memorable short story "The Drover's Wife" — the seed for which was surely in his poem quoted above), hardly in his best style, that also jumped into the attack:

> So you're back from up the country, Mister Lawson, where you went
> And you're cursing all the business in a bitter discontent . . .

There was a jab at one of Lawson's more pessimistic poems —

> (And the women of the homesteads and the men you chanced to
>   meet —
> Were their faces sour and saddened like the faces in the street?)

— but Paterson seemed to get into his stride in the last part of the poem

> Did you heard the silver chiming of the bell-birds on the range?
> But, perchance, the wild birds' music by your senses was despised,
> For you say you'll stay in townships till the bush is civilised.
> Would you make it a tea-garden, and on Sundays have a band
> Where the "blokes" might take their "donahs", with a "public" close
>   at hand?
> You had better stick to Sydney and make merry with the "push",
> For the bush will never suit you, and you'll never suit the bush.

Now that the "twin deities" were hurling bolts at each other, some of the lesser lights of the *Bulletin* group added to the storm, even if with weaker thunder. (It should be noted that there seemed to be rules to the game: the metre to be used was either that of Lawson's first poem or of Paterson's "Clancy".) Thus Edward Dyson's "The Fact of the Matter" in the issue of 30 July (along with one of his best known ballads "The Old Whim Horse"), with an obvious jibe at the "vision splendid":

> I'm wonderin' why those fellers who go buildin' chipper ditties
> 'Bout the rosy times out drovin', an' the dust an' death of cities,
> Don't sling the bloomin' office, strike some drover for a billet
> And soak up all the glory that comes handy while they fill it
> Night watches are delightful when the stars are really splendid
> To the chap who's fresh upon the job, but, you bet, his rapture's
>   ended
> When the rain comes down in sluice heads, or the cuttin' hailstones
>   pelter,
> An' the sheep drift off before the wind, an' the horses strike for
>   shelter . . .

Meanwhile Lawson had been preparing his next sally which came to light (6 August) with an opening couplet sharply aimed —

> It was pleasant up the country, Mr Banjo, where you went
> For you sought the greener patches and you travelled like a gent,

— turning next to the hardships of the bush worker —

> Did you ever guard the cattle when the night was inky black
> And it rained, and icy water trickled gently down your back,
> Till your saddle-weary backbone started aching at the roots

And you almost heard the croaking of the bullfrog in your boots?
Did you shiver in the saddle, curse the restless stock and cough
Till a squatter's blanky dummy cantered up to warn you off?

— and then giving his lines a political turn, attacking the very evils of a
system that Paterson himself had frequently deplored:

Though the bush has been romantic and is nice to sing about,
There's a lot of patriot fervour that the land could do without —
Sort of *British Workman* nonsense that shall perish in the scorn
Of the drover who is driven and the shearer who is shorn —
Of the struggling western farmers who have little time to rest,
Facing ruin on selections in the sheep-infested West;
Droving songs are very pretty, but they call for little thanks
From the people of a country in possession of the Banks.

A fortnight later a clever parody of nine stanzas, "The Overflow of
Clancy", appeared, signed by "H.H.C.C.":

And the pub hath friends to meet him and between the acts they treat
    him
    While he's swapping "fairy twisters" with the "girls behind their
    bars",
And he sees a vista splendid when the ballet is extended
    And at night he's in his glory with the comic opera stars.

I am sitting very weary, on a log before a dreary
    Little fire that's feebly hissing 'neath a heavy fall of rain,
And the wind is cold and nipping and I curse the ceaseless dripping
    As I slosh around for wood to start the embers up again . . .

On 27 August a Brisbane poet Francis Kenna, who used "K" as a
pseudonym for most of his contributions, contributed "Banjo of the
Overflow". Kenna a few years later locked horns with fellow-Queenslander Brunton Stephens in a violent *Bulletin* controversy about the state
of Australian poetry; he was a clever rhymster as his verses showed:

He has clients now to fee him and his friends to come and see him,
    He can ride from morn to evening in the padded hansom cars,
And he sees the beauties blending where the throngs are never ending,
    And at night the wond'rous women in the everlasting bars.

And the bush is very pretty when you view it from the city,
    But it loses all its beauty when you face it "on the pad";
And the wildernesses haunt you, and the plains extended daunt you,
    Till at times you come to fancy that the life will drive you mad.

Lawson's stirring "The Southern Scout" or "The Natives of the Land"
("Ye landlords of the cities that are builded by the sea") appeared in this
same issue.

None of these "outsiders" had taken Paterson's part, but he was quite capable of looking after himself, as he showed in his lines "An Answer to Various Bards" with which, on 10 October, he ended the immediate controversy. It was probably the strongest poem of the series —

> Well, I've waited mighty patient while they all came rolling in,
> Mister Lawson, Mister Dyson, and the others of their kin,
> With their dreadful, dismal stories of the Overlander's camp,
> How his fire is always smoky, and his boots are always damp;
> And they paint it so terrific it would fill one's soul with gloom —
> But you know they're fond of writing about "corpses" and "the tomb".
> So, before they curse the bushland, they should let their fancy range,
> And take something for their livers, and be cheerful for a change.

— with an olive branch to conclude:

> But that ends it, Mr Lawson, and it's time to say good-bye,
> So we must agree to differ in all friendship, you and I.
> Yes, we'll work our own salvation with the stoutest hearts we may,
> And if fortune only favours us we will take the road some day,
> And go droving down the river 'neath the sunshine and the stars,
> And then return to Sydney and vermilionize the bars.

It was as a postscript to these exchanges that Lawson in a later poem, "The Poets of the Tomb", spiritedly refuted the charge that he was fond of writing about "corpses" and "the tomb"; Paterson too harked back to the argument when his "A Voice from the Town" appeared in the *Bulletin* in October 1894:

> I thought, in the days of my droving,
>   Of steps I might hope to retrace,
> To be done with the bush and the roving
>   And settle once more in my place.
> With a heart that was wellnigh to breaking,
>   In the long, lonely rides on the plain,
> I thought of the pleasure of taking
>   The hand of a lady again.
>
> I am back into civilization,
>   Once more in the stir and the strife,
> But the old joys have lost their sensation —
>   The light has gone out of my life;
> The men of my time they have married,
>   Made fortunes or gone to the wall;
> Too long from the scene I have tarried,
>   And, somehow, I'm out of it all.

Many years later his verdict on these events was characteristic and slightly ironical:

... I think that Lawson put his case better than I did, but I had the better case, so that honours (or dishonours) were fairly equal. An undignified affair, but it was a case of "root hog or die".

The truth is that Paterson was on friendly terms with the Lawsons for many years. Once he called at Lawson's home to see how he was getting on: Mrs Lawson said she was happy because her husband was working again.

"What's he working at," I asked, "prose or verse?"
"Oh, no!" she said, "I don't mean writing, I mean working. He's gone back to his trade as a housepainter."[9]

There is also extant a memorandum[10] to A. B. Paterson from Angus & Robertson dated 3 September 1895, reading: "Lawson suggests as 'The Story of Conroy's Gap' is widely known as 'Conroy's Gap', 'The Story of' ought to be dropped. It would look better from a compositor's point of view I think too." Across this Paterson had written: "All right. This suits me. — A. B. Paterson."

Paterson came to Lawson's real assistance in the next few years helping him with his legal agreements and copyright problems free of charge, and showing constant patience with his wayward and feckless "client". Thus, on 19 June 1899, Paterson in his holograph on behalf of "Street and Paterson" wrote to Angus & Robertson as follows:

Mr Lawson has been in to see us. He wishes to sell you a book of verse as follows:

(1) All the verse now in your hands.
(2) "Past Caring", "The Jimmy Woodser" and "Pigeon Toes" of which the first has appeared and the others are about to appear in the *Australian Magazine* and will be submitted in proof.
(3) "The Shakedown on the Floor" which has appeared in *The Freeman's Journal* and "The Green Tide" which is to appear in the *T. & C. Journal* and will be submitted in proof.
(4) Six new pieces in hand not published anywhere which he wishes to sell.

He has certain verses in the *Bulletin*'s hands which he cannot submit for the same reasons that hindered him before, but two, namely "The Darling River" and "The Sliprails" can be included.

He says you can lay your hands on all the published stuff and he wants you to have a look at that and he will then have the six new pieces ready if you wish to deal for them.

He wishes to sell for a cash sum but wishes to keep a small royalty so as to have an interest in the future sale of the book especially in the event of a selected edition coming out.

Yours truly,
STREET & PATERSON[11]

Other correspondence to do with Lawson's agreements appeared from time to time during 1899, including a most revealing letter[12] (in terms of Paterson's relationship with Lawson) from Paterson to George Robertson, marked "private":

> Waltham Buildings,
> Bond Street,
> July 15, 1899.
>
> G. Robertson, Esq.,
> Dear Robertson,
>
> Yours to hand. Lawson does not trouble me much, or rather I have so many other things to think about that he is rather a relief — I have started him off to get the papers signed by the Freeman's Journal and the Town and Country Journal. . . . I think you are too critical as to the quality of his last pieces. What I read were distinctly good: you were very set on getting his work and now that you have got it at your own price you don't like it!
>
> Yours truly,
> A. B. PATERSON.

Since writing the above he has come back with the Freeman and T. & C.J. papers all right!

Lawson the importunate! Then there was the short memo. scribbled by Paterson to Robertson on the next day: "Lawson submits the enclosed for your perusal and would be glad to get an advance of say £5. — A.B.P." On the back of the note, Paterson had scrawled in pencil: "This may suit you to pay a fiver in advance. If not, say so. — A.B.P."

The fact is that both Paterson and Lawson were essential to the period, as indeed they were to Australian literature as a whole — they "found it provincial and left it national". The voice of both was the voice of the country, even if they were two different poeple — different in unbringing and education, in environment, in temperament. H. M. Green puts it that "to Paterson life was a game, played mainly on horseback . . . to Lawson life was a battle . . .";[13] Norman Lindsay, who knew them both, takes the contrast a step further: he sees in Paterson's writing the philosophy of one who "takes life as a high adventure in action, even to the risk of a broken neck. Lawson's self-image, sodden with self-pity, is that of the under-dog."[14] Both Green and Lindsay ignore, or take into insufficient account, that Paterson and Lawson, brought up in the outback and strongly influenced by the ballad-makers, knew, wrote about and respected the bush people — the shearers, drovers and similar types — and proceeded to make a contribution to Australian writing that commemorates them equally in the mind of their readers. Call one a nationalist and one a socialist; one an aristocrat and one an underdog; in the long run it is of little consequence: viewed in the context of their writing and their times Paterson and Lawson are synonymous. There are few writers since to the present day who have not directly or indirectly drawn on Paterson and Lawson whenever they have depicted a truly Australian character or voiced a genuinely national sentiment.

NOTES

[1] In *The Romantic Nineties* (1933).
[2] In *Henry Lawson — the Grey Dreamer* by Denton Prout (1963).
[3] In "Young Paterson and Young Lawson", *Meanjin*, No. 4, 1964.
[4] In *The Bookfellow* (1899).
[5] A. W. Jose (op. cit.).
[6] Denton Prout (op. cit.).
[7] In his *Sydney Morning Herald* reminiscences.
[8] Ibid.
[9] Ibid.
[10] In the Mitchell Library, Sydney.
[11] Ibid.
[12] Ibid.
[13] In his *History of Australian Literature* (1961).
[14] In *Bohemians of the Bulletin* (1965).

CHAPTER VIII

Waltzing Matilda

And his ghost may be heard as it sings in the Billabong
"Who'll come a-waltzing Matilda with me?"

— A. B. PATERSON.

PATERSON'S MOST FAMOUS ballad, in 1966, is certainly "Waltzing Matilda". It is at once bush song, community-singing song, marching song, school song, and folk song, and has frequently been described as Australia's unofficial national anthem. Wherever a group of Australians is gathered in convivial mood in another country the song is bound to be heard, and it assumes for overseas inhabitants the character of a type of tribal song, somewhere between a Maori haka and a school war-cry. It has been translated with various degrees of success into French, Japanese, Italian, Welsh and even dog-Latin:

> Olim sedebat prope ripam fluminis
> Solus grassator sub umbra fagi,
> Et cantabat homo dum aestuaret cortina,
> Veni et saltemus Matilda, veni! . . .[1]

It is generally accepted that Paterson wrote this ballad in Queensland in 1895. Soon after *The Man from Snowy River and Other Verses* was published early in that year, Paterson went north to Queensland partly on business for his law firm, partly to have a holiday. He first of all visited Winton in the central western district of Queensland — nowadays nearly a thousand miles' rail journey from Brisbane, and in those days an exhausting one by rail and horse-and-buggy. He was at that time engaged to a Sarah Riley, whose family owned Vindex Station near Winton, and he had promised to spend part of his holidays there. During this period Sarah Riley met at Winton an old school friend, Christina Macpherson, who, with her sister Jean and father Ewan Macpherson, was on the way from Victoria to Dagworth Station on the Diamantina River to the northwest of Winton, managed by her brother Robert. Sarah Riley and Paterson accepted an invitation to join the Macphersons in their journey and became guests at Dagworth.

With greater or less embellishment, according to various bits of evidence and pseudo-evidence, hearsay, conjecture, and perhaps invention, there are stories differing in detail as to what followed, and the actual circumstances in which Paterson composed his ballad. Christina Macpherson was musically inclined; it is said she was continually humming an old Scottish tune which she had heard played by the local band at a Warrnambool race-meeting while she was still in Victoria. This tune was said to be "Bonnie Wood of Craigielea". Whatever the tune was, it attracted Paterson. In the meantime, riding around the station with Robert Macpherson and his brothers, he came upon a dead sheep along the river, with a forequarter missing — most likely killed, Macpherson explained, by a passing swagman who could not preserve the meat and therefore ate only what he could cook on the spot. Near another waterhole, Paterson was told of a local legend about a "wanted" man who had drowned himself there rather than be captured by the police. Paterson also heard for the first time the phrase "waltzing Matilda" and had its meaning explained as to "carry a swag" or "hump a bluey".

There was an old autoharp (an instrument of the zither family) on the station; Christina played her "Scottish tune" on this at idle moments, while Paterson turned over in his mind the lines of verses to match this tune. Nearby, at a station called Oondooroo, owned by the Ramsays, a demonstration of firefighting equipment* had been arranged. The Dagworth contingent was invited over. Here there was a piano, and Herbert (later Sir Herbert), one of the brothers Ramsay, who sang very well. With Christina at the piano, Paterson writing out the lines and Herbert singing the song, "Waltzing Matilda" came into being. Herbert even dressed up in a swagman's costume to play out the part. During the next month (May), the Winton races were held — a social and picnic occasion for the surrounding district — and here the song was sung as the Dagworth and Winton parties came together again, and many people heard it and passed it on.

This is substantially the account of the composition of the ballad given by Sydney May in his book *The Story of Waltzing Matilda*,[2] and there seems no reason at all to doubt the main thread of it: that Paterson wrote "Waltzing Matilda" here, at this time. There is corroborative evidence for the incidents May describes in that Sir Herbert Ramsay later gave May's daughter this story in detail, and also a copy of a photograph of himself in a swagman's costume at the time, which is reproduced in May's book. May's account is accepted by the ballad authority John Manifold (whose father, the owner of an adjoining station, learned the tune about this time).[3] A version given by Thomas Wood in his book *Cobbers* as a result of a visit to Winton has similar features; a well-known Melbourne journalist and broadcaster, Jerry Waight, also published an account[4] based on information supplied by the Macpherson family which supports May's story. Hugh Paterson, son of A. B. Paterson, has substantiated this account[5] as has also Vince Kelly,[6] Sydney author and journalist, who worked with Paterson on a Sydney newspaper in the 1920s, and with

* Many years later (in a letter to the *Sydney Morning Herald* dated 9 January 1932) Paterson explained that the invention was made up of a steel mat hung from a long pole stretched out in front of a two-horse vehicle. The horses wore leather leggings to protect their legs from burns. "The affair worked better than might have been expected," wrote Paterson, "the steel mat swept burning grass towards the ground already burnt, but it was only effective in clear, open country."

whom Paterson talked about the circumstances of the ballad's composition. (Indeed, Kelly has told me that a few months before his death Paterson told him he had a greater affection for this ballad than for almost all his other verses.) In the Mitchell Library, Sydney, is a letter written by Miss Jeannie Ranken, a close friend of Paterson's sister Gwen, to H. M. Green, the celebrated Australian literary historian. It reads, in part

> Dear Harry,
> I have just left Miss G. A. Paterson (Barty's sister), and have compared her version of the original of *Waltzing Matilda* with mine. We both got our information direct from Barty, and we agree on the matter, so I think you may take it as correct.
>   *Waltzing Matilda* was a name which appealed to Barty very much. He heard it first from an old swagman years ago, but it has been in vogue in the bush for many years, and probably Barty for long intended to use it in a verse story. However, he did not do so until when staying at Dagworth Station, Winton. One night Miss Christina Macpherson was at the piano, and she played an old air. Asked what it was, she said she did not know, but it was very old, and she had heard that it had once been a Scottish hymn tune. Barty was very much struck by it, and said he would like to write words for it, and did write *Waltzing Matilda* to the air. According to what Barty told both his sister and me, he got the idea of writing a song for the tune, and was not "persuaded" to do it.

Finally, there is a piece of corroborative evidence, not before published, supplied by the writer Henry Lamond,[7] which recalls Paterson's visit to the Queensland outback in 1895:

> As I remember him he was tall, tanned, wrinkled, well-balanced on his feet, lithe and active. My father was then an inspector of police. He may have had orders from higher-up; but I do know he went out of his way to give Mr Paterson a full insight into the outback. I do remember Banjo or his sister, and I forget which, lisped when they talked — lisped badly. Early in ninety-six we left by train for Rockhampton, to Cooktown. Banjo had then returned from Winton and he and his sister were on the same train. I remember he showed my father a page of paper. My father read it. He seemed to be delighted with it; he asked permisison to show it to my mother, who came from a pastoral pioneering family in the Gulf country. She read it. I could tell by the light in her eyes, and the smile of appreciation on her face, she enjoyed it. I didn't know then what was written on that paper. Youngsters of ten didn't join in conversation with their elders in those days. But I learned later that was the original of what is now known as Waltzing Matilda. . . . [Clearly, Lamond has confused Paterson's "sister" with Sarah Riley.]

There is evidence that the song circulated in parts of western and central Queensland and in northern New South Wales, but nothing seems to have been heard of it in Sydney (and Paterson does not appear to have mentioned it at all) until 1903 when he sold it (i.e., the text without music) with some other odds and ends of verse ("old junk" he called it) for a token sum to Angus & Robertson Ltd. In the same year this firm sold the musical rights of the verses to the firm of Inglis and Co., tea merchants, of Sydney (their brand "Billy" tea was famous even in those years). It seems, as John Manifold has remarked, that "Mr Inglis had notions in advance of his time and proposed to use 'Waltzing Matilda' to advertise his product".[8] (The first "singing commercial" perhaps.) Mrs Marie Cowan, the wife of the manager for Inglis and Co., who was a gifted amateur musician, set the words to music. (Her husband is said to have recalled that Paterson told him he was very happy about the song, and that "Mrs Cowan has done a good job, good luck to her".) It is important to note that the first editions of the song as published by Inglis and Co. stated that the music was *arranged* by Marie Cowan; in later editions the word was changed to *composed*.

Certainly the publication of the song at this time, and some years later (1911) in a collection called *The Australasian Students' Song Book* edited and published by a committee of Sydney University students under the chairmanship of Frederick Todd, who later became Professor of Latin at the University, helped considerably in making the song popular. The song-book sold about 5,000 copies. Nevertheless the song does not appear to have been sung very much during World War I—as against its tremendous popularity in the years to follow. This was sparked off by its publication by Dr Thomas Wood in *Cobbers*, which had a remarkable sale as the first "best-seller" travel book on Australia, and the climax of the song's popularity was reached during World War II among Australian troops in all theatres of the War.

Perhaps it has been this very popularity that has prompted in more recent years speculation and doubt about the origins both of the tune and the words of this ballad. As for the tune, there have been undoubtedly conflicting pieces of evidence and a number of puzzling aspects in the story. Largely through the indefatigable and enthusiastic researches of Oscar Mendelsohn, a well-known author and by profession one of Australia's foremost authorities as an examiner of questioned documents, there is at least an alternative and acceptable explanation of the origin of the tune as set out in his book *A Waltz with Matilda* (1966).

There have always been difficulties about accepting that the tune of "Waltzing Matilda" was based on "Bonnie Wood of Craigielea". The principal stumbling block is that, as Mendelsohn has so convincingly explained, the rhythm and melody line of the latter song bear little recognizable resemblance to "Waltzing Matilda". Another theory about the musical origins of the song bases it on an English folk-song called "The Bold Fusilier" said to derive from the days of Marlborough, when it was a marching song. This view was put forward by the Australian historian and author M. H. Ellis, and has also been accepted by authorities such as Dr Russel Ward, Frederick Macartney, and others. The difficulty, however, is that there seems to be little evidence of the existence of this song in English folk-lore, and although different versions of the words have been put forward by those who subscribe to this theory (and there is marked correspondence, in rhythm, with the words of "Waltzing Matilda"), there is no version of the tune available with which to make a comparison.

Oscar Mendelsohn in 1955 was told by the Mitchell Library that a manuscript copy of "Waltzing Matilda" had been presented to it by Miss Dorothy Sanders of Newcastle. The cover sheet read: "Waltzing Matilda, words by A. B. Paterson. This composition of music entirely by Harry A. Nathan. Copyright deferred. To my old friend W. A. Renwick, 10th August, 1905. Composed 1900, copyright 1903." Mendelsohn inspected the manuscript, satisfied himself that it was genuine, and talked to Mrs Sanders, who turned out to be the daughter of "my old friend, W. A. Renwick", a commercial traveller, Mrs Sanders explained, whose business took him far into northern N.S.W. and to Toowoomba in Queensland. After a great deal of patient research, interviewing and detective work, Mendelsohn established that Nathan was a choirmaster and organist in a small church in Toowoomba at the turn of this century, and a descendant, like the conductor-composer Charles Mackerras, of Isaac Nathan, Byron's friend who wrote the music of Byron's "Hebrew Melodies". Henry Alfred Nathan was born in Sydney in 1866 and died near Brisbane in 1906. The notation and harmonization of the manuscript song shows a high degree of professionalism; there is evidence quoted by Mendelsohn that Nathan was playing and singing his "Waltzing Matilda" around the turn of this century; and the hypothesis is reasonable that, the words of the ballad having reached his ears, he set it to a suitable melody. It is a reasonable assumption, Mendelsohn claims, that he made contact with Paterson about the clearance of the words.

The arguments against Mendelsohn's explanation seem to me to be threefold. What then was the tune that Christina Macpherson played and Herbert Ramsay sang — and sing he did — and which certainly must have been the basis of the song as it spread in the five years till 1900? Was it, by some coincidence, similar to Nathan's version, or did he perhaps "arrange" the existing version (there might be some justification for this view in the fact that there appears at the end of the manuscript the note "Harmonized by Harry A. Nathan")? If Nathan's was the basis of the song as we know it, by what means was it spread abroad to gain popular acceptance? (Nor can one overlook May's statement in his book that he himself recalled hearing it sung on a station in New South Wales in 1899, a year *before* Nathan claims to have composed it.) And finally if Nathan *had* been in touch with Paterson, and Paterson knew he had composed the tune, surely Paterson, as the honest and forthright man he was, would have told the Inglises and the Cowans in 1903 that Nathan's music already existed. One is not worried, of course, by the version of Marie Cowan — since John Manifold has pointed up the obvious: that she had heard the tune at some time or other and simply set down a version of it, perhaps embellishing and improving on it slightly — which is why, at the beginning at any rate, she only claimed the credit for having "arranged" it.

The strongest argument, I think, that Mendelsohn advances for

Nathan's claim to the composition is that the words on his manuscript are similar to the version that Paterson gave his signature to — and since this version could not possibly have been known in such detail to Nathan in 1900 (it was printed only in 1917 in *Saltbush Bill J.P. and Other Verses*), this does make it strongly probable that there may have been some contact between Nathan and Paterson: the former, as Mendelsohn points out was the organist at Townsville Cathedral around 1899 and Townsville is not far from Winton, to which town Paterson was making occasional visits at the time.

Comparing the words of Paterson's original as preserved in his *Collected Verse* (P), the words on Nathan's manuscript (N), and the Inglis version (I) as circulated in 1906 (substantially the version as we know it today),* one notes, apart from the basic similarity of the first two, that the Inglis, i.e., the present day form of the ballad, is much more singable; time and frequent performance, like water over a stone, have made it smoother and more acceptable. This is the way of folk-songs, and the music of the song as we sing it now too is more polished and harmonious than Nathan's version.

Verse 1
P: Oh! there once was a swagman camped in a Billabong,
N: Once a jolly swagman camp'd by a Billabong
I: Once a jolly Swagman camped by a Billabong

P: Under the shade of a Coolabah tree;
N: Under the shade of a Coolabah tree
I: Under the shade of a Coolibah tree,

And he sang as he looked at his old billy boiling,
And he sang as he sat and waited till his billy boiled
And he sang as he watched and waited till his "Billy" boiled

"Who'll come a-waltzing Matilda with me?"
You'll come a-waltzing Matilda with me.
You'll come a-waltzing Matilda with me.

Who'll come a-waltzing Matilda, my darling,
Waltzing Matilda, Matilda my Darling,
Waltzing Matilda, Waltzing Matilda,

Who'll come a-waltzing Matilda with me?
You'll come a-waltzing Matilda with me,
You'll come a-waltzing Matilda with me

Waltzing Matilda and leading a water-bag —
And he sang as he sat and waited till his billy boiled
And he sang as he watched and waited till his "Billy" boiled

---

* Grateful acknowledgement is made to Allans (Music) Australia Pty. Ltd. for permission to reproduce their copyright version of "Waltzing Matilda".

Who'll come a-waltzing Matilda with me?
You'll come a-waltzing Matilda with me.
You'll come a-waltzing Matilda with me.

Verse 2

Down came a jumbuck to drink at the water-hole,
Down came a jumbuck to drink at the Billabong,
Down came a jumbuck to drink at that Billabong

Up jumped the swagman and grabbed him in glee;
Up jumped the swagman and grabbed him with glee,
Up jumped the Swagman and grabbed him with glee,

And he sang as he stowed him away in his tucker-bag,
And he sang as he shoved the jumbuck in his tuckerbag
And he sang as he shoved that jumbuck in his tuckerbag

"You'll come a-waltzing Matilda with me."
You'll come a-waltzing Matilda with me.
You'll come a-waltzing Matilda with me.

Verse 3

Down came the Squatter a-riding his thoroughbred;
Down came a Squatter mounted on a thoroughbred
Up rode the squatter mounted on his thoroughbred

Down came Policemen — one, two and three.
Down came Troopers one two and three.
Down came the troopers, one, two, three.

Whose is the jumbuck you've got in the tucker-bag?
Whose is the Jumbuck you've got in your tucker bag?
Whose that jolly jumbuck you've got in your tucker-bag?

"You'll come a-waltzing Matilda with me."
You'll come a-waltzing Matilda with me.
You'll come a-waltzing Matilda with me.

Verse 4

But the swagman, he up and he jumped in the water-hole,
Up jumped the Swagman, sprang into the Billabong
Up jumped the Swagman and sprang into the billabong

Drowning himself by the Coolabah tree;
Drowning himself neath the Coolabah tree.
You'll never catch me alive said he.

And his ghost may be heard as it sings in the Billabong
And his ghost may be heard as you walk around the Billabong
And his Ghost may be heard as you pass by that Billabong;

"Who'll come a-waltzing Matilda with me?"
You'll come a-waltzing Matilda with me.
You'll come a-waltzing Matilda with me.

There remains one red herring, as it were, the "Buderim" variant of "Waltzing Matilda". This is a very beautiful, haunting tune, which has absolutely nothing in common with the melody as we know it. According to John Manifold it was given to him by John O'Neil of Buderim (a town to the north of Brisbane), and it preserves, like Nathan's manuscript, the original Paterson words. John O'Neil claims that he learned the tune and words from his father in 1915 before the Paterson verses were officially published in 1917. Manifold's explanation is obviously correct: the words of the song, probably early in the piece, became detached from the original tune (a non-singer obviously broke the chain) "and grew itself a perfectly distinct and very beautiful tune, possibly but not certainly somewhere in the Brisbane River valley . . .".[9]

So much for the music then (the words and music by the way are copyrighted at present by Messrs. Allans Ltd. — sold to them by Angus & Robertson on January 20, 1931). What is more important, are the words of the song, and a consideration of the arguments advanced of late quite seriously by responsible scholars and researchers that Paterson did *not* after all write "Waltzing Matilda".

In the 1930s I worked under Dr Charles Fenner, then Director of Education in South Australia. I remember he told me once, cryptically, that Banjo Paterson might not have written "Waltzing Matilda". This heresy did not impress me at the time — but Sydney May in his book explains the matter more fully, since Dr Fenner had written to him in 1944 to tell him that D. H. Souter had claimed the authorship in a journal called *Country Life*. But careful research and the help of Souter's relatives finally unearthed a poem Souter had written in 1925 about a swagman, which, however, did not even remotely resemble "Waltzing Matilda". The incident is worth mentioning in the context of hearsay which surrounds some of the argument denying Paterson's authorship of the ballad.

It is possible that Professor Russel Ward was the first critic of any authority to question authorship.[10] Mendelsohn in his book mentions that the balladist E. J. Brady had written to him in 1946 claiming that "Banjo never wrote it at all" and that he (Brady) had heard it sung in the bush when he was a boy (Brady was born in 1869 so this certainly antedated Paterson), but he offered no further evidence beyond emphasizing that Paterson had never ever at any time claimed to be the author of the ballad.

But Russel Ward offered a much more scholarly treatise. He explained that its unique popularity stemmed from its use of the folk tradition embodied in "Wild Colonial Boy" and other bush songs, in which robbery of wealthy squatters was always regarded as "a national and noble act". He felt this was unusual and out of character in Paterson, who invariably portrayed his bushmen as noble, romantic or at least appealing figures. He stressed too that the lilting rhythm of "Waltzing Matilda" demanded

that it be sung rather than declaimed — whereas the latter method of
expression was the rule with most of Paterson's verse. There was further
the use of the incremental refrain in this ballad — and only once elsewhere (in "A Bushman's Song") had Paterson used this device. Then
there was the evidence of publication: that Paterson took no steps to have
the ballad published until 1917; also the fact that the 1903 "Billy Tea"
version which is now sung and recited is poetically ever so much better
than the version he chose to leave to posterity above his signature. All
these facts, Ward concludes

> . . . suggest the probability that there was a folk version of "Waltzing
> Matilda" current in the outback during the 1870s and 1880s. If there
> was, Paterson may well have heard it once or twice during his boy-
> hood on the Monaro Tableland, and retained it shadowly in his
> subconscious mind. When, as a young man of twenty-six, he heard
> the tune again, he would have been reminded of the forgotten bush
> ballad. In writing down the words, after the lapse of so many years,
> he might well have been uncertain how much he remembered and
> how much he improvised on the spot but, being an honest man, he
> took no steps to publish the song as his own. This would not be
> inconsistent with his having allowed the young ladies at the station
> to believe, for the occasion, that the poem was entirely his. When
> twenty-two years later it was published, by those who had purchased
> it, in a book of his verse, he possibly took steps to see that it was in
> a form as different as possible from what he had by then remembered
> of the words of the folk ballad.

Oscar Mendelsohn goes further in his book: he states as his "firm belief"
that Paterson "did not write the words of 'Waltzing Matilda' ". He quotes
Professor Ward's arguments and adds a few more of his own — including
the Brady reminiscence already referred to; an interview with M. H. Ellis,
who knew Paterson and had tried, unsuccessfully, to get from him the
manuscript of the poem to present to the War Memorial Library of his
old school, eventually asking him point-blank, "Banjo, did you or did you
not write the thing?" To this, Mendelsohn says, "Paterson made no reply
but gave a laugh and walked away." (Ellis has told me since that he tried
on several occasions to get the manuscript from Paterson; eventually he
offered £25 for a holograph copy. Paterson showed a flicker of interest at
this, but Ellis heard no more from him about it.)

Mendelsohn also makes play of Paterson's silence about the ballad:
that he did not, for instance, discuss it with the Cowans when Marie
Cowan became famous as the arranger or composer; that it was significant that about the time he "wrote" the ballad he was engaged in collecting and "doctoring" old bush songs for the anthology he subsequently
edited in 1905. He also finds it "remarkable" that in his *Sydney Morning
Herald* reminiscences Paterson made no mention of "Waltzing Matilda":
it was almost as if, suggests Mendelsohn, knowing he was not the writer,
"he would be anxious to soft-pedal the whole affair".

None of these arguments is, I consider, unanswerable; most of them can be demolished, and a few where the reasoning is hypothetical can be answered by counter-arguments of equal weight. Dealing with them, not necessarily in the order they have been mentioned:

1. Paterson was a man of the highest integrity and honesty. This is proved over and over again in the facts available about his life. He would never have allowed a lie to be perpetuated, i.e., that he had written something he hadn't; he sold the copyright of the ballad to Angus & Robertson even if he regarded it as "junk"; furthermore, he left his son Hugh, his sisters and his journalist colleague Vince Kelly firmly with the impression that he had written the ballad. Quite recently Sir Daryl Lindsay has told me that at an army staging camp at Randwick Racecourse at the beginning of World War I he was with Paterson watching troops parading, and some of the men began to sing "Waltzing Matilda". "Well, Daryl," said Paterson wryly, "I only got a fiver for the song, but it's worth a million to me to hear it sung like this!"

2. The circumstances of the composition of the ballad have been confirmed by those who were present at the time — notably Sir Herbert Ramsay, members of the Macpherson family and their employees — and, of course, by Paterson himself (to his son, his sisters, Vince Kelly, etc.).

3. There is nothing sinister in the fact that he was collecting and "doctoring" old bush songs at this time. If it is argued that he was likely to slip one old song in his pocket, and produce it later as his own, then he was as likely to have done so with half a dozen others. Is there any evidence of this? Of course not! There is every reason, on the other hand, to take the opposite view because of our knowledge of Paterson's probity and honesty: that had he discovered "Waltzing Matilda" as an old bush song, he would most certainly have included it in the collection.

4. As for the unique "singability" of the ballad compared with his other verse, surely the circumstances of its composition explain that: the words were set to a tune, and this was not Paterson's normal method of composition. Obviously, then, the ballad was bound to have a different quality about it, even unto the "incremental refrain" commented upon by Professor Ward. Mendelsohn quotes an article written in 1964 by A. A. Phillips[11] in support of his arguments. Phillips commented: "One cannot believe that Paterson composed it; it is quite outside his normal range . . .". But Phillips later in his article then turns turtle by saying: "Was it a case of the music imposing its style on the words?"* Precisely!

---

* However Phillips later admitted (*Meanjin*, No. 3, 1965) that his ground for doubt had now vanished: "I had forgotten that, according to the story, Paterson wrote the words of 'Waltzing Matilda' to fit an already chosen tune."

5. There is nothing strange about the deferring of the printing of the ballad until the 1917 edition of poems. The same thing happened with two of Paterson's best-known ballads, written as far back as 1886. "A Dream of the Melbourne Cup" and "The Mylora Elopement" did not appear until the same edition; nor did "An Answer to Various Bards", which was written in 1892. Paterson (or his publishers) showed little system and order in the collecting of his verse — a fact commented upon by those who have troubled to show some bibliographical interest in his writing.

6. There seems no reason for Paterson to have taken the matter up with the Cowans since the tune which Mrs Cowan arranged was presumably similar to that already in vogue.

7. That Paterson did not mention "Waltzing Matilda" in his 1939 *Sydney Morning Herald* reminiscences has little significance. It is one of the tragedies of latter day biography that Paterson, presented with such a magnificent opportunity as was offered in the columns of this newspaper, made such little use of it. His reminiscences are scrappy and anecdotal; he deals with odd incidents and people, some of them of minor interest, but not at all with so many of his experiences that would have been of such value to a better understanding of his life and work: his relationships with and recollections of his contemporaries of the 1890s, his adventures in World War I, his years as an editor and journalist in the thriving days of the Sydney newspaper world, and so on.

8. Paterson's silence about the song and his disinclination to talk about the circumstances of the writing of it need not be related to any hypothesis that he had guilty feelings about having plagiarized an old bush song. Vince Kelly has recalled that Paterson had a greater affection for this ballad than most of his others; others have mentioned that Winton and Dagworth had "sad memories for Paterson". The reason, then, is surely simple. He did not marry Sarah Riley; he was a most handsome and eligible young man as we know, and my guess is that John Manifold is not wide of the mark when he suggests that a quarrel with Sarah over Christina Macpherson or vice versa, could have explained most of his reluctance to discuss the Dagworth days; the memory of it was better locked away, like "Waltzing Matilda", among its odds and ends in a tin box. And since, in 1902, he met Alice Walker of Tenterfield, and married her in 1903, this was a further reason for him not to revive the song, nor the memories and incidents associated with it.

9. To have doubts about Paterson's authorship of "Waltzing Matilda" because the note of "social protest" basic to it is, as Russell Ward suggests, "conspicuously absent from most of Paterson's published verse" seems to me unjustified on two counts. First of all, as Gavin Long quite recently wrote[12] (apropos Denton Prout's description[13] of Paterson as "the spokesman of the squattocracy and the station

owners") : "It is difficult to see how this widely-shared notion ever
got about. In fact, Paterson wrote about the bush workers and about
the underdogs of city and country . . ." and this is true, whether it
is of ". . . the horse thief, Andy Regan, that was hunted like a dog /
By the troopers of the Upper Murray side . . .,[14] the out-of-luck
jockey and down-at-heel drover, or the "wretched woman detected /
In stealing her children some bread".[15] And surely there is a
general philosophy of affection and respect for the wanderer and
rover implicit in such of his lines as

> . . . through our blood there runs
> The vagabonding love of change
> That drove us westward of the range
> And westward of the sun . . .[16]

But, in the case of "Waltzing Matilda", the point is that if we
accept the circumstances surrounding the writing of the song (and
I submit there is no reason why we should not) , then, social protest
or not, here was a story of a swagman jumping into a billabong to
defeat the law, and, like any creative writer, Paterson accepted the
story put in front of him, embellished it with his imagination as
he thought fit, and simply made a ballad out of it. Why blow it up,
then, into an argument as to whether it fits or not into the general
tenor of his writing? Even his old ballads on bushrangers are written
from both sides of the law.

10. But the clinching argument against the theory that "Waltzing
Matilda" was an old bush song "doctored up" is: Where then is
the old bush song? If Paterson got his hands on the version, someone must have known something about it, someone who would
have surely spoken up when it appeared as Paterson's own ballad.
E. J. Brady said (at the age of seventy-seven) that he used to sing it
in the bush when he was a boy. But, as the incident quoted above
concerning Dr Charles Fenner and D. H. Souter shows, memories of
old men, even if they are writers, play tricks. Nobody that I am aware
of has ever turned up with another version of "Waltzing Matilda"
(a phrase by the way admitted to have had only a restricted use,
geographically and temporally, in western and central Queensland,
which fact in itself tends to contradict any suggestion that such a
song was in general circulation) ; nor, I suspect, is this ever likely to
happen. In any case, there is extant among the publisher's papers a
list of songs and their origins compiled by Paterson himself for *Old
Bush Songs*. "Waltzing Matilda" is *not* included. In other words,
"Waltzing Matilda" is well and truly Banjo Paterson's.*

* In a vigorous defence of Paterson's authorship of the song ("Jostling Matilda",
Meanjin, No. 3, 1965) , which came to my notice after I had written this summary,
Frederick Macartney uses arguments substantially similar, especially the fact that there
is no evidence of an earlier "Waltzing Matilda" and that, apart from "the additional
weight of motive and character", any court on the available evidence "would at once
dismiss any notion of duplicity on his part".

"Waltzing Matilda's" popularity was inevitable, and there is no mystery about why that should be. Apart from the contributing factors mentioned, including its emergence in World War II as a troop and marching song, the whole tendency of popular music from the 1930s on was towards melodies of a simple and repetitive type — something which has been insufficiently emphasized in this context — and "Waltzing Matilda" filled this pattern admirably. And as much as the purists may shudder at the idea, "Waltzing Matilda" *is* the nearest thing we have to a national anthem, and in the minds of many Australians it is automatically that. It is learned at school and sung with pleasure, and becomes the one song that adults sing, as a group, naturally and unselfconsciously. The words satisfy a certain instinct for nationalism: every Australian knows what "waltzing Matilda", "jumbuck", "tucker-bag" and "billabong" mean, so that the song is almost a password in foreign countries. And the elements of "fair go", of the little man against the big man, of anti-authority, of bravado and of the setting of the outback give the song that added appeal to the average Australian conscious of his colonial beginnings. "The words," writes Oscar Mendelsohn justly, "have been more responsible than the melody for the prodigious success of 'Waltzing Matilda'."

Yet the signal achievement of this ballad was that it got off the printed page and became part of folk-song. Usually folk-songs and ballads circulating by word of mouth are collected and finally achieve printed form; Paterson, with "Waltzing Matilda", reversed the process: once it had been written down and sung, it went walkabout. Tens of thousands of Australians have learned it without ever having seen it on the printed page. Two of Paterson's other ballads achieved oral circulation too: "A Bushman's Song" (which became, as John Manifold has remarked, "without capitals or quotation marks genuinely a bushman's song")[17] and one of his last published verses, "The Billygoat Overland", which is sung to the tune of "The Lincolnshire Poacher". The same happened with at least two of Henry Lawson's poems, "Andy's Gone with Cattle" and "Freedom on the Wallaby". Both Paterson and Lawson with these verses seemed to have struck the pure and authentic note of Australian folk and bush song.

But "Waltzing Matilda" is of all bush songs, the best remembered. And while there may be reason for doubt about its musical origins, there need be none about the words and their writer — A. B. "Banjo" Paterson.

NOTES

[1] From the Xavier College (Melbourne) school magazine, quoted by Oscar Mendelsohn in *A Waltz with Matilda* (1966).

[2] First published in 1944; a second enlarged edition printed in 1955.

[3] In *Who Wrote the Ballads?* (1964).

[4] In *ABC Weekly*, 22 May 1941.

[5] In an ABC documentary broadcast in 1964 to mark the 100th anniversary of Paterson's birth.

[6] In conversations with the author, and in various letters and published accounts, especially in the article "Old Scottish Hymn Tune was Waltzing Matilda's Inspiration" (Sydney *Sun*, 12 January 1943).

[7] For use in the ABC documentary referred to above.
[8] Op. cit.
[9] Op. cit.
[10] In his article "Waltzing Matilda" in the anthology *Australian Signpost*, ed. T. Hungerford (1956).
[11] In *Meanjin*, No. 4, 1964.
[12] Ibid.
[13] In *Henry Lawson — The Grey Dreamer* (1963).
[14] "Father Riley's Horse."
[15] "Our Mat."
[16] "Old Australian Ways."
[17] Op. cit.

CHAPTER IX

At the Boer War

Ay! we that saw that stirring march are proud that we can say
We went with French to Kimberley to drive the Boers away . . .

— A. B. PATERSON.

THE FIRST DIARY entry recorded by A. B. Paterson, officially accredited war correspondent for the *Sydney Morning Herald* and the Melbourne *Argus* travelling on the troopship *Kent* with the New South Wales Lancers, reads:

> November 1899 — En route for South African War. By all accounts, these Boers are only part human. There is an ambulance outfit on board, and I ask an ambulance orderly — a retired sergeant-major of British infantry — whether the Boers will fire on the ambulances.
> He says: "Of course, they'll fire on the hambulances. They 'ave no respect for the 'elpless. They've even been known to fire on the cavalry."
> Colonel Williams, commander of our hospital outfit, fully believes this, and is training his men in rifle-shooting at a box towed over the stern, and with revolvers at bottles thrown overside. No-one has as yet sunk a bottle, and some of the shooters have even missed the Indian Ocean.[1]

His first dispatch, printed in the *Sydney Morning Herald* on 18 November, was "A Rough Passage Across the Australian Bight"

Paterson's chief impressions of the voyage to Capetown were of the immaturity of the troops and the rivalry between their various sections. The army medical men barricaded themselves in part of the ship; the machine-gunners and signallers squabbled for space for their drills; all stores were below decks, with only the chief officer, the boatswain and the carpenter having access — consequently they were the three great powers. Thus, wrote Paterson, "we fared across the Indian Ocean, toiling, rejoicing, and borrowing gear and equipment — generally without the knowledge or consent of the lender".[2]

In Capetown at the end of November, Paterson "as green as grass in the ways of the world" began to experience something of the politics of war time; he was most impressed with Sir Alfred Milner, Governor of

Cape Colony — "a long dark wiry man, with a somewhat high-strung temperament; but he has been a pressman so nothing ought to rattle him".[3] Paterson asked Milner if he could get to the front as a correspondent with the Australian troops; Milner jokingly remarked that there would soon be more correspondents than fighting men at the front, but nevertheless gave him a letter to the Chief Press Censor suggesting that the Australians ought to have a man of their own to report the exploits of the soldiers to the various parts of Australia from which they came.

During his several weeks' stay in Capetown Paterson had his first taste of English "society" — Milner asked him to take two ladies on a jackal-hunt that was being arranged with a pack of English hounds. First of all, however, he had to get a horse; by a stroke of luck the groom in charge of the officers' horses had been in Australia and had looked after a horse Paterson had ridden in a race, and Paterson bribed him to borrow one of a number of Argentine horses specially imported to South Africa. It turned out that Paterson's charges for the day were the Duchess of Westminster and Lady Charles Bentinck; ". . . both were young and attractive women", Paterson wrote with a curious colonialism, ". . . and their features had all the repose that marks the cast of Vere de Vere. Both carried whiskey and water in hunting flacks, and they both smoked cigarettes . . .". Nor did it take him long to discover that ". . . they looked upon me as the Wild Colonial Boy, the broncobuster from the Barcoo, and I determined to act up to it". He found the only common interest he had with them was horses — so horses he talked with them. At other times he listened to their cynical and knowledgeable comments about the various members of the High Command: which general wore rouge, and which stays, and who was a friend of the Prince of Wales, and so on. He came to the conclusion that "military appointments were like the Order of the Garter — there was no damned merit about them". He managed, however, to hold his own at the hunt and was in at the kill.

He also became friendly with the Duke of Teck, then director of remounts, who complained bitterly about his job; he said he had issued ten thousand horses since he had been in the job and according to the army had not issued a good one. Paterson was amused to find the word "Stellenbosched" coined; the large army remount camp was at Stellenbosch, and Lord Roberts, the C.I.C., had the habit of relieving of his command any senior officer who displeased him and relegating him to take charge of the Stellenbosch camp. Paterson also recorded with wry humour that "Australian horse-thief" was a popular phrase, due to "the all-round reputation that the Australians had made for themselves from the moment they arrived".[4]

During this period of enforced idleness Paterson occupied himself with stray bits of journalism, gradually building that style and reporting instinct which he was to consolidate in the newspaper world later on. A little-known gem was his ironical send-up of Imperial Army-Australian relations which he wrote back for the *Bulletin*;[5] his short stay among the red-tabbed brass of British H.Q. in Capetown had sharpened his satirical sense as well as his observation. The piece was entitled "A War Office in Trouble", and having set the scene of telephones ringing, typewriters clacking and passages full of military hangers-on, newspaper reporters, messengers and inventors of various types of equipment, he continued:

> . . . In the innermost room of all a much-decorated military veteran with a bald head, a grizzled moustache and an eye-glass is dictating to three shorthand-writers at once, while clerks rush in and out with cablegrams, letters, and cards from people waiting. On the table are littered a heap of lists of troops, army-contracts, and tenders for supplies, all marked "Urgent".
>
> A clerk rushes in: "Cablegram from Australia offering troops, sir!"
>
> Military Veteran: "No! can't have 'em. It has been decided not to use blacks, except as a last resource."
>
> Clerk: "But these are white troops, sir — the local forces. It is officially desired that they be taken if possible."
>
> Military Veteran: "Who is the Australian Commander-in-Chief? I didn't know they had an army at all. I knew they had police, of course!"
>
> Clerk: "There are seven distinct cablegrams, sir; seven distinct Commanders-in-Chief all offering troops."
>
> M.V. (roused to excitement) : "Great Heavens! are they going to take the war off our hands? *Seven* Commanders-in-Chief! They must have been quietly breeding armies all these years in Australia. Let's have a look at the cables. Where's this from?"
>
> C.: "Tasmania, sir. They offer to send a Commander-in-Chief and" — pauses, aghast — "and *eighty-five* men!"
>
> M.V. (jumping to his feet) : "What! Have I wasted all this time talking about 85 men! You must be making a mistake!"
>
> C.: "No, sir. It says 85 men!"
>
> M.V.: "Well I am damned! Eighty-five men! You cable back and say that I've seen bigger armies on the stage at Drury Lane Theatre. Just wire and say this isn't a pantomime. They haven't got to march round and round a piece of scenery. Tell 'em to stop at home and breed!" [Resumes dictation.] "At least five thousand extra men should be sent from India in addition to . . ."
>
> C.: "Cabinet instructions are to take these troops, whether they're any good or not, sir. Political reasons!"
>
> M.V. (with a sigh) : "Well, let 'em come. Let 'em all come — the whole eighty-five! But don't let it leak out, or the Boers will say we're not playing 'em fair. Tell 'em to send infantry anyhow; we don't want horses eating their heads off."
>
> C. (interrupts again) : "These other colonies, sir — are we to accept 'em all?"
>
> M.V.: "Yes! Didn't I say let 'em all come. There'll be plenty of room for 'em in South Africa. They won't feel crowded." [Resumes dictation.] "The expenditure of a hundred thousand pounds at least will be needed to . . ."
>
> C.: "They want to know, if they pay the men's fares over, will the British Government pay their return fares?"
>
> M.V.: "Yes! I should think we would. We'll put 'em in the front and

there won't be so many of 'em left to go back. If the colonies had any sense they'd have paid the return fares. Now please go away and let me get to work."

Ten minutes later. Clerk timidly re-appears.

"If you please, sir, another cable from New South Wales. They say they would sooner send artillery!"

M.V.: "Oh, blast it all! What does their artillery amount to?"

C.: "One battery, sir."

M.V.: "One battery! Well, they've got to come, I suppose. 'Cry havoc and let slip the dogs of war.' Stop their one battery if you can; but if not, let it come. And now go, and don't let me have any more of you." Resumes dictation and has got to "purchase of ten thousand horses", when the Clerk re-appears.

C.: "Fresh cable, sir! Two circus-proprietors in Sydney have presented six circus horses . . ."

M.V.: "Shivering Sheol! This is the climax! Six circus horses! Didn't they say anything about a clown and pantaloon? Surely they wouldn't see the Empire hurled to ruin for want of a clown! Perhaps they could let us have a few sword-swallowers to get off with the Boers' weapons? Look here, now — hand the whole thing over to one of the senior clerks, and tell him to do exactly what he d—— well pleases in the matter, but that if he comes in here to ask any questions about it, I'll have him shot! Now go and don't you come here any more, or I'll have you shot too! Take this cheque for a hundred thousand to the petty-cash department, and tell that contractor outside that his tender is two millions over the estimate, and don't let me hear any more of this blessed Australian army."

Cable message: "Some difficulty exists in ascertaining from the War Office whether the colonial troops will be expected to take their own saddles or not, and whether the officer commanding shall take one horse or two. It is not definitely known whether the offer of Fitzgerald's six circus-horses will be accepted. Great enthusiasm prevails."

About this time, too, Paterson sent back his first Boer War poem, "The Reveille", published in the *Sydney Mail*. It was, with good reason, not included in his later collected verse; it is naïvely jingoistic and cliché-ridden. Paterson could never be himself on formal poetic occasions.

> Trumpets of the Lancer Corps
>   Sound a loud reveille;
> Sound it over Sydney shore,
> Send the message far and wide
> Down the Richmond River side,
> Boot and saddle, mount and ride
>   Sound a loud reveille.
>
> Whither go ye, Lancers gay,
>   With your bold reveille?
> O'er the ocean far away

From your sunny southern home
Over leagues of trackless foam,
In a foreign land and roam,
With your bold reveille.

Paterson has left a detailed record of his adventures during the war
through a brilliant series of dispatches back to his Australian newspapers,
supplemented by more general accounts in his *Happy Dispatches*, written
in retrospect some thirty-five years afterwards. Paterson emerged with
much credit from the campaign; he was with the Lancers in their long
treks through country that was as dry, thirsty and inhospitable as his own
Australian outback, and shared their constant dangers from Boer
ambushes and the ever-present snipers. He was the first war correspondent
into Bloemfontein, and he won recognition for dispatch-riding through
country occupied by Boers on the surrender of Johannesburg and the fall
of Pretoria. Some general idea of his achievements can be seen from a
summary of his reports back to Australia as published in the *Sydney*
Morning Herald, most of them covering at least two full-page columns:

DECEMBER: Arrival of the New South Wales troops; reception at Port
Elizabeth and impressions. Landing at Capetown and difficulties with
the first camp.
JANUARY: Three dispatches, dramatically headed "From the Seat of
War"; Australians rushed to the front; New South Wales and New
Zealand forces under fire; capture of a Boer homestead and attack on
a kopje; troops engaged at Arundel.
Paterson also included a fine account of a visit to the Orange River
country, and his impressions of the character of the country.
FEBRUARY: Seven dispatches, all lively accounts of actions in which
the Lancers were involved. Paterson's best piece of journalism during
this month was undoubtedly his long interview with Olive Schreiner,
under the heading of "From the Boer Side" (17 February). He
wrote:

. . . She is a little woman, small in stature, but of very strong
physique, broad and powerful: her face olive-complexioned with
bright restless eyes and a quick mobile mouth. She talks fluently
and with tremendous energy . . . emphasizing her remarks with up-
lifted finger. "You Australians and New Zealanders and Canadians," she said, "I cannot understand it at all, why you come
here lightheartedly to shoot down other colonists of whom you
know nothing — it is terrible. Such fine men too — fine fellows."

Paterson considered there was no doubt of her sincerity — it seemed
a pity to him that this woman who was "no doubt a great literary
genius" should be wasting her time and energy on the Boer War
question "instead of giving us another book as good as her first
one . . ."
MARCH: His five dispatches included graphic accounts of French's

dash on Kimberley and the relief of that city.

APRIL: Seven dispatches covered the Modder River engagements, the surrender of General Cronje and the entry into and capture of Bloemfontein.

MAY: This was Paterson's best month in the *Herald*. Nine of his dispatches were published, covering the skirmishes around Bloemfontein. As colour pieces, he discussed the Kaffir question,. various phases of veldt-warfare and the Rainy Season. Most interesting of all was his account (12 May) of his meeting with Kipling near Bloemfontein. Headed "Personality of Kipling — The Man Who Fans Patriotism", it was the basis of his subsequent account in *Happy Dispatches*.

JUNE: Five dispatches covered the Boers in flight and the capture of Kroonstad.

JULY: Three dispatches, centred mainly around Johannesburg.

A short passage from the dispatch published on 13 July ("At the Front. Outside Johannesburg," 30 May) reveals Paterson as still very much the countryman:

> We pushed on through the open veldt, the long grass brushing the horses' knees, and forming a dense carpet under their feet. This is the most wonderful grassed country I have ever seen. At all farms the rafters were hung with tobacco leaves, making a pleasant fragrance and we got ducks, fowls and turkeys galore . . .

AUGUST: Six dispatches covering the campaign around Pretoria during June, the taking of that city and the pursuit of General de Wet.

SEPTEMBER: Three dispatches, including a fine piece of writing published on 7 September headed "Surrender of General Prinsloo — A Melancholy Procession of Burghers" (Fouriesberg, 30 July), where Paterson showed a dramatic reporting sense:

> This morning brings no abatement of excitement. Boers ride in every few minutes and lay down their arms. At about 10 oclock the infantry and guns are lined up, and General Prinsloo rides in from the Boer laager. He is an old greybearded farmer clad in long, check tail coat, dark tweed trousers barely reaching the tops of his boots, and a shining pair of spurs. Hunter receives him with due ceremony and talk begins. Prinsloo can talk no English, so an interpreter is employed, and at once it appears that there is a hitch. What do they say? It appears that Prinsloo says he was led to believe that all his men would be sent back to their farms. He is a fuzzle-headed old fellow this Prinsloo, and keeps repeating himself . . .

In his account of the march to Kimberley, when his unit joined up at the Modder River with French's forces, Paterson told how the horses were dying of cold and of suffocation from the dust and soldiers dropped out of the ranks delirious with heat and thirst. Yet it was the horses he kept going back to; it was of less concern to him that there were limited rations, more that there was no horse-feed since the Boers had fired the grass, and smoke added to the misery of the dust and the heat. The big English horses of the Scots Greys, he noted, did not stand up to the conditions anywhere near as well as the wiry Australian "whalers": gun-horses dropped in their harness, and the pistol-shots constantly marked the sad end of their misery. Paterson also got his experience here of mules and mule-wagons (of great importance to him during World War I) ; indeed, he recalled that the march to Kimberley "was a sort of baptism of fire for my future career as a remount officer". But his "baptism of fire" was often of a much more particular variety than that. During his march with French's men he took part in a major engagement, his account of which remains, by any standards of war-reporting, as exciting as it is memorable:

This is something like sport, this shooting at human game with cannon over three thousand yards of country. "Hooray! Give 'em another!" The second gun fires and the shell whizzes away, and the same dead silence reigns, when suddenly another note is struck — a discordant note this time. From the rocky tree-covered hill in the direct front only half a mile off, comes a clear tock-tock-tock-tock — a couple of clear double reports, and something seems to whistle by the gunners, making a noise, like a heavy wind blowing through a very small creak in the door. Pee-u-u-w! It is the thinnest, shrillest sound, this whistle of a bullet at short range. Most of the men duck instinctively as the first bullet goes over. Pee-u-u-u-w! Pee-u-u-u-w! They come by thick enough now, and each man's heart sinks as he sees what the column is let in for. Here we have marched all the guns and horses, without cover, to within half a mile of a hill and the Boers have seized it while we were shooting at their mounted men! Pee-u-u-u-w! Pee-u-u-u-w! That fellow was close!

The General sees the trouble at once. "Dismount, all you men with carbines! Get the horses back. Keep the guns working!" and he and his staff turn away as the men jump off their horses and run up to the front and lie down in a long row, from which a rippling, rattling fire soon breaks out. The horses are taken back, and the guns and the dismounted men are left alone for a duel to the death with the foe in the hill. Now is the time to see the Royal Horse Artillery at its best! All the years of training, all the hard toil of drilling and practising reap their reward here now. The men serve the guns with machine-like precision; the battery major, with his hands behind his back, stalks up and down behind his guns exactly as a gamecock stalks about his barn-yard; there is defiance in every motion as he marches quickly from gun to gun, watching where the shells are landing and giving quick directions as he passes. The R.H.A. will "take on" any living kind of gun that will stand up to them within their range. To go into action under heavy rifle fire at 800 yards is suicide according to the drill books, but here they do it with a light heart. "Shoot, and be ——" is the motto of the R.H.A. "Let us see who will get sick of it first!" and they send the shells as fast as ever the guns can be worked, whizzing into the hill, where the steady tock-tock, tock-tock still keeps up, and they never flinch, though the hurried white-faced stretcher-bearers run up and carry man after man wounded to the rear.[6]

At the relief of Kimberley again it was not the moments of glory and success that he remembered, but the horses, exhausted from heat and over-work, being shot as they collapsed. Starving Kaffirs hung around the lines like vultures, descending on the carcases as they were thrown aside, stripping them of flesh in a matter of minutes. Because of the confusion it was impossible to send messages out of Kimberley; Paterson made a bold dash by horse back to the Modder River and got his dispatch away; it scooped all other correspondents and was headlined in the London *Times* and other international newspapers.

His memories, carried forward over thirty years later to *Happy Dispatches*, tended to be of places and people rather than action. Here for instance was one countryman admiring the property of another:

This is the best bit of country we have seen in Africa. We are camped on a high ridge, which is (like nearly all the rest of Africa that we have seen) perfectly bare of trees. The grass is knee-deep, almost exactly like our kangaroo-grass. Below is a flat of about six hundred acres covered with maize, growing very well, and about eight feet high. All among the maize there are thousands of melons — and pumpkins; the fruit is so thick that a horse can hardly avoid smashing it as we ride through the rows of corn. From this ridge, at least six houses are in sight, each with its dam of water, its mass of willows and poplars, and its fruit garden. The soil is a rich red loam; and the grass is so good that horses, when turned loose to graze, hardly move ten yards from the same spot.

He recalled, too, the time when he rode with an ambulance corps into the middle of a Boer commando unit and interviewed a fifteen-year-old lad who told him he would fight "till the last Afrikander is killed. If there is only he and I left we will fight till we are both killed and then you will have the land. Till then, no . . ."

All these experiences were important stages in Paterson's development as a first-class pressman. He soon appreciated the need for swift reporting, and, in the days when communication by cable was not as prodigally developed as it is in these days of press telegrams (and on-the-spot voice-casting of long and windy purple prose by means of recording machines was an electronic dream), terse, meaty messages were the nub of success-ful news dispatches. Thus he served an apprenticeship that worked miracles with his prose style. As his many dispatches back showed, there were few more indefatigable correspondents in South Africa: even Lord Stanley (later Lord Derby), who was chief press censor for Lord Roberts, complimented him for his enthusiasm. Once Paterson woke Lord Stanley up at three o'clock in the morning to get a message censored; the latter

drily commented that Churchill, who thought he was the only correspondent who got through with the news, would curse about it.

Paterson's work as a war reporter attracted the attention of one
Gwynne, the chief Reuter representative in South Africa (later editor of
the London *Morning Post*). Gwynne appointed Paterson as an extra man
for Reuter to report especially on the actions involving Australians and
New Zealanders — an honour which in later life Paterson treasured very
greatly and which put the seal on his determination to make a career of
journalism.

Yet characteristically, both as a journalist and as a writer who found
the best material for his verse and prose in personalities and men of
action, Paterson retained from his Boer War experiences memorable pen-
pictures of the celebrities he met. Modestly he explains that he got to
know Lord Roberts, Haig, French, the Duke of Marlborough, Winston
Churchill and the rest principally because of his "probably fictitious"
reputation as "an Australian, a steeplechase rider and polo player" and
hence "a judge of a horse". He was constantly asked to help officers pick
horses from remount depots, thus, he wrote,[7] "attaining a status in the
army that I would never have reached as a correspondent". The horses,
indeed, became "the key to more valuable acquaintanceships and good
friendships than either rank or riches".

He met Winston Churchill first in Capetown when the latter arrived
as correspondent for the *Morning Post*, tabbed him immediately ". . . with
his great social influence, his aggressiveness and undoubted ability" as a
man "to be feared if not liked". He was a reluctantly admiring witness of
Churchill's bearding of General French about some failures in the
campaign; began to understand the "curious combination of ability and
swagger" with which Churchill boasted to him about his political
ambitions ("I am going to plaster the *Morning Post* with cables about our
correspondent Mr Winston Churchill. . . . when I go up for Parliament
again, I'll fly in . . ."), and remarked the phenomenon of Churchill and
his cousin the Duke of Marlborough drinking a bottle of beer for breakfast each morning — "an unholy rite," recorded Paterson, "that is the
prerogative of men who have been to a certain school or college".[8]

Lord Roberts, Paterson felt, ran the war as a "one-man job"; his staff
were "nearly all titled men"; he admired him nevertheless because,
although he was seventy, this "small, grizzled old man" sat his horse "like
a youngster". He "broke" generals and "red-collared popinjays of staff
officers" with equal facility. Paterson was less impressed with Kitchener;
he wrote of him that he had "the aloof air and the fixed expression of a
golf champion", and left an interesting account[9] of an incident near
Paardeburg after Kitchener had launched a suicidal attack on General
Cronje's forces, with 1100 men killed or wounded. Kitchener personally
ordered a small group of tired and exhausted New South Wales riflemen
under Captain Antill to attack an entrenched kopje, even though Antill
pointed out that his men and horses had been without food for two days.
They held on gallantly for several hours until Kitchener, wrote Paterson,
"sent 3,000 men to help them in a task which he had asked 100 men to do
before breakfast". Antill and his men, near collapse, could not then find

their supply wagon, and were refused rations by other units; eventually Kitchener, noting their plight, scribbled a chit for them to be fed. "That was one good thing about Kitchener", noted Paterson with nice irony. "He trampled on red tape when necessary."

Nor did French impress Paterson particularly. There was a prim and proper morality about Paterson in his writings (someone said once that "the Banjo never talked sex"), which emerges even in his recollections of these military leaders. Seldom has any man of eminence been more effectively and categorically damned for his private shortcomings than was French in Paterson's short sentences:

> . . . his troubles through life had been mostly female and financial. It must be admitted that the world owes a great deal to the Jewish race; French at one time and another had owed them a good deal too . . .[10]

Elsewhere he had mentioned that French "took all things as they came, especially women".

Paterson considered that, had it not been for "having the cool clear-headed Haig at his elbow", French could well have failed, and some other general would have been left to command the British Army in France in World War I; "Haig carries French's brains", the Tommies used to say. Paterson was perhaps a little biased because he had seen Haig play polo in Australia; nevertheless he obviously and sincerely admired Haig for his qualities in command, for his "capacity to take infinite pains", the clarity and succinctness of his instructions. He got to know Haig well on a personal basis; Haig gave him fatherly advice about his duties as a war correspondent. "Don't try to be too clever, and you'll get along all right. . . . if you want any information come to me and I'll tell you — if I have time. Don't worry the General."[11] Clearly Haig gave him what Paterson might have described as a "rails run"; Paterson, in return, left for posterity an impression that was favourable to a degree, even if subsequent historical assessment flatly contradicts it: "he might have been a great public-school teacher or a great judge. . . ." Still, Paterson, the sportsman and man of the outdoors, saw army leaders in his own terms: a typical Banjoism was his speculation on the rating the handicapper would give French and Haig as generals compared with, say, Napoleon and Julius Caesar. In fine, he saw generals as horsemen, polo-players, even as cricketers. "If they make one bad stroke and get caught they are out — and they very seldom get a second innings."[12]

Nevertheless, of all the military leaders and potential leaders he met during the Boer War, the one on whom Paterson was clearly prepared to wager his money was a young cavalry major, Dudley Allenby, to whom he had been introduced soon after he arrived in South Africa, and to whom he had taken an instant liking. Later on, at Bloemfontein, when a squadron of New South Wales Lancers was bogged down without a leader (their major had taken ill) and discipline was very slack, Allenby was detailed to lick it into shape. He arrived one dark and rainy night when the officers, having drawn their own and their batmen's rum issue, had settled down to overcome their boredom with what developed into a drunken revel. In the middle of it all Allenby arrived — and in the horrified silence that followed his entrance Paterson saved the day by interposing, as a civilian, to explain the situation. Allenby recognized Paterson and stayed his wrath — ordering lights out in five minutes. Paterson's portrait that follows this incident is one of the best descriptions of the younger Allenby that exists:[13]

> Daylight revealed him as a sinewy well-set-up man, at least six feet high, and broad and strong as a London policeman. In facial contour he bore a distinct resemblance to Kitchener, but he smiled often and his expression was free from the secret sorrow that always seemed to harry Kitchener's soul. He set about the reorganization of the squadron with the enthusiasm of a scientist experimenting with a new sort of beetle. He neither bounced nor bullied anybody, but explained things as carefully as a school-teacher dealing with a lot of children. He got hold of the blacksmiths, and told them that he would give them a certain time to get all the horses properly shod and that then he would come round to see that they had done it. He stirred up the cooks, and if he found any dirty utensils on an inspection, the man responsible was for it. He made the young officers take a pride in their troops; if a man was slovenly dressed, or a horse not properly cleaned, trouble always followed.

An English infantry colonel prophesied to Paterson at this time that Allenby would one day be a field-marshal, but whether Paterson believed this or not, he probably little realized that his friendship with Allenby would stand him in such good stead some sixteen or seventeen years on.

But the most affectionate, and from the literary standpoint, the most useful relationship established by Paterson in South Africa, was with Rudyard Kipling whom he met on 25 March 1900 at Bloemfontein. Kipling had come out to South Africa partly "to see what the war was like", partly for convalescence after a severe illness. It is clear that he and Paterson warmed to each other, and a friendship began which was renewed a few years later, when Paterson went to London. Kipling talked constantly of the war, and of the future of South Africa. He felt the country had an enormous potential which railways, irrigation, mills and more efficient mines could develop out of all knowledge. The British, nor any other nation, could hardly afford to leave the country for the Boers "to sleep in". Paterson's portrait of him is unforgettable:

> . . . a little, square-built, sturdy man of about forty . . . His talk is a gabble, a chatter, a constant jumping from one point to another. In manner he is more like a business man than a literary celebrity. There is nothing of the dreamer about him. The last thing anyone could believe is that the little, square-figured man with the thick black eyebrows and the round glasses is the creator of Mowgli, the Jungle Boy . . .[14]

Paterson was intrigued by his "Americanized" language, his use of "yep" for "yes", his stories of adventures from the Indian frontier to New York.

For it was Kipling as author that he was most interested in: how did he get his material? "Some of it I saw; some of it I was. As for the rest — I asked questions." And this, after all, was Paterson's own approach to writing. The highest compliment Paterson, the Australian, the believer in the outback and the bush making men, could pay was that

> . . . you could have dumped Kipling down in a splitters' camp in the backblocks of Australia and he would have been quite at home; and would have gone away leaving the impression that he was a decent sort of bloke that asked a lot of questions . . .[15]

Although it is frequently said that Paterson wrote eight ballads from his Boer War experiences, he did in fact write twelve. Ten are included in his *Collected Verse* ("Driver Smith", "Jock", "Johnny Boer", "Right in Front of the Army", "That V.C.", "On the Trek", "The Last Parade", "There's Another Horse Fell Down", "The Scottish Engineer", and "With French to Kimberley"), apart from "The Reveille" already referred to, and the little-known "Now Listen to me and I'll Tell you my views concerning the African War", which was published in the London *Reynold's News* towards the end of 1902, and repeated in the *Bulletin* of 29 March 1902 under the heading, "Bit of War Verse by Australian Banjo Paterson in *Reynold's News*".

Some of the ten poems now collected were published in Sydney journals and newspapers; "That V.C." for instance appeared in the *Bulletin* of 19 May 1900, although it was previously published in a journal called *The Friend* which Lord Roberts sponsored in Bloemfontein. *The Friend* was probably a misprint for *The Fiend* surmised the *Bulletin*. Noting that, whereas the old motto of the Free State had been "All will come right", the new motto was "All has come right" with the addition that "The British are here to stay", the *Bulletin* commented sardonically that this was probably true since "they never yet took a return ticket when, gun in hand, they visited a rich country".[16] "With French to Kimberley" appeared in the *Sydney Morning Herald* of 29 September in the same year. It must be said that most of this verse, anyhow, ranges from the mediocre to the execrable. Paterson was a balladist of the bush and the outback: he hardly ever rose to "special occasion" verse; immediately he attempted this, the natural flow and ease of his versifying was inhibited.

So it is that Paterson has written few lines worse than in this excerpt from "That V.C.":

> A wounded soldier on the ground
>   Was lying hid behind a hummock;
> He proved the good old proverb sound —
>   An army travels on its stomach.
>
> He lay as flat as any fish;
>   His nose had worn a little furrow;
> He only had one frantic wish,
>   That like an ant-bear he could burrow.

(These stanzas rank, surely, in poetic triteness with Wordsworth's lines, "For still, the more he works, the more / Do his weak ankles swell".) Or these lines from "Jock":

> Yes the Jocks — Scotch Jocks,
> With their music that'd terrify an ox!

— even though the latter poem is a sincere attempt to pay tribute to the Scotch Greys.

Paterson commemorated, too, his brief moment of adventure with an ambulance corps in "Driver Smith", a cheerful fantasy about a Sydney ambulance-driver who captured Kruger and "ended the blooming war".

But the most interesting aspect of these War verses was the growing sympathy and respect Paterson came to feel for the Boers, the enemy. For the dry plains and the barren kopjes of South Africa were akin to his own outback; the outlanders were overlanders too; veldcraft, in Paterson's book,. was as worthy a talent as bushcraft. "Johnny Boer" (there is even affection in the reference to "old Johnny" and "the beggar") was a worthy adversary.

> On rocks a goat could scarcely climb, steep as the walls of Troy,
> He wheels a four-point-seven about as easy as a toy;
> With bullocks yoked and drag-ropes manned, he lifts her up the rocks
> And shifts her every now and then, as cunning as a fox.
> At night you mark her right ahead, you see her clean and clear,
> Next day at dawn — "What, ho! she bumps" — from somewhere in
>   the rear.
> Or else the keenest-eyed patrol will miss him with the glass —
> He's lying hidden in the rocks to let the leaders pass;
> But when the mainguard comes along he opens up the fun;
> There's lots of ammunition for the little Maxim gun.

And as the war dragged on, Paterson's respect for Johnny Boer grew almost to admiration; and his anger at the propaganda used about and against the Boers prompted him to write, with indignation and savage irony mingling at white-heat — a most rare occurrence with the usually imperturbable and detached Paterson — his lines (with Kipling overtones) giving his views concerning the African War:

> And first let us shriek the unstinted abuse that the Tory press prefer —
> De Wet is a madman, and Steyn is a liar, and Kruger a pitiful cur!
> (Though I think if Dom Paul — as old as he is — were to walk down
>   the Strand with his gun,
> A lot of these heroes would hide in the sewers or take to their heels
>   and run!
> For Paul he has fought like a man in his days, but now that he's
>   feeble and weak,
> And tired, and lonely, and old and grey, of course it's quite safe to
>   shriek!)

And next let us join in the bloodthirsty shriek, Hooray for Lord
  Kitchener's bag"!
For the fireman's torch and the hangman's cord — they are hung on
  the English Flag!
In the front of our brave old army! Whoop! the farmhouse blazes
  bright
And their women weep and their children die — how dare they
  presume to fight!
For none of them dress in a uniform, the same as by rights they ought,
They're fighting in rags and in naked feet, like Wallace's Scotchmen
  fought!
(And they clothe themselves from our captured troops — and they're
  catching them every week;
And they don't hang *them* — and the shame is ours, but we cover
  the shame with a shriek.)

If this had been published in the *Worker*, commented that journal sourly
(22 March 1902), ". . . it would probably land us in one of Rutledge's*
Jingo gaols".

Nevertheless, the only ballad from his war experiences that can
possibly be said to rank with his better work was "With French to
Kimberley", where in the best Patersonian style, action is linked with
rhythm to convey almost breathlessly an experience in which he had
shared and which in this ballad he recounted in every exciting detail:

He crossed the Reit and fought his way towards the Modder bank.
The foeman closed behind his march, and hung upon the flank.
The long, dry grass was all ablaze (and fierce the veldt fire runs) ;
He fought them through a wall of flame that blazed around the guns!
Then limbered up and drove at speed, though horses fell and died;
We might not halt for man nor beast on that wild, daring ride.
Black with the smoke and parched with thirst, we pressed the livelong
  day
Our headlong march to Kimberley to drive the Boers away.

But if Paterson's experiences during the Boer War returned no great
dividends in ballads, his knowledge of and interest in horses profited
materially. His outstanding success as a remount officer in World War I
traces directly to his observations in South Africa. In reviewing some of
the events of the War in which he participated, and relying on his general
impressions, he maintained that from the beginning there had been a
wrong demand for infantry by the English War Office: that in the tèrrain
of battle — vast treeless expanses of level plain, dotted here and there by
the hills of kopjes, rock- and scrub-crested and thus naturally fortified —
mobility was the first requirement, and five or six thousand mounted
Australians were worth ten to fifteen thousand infantry.

* Probably Arthur Rutledge, Attorney-General in Queensland in the 1880s, who
represented Queensland at the National Australasian Convention in Sydney in 1891.

In carrying on these "moveable" fights, [he wrote] . . . the greatest
qualities needed for the troops were mobility, dash and intelligence,
and in all these qualities the Australian and New Zealand regiments
without exception proved their excellence. It must never be forgotten
that the Australians were accustomed all their lives to finding their
way in the open, to noticing what was taking place around them, and
to relying on themselves at a pinch; the English "Tommies" were
drilled and trained to obey orders, and there their ideas stopped. It
was not that the Australians were any braver than the English, but
that the latter were less intelligent and had less practical outdoor
experience . . .[17]

"Outdoor experience", "mobility" — these were concepts relating wholly
to horses in warfare, and Paterson wrote thoughtful essays on the subject.
He considered that a first-class Australian steeplechase horse made an
ideal cavalry horse, but there were insufficient inducements to breed in
quantity for army use. Admittedly the New South Wales Lancers could
not have been better mounted, but they had police horses which were the
best available. Generally speaking, however, the English cavalry horses,
much more solidly bred, were better weight-carriers: they could carry to
seventeen or eighteen stone on their backs — weights which distressed the
more lightly-framed, weedier looking Australian horses. But Paterson was
scathing about the conditions endured by horses in South Africa. He had
made careful notes. On a hard day's march, horses were given a meagre
meal, at dawn, of a handful of hard, uncrushed Indian corn. Then they
stood saddled with six stone of equipment often into the blazing noon,
while their riders waited for orders. After a little maize or raw oats at mid-
day they were galloped or cantered most of the afternoon over rocky
kopjes, then often tied together all night. They were frequently left for
forty-eight hours with their saddles on, and no opportunity to rest after
that. There were no glorious, daring sallies at the foe, who did not keep
in any one place long enough for these exercises; such charges usually
degenerated into the sorry spectacle of a long drawn out string of weak
and weary horses plodding hopelessly across the veldt at a heavy canter.
Paterson wrote:

The fact is that all well-bred horses were too delicate to stand starva-
tion, sickness and mismanagement. They became sick, refused their
food, and, of course, soon died. The English horses fared no better
than ours, and, indeed, it would have taken a lot of iron horses to
stand the vicious mishandling to which the poor four-footed servants
of the Army were subjected. Good horse, or bad horse, right type or
wrong type, the ill-treatment and hardships they had to undergo
brought them all to one level and the "five-pound scrubber" was
quite as likely to survive as the finest specimen of the weight carrying
charger. It was not the severity of the work they had to do which
killed them; but it was the wretched conditions under which they
did their work. If our horses could have been kept free from sickness,
and have been properly fed, they could have done all the Army work
with the greatest of ease. As it was, they died like flies . . .[18]

Paterson was determined that he would do everything in his power to see that such misuse of the horse in warfare was avoided in the future.

He returned to Australia in the latter part of 1900 and embarked on a series of lectures about his Boer War experiences, travelling to the far north of Queensland, and south to Tasmania. His journeying was not without its difficulties. He wrote to George Robertson[19] from Launceston, in Tasmania, *en route* to Dunedin, New Zealand:

> . . . I am in very miserable health since I came back, can't get enough exercise. The days I should have to myself I have to wait in to see interviewers. I think as soon as this tour is over I will be off to China or else buy a pig-farm in the country and never move off it. . . . The lecturing is not so bad but the lonely travelling is awful. Anyhow the money is good which is the main thing . . .

As for his lectures, Paterson showed a good deal of moral courage in presenting both sides of the campaign, and in some places was taunted and jeered at as "pro-Boer". Nevertheless, at least one cheerful account of his lectures remains, from an occasion in the far north of Queensland:

> "Banjo" Paterson was speaking his little piece about the Boer War the other day, and everybody went to see him. When he came casually on to the stage and opened out about the gory business in South Africa without any preliminary frill, he quite won our admiration. "No guyver about him; he jest sparred on to the platform and bogged into the war, my oath!" said Hogan's nephew. But his eloquence was not level with the intelligence of his audience. They wanted gore, and Queensland gore at that. Paterson's neat little pictures amid the dust and carnage were lost hopelessly on a crowd anxious to hear "How Ginger Mick won the 'Southern Cross' ". "Ginger" was a local bloke. Open mouths and long breaths were the order of the hour, but it used to take the audience so long to assimilate the gist of "Banjo's" talk — or his points slipped by so rapidly — that some of the listeners would break suddenly out into an irrelevant volley of applause some minutes after the applause-place had been passed. Then the brighter section of the audience used to reprove the guilty disturbers with many aspersions on their intelligence, sprinkled with blanky. When the lecturer told of the successful commandeering exploits of Queens- landers, the O'Guire family — with vivid memories of losses sustained — opined that Ginger "done" 18 months for duffing before he went to duff for Chamberlain. This led to another difference among the audience. Towards the end Sweater Mac. caused a commotion by asking dubiously, "Well, I wonder if he really was at the war?" Sweater nearly got hurt.[20]

There remains an anti-climactic postscript to his Boer War experiences, recorded in 1905. Lieutenant-Colonel George Leonard Lee, who, as Major Lee commanded the New South Wales Lancers, was summoned before a Court of Inquiry to answer a complaint about his disbursement of £700 remitted by the New South Wales Treasury to South Africa to be used as advances to the officers and men of the contingent. The Chief Inspector of Public Accounts (Mr Brodie) claimed that, as the men were subsequently paid in full, the whole of the £700 should have been refunded by Major Lee, instead of an amount of £89 10s. 6d. — Colonel Lee claiming that he had in general used the money for "such purposes as [he] thought best in the interest of the troops".

Paterson was among the witnesses called: he was asked to explain an entry of £3 alleged to have been "improperly" advanced to him on 30 March 1900. Paterson's explanation[21] read:

> The only financial affairs between Colonel Lee and I consisted of mess accounts. Sometimes I bought the turkeys and sometimes Colonel Lee bought them; sometimes Lieutenant Osborne would buy some. We adjusted accounts as best we could and sometimes I had to pay up, and sometimes the others. . . .

Paterson was criticized by one newspaper of the day for his grammar (". . . does not that exceedingly brilliant man of letters, Banjo, know that 'between' is a preposition and that it therefore governs the objective case?"), but since he was at that time editing a rival newspaper, one observes that the internal and external politics of press practice were not substantially different even sixty years ago. The Court found he had "satisfactorily explained" the matter, and found also in Colonel Lee's favour on the whole issue.

NOTES

[1] In *Happy Dispatches* (1934).
[2] Ibid.
[3] Ibid.
[4] Ibid., as for all quotations in previous paragraph.
[5] *Bulletin*, 4 November 1899.
[6] *Sydney Morning Herald*, 11 August 1900.
[7] In *Happy Dispatches*.
[8] Ibid., as for other quotations in this paragraph.
[9] In "The Offer of Troops" (*The Story of South Africa*, 1899).
[10] In *Happy Dispatches*.
[11] Ibid.
[12] Ibid.
[13] Ibid.
[14] Ibid.
[15] Ibid.
[16] *Bulletin*, 19 May 1900.
[17] In "The Offer of Troops".
[18] In "Horses in Warfare" (*The Story of South Africa*, 1899).
[19] In a letter dated 30 October 1900 in the Mitchell Library, Sydney.
[20] *Bulletin*, 9 March 1901.
[21] These accounts and comments are taken from the *Star*, 8 October 1905.

A. B. Paterson at the age of eleven. (Courtesy *Sydney Morning Herald*)

A. B. Paterson in his *Bulletin* days. (Courtesy Mitchell Library)

Sketch of A. B. Paterson, polo player — better known as the author of "The Man from Snowy River". (Courtesy Mitchell Library)

A. B. Paterson about to take part in a hunt near Sydney, 1898. (Courtesy Hugh Paterson)

Waltham Buildings,
Bond Street

Sydney, 14 July 1899.

Mess Angus & Robertson

Dear Sirs,

Lawson's Agreement

Mr Lawson has called here and states that he submits the (8) pieces of verse now in your hands in accordance with your letter of 22nd June wherein you offered him £75 for the verses noted in ours of 19th and in addition usual rates for the six pieces he is at work on. He says that the material last sent you is the six pieces of original verse but he has submitted 8 instead of six. He wants to know definitely whether you adhere to your letter and what offer you make him for the serial sale of the unpublished work now in your hands. We did not make him any other offer nor give him any money. Please let us have answer by the morning stating what sum (if any) you will give for the serial sale of the six pieces

Yours truly
Street & Paterson

A. B. Paterson acting as solicitor for Henry Lawson. (Courtesy Mitchell Library)

24 Bond St Sydney
3 August 1899

George Robertson Esq
    Angus & Robertson

Dear Robertson,

Herewith the balance of the book. It is not all typed but I send it on as I want to let you see it and you can easily read the sense of it. There are heaps of alterations & improvements to be made but we will discuss those later on. You might think over some names for it. "Red Mick & his relatives" "A mountain station" "In No Man's Land" "The findings of Christina" and so on. Anyhow I will look in about Monday if you can then spare time to settle the question of what wants writing up most, & the more important question of what wants writing down. I fear the love-making is very flat, & there is too much fight & drink all through it. Still I have to please a large section of the public & if we do that the critics won't break our hearts. Yours truly A B Paterson.

Letter to George Robertson about Paterson's first novel. The novel was eventually published in 1906 with the title *An Outback Marriage*. (Courtesy Mitchell Library)

A. B. Paterson after returning from the Boer War, about 1901. (Courtesy Mitchell Library)

A. B. Paterson with his wife and daughter Grace. They are in the grounds of his house West Hall in Queen Street, Woollahra, Sydney, about 1904. (Courtesy Hugh Paterson)

A. B. Paterson with his daughter Grace at West Hall, Woollahra, about 1904. (Courtesy Hugh Paterson)

Motorized horsepower also attracted Paterson. Here, he is riding beside Colonel Arnott in the Colonel's Minerva near Hyde Park, Sydney in 1910. Paterson had travelled with Arnott in an Innes car in the first reliability trial from Sydney to Melbourne in 1905. (Courtesy Hugh Paterson)

A. B. Paterson and his wife in horse and trap at his Coodra Vale property in New South Wales, about 1911. (Courtesy Hugh Paterson)

Major Paterson at Moascar, Egypt, about 1917. He was in charge of the Remount Division of the A.I.F. (Courtesy Hugh Paterson)

A. B. Paterson in the late 1930s. (Courtesy *Sydney Morning Herald*)

Portrait of A. B. Paterson. (Courtesy Australian Club, Sydney)

CHAPTER X

Paterson and Morant

"Station songs and droving ditties!"
Strung together on the track
Far away from coastal cities
In the droving days — outback;

Jingles! — neither good nor clever —
Just a rover's random rhymes,
But they'll serve their turn if ever
They recall the old bush times,

When a bushman, in his leisure,
Reads them 'neath the shady pine;
Or they give one moment's pleasure
To some old bush mate o' mine!

— HARRY ("THE BREAKER") MORANT.

ON 19 APRIL 1902 there appeared a violently polemical leading article on the Red Page of the *Bulletin* (by "F.R.") headed "Beatification of 'The Breaker' — with some Literary Remains". It was an attack on the manner in which Harry ("The Breaker") Morant had met his death by a British firing-squad, within eighteen hours of his court martial, for having, according to the article, killed "a German missionary". Handcock, another Australian, was executed with Morant. The writer claimed that these soldiers had been shot "to whitewash the British Army", since, as Morant swore in evidence during his trial, the practice of shooting Boer prisoners was universal.

The facts are not quite as simple as that. But there is no doubt, in the story of the Australian ballad, that Harry Harbord Morant ("The Breaker") is of the stuff that legends, even heroes, are made. "Romantic" is a much abused word, but it sums up the impression which Morant made on the minds and imaginations of those with whom he came in contact from the time he first arrived in Australia, probably about 1884, and even then, as Will Ogilvie later described him,

A chivalrous, wild and reckless lad
A knight born out of his time.

Morant's origins have never been satisfactorily explained. It was said he was the son of Admiral Sir George Digby Morant (this was denied by Admiral Morant); but there seems little doubt that he came from an upper-class home in Devon where he was born in 1864; that he was given the early education appropriate to the son of an English gentleman, and went into the Royal Naval College; that there was some trouble there, and he was sent to Australia to make a fresh start. He first appeared in the Charters Towers district of Queensland and started work on a station property, drawn irresistibly to horses since he had been in early youth a keen horseman.

He drifted about Queensland doing odd jobs, worked on a newspaper in Hughenden at one time, got into various scrapes with the law, and, in an outback life where hard drinking and hard living were the order of existence, found his restlessness best appeased by droving and horse-breaking in the cattle country. His reputation as a horse-breaker spread far and wide in central and western Queensland — and this was responsible for the legend that was built up about him, as well as for his nick-name.

He used to boast that he knew every country pub and hospital (since broken bones were inevitable in his occupation) in the outback; he was, it is certain, a horseman of uncanny ability. Frank Fox wrote[1] of an occasion when, near Clarendon, in New South Wales, he put his horse, for a wager, over a seven-foot-high fence, and won his bet; on another occasion, in Parkes, at the dead of night he put his horse over a solid four-railed fence nearly four feet high at the back of a hotel, with a six-foot area on the other side, and successfully turned the horse around and cleared the fence again — with a clean jump each time.

Since he "rarely rode the bush without a book of poems in his saddle bag",[2] it was his chief delight to recite verse aloud as he rode on his lonely rounds, and sometimes he would

> . . . in the right mood compose aloud to a mate a string of verses to beguile the hot, dry, dusty hours behind some mob of cattle "on the track"; and occasionally, if pleased with his conceit, he would in camp rip off the paper cover around a jam tin and write the lines out to send to the *Bulletin* . . .[3]

His first verses were published in the *Bulletin* in September 1891. Thereafter, until his death in 1901, he wrote over sixty poems and ballads published in that journal. This success attracted him to Sydney in the early 1890s. Whenever he could accompany a rail-load of cattle for market to that city he did so

> and when they're sold at Homebush, and the agents settle up, Sing hey! a spell in Sydney town and Melbourne for the Cup!

and thus he became one of the confraternity of ballad-writers — Ogilvie, Dyson, Lawson, and the rest — congregated around the *Bulletin* office. And especially Banjo Paterson. There is no doubt that they became

friends, at least to the extent that they shared a common enthusiasm for
horses and horse-riding. They rode together in hunt-club meets over the
post-and-rail country on the city's outskirts, and rode against each other at
amateur race meetings. Until 1898 Morant rode for several years in the
annual Sydney Hunt Club Steeplechase at Randwick. He shared also with
Paterson a great love for polo and formed a polo team at North Rich-
mond, into which he pressed anyone who owned a pony in the Kurrajong
district. George Lambert, as well as Paterson, played with and against him
whenever Morant could organize a match on his occasional visits to the
city. Above all Morant was accepted by the ballad fraternity for the
quality of his writing in that genre. Impatient of revision once his lines
were set down, nevertheless his grace of language and his instinct for
rhyme and rhythm have guaranteed his place in the top flight of balladists
of the period.

While he had some affinities with Ogilvie in mood as well as in subject
matter, he is probably closer than any other balladist of his day to Paterson. For one thing, he saw the bush always at its best, scenically, musically,
physically — and like Paterson this was not a pose because he genuinely
and passionately loved the outback and its people — on the track, and in
camp

> From sunrise unto sunset through the summer days we'd ride,
> And stockyard rails were up and pegged with cattle safe inside,
> When 'twixt the gloaming and the dark we'd hear the welcome note
> Of boisterous, pealing laughter from the kookaburra's throat.
> Camped out beneath the starlit skies — the treetops overhead,
> A saddle for a pillow and a blanket for a bed,
> 'Twas pleasant, mate, to listen to the soughing of the breeze
> And learn the lilting lullabies that stirred the mulga trees.

and indeed wherever mateship flourished . . .

> We'll light our campfires while we may, and yarn beside the blaze,
> The jingling hobble-chains shall make a music through the days;

His equestrian ballads, at their best, had all the vigour of Paterson's
and a real feeling for the craftsmanship of verse.

> He raced to her side ere she crossed the plain;
>   then into the scrub they dashed,
> When the brigalow snapped on his saddle-pads,
>   and the rotten deadwood crashed
> 'Neath his horse's hoofs, and the young boughs bent,
>   and the brittle branches smashed.
>
> The foam-flakes flew, and the flowers beneath
>   were stained by many a fleck,
> But Bill ne'er steadied, and horse ne'er fell! —
>   'tis little that riders reck,
> When racing hard on a warrigal's flank,
>   for the risk of a broken neck.

Like Paterson, with his Dandaloo, Booligal and Kiley's Hill, Morant
had that same warmly nostalgic and sentimental feeling for place — the
outback townships and signposts of the scattered communities:

> We came through Eulo township and camped to see 'the Queen'
> (As every drover man has done who has through Eulo been!)
> We left the Warrego behind, came through the Border fence
> And crossed to where in Culgoa swamps the lignum's high and dense.

> We loitered through Macpherson's run, the braw old Scotsman said:
> That there'll be grass on Gunga run when all of us are dead!
> We hurried by Damdismal — for Crossbred looks askew
> At cattle passing through his place — and dogs the drover through!

He had Paterson's sardonic humour, probably in greater measure, and
one remembers especially Morant's lines of the lonely stockman thinking
of "his light o' love of a year ago", musing to his cattle dog Bluey: "tell
us what games are their candles worth?"

> One eye opens and two ears prick:
> "Not very many, boss," grins the dog;
> "Sweethearting's vanity — best to stick
> To good tobacco and decent grog."

Morant, with his daredevil and reckless attitudes, in fact was in many
ways the *alter ego* of the temperamentally more mature Paterson; but his
love for space and the open air, and his streak of genuine poetic talent,
brought him close to Paterson in their periods of companionship in
Sydney. However, at the end of 1898 a droving job across the Darling set
him wandering further west, and he found himself in the Murray Valley
of South Australia where he took employment on a cattle station at
Paringa, near Renmark. Here he was when the Boer War began, and he
enlisted straight away with the South Australian Mounted Rifles. His
personality and horsemanship won him quick promotion, so that by the
time he reached Capetown early in 1900, soon after Paterson, he had his
sergeant's stripes. In October 1900 his period of enlistment was up; he
transferred as a lieutenant into the British Army's Transvaal Constabu-
lary and was given a period of leave in England. For several glorious
months he hunted and played polo in Devon. He became a firm friend of
a Captain Hunt, who invited him to join a special service unit called the
Bush Veldt Carbineers under an Australian, Major Lenehan, who knew
Morant from his Sydney days. Back in Africa they went into action in
April 1901; in August in an attack on a Boer outpost Captain Hunt was
killed and cruelly mutilated, and Morant seemed emotionally changed at
the death of his friend. There were several incidents in which prisoners
were shot and a German missionary was also killed. In October Morant,
along with two other Australians, Lieutenants Handcock and Witton,
and an Englishman, Lieutenant Picton, were arrested, charged with
shooting Boer prisoners and the German missionary, and after a long
period of detention and inquiry, were court-martialled early in 1902. They

were found not guilty on the charge concerning the missionary, but guilty
on the other charges. The first three were sentenced to be shot; Witton's
sentence was commuted to life imprisonment by Lord Kitchener, who
however endorsed the verdicts against the other two, and they were shot
within eighteen hours of the verdict being given. There was an outcry in
Australia when the news reached there, but no particular action was
taken. It can safely be said, after the various accounts are read, that the
court martial was a travesty of justice, that Morant and Handcock were
scapegoats to appease complaints made by the German authorities, and
that Kitchener's conduct of the matter in hastily signing the death war-
rants and ignoring, and indeed suppressing, immediate requests and
petitions on behalf of the convicted men was inhuman and outrageous. A
telegram which he sent later to the Governor-General of Australia on
7 April 1902 (published throughout the Australian press), in which he
set out to justify the sentences, was an utterly callous and unscrupulous
distortion of the facts revealed in the record of the court martial. When
Kitchener visited Australia in 1910, he was asked to unveil a war
memorial at Bathurst, which listed the men in that district who fought in
the Boer War, including Handcock. Kitchener refused to do this unless
the name of Handcock was removed from the roll. So removed it was.*

Morant, in the Australian idiom, died game. He refused to have his
eyes bandaged. "Shoot straight, you——!" he said to the firing party.
"Don't make a mess of it." Just before he died he wrote some grim and
sardonic lines, "Butchered to make a Dutchman's Holiday" — "a final
rhyme," he called it, "while awaiting crucifixion":

> And if you'd earn a D.S.O. —
> Why every British sinner
> Should know the proper way to go
> Is: *"Ask the Boer to dinner!"*
>
> Let's toss a bumper down our throat
> Before we pass to Heaven,
> And toast: "The trim-set petticoat
> We leave behind in Devon."

Following the *Bulletin* article referred to at the beginning of this
chapter, several correspondents offered views in support, and then, on
10 May 1902, Paterson wrote to the *Bulletin* explaining that he had, from
a mass of old correspondence, turned up several letters from Morant
written during 1895. Paterson recalled that he had first met Morant at a
hunt near Sydney and had also seen him ride in steeplechases. "From
what I saw of Morant," he continued, "I find it hard to believe that he
killed anybody for gain. Reckless ne'er-do-well he was, but one finds it
very difficult to think of him as a murderer . . ."4 He then quoted the
first of these letters:

* As a result of a long campaign by the Bathurst Sub-Branch of the R.S.L. (Returned
Sailors', Soldiers' & Airmen's Imperial League of Australia Inc.), the Bathurst City
Council eventually agreed to Handcock's name being restored to the Memorial, and this
was done on 1 March 1964 when a small bronze plaque bearing Handcock's name was
placed at the foot of the Roll of Honour.

Enngonia, Bourke, 3/8/'95

Dear Paterson — Your letter (*re* Hunt Club races) came along all right, as welcome as a thunderstorm, and set a man yearning for a ride over fences. Would have written you ere this, but a bit of sandal-wood in my right (or should I say "write"?) hand has made me economical about ink. I have a dingo-skin here, the biggest I have ever seen, and all the local liars say the same of it, which same I will send down to you at the first opportunity. Do for a mat — head, pads and all attached. Considering the "strychnine and stiffening" character of the country my dingo died a sporting death. The local talent had tried with poison since Christmas last to kill him, but I pulled him down with a couple of cattle-dogs in the moonlight about a week ago, after a couple or three miles gallop, finishing him with that good old weapon, the stirrup-iron. Killed him within a few hundred yards of a tank-sinker's camp, the pick and shovel men turning out of their bunks,

"In a mixed kind of costume, half Pontificalibus."
"Half what scholars denominate 'Pure naturalibus' "
like Sir Thomas's household in "Ingoldsby".

Filled up some leisure by breaking in a four-year old colt by The Levite (a Yattendon horse) out of an old mare by The Drummer. The colt was a man-eater when I first tackled him, but has turned out a beautiful horse to ride, and I may get a race out of him, as his old mother has won both over hurdles and on the flat.

Like Joseph and John Bunyan of old, "I dreamed a dream" — to the effect that The Admiral had won the Cup, whence came the doggerel you possibly read in "Sporting Notions" a week or so since.

Everything in these parts is devilish dry, and there is small chance of my starting for down the Macquarie with cattle, though I would like to come down and have a ride on Queen Mab. Talking of rhymes, though Lawson's book sold so readily, I fancy his work is very unequal, and, strange to say, his latter jingles and sketches are not all popular with men who have spoken of them to me up here. His best, or, to be correct, his most popular scribbles have appeared over his "Joe Swallow" penname, and his identity with that name is, I fancy, mostly unknown.

Had an English letter the other day from an old schoolfellow, who is at present yachting in the Hebrides to put in the time ere stag-hunting commences in Devon. Stag-hunting starts this week there. How I hate this —— brigalow desert sometimes! Thirty years next Christmas, but feel fifty! Would like one whole open season, well-carried, in Leicestershire, and wouldn't growl at a broken neck at the finish. A better lot than dreary years in the bush with periodical drinks!

Owing to literally going in bandages, my fist is even more illegible than usual. It would be charitable to speedily finish this scrawl.

Yours in the Brigalow,

HARRY H. MORANT.

Another letter, undated, read:

Writing Sydney letters to-day, so send a line. Everything up these parts is dry and damnable. Little grass, less water. Stock poor and men poorer. If it were to rain shortly I should be able to get down to Sydney, as I have some cattle to shift down from an adjacent place to some fellow's paddocks down Warren way.

There are a few scrubbers (cleanskins) yet remaining in an adjoining ten-mile block. The country is fairly dense brigalow and gidgee, and it's not the easiest thing in the world to get them — in fact, we cannot yard them, so whenever we want beef here we go out and shoot or "rip"—do you know the latter performance?—and butcher some cheap beef on the beast's hide. Last week my mate and I went beef-hunting. We were riding colts, and had but four revolver cartridges; four bullets failed to drop the clean-skin heifer we selected, and I got alongside the heifer to knife her. She turned and charged in her tracks, and the colt, not being up to the game, his bowels came out instead of the heifer's, whilst I was hurled headlong. The colt went off (died that night, poor brute!), and I just managed to put a tree between me and the heifer as she charged. After one or two narrow squeaks — though no beast can catch a man if there is a tree handy — I managed to hamstring her, and the cuddy's misfortune was avenged. Were Frank Mahony about at the time, I guess that illustrations of "Beef-Hunting on the Border" might be worthy of Christmas publication.

I brought a Lancer's spear back with me from Sydney, and find it a first-class weapon for pigs, which are fairly numerous in the lignum of the Culgoa. With a handy horse, pigsticking is not bad fun.

I should like to get down for the Hunt Club Steeple and Point-to-Point, and if rain falls soon I intend to. Trusting that you are all well,

Yours, up country,

HARRY H. MORANT.

At Christmas 1896, Morant wrote this letter to Paterson:

Dear Paterson — Another Christmas evaporated, thermometer registering something over 110 in the shade each day in the past fortnight. My dislocated shoulder is now as fit as ever. They have an outlawed mare, the Witch, over at Bundaleer station. The boss there gave a fellow a note to ride her twelve months ago. She slung him, and had been spelling since. She was in the yards, the other day, and I had a go at her. I have not, as a rule, much respect for sheep-station outlaws, but this one was pretty bad. Up on her hind legs, then backward bucks, and occasionally one or other stirrup banged on the ground. The worst part of her was that one couldn't pull an ounce on her mouth. If you did, the brute would come back with you. I rode her for about an hour, and she was just as bad at the finish as when I got on her, though she would stop when she got the double of a whip round her. I'm not keen on riding her again, anyhow.

In the course of a month or six weeks, I intend departing from these regions to try Coolgardie. If I don't find it prosperous over there, next Christmas will find one prodigal turning up in England with a request for prime veal.

So long . . .

Finally, there was an extract from a last letter — "the aftermath," said Paterson, "of one of his periodical drunks":

When I came over here the other day, it was t0 participate in a hurrah spree to finish the bachelor days of the manager here. He is about to take unto himself a wife of his own! Most fellows up here generally get shook on, or content with, some other fellow's spouse. Anyhow, I was unsteadily tripping across to my bedroom in the small, murky hours of the morning, and went headlong down some 18 ft. of a cellar. Left shoulder dislocated was the result. An amateur surgeon pulled it in again without chloroform next morning, but a ten days complete rest, mostly camping under the flow of an artesian bore, and frequent applications of arnica have put me pretty right once more. I go back to old Morton at the end of this week.

Apropos of "The Man from Snowy River", there is a small, sultry border township, Barrinhun to wit, where, just a year ago, a horse owned by an alleged steward ran a bad second to a shearer's moke, and was declared the winner by the biassed judge.

I have done a bit of brumby running in mountain country, although most of my cleanskin experience has been in mulga or brigalow, and I have noticed that a good man on a plucky horse can always beat brumbies when doing down a declivity. A horse with a rider on his back goes with confidence, whilst brumbies are never all out then. When going uphill the naked horse gets away. Weight tells then, I suppose, though, of course, there is the chance of a smash going down.

I must now saddle-up for my ride home. With best wishes — Yours truly,

H. H. MORANT.

It must be said at once that the warmth and friendliness and indeed artlessness of these letters make Paterson's description of him as a ne'er-do-well seem at least ungracious; furthermore, the letters reveal, even more convincingly than his poems, how Morant's interests were similar to those of Paterson.

Had Paterson left, even as patronizingly as he did, the relationship between himself and Morant as one between a man of standing and substance and a "ne'er-do-well" and wandering outback station-hand, there would be no great reason for further comment.

But Paterson, forty-four years later, in his reminiscences, seemed to go out of his way to blacken and ridicule Morant, and for a man who throughout his life was upright and charitable in his dealings with his fellowmen, this one lapse seems the more puzzling. He met Morant first, he said, as a result of a letter from his uncle, Arthur Barton, a Queensland grazier.

> There is a man going down from here to Sydney [Barton wrote] and he says he is going to call on you. His name is Morant. He says he is the son of an English Admiral, and he has good manners and education. He can do anything better than most people: can write verses; break in horses; trap dingoes; yard scrub cattle; dance, run, fight, drink, and borrow money; anything except work. I don't know what is the matter with the chap. He seems to be brimming over with flashness, for he will do any dare-devil thing so long as there is a crowd to watch him. He jumped a horse over a stiff three-rail fence one dark night by the light of two matches which he had placed on the post![5]

Paterson then described his first meeting with Morant — "a bronzed, clean-shaven man of about thirty, well set up, with the quick walk of a man used to getting on young horses, clear confident eyes, radiating health and vitality . . ." he told how they talked of the outback, hunting and race-riding and how Morant before he left tried (unsuccessfully) to borrow five pounds. Then followed a story of a confidence trick played by Morant on a gymkhana committee, and how he presented a pony to a small boy which, however, was later claimed by the rightful owner. "Such was the man," wrote Paterson scornfully, "who was shot by the British army after a court martial for defying army orders and shooting a prisoner in revenge for the death of one of his best friends. . . ." Paterson claimed to know "all that was to be known" about Morant's trial and execution, allegedly through a lawyer who defended him, "one J. F. Thomas of Tenterfield" (it was of course quite true that Major J. F. Thomas of the New South Wales Mounted Rifles, a country solicitor in private life, defended the soldiers charged), and Paterson's account continued:

> This was the story of the Morant affair, told me by Thomas, and confirmed by reference to his bundle of papers:—
>
> "Morant," he said, "was detached from his own command in South Africa, and was acting under the orders of a civilian official named Taylor, who knew the country and had been appointed by the Army to go round the outlying farms requisitioning cattle, so that was how he was put on the job. He had a few men under him, and pretty well a free hand in anything he did. They had to keep their eyes open, for wandering bands of the enemy used sometimes to have a shot at them, and in one of these skirmishes a mate of Morant was killed.
>
> "Morant told me," said Thomas, "that he had orders not to let all and sundry wander about the country without proper permits. He questioned a man who was driving across country in a Cape cart on some business or other. According to Morant, he thought that

this man was acting as a spy. It so happened that Morant had just
seen the body of his mate, and claimed that it had been disfigured;
that somebody had trodden on the face. Of course, everybody was
excited, not knowing when there might be another skirmish. Morant
told his men that he had orders to shoot anybody in reprisal for a
murder or for disfiguring the dead or for spying. So he took this man
out of his Cape cart and shot him! Unfortunately, the victim turned
out to be a Dutch padre." Somehow, I seemed to see the whole thing
— the little group of anxious-faced men, the half-comprehending
Dutchman, standing by, and Morant, drunk with his one day of
power. For days he had shifted and battled and contrived; had been
always the underdog; and now he was up in the stirrups. It went to
his head like wine. . . .[6]

Now, if Paterson had really read the "bundle of papers" given him by
J. F. Thomas, and if these papers were a true account of the proceedings
and findings (and presumably they must have been), then Paterson's
version is a distortion of the truth. As far as the missionary was concerned,
the evidence of the court martial confirmed that he was a German named
Hesse, not a "Dutch padre". Morant, as well as Handcock, was *acquitted*
by the court martial of having shot him; Morant, as the evidence clearly
showed, was nowhere in the vicinity of the place where the missionary
was shot. Where on earth then could Paterson have got his story that
Morant "took this man out of his Cape cart and shot him"? Surely it was
just as much part of Paterson's own imagination as was his re-creation
of the scene described above: "I seemed to see the whole thing . . .".

F. M. Cutlack wrote[7] indignantly to the *Sydney Morning Herald* after
Paterson published his account:

One takes a man as he finds him in his life, especially in the bush,
but as one who knew Harry Harbord Morant well and affectionately
— adventurer as he was — I deplore that "Banjo" Paterson does not
even remember his universally known nickname of "The Breaker",
the name with which for years he signed his verses in "The Bulletin". Perhaps he deceived some people, and left them angry; but he
was known in all the back country from Queensland to the Lower
Murray, and great numbers of other people of careless habits — or
even of some scrupulous rectitude — loved him despite his faults.

It is quite true. Paterson's failure to mention Morant as a brother
balladist is inexcusable and seems to have been deliberate. Though it is
hard to say it, Morant must have been a blind spot in Paterson's recollection: he had let dislike turn into uncharitableness and unjust condem-
nation, and it is difficult to avoid the thought that this may have grown
from simple jealousy of a man who was, like himself, a splendid horseman
and dedicated bushman, and in politer society a handsome and dashing
personality (with the rumoured *cachet* of English county), an amateur
race-rider, accomplished polo-player, and, to boot, also a successful *Bulletin* balladist who had gone to the Boer War to fight and die as a soldier.

And if Paterson knew Major Thomas as well as he claimed to have done (and there is no reason to doubt this), he must have known that Thomas regarded Morant's death as an injustice and indeed had grave doubts about his guilt. For Thomas had written immediately to Australia from Pretoria on 27 February 1902:

Have you heard the news — the awful news? Poor Morant and Handcock were shot this morning at 6 a.m. It has broken me completely. . . . Poor Handcock was right when he wrote, "Our graves were dug before we left the Spelonken". They were dug: I see it all clearly now and why. I know what I cannot write in this accursed military-ridden country. Poor Handcock! A brave, true, simple man! And Morant, brave but hot-headed! They took their sentence with marvellous braveness. Their pluck astonished all. . . . Morant and Handcock were doomed — politically doomed — through the iniquities of the court of inquiry, proceedings of which got to Germany, I believe.

I am full of bitterness. I cannot here express my feelings . . .

But though not guilty Morant and Handcock have died over that case because our own (no, not our own, altogether) people would have them convicted before a trial . . .

A postscript to this unhappy lapse on Paterson's part was a letter which was written to the *Sydney Morning Herald*[8] immediately after his reminiscence of Morant had appeared:

Sir,

I was surprised that Banjo Paterson in his article in Saturday's *Herald* had not made sure of his statement that Mr. J. F. Thomas of Tenterfield ". . . died years ago and had taken his troubles to a Higher Tribunal".

I have been in close association with Mr Thomas at Tenterfield for the past three years. He is very much alive. Mr Paterson's version does not tally in several details with the account told me by Mr Thomas. I hope Mr Paterson will correct details of a terrible injustice where an Australian scapegoat had to be found to placate Germany. The so-called "Dutch padre" was Dr Hesse, a German missionary, and on the charge of shooting him, all three of the accused men were exonerated by courtmartial.

Yours etc.

W. H. NASH.

Turramurra, February 27, 1939.

It was clearly unanswerable; nor did Paterson as far as I can find out ever make a reply.

NOTES

[1] In *Bushman and Buccaneer* (1902).
[2] F. M. Cutlack, in *Breaker Morant — A Horseman Who Made History* (1962).
[3] Ibid.

4 In his *Sydney Morning Herald* reminiscences.
5 Ibid.
6 Ibid.
7 This letter was published in the *Sydney Morning Herald* at the end of Paterson's article about Morant.
8 *Sydney Morning Herald*, 28 February 1939

CHAPTER XI

Travels and Adventures: 1901-2

*. . . [Paterson] preferred to consort with men of action,
whether these had to do with affairs constructive or destruc-
tive. Wherever there was a war or a revolution, or any other
state of human conflict he was first in the ring . . .*

— NORMAN LINDSAY.[1]

PATERSON'S THIRST for excitement and adventure, unslaked by his brief
period of travelling in parts of Australia* to lecture about the Boer War,
turned his attention to the East, and especially to China, where the Boxer
War offered him further opportunities as a war correspondent. Furthermore, Paterson admired especially that fellow man-of-action, the Vic-
torian-born Dr George Ernest Morrison — more famous as "Chinese"
Morrison — whose exploits even before he reached China would have
satisfied an ordinary man for a lifetime. Morrison as a youth paddled a
canoe 1,500 miles down the River Murray, then shipped as a seaman in
the Islands Kanaka trade; at the age of twenty he walked from the Gulf
of Carpentaria, often through the most inhospitable desert country, to
Geelong (over 2,000 miles) and then led an expedition to New Guinea,
where he was speared by hostile natives. ("He got his black boy to cut
off the shaft of the spear," wrote Paterson,[2] "but never had the head of
the spear taken out till he got to Melbourne. A man like that takes some
stopping . . .") Later he travelled through Spain, Morocco and other
parts of North Africa before beginning his celebrated journeys through
China in 1894. Morrison had become famous as a roving journalist —
correspondent for the London *Times* — and this was a further incentive
to Paterson to meet him, Paterson by this time having become determined
to follow journalism as a career.

The other reason prompting Paterson's wish to travel again was that he
was resolved to visit London: he still corresponded with Phil May, now
living in delightful eccentricity in London's Bohemia, and especially with

---

* At one stage, soon after his return from the Boer War, he thought seriously of
turning to politics; it is recorded that he attended a political meeting at Burrowa and
"dealt with a variety of political questions and was very well received". (*Bulletin*, 30
May 1901.) He was asked to contest the seat at the forthcoming elections but would not
give a definite answer. Exactly ten years before, in June 1891, the *Bulletin* had reported
that Paterson proposed to stand for the electorate of Yass Plains "in the democratic
interest", but then, too, he had changed his mind.

Kipling, who had given Paterson a standing invitation to visit him.
Kipling wrote to Paterson on a variety of subjects; in one letter he urged
him to start a campaign for more money for officers in the Australian
army, pointing out that young subalterns would soon be "frozen out" by
mess expenses and the various subscriptions they were required to make.

Meanwhile, however, Paterson, on his return from South Africa, had
attracted the notice and friendship of Sir James Reading Fairfax, proprietor of the *Sydney Morning Herald*, whose great personal interest was
in the development and settlement of the many as yet virgin but fertile
areas of eastern Australia. Sir James was a man after Paterson's heart. "He
believed in the development of the country," Paterson later recalled,[3] "and
he held that while the country was progressing the town would look after
itself." Sir James commissioned Paterson to write a series of articles for
his newspaper entitled "Good Districts", with the object of "restoring
confidence" in the future of the State. As a result Paterson spent a number
of weeks touring the seaboard from the dairying country of the South
Coast, through the orange-growing districts of Gosford to the tropical
North Coast with its potential for sugar- and banana-growing. Paterson
reported that there was a "gold-mine" in these coastal districts.

Sir James Fairfax, delighted with this venture, immediately gave Paterson a further commission:

> I want you to go and find what is doing in the matter of irrigation.
> I know that Colonel Home has recorded some scheme but it appears
> to have dropped out of sight. I think irrigation is one of the most
> important matters for this country, and if there is any practicable
> scheme, the *Herald* will support it.[4]

Paterson inquired at the Public Works Office. He found there was an
Irrigation Section, and there was a scheme, but it was a dead letter. The
only way to get something done with it, they told Paterson, was to stir up
the politicians and the public. They pulled out dusty plans and speci-
fications from pigeon holes and showed him what the ideas were. Paterson lost no time, together with a *Herald* representative and photographer,
in making "a frightful climb through granite gorges" to get photographs
of the site of the proposed huge dam between two mountains known as
Barren Jack and Black Andrew. The *Herald* then ran the photographs
and plans with an accompanying report.

Paterson maintained that it was Sir James Fairfax's enthusiasm and
active support which undoubtedly led to the eventual building of the
dam. Public enthusiasm mounted; politicians stuck for a catchphrase took
up the cry, "I believe in irrigation and the Barren Jack Dam". (The name
of Barren Jack, Paterson claimed, was changed to Burrinjuck lest the
word "barren" deter English settlers! Times do not change it seems.)
Paterson wrote:

> The late W. E. O'Sullivan was then Minister for Public Works — a
> man of large ideas who kept his ear pretty close to the ground for
> indications of public feeling. Like Horace he stepped nobly up to

the bridge and said, "I will build the Barren Jack Dam" — and that, as the Americans say, was all there was to it.[5]

Perhaps it was not quite so uncomplicated, but certainly history supports Paterson inasmuch as an Act was passed in 1902 authorizing the spending of £1,000,000 on "hydraulic works", and eventually an Act in 1906 authorized the building of the Burrinjuck Dam itself.

As a result of these successful assignments, the *Sydney Morning Herald* management readily agreed to underwrite Paterson in another overseas mission and on 27 July 1901 the newspaper announced (over-optimistically as it turned out) :

> Mr A. B. Paterson ("Banjo") will be a passenger to China by the China Navigation Company's steamer Changsha, sailing on Monday next. His exploits as our special correspondent in the South African war will be fresh in the memory of our readers including his fine description of French's relief of Kimberley, followed promptly by the ride from Kimberley to Modder River. His successful race for the honour of being first into Bloemfontein, and his despatch riding through country occupied by the enemy on the surrender of Johannesburg and the fall of Pretoria, and later the surrender of Prinsloo and his army near the Basuto frontier, were also included in his letters. Mr Paterson intends now to visit China and Japan, and then take the Trans-Siberian railway to St. Petersburg.* He will contribute articles to the "Sydney Morning Herald", and the "Sydney Mail". Those intended for the latter will be accompanied with illustrations, for producing which he will take a photographic outfit. In the event of war breaking out in the East, Mr Paterson will be at hand to act for the "Herald" as occasion may require.

Paterson, in fact, had considerable ambitions as a war correspondent; he treasured a letter of commendation he had received from Baron Reuter for his work as a correspondent in the Boer War and he had the idea that he might get a job with Reuter's on either side (he was not particular) of any war that might happen. He confessed, though, that he preferred to be with a white army; he had the idea "that Chinese impaled correspondents on bamboos". As it turned out, by the time he reached the mainland of China the prospects of war had fizzled out.

In the meantime he set off on his voyage in the *Changsha*. The first port of call was Thursday Island, a place which captivated Paterson — a little bit of the East it seemed to him, with "more nationalities than there were at the Tower of Babel — every Caucasian nation, local blacks, Kanakas, Chinese, Japanese, Javanese, Malays, New Guinea boys . . .[7] This was the sort of environment to make Paterson's pulse quicken; many

---

* Paterson did not follow this itinerary and certainly did not go to Russia. Yet thirty years later, he wrote: ". . . judging what I have seen in other countries such as the Philippine Islands, Borneo, the Yangtse Valley of South China and in the South of Russia . . ."[8] — a slip of the pen that many more eminent men than Paterson have just as inadvertently allowed.

years later he wrote a lively account of the place with the title "Thirsty
Island" in his book of stories and sketches *Three Elephant Power.*

At Manila, when the ship berthed there towards the end of August
1901, Paterson's now well-developed journalistic instinct took him like a
homing-pigeon in search of a "star" interview, and he set his sights on
General Chaffee, the officer commanding the American forces against the
Filipinos. Or perhaps it was because the ship's doctor had whetted his
curiosity. "This war between the Americans and the Filipinos," said the
doctor, "has a comic opera skinned to death. When you go ashore you go
and see old General Chaffee, and ask him whether he'd sooner fight Boers
or fight Filipinos."[8] Paterson sought out the General; he found to his
surprise that his letter from the Premier of New South Wales recommend-
ing him as a correspondent readily secured him audience with "a kindly
and much-worried veteran who seemed quite glad to hear about somebody else's troubles in South Africa". The General who, with his heavy
eyebrows, grizzled moustache and manner of speech like a man rehearsing
a lecture, reminded Paterson of Mark Twain, gave him a graphically
colloquial account of his problems. Paterson's journalistic flair in recording what were ostensibly the General's own words, is apparent in his
account:

> "Say," he said, "you've seen this country, all mountain and jungle
> that a dog couldn't open his mouth to bark in? You'll understand the
> trouble. They don't understand it in the States. They don't under-
> stand why I don't get this war over with and come home. Do you
> know who are shooting my men? The wharflabourers that are load-
> ing your ship! They've all got rifles hidden in the thatch of their
> houses and they take them out of a night and shoot into my camp.
> I can't burn all the thatched houses in Manila. Our people wouldn't
> stand for it. And those Moros back in the hills! If we go up there
> after them all we hear is a bullet coming from way off through the
> scrub.
>
> "If we catch any of 'em all we can do is to tie them down and fill 'em
> with watta till they show us their villages. I've got most of the
> generals, that there is anything to, cleaned up right now. But we
> daren't go away. If we went away there'd be hell with the lid off here
> in a week . . ."[9]

But the high point in Paterson's Eastern journey was on the Chinese
mainland, where he recorded the colour, movement and exoticism of a
new and exciting environment with an eye for the unexpected and
revealing detail: the fat Chinese shop-keeper who spoke English, with an
affable hate for white people; the hordes of shrieking, howling beggars
"with every malformation known to science". But above all, Paterson
met "Chinese" Morrison in Chefoo, and in so doing left a sort of historical document for posterity, though it should be qualified by the observation that Morrison's recollection of the interview did not tally in all
respects with Paterson's.*

---

* According to Cyril Pearl, who at the time he told me this was writing a book on
the life of Morrison.

Paterson, looking back on his recollections of Morrison, felt that of the three "great men of affairs" he had met up to that time — Morrison, Cecil Rhodes and Winston Churchill — Morrison had the most impressive record since he had gone into China almost unknown and had "outclassed the smartest political agents of the world". His first impressions on meeting Morrison were unfavourable: he talked too much, about women. ("Paterson never talked about women" is a remark made time and time again to me by those who knew him.) Nor did he make a very good impression in the flesh: "a tall, ungainly man with a dour Scotch face and a curious droop at the corner of his mouth. . . ." But as Paterson fired question after question at him (an English doctor named Molyneux was also present, who "acted as a sort of Dr Watson to Morrison's Sherlock Holmes"), he soon had Morrison talking freely and "it was an education to listen to him". On the Boxers: ". . . The Boxers were just a rabble, washermen and rickshaw coolies. Old Napoleon with his whiff of grapeshot would have settled the Boxers before lunch . . ." On the potential of the China trade: "You can't conceive the amount of trade there is here, and everybody wanting to have a go at it. And it's nothing to what it will be. There's gold-mines and tin-mines and quicksilver and all sorts of minerals in the interior, and it's very lightly inhabited. There's all this wonderful agricultural land on the coast, and there are hills all over blue grass, splendid grazing-land in the interior . . .". The English, he claimed, had missed the chance of a lifetime. They had frittered away their time and resources at the Boer War:

> ". . . The next thing was that they had to send men-of-war and troops here whether they liked it or not. But instead of running the show themselves and being top dog, they just had to snap and bite along with the rest of the pack.
>   "They might have taken the job on only for the missionaries," he went on. "The missionaries all wrote home and said that if the English tried to govern China the dear little converts would all get their throats cut. . . . But I didn't suggest that the English should govern China. I said to let the Chinese govern it, nominally, and we could have enough troops here to back them up . . ."[10]

Paterson when he saw for himself the astonishing spectacle of trading steamers from every country jostling in the Chinese ports, and met concession-hunters, bankers and politicians from every country "hustling" for trade and influence, wrote:

> Perhaps Morrison was right. We should have walked in and taken the boss mandarin's seat at the top of the table.[11]

Before he left China *en route* for London, Paterson met a number of soldiers of fortune, watched all-nations' drinking bouts at a country club in Shanghai ("the Russians are in a class by themselves", he observed),

rode a Chinese pony in a memorable race-meeting at Chefoo, and saw
warships of all nations at anchor in Weihaiwei harbour at night, "using
their searchlights like great pencils of flame". On the P. & O. steamer
Admiral Curzon towards the end of October 1901, he met Marie Lloyd
the famous music-hall star when she boarded the ship at Singapore with
her entourage — ". . . a Juno of a woman", he described her as, ". . . with
the physique of a ploughman, a great broad face, and eyes very wide
apart. She walks into a room as a dreadnought steams into a harbour,
followed by a fleet of smaller vessels in the shape of sycophants and
hangers on".[12] She asked Paterson to write a song or two for her; he was
more amused than flattered, and described sardonically the language and
behaviour of her Cockney retinue.

In London at the beginning of November he was welcomed with open
arms by his old friend Phil May. Here Paterson had a brief and glorious
introduction to Bohemia. There were stage-plays and musical shows in
the West End (the theatrical profession, as Paterson recalled, regarded
May as a sort of Aladdin) ; late-night restaurant suppers where May introduced him to many London celebrities (May's caricatures on the backs
of menus were in great demand) ; pub-crawls with May and his bulldog,
his proudest possession. Paterson has left a magnificent account of this
eccentricity:

> Americans who recognized him by his portraits would introduce
> themselves and say:
>   "Ah must have a drink with Mr Phil May."
>   While I was arguing the point, and saying that he did not want
> any more drinks, the bulldog would brush against somebody's leg;
> the owner of the leg, looking down into the cavern of ivory and red
> flesh which the bulldog called a mouth, would go faint all over.
> Then there would have to be drinks to bring this man round, and to
> insure the others against a similar collapse. After a couple of hours
> of this, Phil would call a cab and say:
>   "Take this dog home to St John's Wood for me, will you?"
>   The dog loved riding in cabs, and evidently had the idea that
> when he entered a cab he bought it; for if there happened to be
> nobody at home when he arrived there, he would refuse to leave the
> cab and the cabman had to sit on the box and wait, perhaps for an
> hour or two, until Mrs May came home. No wonder that Phil was
> chronically hard-up![13]

Paterson became an honoured guest at the National Sporting Club,
where he met again a sporting celebrity of the time in Bob Beresford,
whom he had known in South Africa — a Queensberry Cup winner, a
champion billiards player, and said to be one of the best pigeon-shots in
the world. He and Paterson got on famously. Paterson was invited to the
Junior Carlton and also to the Yorick Club, where he was asked to speak
and brought down the house by reciting his lines, "Lay of the Motor Car",
especially written for the occasion:

> We're away! and the wind whistles shrewd
>   In our whiskers and teeth;
> And the granite-like grey of the road
>   Seems to slide underneath.
> As an eagle might sweep through the sky,
>   So we sweep through the land;
> And the pallid pedestrians fly
>   When they hear us at hand.
>
> We outpace, we outlast, we outstrip!
>   Not the fast-fleeing hare,
> Not the racehorses under the whip,
>   Nor the birds of the air
> Can compete with our swiftness sublime,
>   Our ease and our grace.
> We annihilate chickens and time
>   And policemen and space . . .

Still keen to advance his career in journalism, Paterson wrote to *The Times* and was granted an interview; a "very severe ordeal" he found it, satirically recalling that a haughty menial piloted him around the whole building — apparently the rules did not allow of anyone going straight up and down the stairs by the quickest route. But he was elated by the outcome of his interview, and wrote off to George Robertson[14] in Sydney:

> 1 King St.,
> St James Square,
> London.
> 28 Nov. '01.

Dear Robertson,
   I am to be appointed Australian correspondent for the Times; the matter is now in course of arrangement and unless the show bursts up I am sure of it. The Times work very slowly I can assure you: this will give me a good position to try and put some new ideas about Australia into the heads of these English who are quite in the dark about us and our ideas. Their one idea is that the visit of the Duke of York "marked an epoch in the history of Australia". I longed to say, "Yes, he got nearly as big a reception as Bill Beach, the sculler", but I would have been fired forthwith. I am very "down" over being blocked in Siberia and if it were not for the Times job I would try to hang on till the ice melts and go back that way, but as it is I must get back soon—that is if the thing doesn't fall through . . .

Alas, the thing *did* "fall through", and it was one of Paterson's keenest disappointments; having worked, even if briefly, for Reuter's, he would have valued a *Times* job to the same degree as any dedicated newspaperman of his day. It was rather an anti-climax that the only London newspaper where he was able to get contributions accepted was the *Pink 'Un*.
   But as his letter to Robertson implied, London and its people rather

baffled Paterson, though he could not but admire their serene self-complacency. Even their fogs were a mark of superiority: ". . . this awful yellow shroud choked everything . . .", Paterson wrote in another letter back from London in December 1901,[15] ". . . and yet, talking it over with an English bus driver next morning he said with the greatest pride, 'Ah! You don't see fogs like that in no other part of the world. . . .' " And as the bus driver boasted of the skill of his fellow-drivers in the fog, Paterson "thought of various little bits of driving that I had seen some of Cobb and Co.'s men do on dark nights with unbroken horses in very broken country; but I didn't try to tell the busman about them". He found remarkable the apathy of the average Londoner to momentous public affairs, and realized, as he had in South Africa, that this was brought about by the contemptuous disregard for the public interest by those in power. He wrote:

> England and Australia are the two extremes in political matters. Here a general may half wreck an Empire and no one does anything; with us if a sergeant of Volunteers is disrated for drunkenness there is a Labour member to demand a special committee of the House to inquire into it. Those are the two systems and each has its drawbacks. You pay your money and don't have any choice.

It is interesting, too, to recall Paterson's observations on the Australian expatriates in London; times have not significantly changed even in sixty years. Australian artists, he noted, arrived in London and grimly set to work for any money they could get. Most of them got steady work out of it; a few reached the top, like Melba, Ada Crossley, Florence Schmidt, always ready nevertheless to give a helping hand to their struggling countrywomen. It was one of the greatest fascinations of London life, Paterson felt (as many have since), that everyone has a chance, since everyone is treated alike with indifference and there is no royal road to success. Nor have Australians in London changed much since Paterson's time. He wrote:

> We get good fun out of meeting men from other parts of the world sometimes; each gets telling the other about the place he comes from, and before long each tries to outdo the other in stories. The latest is that an Australian and an Indian met at a club, and the talk was on grass. "Grass? my dear fellow," said the Indian, "I've positively seen grass so high and thick that the elephants couldn't force their way through it. Positively, couldn't get along, I assure you." The Australian drew at his pipe for one second and then said in a hushed voice, "Would you mind changing the subject? Ever since I was out in the Territory (pause) — and a blade of grass fell on a friend of mine and killed him — I hate talking about grass."[16]

But the event Paterson most looked forward to during his visit to England was his stay with Kipling, since he was about to take up the invitation Kipling had extended him in South Africa. Paterson found him living in "an unpretentious house at Rottingdean, Brighton" and was made very welcome by Kipling and his American-born wife. Kipling insisted on two or three hours of work a day and let nothing, not even Paterson, interfere with that, but thereafter gave his full time to conversations with and the entertainment of his guest. This included a drive in a new Lanchester car he had just had delivered, which intrigued Paterson enormously. "Out we went, scattering tourists right and left, and away over the Sussex downs . . ."[17] In the course of his stay he found out that Kipling hated publicity: ". . . in private life he was just a hard-working commonsense, level-headed man, without any redeeming vices . . . less of a quack, less of a showman, and less of a time-server than any public man I ever met."[18] They talked a good deal about writing and the subject-matter of writing. Kipling was writing some lines on Australia in which he mentioned a "fruit-farm on Hunter's River . . ."; Paterson told him fruit-farms in Australia were "orchards", and gave him the correct form of "Hunter River". Nor did he hold it against Kipling that he once described the Maribyrnong Plate as a steeplechase. As a horseman Paterson admired the lines from "Ballad of East and West":

> The dun he leaned against the bit and slugged his head above,
> But the red mare played with the snaffle-bars, as a maiden plays with
>   a glove.

It was the very picture of the way horses galloped, and he asked Kipling, since he was not a horseman, how he could have managed to write such convincing lines. Kipling replied that it was "observation": that he must have noticed the action of horses without knowing that he noticed it. Paterson was also intrigued to know how he had come to write *Kim* with its mass of material and detail:

> "Oh," he said, "the material was just lying about there in heaps. All
> I had to do was to take it and fit it together. . . ."[19]

But Paterson came to admire and respect Kipling most of all for his unswerving devotion to the cause of Empire. While Paterson did not go along with this — he felt that Australians would always put Australia first ". . . and that the young Africans did not care a hoot about the Dutch — they were Afrikanders first, last and all the time . . ." — he nevertheless admitted that Kipling's was "the large view".[20]

Paterson cherished all his life these brief experiences in London, and thirteen years later, with much more confidence, made this city the base for a more comprehensive look at life in the British Isles. But in the meantime the holiday was over —

> The London lights are far abeam
>   Behind a bank of cloud,
> Along the shore the gaslights gleam,
>   The gale is piping loud;
> And down the Channel, groping blind,

We drive her through the haze
Towards the land we left behind —
The good old land of "never mind",
And old Australian ways.

— and he arrived back in Sydney in April 1902. His first move was to
confer with his publishers, Angus & Robertson, about the issue of a second
book of verse later in the year; he also took up the threads of his journalistic career again, and in May travelled up to Coonamble, in northern
New South Wales, and the surrounding districts to cover a shearing strike
there for the *Sydney Morning Herald*. But another major adventure was
round the corner. When he returned to Sydney Sir James Burns, of the
trading firm of Burns, Philp & Co., one of the largest companies of its type
in the Southern Hemisphere, asked Paterson to call and see him. Paterson
has left a memorable description of Sir James ("as near to an Empire
builder as we ever saw in these parts . . .") and the early operations of
his firm,

> A thin and austere Scotsman of the old son-of-the-manse type, few
> people would have taken him for what he was — an outstanding
> financial genius.
>   The great O'Sullivan might toss missions about with the abandon
> of an elephant throwing hay; but James Burns risked his company's
> money, and his own, in ventures which required a lot of pluck and
> a lot of foresight. They were merchants, ship-owners, island traders,
> and graziers; putting the firm's money behind settlers away up on
> the Queensland rivers where they were liable to be scuppered by
> blacks at any time; financing storekeepers in little one-pub towns,
> where these storekeepers found grubstakes for prospectors and
> miners; sending their vessels to the islands where no boat's crew
> dared land unless the bow-man had a loaded rifle; running small
> steamers to places where there were no wharves, and the boat just
> tied up alongside the bank. Anywhere that there was a risk to be run
> and money to be made you would see the flag of James Burns. If he
> had been dealing in diamonds instead of copra and bananas, he
> might have been another Cecil Rhodes's understudy . . .[21]

It appeared that Burns, Philp & Co. had taken over the affairs of a
Scottish company which had pioneered settlement in the New Hebrides
Islands; in addition, the company had bought thousands of acres from
the natives, paying the chiefs in trade goods. But since France had a joint
interest in the islands, French investors had bought land too, in some
cases from the same native chiefs. All sorts of conflicts arose — conflicts
about boundaries, prior rights of purchase, the rights of the native chiefs
to sell the land — nor could the French and English holders even agree on
the setting up of a court to settle their differences. With some of the
richest land waiting to be occupied, no one dared spend any money — for
equipment, planting or to build permanently. Some of the land claimed
by both sides was inhabited by natives so fierce that only armed parties

dared go ashore. Sir James explained to Paterson that his firm had decided that the man in possession would have the best chance of getting the land, and it had called for volunteers to settle in the New Hebrides — offering them the land free. He invited Paterson to accompany this group as a watchdog and reporter; and since, in Paterson's words, it "promised some adventure", he agreed to go, with these "Australian Pilgrim Fathers" or "Argonauts in search of the Golden Cocoanut", as he later on ironically referred to them.

Paterson's account,* based on extracts from a diary he kept, is in itself a fascinating if little known chapter in our history:

> *May 31 1902.* I join the Australian argonauts in their search for the land of the golden cocoa-nut. They are the genuine article all right — hard-handed anxious-faced men — shearers, mechanics, miners, farmers, prospectors, out-back men, and a few born wanderers never happy unless they are on the move. In all Australian black tribes there were men who would not stop in camp, but would "go walk-about" as they called it, visiting other tribes and sometimes going hundreds of miles. They very often got a spear through them, and they invariably had a bad time but they saw the world. A lot of these settlers were like walk-about blacks and if a new venture were started at the North Pole they would be off to it. One man was asked why he joined the expedition and he said "We only had six inches of rain on our farm last year, so I am leaving my brother to stand off the Bank Manager while I go down to see what this place is like."

At Norfolk Island the settlers saw for the first time tropic abundance, so much so that some of them were inclined to stop there and not go on. Why should they kill themselves working? Here was fifty inches of rain a year and every kind of fruit and vegetable. But Paterson, the humourist, remembers drily a dentist he met there:

> "Nobody is properly awake in Norfolk Island until about twelve o'clock," he said, "not even the horses. If you want to go for a ride you prod your horse with a nail in the end of a bit of board until he wiggles his upper lip. Then you know that he is awake and can safely be mounted . . ." This dentist showed them several scars in his arm which he said had been made by sticking a knife into himself in Norfolk Island to find out whether he were dead or alive.

Indeed, Paterson extracted as much humour from the situation as he could; there was his recollection of the tough character who had been a sleeper-cutter on the Johnston River in Queensland and was not worried about the humidity of the climate: he told how he and his mate used to wrap their matches in flannel and put them in a little bottle, then wrap that bottle in flannel and put it in a pickle bottle, then put the pickle bottle in their coats — and the matches were still wet. "Bring on the humidity," he said.

* This and the following accounts were quoted by Paterson in two scripts, "The Pioneers", written for broadcasting by the A.B.C. in 1935, hitherto unpublished.

Arrived at the New Hebrides, the settlers were immediately captivated by the richness of the country, with its crops of cocoanuts, bananas, maize, coffee and spices. They found missionaries devoted to their work among the natives, traders hanging on precariously at outlying stations, settlers, both French and English, cultivating their lush crops against the wild growth that threatened constantly to engulf them, and against the unpredictable natives alternating between friendship and hostility. Paterson found a curious parallel in the experiences of the American Pilgrim Fathers confronted by cunning and treacherous Indians, and in the trouble with land titles that was the lot of the Dutch pioneers settled on the land that is now New York, who discovered that Charles II of England had already presented the land to his brother James of York.

Paterson conceived great admiration for the missionaries. He wrote:

> The British missionaries were all Scotch . . . hard, black Scotch, with short teeth; combative Scotch, fighting the black man's battle all the time. Most of them held medical degrees as well as their degrees in Divinity; and the healing of the flesh took up the greater part of their time. . . . these Scotch never let go their grip. They physicked and drenched and operated and preached, day in and day out, in a climate where their own children sometimes developed malaria before they were a couple of months old. It was the same with the French missionaries who concentrated on trying to save the children . . .

And he was utterly delighted at the spectacle of children of five and six acting as interpreters between grown men: the missionaries' children learned the local language from their native nurses faster than their fathers could learn it.

The French and Australian immigrants adjusted to each other quite amicably. They visited a newly-arrived French settler who, with his wife, was hacking out his plantation in the most primitive surroundings, and shared with him his Spartan meal; they visited another French planter who had after many years achieved prosperity. Dressed in a suit of pyjamas and a solar topee:

> . . . he took the settlers to a ten-roomed house, with cool deep verandahs, sheltered by climbing roses; he sat them down in lounge-chairs before an assortment of liquors undreamed of in their philosophy; and at intervals he roared French marching songs or played, impartially, French and English records on a gramophone.

This, recorded Paterson, was all the incentive the Australians needed:

> Anything that could be done by a middle-aged Frenchman with a slightly protuberant outline could surely be done by these hard-handed men who had milked cows and shorn sheep and watched over travelling mobs of cattle on the dry stages of the outback. They decided to finish the inspection of their own land next day and then

to draw lots for the choice of blocks. "I never knew that Frenchies were like that," said one man; "I always thought that they lived on cigarettes and absinthe and that hard work was a stranger to them. Fancy sixty bushels of maize to the acre — that's fifteen bags at five bob a bag and three crops a year; that's eleven pound five a year per acre from maize and this Frenchman says it doesn't interfere with the cocoanuts for two years. It'll do us!"

... they saw the future through a mist of French liqueurs. They were prepared to live on bananas, bread-fruit, fish and the flesh of wild pigs, until their returns came in. One man suggested that he would sell the rights of shooting wild pigs on his estate to sportsmen from Sydney ...

Paterson returned to Australia after a couple of months and reported to Sir James Burns that the settlers seemed certain to make a success of the venture. As it turned out, however, his optimism was premature. After some years, tariff barriers set up by a number of countries destroyed export markets; the settlers were left with their copra and maize which nobody seemed to want. Paterson's 1935 postscript read as follows:

Some of the settlers came home; others went in for trading or beche-de-mer fishing; others are still there, hoping that the pendulum will swing back again; but they are old men now and if any great reward should ever come to this venture it will come to the younger generation. So we may leave this little side-line of our history, saying only that though these men failed to command success, at any rate they deserved it.

Paterson was asked to undertake some further lecturing on the Boer War in the latter months of 1902, and during a visit to the New South Wales town of Tenterfield, he met and fell in love with Alice Walker, the daughter of a local grazier. (His previous engagement to Sarah Riley had petered out after seven years.) With marriage ahead of him, and a more settled career in journalism offering, Paterson's days of wandering were over.

NOTES

[1] In *Bohemians of the Bulletin* (1965).
[2] In *Happy Dispatches* (1935).
[3] In a letter to the *Sydney Morning Herald*, 18 April 1931.
[4] Ibid.
[5] Ibid.
[6] In a letter to the *Sydney Morning Herald*, 21 January 1931.
[7] In *Happy Dispatches*.
[8] Ibid.
[9] Ibid.
[10] Ibid., for this and previous quotations.
[11] Ibid.
[12] Ibid.
[13] Ibid.

[14] Letter in the Mitchell Library, Sydney.
[15] In the *Sydney Morning Herald*, 20 January 1902.
[16] Ibid.
[17] In *Happy Dispatches*.
[18] Ibid.
[19] Ibid.
[20] Ibid.
[21] In his *Sydney Morning Herald* reminiscences.

CHAPTER XII

From Sydney to the Bush

. . . a good news-hound, a man with a nose for news, may not show his head above ground very much, but few lives are more interesting . . .

— A. B. PATERSON.[1]

Here in my mountain home
On rugged hills and steep

— A. B. PATERSON.

PATERSON, ACCORDING TO George Robertson of Angus & Robertson, his publishers, was somewhat apprehensive about the selection of ballads for his second collection, *Rio Grande's Last Race and Other Verses*, published in 1902. A letter[2] from Robertson, undated, but obviously written just before the verses were published, makes this clear:

HALSTEAD

BLACKHEATH.

Friday night.

Dear Thomson,

ABP seems unhappy about "Rio Grande" and asked me whether I could suggest someone to run through the proofs with an eye to rejection of unworthy pieces. I have given the matter some thought in the train and can think of no one more fit than MacCallum. In order to prevent loss of time — MacCallum would do the work on Saturday and Sunday — I scribble this against time. I take it that ABP wishes independent judgment brought to bear on the job — that of someone capable of steering between his own forebodings and his publishers' natural wish to make a fat 5/- volume. He ought to be perfectly satisfied if nothing below the standard of Snowy River goes in — I don't mean below the highest standard in Snowy, but generally speaking. MacCallum knows the Snowy book well, he knows what the reviews praised and blamed, and he has a good idea of what the general public approved in it. Ask him to take the proofs and size up the various pieces with reference to the Snowy standard — and let you have them on Monday. 42p. job I am afraid. M. has considerable knowledge of technique (an opinion isn't considered worth a damn unless this word is dragged in) and if he will only remember that Paterson isn't, never will be and isn't wanted (by either the Public to whom he appeals or his Publishers) to be a Keats or a Milton he'll do it all right. The only question he has to answer about each "pome" is — Is it as good as the poorest piece of the same sort in Snowy River. Some, we know, are quite as good and if nothing poorer than the poorest Snowy gets in it will be all right.

I could write all night but the driver is waiting to take this to post.

Yours faithfully,

(Sgd.)   G.   R.

Show this to Paterson & MacCallum if you like — I mean the W.S. & Co. man — not the Professor of course. Curiously enough both Jose and MacCallum thought very little of Snowy when it was passing through to the press. Jose preferred Dyson! But they were wrong because ABP has gained not only cash but fame by the book. You have to think of the people you are appealing to — and it isn't the Keats crowd.

Paterson's doubts were groundless, as it turned out, since the volume had almost as enthusiastic a response as *The Man From Snowy River*; the first edition sold very quickly, subsequent printings were rushed and the returned wanderer had another success on his hands. Two of Paterson's best known characters, Salt Bush Bill ("Saltbush Bill's Gamecock" and "Saltbush Bill's Second Fight") and Mulga Bill, appeared in this volume; it also included much of the verse Paterson had written as a result of his experiences in the past few years: "With French to Kimberley", "The Scottish Engineer", "By the Grey Gulf Water", "The Pearl Diver", and the ballad "Song of the Artesian Water" inspired perhaps by Kipling's admiration of the line "Till I drink artesian water from a thousand feet below" in "A Bushman's Song".

But it's hark! the whistle's blowing with a wild, exultant blast,
And the boys are madly cheering, for they've struck the flow at last;
And it's rushing up the tubing from four thousand feet below
Till it spouts above the casing in a million-gallon flow.
     And it's down, deeper down —
     Oh, it comes from deeper down;
It is flowing, ever flowing, in a free, unstinted measure
From the silent hidden places where the old earth hides her treasure—
Where the old earth hides her treasures deeper down.

Australian newspapers and journals praised lavishly in their reviews; there was an approving nod from A. G. Stephens;[*] but it is perhaps more interesting to look at the opinions of a responsible English journal, the *Athenaeum*:[3]

---

[*] ". . . But it is in the old alliance of humour and horse that Paterson is most successful. No other local writer can get such twinkling, genial fun from the play of fancy over four hoofs and a hide — the Australian microcosm . . ." (*Bulletin*, 27 December 1902.)

The majority of the pieces are vigorous bits of verse journalism, transcripts of racecourse humour, episodes of life in the backwoods [sic] . . . They invariably lay more stress upon the content of a story than upon the way in which it is told . . . The literary tradition has only filtered to them through the irregular channel of Mr Kipling. Occasionally however Mr Paterson endeavours a higher flight and interprets to us the heart and temper and not merely the local colour of

> The land where the kangaroo
> Barks loud at dawn and the white-eyed crow
> Uplifts his song on the stockyard fence
> As he watches the lambkins passing hence . . .

It is the Australia of the second generation. Mr Paterson is no exile singing the song of nostalgia . . . he is the free man of the free Commonwealth, conscious, not without pride, of filling his own place, and no mean place in the order of things. He is an Anglo-Saxon, but no longer an Anglo-Saxon out of joint . . .

Nor was he an Australian out of joint. He soon caught up in Sydney with his former interests, especially horse-riding, and with his closer acquaintances. Norman Lindsay, who first got to know him about this time and saw a good deal of him, doubted if Paterson was ever really an intimate friend of anyone — he seemed to have little use for "confidential exchanges of a personal nature". Lindsay has recorded this trait of Paterson at the time:

> . . . he rarely bothered to put [his] acceptance or rejection of you into words, though he did that incisively enough by the casual glance which either accepted you or dismissed you. He spoke slowly, with a slight drawl, which had a saturnine inflection. Saturnine is another definitive label which must be added to his portrait. Every line in his dark-textured face defined it.[4]

Paterson seldom unbent even within his own circle of writers and artists.* Norman Lindsay recalled the occasion about this time when Steele Rudd made his first visit from Queensland to Sydney, by this time an established author. His fellow-writers gave him a dinner of welcome at the Paris House, with Paterson in the chair. The latter made a short conventional speech of welcome, and left as soon as the dinner was over. "His departure from the dinner," wrote Lindsay, "relieved it of tension, and we sat on till late over the wine . . .".[5] It was an interesting contrast in a number of ways:

> . . . Well, Steele Rudd was the opposite sort of bushman to Banjo. Banjo was squattocracy, he came from a class with a definite class distinction. Steele was typical cocky farmer. Slow drawl you know; "I

---

*Nevertheless it should be recorded that Paterson was not lacking in charity towards his fellow-writers; apart from his assistance to Lawson, previously noted, he was one of the organizers of the Victor Daley Testimonial Fund launched in April 1903. He served on a committee with J. F. Archibald, A. G. Stephens, J. C. Williamson, D. H. Souter, Roderic Quinn and others.

don't know as if one horse is better than another. A little brown horse you know, bushmen think most of little brown horses and white horses are pretty safe" — that's the way he talked, but Banjo's talk was crisp, clean and precise . . .[6]

Paterson was married early in April 1903 to Alice Walker at Tenterfield.† His marriage was destined to be a completely happy and harmonious one. His wife, much younger than he, is remembered as a quiet and charming woman, a splendid horsewoman and sportswoman (she was an accomplished tennis player) , who shared many of Paterson's interests. They made their home in Sydney, for Paterson had now been appointed to a responsible and important position in the city newspaper world — the editorship of the *Evening News*.

The *Westminster Gazette* reported on 28 February 1903:

> The *Sydney Evening News* of which the leading Australian poet Mr A. B. Paterson has just been appointed editor is a flourishing journalistic property which sprang from the ashes of the *Empire*, the ambitious Sydney morning paper founded and edited for some years by the late Sir Henry Parkes. The *Empire* was a success in the literary sense but succumbed to bad business management . . .

Paterson in fact took over the editorship at the beginning of January of that year. In a sense his stars had already strangely crossed with those of this newspaper and its antecedents. Mr Justice Windeyer had clashed violently with the *Evening News* during the 1880s when the newspaper had campaigned against him — and the Windeyers were close friends of Mrs Emily Barton, and Paterson as a youth had met them on many occasions. And Paterson had also known Sir Henry Parkes, of whom he left this vignette:[7]

> Sir Henry Parkes, with his mane of silvery hair and his Nestorian beard, adopted the role of the aloof potentate; in the argot of the prize-ring, he let the other fellow do the leading, and then countered him heavily.
>
> It is said that a field-marshal in war cannot afford to have any friends, and Parkes was a field-marshal, plus. Not but what he could relax on occasion, but always in an aloof, Jupiterish sort of way. I

† The Presbyterian Church at Tenterfield was filled with people from the surrounding parts of the district on 8 April, all anxious to witness the marriage of Mr A. B. Paterson to Miss Alice Walker, eldest unmarried daughter of the late Mr W. H. Walker of Tenterfield Station. The ceremony was performed by the Rev. Richard Dill Macky. Miss Bessie Walker was the only bridesmaid and Mr W. H. Kelly acted as best man. After the ceremony a few intimate friends of the house party were entertained at the Homestead where a large number of the employees and their families had gathered in order to present the bride with a silver salver. On behalf of the bride the bridegroom returned thanks in a few well-chosen words. The interior of the church was tastefully decorated for the occasion by the employees of the station many of whom had known Miss Walker since childhood. Among those present were Miss Edith Walker, Miss Nesta Drury (Brisbane) , Mr & Mrs F. W. Everett, Mrs Jeffreys, Miss May Walker, and the Messrs. Tom, Lionel and Wallace Walker. Mr and Mrs Paterson left later in the day for Bombala and the southern mountains where the honeymoon is to be passed." (*Evening News*, 10 April 1903.)

remember seeing him at a public dinner when the waiter poured him out a glass of champagne from a full bottle, and then moved off with it.

"Leave that bottle," said the statesman, who always got the temperance vote, "I'll finish that and probably another after it."

The old man never had any money, though goodness knows he had opportunities enough of getting it "on the side" had he been so minded. On various occasions he came into the lawyer's office where I was employed always full of dignity, in a frock coat and a tall hat, to discuss his pecuniary complications. But personal finance bored him. He despised money; he was Sir Henry Parkes . . .

The *Evening News* had been founded on 29 July 1867 by Samuel Bennett, a vigorous and single-minded newspaper proprietor who was one of the forerunners of the dynamic if unpredictable press barons who have variously distinguished Australian journalism. As a young Cornishman he had emigrated to Australia in 1841 after having, as a printing apprentice and journeyman, become expert in most aspects of publishing. He worked in the printing office of the *Sydney Morning Herald* for seventeen years, and realized his dream of owning a newspaper when Parkes's *Empire* (a daily newspaper he had begun in 1850) came on the market in 1858, and Bennett became its sole proprietor. For several years he ran it as editor and leader-writer: he specialized in research articles on the early history of the Colony, and, indeed, these were collected together and published as *A History of Australian Discovery and Colonization*, in a volume of 661 pages. But he had become obsessed with the idea of introducing an evening paper to Sydney (the first evening paper in England had appeared only a few years before Bennett began his), and in 1867 he launched the paper with an initial circulation of 2,000.*

The venture prospered. He declared that the aim of his new paper was "to be true to those principles of liberalism of which Sir Henry Parkes was so distinguished an exponent. It turned neither to conservatism on the right nor to socialism on the left. It was neither reactionary nor revolutionary. It stood for the right of every man to work out his own salvation with the least possible interference from the Government or bodies of men."[8]

Paterson, historically, was in distinguished company. James Hogue, who was Bennett's first editor, was a brilliant polemicist and leader-writer who entered the New South Wales Parliament as the Member for Glebe, and eventually became Minister for Education. C. E. Dekker, who succeeded him in 1895, and was Paterson's immediate predecessor, had been trained in England, and was an authority on foreign affairs. Some notable journalists were associated with the newspaper after Paterson. Walter Jeffery, a sailor who had served both in the navy and merchant service and later became a lighthouse-keeper, fireman, farmer and coal-miner, specialized in early Australian naval history and left much material for researchers in subsequent years. He also collaborated with Louis Becke in writing the novel *The Mutineer*. H. E. Taperell was a witty and ironical

* The newspaper lasted until March 1931.

journalist; E. G. Knox had a brilliant military career with the A.I.F. in the First World War, and emerged as a major on the General Staff of the Air Force.

Paterson was none of these things; he was "the poet, whose Pegasus found himself in a strange pound . . .",[9] the master of the destinies of an eight-page, folio-sized penny newspaper, with a comfortable supremacy in sales and advertising over its only competitor, the *Star*. "*The Evening News*," writes a press historian of the newspaper in these years, "supplied the rapes and garrottings, but not enough of them."[10] This was probably true, as a glance at the headlines during the month (January) that Paterson took over will show: "Youth's Horrible Death"; "Awful Accident"; "Shocking Discovery at Belmore"; "Beat His Wife with a Shovel"; "Garrotted in Erskine St."; "Hanged Himself in a Stable"; "Madman in Chains"; "Maimed for Life"; "An Eye Taken Out"; "Shot Himself at 77" (they in fact covered news stories culled from remote parts of the world as well as from Australia). The style of the reporting can be gauged from the account of the execution of one Patrick Kenniff, a Brisbane murderer:

> . . . the body was lowered into a handsome cedar coffin elaborately silver-mounted. The authorities had granted permission to the father of the prisoner to hold a private funeral, and accordingly the old man and his friends had provided this gorgeous coffin . . .[11]

The format of the newspaper was stereotyped. Advertisements covered the front and back pages. Page 4 featured three or four short pithy leaders, usually heavily political; they were written to a set pattern — so much so that a contemporary has recalled that the leader-writers (there were three of them) were usually out of the office by 10 a.m. Page 5 had a regular column "To-day's Divorces". On Saturdays a special four-page supplement presented, in a rather scrappy magazine form, such regular features as "Stageland", "Recent Publications", "Social Items", etc. As for news proper, it was generally a one-story issue; the star reporter was Tom Spencer, who was invariably given the day's biggest news break to cover. (He was the son of Thomas E. Spencer, who wrote that recitative *pièce de résistance* of most bush concerts, "How McDougal Topped the Score".)

Yet, despite his inexperience, and although he did not change materially the format of the paper nor its policy of sensationalism in news and headline presentation, Paterson made a number of notable improvements and extended the paper's readability. He revamped the Saturday supplement, introducing a series of articles on Australian wild-life (always one of his particular interests) by Edward Sorensen; a weekly cartoon by Taylor, "Horrors of the Backblocks" (a nervous gentlemen dressed in a jockey's costume with the legend "Mr Podger will recite 'How we Beat the Favourite'"; an untidy backblocks pub-keeper knocking on a door with a boot, "Say Boss, was it you I had ter wake at 5 o'clock?"); a weekly article, "Tales of Far Countries by Men Who Have Been There"; a regular budget of military news under the title "Khaki Column". As a magazine section, it was improved out of sight.

As for the paper generally, his best-remembered contribution was to persuade Lionel Lindsay to join the staff as its political cartoonist, or, as he was referred to in those days, "our special artist"; there were thus two such cartoonists in the Sydney daily press, since Hal Eyre was similarly employed by the *Daily Telegraph*. At one stage, too, Lindsay ran an amusing series of drawings, "Places I Have Never Visited". He portrayed Rome as seven hills, on each of which was a barrel-organist, complete with monkey, grinding away at his tunes. (This greatly annoyed the Sydney artist and Garibaldian Dattilo Rubbo, who challenged Lindsay to a duel.)

Paterson gave some rein to his own interests. He turned page 2 into a full sporting page, covering most sports, but always with pride of place to horse-racing. ("Randwick Track Notes" continued to have its special place on the leader page.) He also ran a campaign for drought relief during 1903, which brought in nearly £10,000 — a considerable sum in those days. He did not, except on very rare occasions, write articles with his own by-line. But quite frequently the Patersonian hand was discernible. An article on "The Duties of Racing Stewards", another on "The Death of Gilbert the Bushranger", with some personal anecdotes of the Binalong district, were distinctly Paterson's in style. When the news was received at the end of March 1903 of General Sir Hector McDonald's suicide, a "Personal Recollection" was quite clearly Paterson's, since, as he later recorded in *Happy Dispatches*, he had greatly admired the General in South Africa.* "South Africa is called the grave of military reputations," said this *Evening News* article, "but it added to that of McDonald". It was also recalled that Sir Hector had visited Sydney towards the end of 1901 and had won the affection of leading people of the city. Again, there was an article[12] commenting on the action of General Hutton in Melbourne, who, resenting some press criticism, hailed before him the offending editor of the Melbourne paper concerned, and ceremoniously "dismissed him from his gilded eminence as a colonel of volunteers". Quite obviously it was Paterson, writing as an editor, a war correspondent and a satirist of British Brass Hats (as in "A War Office in Trouble"), who commented that the sensitiveness of a British General to press criticism was a subject for psychologists. "Put him on a battlefield with a pair of crossed swords on his shoulders, and his field glasses in his hand, and lo he walks undismayed among the shot and shell — he laughs at the Boer pom-pom; but print any criticism of his administration and he makes the welkin ring with his squeals of dismay and anger."

As for the occasional contributions under his own name, the best example, and one which he clearly most enjoyed, appeared soon after he took over the editorship of the paper, when "Chinese" Morrison, whom Paterson so much admired, paid a visit to Australia. Under the heading of "Dr Morrison: A Notable Australian: Some Personal Details", and his

---

* In a despatch to the *Sydney Morning Herald* (12 May 1900) from South Africa, Paterson wrote of McDonald: ". . . He is quite young-looking, pleasant-faced, with quick eyes and a mobile mouth and a general expression of light-heartedness — a man with a regular devil-may-care look in his eye, a man who looked as if he would fight a policeman on his way from dinner and think nothing of it . . ."

own name as author, Paterson began:[13] ". . . It is necessary to visit China itself to get any clear idea of the responsibilities and difficulties of Dr Morrison's position . . .", and then outlined the international position, and the astonishing trade growth, even from the few treaty ports; the American, German, French, British and Japanese involvement; and the activities of the restless crowds of adventurers. Paterson continued:

> There are rumours, lies, threats, open violence to be encountered, and among this tumult and strife there moves one man to whose knowledge all white men — Russian, American, German and Jew alike — defer, Morrison, the Australian who represents the *Times* in China . . .
>
> Dr Morrison lives for the most part in Pekin where he is in touch with the best informed Chinese circles. But he moves constantly about, travelling in men-of-war, on tramp steamers, on mule-litters, on pony-back, or on his feet as occasion demands. He is a powerful, wiry man of solid and imposing presence, and those who know him best in China say he has mastered the secret of all Chinese diplomacy — bluff. In China you must "save your face", i.e., preserve your dignity at all costs. He never allows any Chinaman however important to assume for a moment that he (the Chinaman) is in any way the equal of the *Times* correspondent in China. He has been known, so his friends say, to pull a Chinese mandarin out of his chair of state and seat himself in it, in order to impress upon that Chinese and his friends the transcendental amount of "face" possessed by the *Times* correspondent. For the rest, a keen knowledge of men, a gift of diplomacy and a dogged Scotch persistency, pull him through his difficulty . . .

Paterson concluded his article with a fine sweep:

> Dr Morrison's movements are timed to take him back to China in the Spring, when the gentle Chinese and the Russian and the Manchu awaken from their winter sleep and resume their game of swapping concessions and privileges; when the German starts to undersell his English competitor, and the river highways teem with human life, and the fishing junks go out to sea from Swatow in a cluster as thick as sailing boats at a Balmain Regatta. China is the theatre of the world's chief performance of the next few years, and we may watch the unfolding of the drama with added interest from the fact that the man who is to tell us most about it is an Australian.

As for Paterson in his role of working editor, one of the most memorable recollections is that of Claude McKay, who worked as a casual journalist on the *Evening News* at the time, and recalls Paterson in his "office lean and dingy", with a roller-top desk taking up most of the space in it, the pigeon-holes crammed with odds and ends of letters and clippings, ". . . the writing surface of his desk littered high with old proof sheets, out of date newspapers opened and unopened leaving him little elbow-room at his near-submerged writing blotter-pad."[14] Paterson hated being left to himself; most visitors were treated like long-lost brothers as the editor settled back comfortably for a yarn; thrice-welcomed was the outback visitor with his cattle-dog — and usually the dog sized up the situation by curling up and going to sleep. Walter Jeffery was, in those years, general manager of the newspaper (passing his time, says McKay, reading Conrad and writing of the sea). At peak-hours and times of great urgency, Jeffery and Paterson invariably escaped into some remote office corner, "exchanging confidences of far horizons — of sunlit plains extended and palm-fringed South Sea Islands".[15]

Paterson found that the editorship of an evening paper had its ups and downs; furthermore, his competitors were not slow to seize on his short-comings — he was referred to as "the man from Joey River", and his newspaper as the "Snooze". On one occasion he reported a football match and the "ferocious" and "ruffian" doings of one "Bull" Joyce, a star Glebe player. According to the *Star*,[16] a deputation of indignant Glebeites

> . . . burst into his sanctum. Professional esprit de corps prevents us referring to what transpired in the editorial holy of holies — the fire escape successfully negotiated at the rear of the building is sufficient to show that things were sultry for a time. Thursday's issue of the "Snooze" contained a very ingenious apology to the outraged footballers . . .

On a later occasion the *Daily Telegraph*[17] made capital out of trouble Paterson experienced with the Italian community because of an allegedly insulting cartoon.

> All the Dagos in the metropolitan area are after his scalp in conse-quence. In Thursday's issue of the "Snooze" Banjoey rises to explain that it was only a joke. "A sense of humour does not seem to be characteristic of the Italian people", claims the plaintive humourist. The famous Banjoey himself is not an Italian. His frozen humour, however, is characteristic of imitation hokey-pokey compounded from the mountain snows amongst which he sought his saddened inspiration.

Paterson was greatly loved by the *Evening News* staff. And casual con-tributors, paid by the line, were grateful that he had begun life as a lawyer, since he marked contributions for payment with a professional fee: a paragraph, 3/4; a short cross-head, 6/8; half a column, half a guinea; a column, a guinea. Most appreciated, however, was his sense of humour and his kindliness to his colleagues and employees, splendidly commemorated in McKay's account of a sub-editor of the time who was a noted gourmand:

> . . . Every banquet to which a reporter was called in Sydney he attended. No ticket for one ever got past him. He got rounder and

ruddier until his doctor warned him off the perils of the table and put him on a strict diet. He sadly told Banjo of the blow:

"I'm not to eat cabbage, Barty," he wailed. "I'm fond of cabbage, dished up and cut across, with pepper and butter. And I'm fond of mashed potatoes, with plenty of pepper and butter. I'm ordered to have neither. I think," he added, reflecting on his fate, "I can give up cabbage, Barty, but I can't, I can't (Caruso sob), I can't give up mashed potatoes!"

Paterson, his long weatherbeaten face lighting up with that attractive, humorous smile of his, used to repeat poor Mr Leighton-Bailey's tale of woe . . .[18]

Perhaps the episode during his editorship that Paterson remembered with most pleasure was the occasion when he assigned himself to cover the first motor-car reliability trial from Sydney to Melbourne. This took place between 21 and 25 February 1905.* Paterson had made the transition from horseback to motor-car seat with little difficulty.

". . . the motorist," he wrote, "is just like the hunting man that always jumps the biggest fence. Each motorist, by his own account, has used less petrol and less spark and has been in bigger ruts and his car has jumped higher and sidestepped more than any other car . . ."[19]

He was most enthusiastic about the future of the motor-car, and later on was to write a brilliant short story on the subject, "Three Elephant Power", which gave the title to his book of stories and sketches.

Paterson travelled with one of the competitors, J. M. Arnott, in an Innes car; other celebrities who took part included C. B. Kellow (later famous as the owner of the racehorse "Heroic"), Harry Skinner, a well-known theatrical entrepreneur of the time, and a crack French racing-driver, F. B. Maillard, who drove a Richard-Brazier. Years later Paterson recalled that Maillard

. . . was a hot favourite for the event . . . and beat everyone to Goulburn. On leaving Goulburn he went past the other cars like an express train, but unfortunately he had no knowledge of Australian roads. He could not even speak English.

In those days the roads beyond Goulburn were crossed here and there by steep gutters to drain off the water.

They were quite invisible from a distance, and all the experienced drivers had their passengers standing up on the back seats to yell out "gutter" when one hove in sight. The poor little Frenchman, blissfully unconscious of this, hit the first gutter at fifty miles an hour, sending his car up in the air like a hurdle horse which has hit a jump. Parts of the car were scattered all over the road, and the Frenchman

* The trial, for the record, was won by a young American, H. L. Stevens, driving a 14 h.p. Darracq.

ran from one to another shouting: "Pourquoi les canivaux?" (why are the gutters there?). As I had some sort of Surry Hills knowledge of French I did my best to explain things, but the only result was to make him cry worse than ever.[20]

Paterson sent back pithy despatches to *Evening News* readers, and also, while the event was in progress, wrote a series of feature articles on it, "Motoring to Melbourne: A Reliability Trial: The History of the Haste Wagons",[21] in which he was at his journalistic best, and was well assisted by Lionel Lindsay's drawings. One of its paragraphs, "The Joy of Motoring", as well as demonstrating the racy and attractive style of writing Paterson had developed with his newspaper experience, also indicated quite clearly why Paterson the horseman found such enjoyment in this new sport:

It is only now and again that you get the full advantages that motoring can offer. When you get a bit of really good road, clear away as far as you can see — smooth gravel for choice — and the car is at her best, the engine working with a rhythmic hum, but everything else as noiseless as the tomb, and you feel her answer to every least touch of acceleration, while the milestones slip past one after another in surprisingly rapid fashion, and you put the watch on her and find she is doing thirty miles an hour, and only sauntering along at that. Then one knows for a few brief minutes what motoring really is. But when the smooth-looking stretch of road is constantly crossed by the apparently harmless waterways, that rack and jolt the car two or three feet in the air, if you let her rush into them; or when the hills are long and steep, and dusty, and loose metal lies thickly, and she doesn't seem to answer properly when you liven her up a little, that is the depressing side of the sport. But one gets a glorious rush through fresh air, laden with scent of half dry gum leaves, and sees the homesteads flying past, and catches glimpses of far-off blue hills and deep gullies, that makes the ride worth having, even if there were no race or trial at all. The car is like an untiring horse, that breasts the hills gallantly and then flies away again as fresh as ever on each stretch of smooth road.

In the main, Paterson's three years as editor of the *Evening News* were hardly eventful; in later life he made few references to them. Claude McKay, in his recent autobiography, records instances in which, though offered the "stories", Paterson allowed his paper to be scooped by the *Sunday Times* and the *Daily Telegraph*; McKay remarks that "for news, Paterson had no instinct whatsoever". Probably Paterson was much more interested in his collection of old bush songs, on which he was steadily working over these years, and its publication in 1905 was certainly of greater moment as far as he was concerned, than the *Evening News's* installation in the same year of the first Hoe press, a machine capable of turning out an eight-page paper at the rate of 48,000 copies an hour.

His *Old Bush Songs* was well received and added considerably to his own stature and reputation. It marked for this period the swan-song of the Australian ballad; thereafter the genre declined considerably and rapidly in popular favour. Paterson had worked for nearly ten years on his collection. As early as 1898, in a letter[22] dated 26 May, he had written to his publishers in terms in which the bushman and bush-song enthusiast were nicely balanced with the lawyer's caution:

> . . . I have been working on these songs — there is a terrible lot of patching and altering to do to make them readable. Several versions of each well-known song come in and it is difficult to patch the verses together. Some of the songs sent in (and these are some of the best) I *know* to be copyrighted and no doubt the publishers would be only too glad to go at you if you give them a chance. Others I am now hunting up and expect to find someone ready to claim copyright. Several have been in the *Bulletin*. When you publish the book you can't copyright it as the mere fact of a song being sent to you from a man from say Kiama does not give you the right to it against the owner and writer of it who may be lying low at Bourke. I will come up and have a talk with you about it . . .

(Years later, in 1919, Professor Todd wrote to Paterson to say that, despite the fact that he had had permission to use three songs from *Old Bush Songs* in his *Australasian Students' Song Book*, G. H. Gibson ("Ironbark"), a *Bulletin* writer of the time, was threatening action. Paterson, by his personal intervention, smoothed the matter over. Explaining this, in a letter[23] to Angus & Robertson dated 17 December, Paterson wrote: ". . . I have often wondered that we did not get sued by somebody over those *Old Bush Songs* . . .")

Paterson had made a number of visits to the New South Wales back country and to Queensland in his search for songs. Many of his friends and admirers, sometimes total strangers who had heard of his project, sent him verses collected from all over Australia; in some cases as he implied in the letter quoted above he was sent as many as three and four versions of the same ballad. The list of sources[24] of these songs is an interesting one: from South Australia C. H. Souter sent him "Flash Jack from Gundagai" and "Five Miles from Gundagai"; from Sir Matthew Henry Stephen, at the time Acting Chief Justice of New South Wales, who was a keen student of the ballad, came "Song of the Emigrants"; and Paterson took from the columns of the *Queenslander* "The Freehold on the Plain", and from the Melbourne *Weekly Times*, "Song of the Billy".

Altogether he set down fifty-five songs, beginning with an aboriginal song in an anglicized form of the dialect (with a note that not even the contributor knew what the words meant, and he doubted "if the blacks themselves knew"), and including such classics of Australian folk-song as "Bold Jack Donahoo", "The Wild Colonial Boy", "The Old Bark Hut" and "The Eumerella Shore". There were frequent footnotes in the form of glossaries, geographical information and even the names of established melodies to which the songs were set (e.g., "Air: 'Wearing of the Green'"). His explanations were often models of simplicity and clarity

— as in his definition of a jackaroo (as a note to the song "Jimmy Sago, Jackaroo") :

> A jackaroo is a young man who comes to a station to get experience. He occupies a position much like that of an apprentice on a ship, and has to work with the men though supposed to be above them in social status. Hence those sneers at the Jackaroo . . .

The newspapers and journals in Australia vigorously applauded Paterson for his achievement in rescuing these old songs (many of which would otherwise have been forgotten) and recording them for posterity. The comment of the Melbourne *Argus*[25] was typical:

> To appreciate these ballads properly you must exercise your imagination a little; you must fancy them being chanted in the shearing shed "to an accompaniment of clashing shears" as Mr Paterson says, or droned out by drovers to soothe a mob of restless cattle. There is real rhythmic vigour in "The Eumerella Shore" and a score besides of the songs in Mr Paterson's collection. And for the most part their interest is an historic interest; they have the romantic savour of everything that reminds us of the "old colonial days".

It is not surprising that over 5,000 copies of the book were sold in the first year of publication.

1906 was an eventful year too — it saw the publication of his first novel *An Outback Marriage*. It was reviewed kindly in most Australian newspapers and journals. The *Sydney Morning Herald,* for instance, described it[26] as "a capital story of Australian life", suggesting that ". . . the chief interest in the story lies in the fine descriptions of Australian bush life. The author makes every page live when he is telling of those things, or when he introduces his readers to 'push' life in Sydney or to the awe-inspiring proceedings of the Supreme Court . . . The story is brimful of interest as it is racy of the soil." Years later Florence Earle Hooper remarked: ". . . the adventures, country scenes and characters are so very good that the book is refreshing; it should make a fine film, though I suppose someone would have to make the love passages more juicy, and it might be difficult to get a hero to risk the buffalo hunting . . ."[27]

Paterson had worked on the novel for over eight years; according to Arthur Jose[28] Paterson had first given Angus & Robertson a rough manuscript of the book as early as 1899 — rather disconnected, but with a series of well-described incidents of outback life especially. There was some discussion about it, and Jose was called in for advice. He suggested the title *In No Man's Land,* and Paterson was left to revise and re-write parts of the book. This is probably substantially true, but Paterson's correspondence with George Robertson[29] about the novel, which, beginning in 1899, went on for seven years, suggests that he did not see eye to eye with Jose; he took the advice of others including his friend and fellow-writer John Farrell; and he worried all the time about titles (suggesting, as usual, some that were far from apt) :

24 Bond St.,
Sydney.
3 Aug., 1899.

George Robertson, Esq.,
Angus & Robertson.
Dear Robertson,
    Herewith the balance of the book. It is not all typed but I send
it on as I want to let you see it and you can easily read the sense of
it. There are heaps of alterations to be made, but we will discuss
these later on. You might think over some names for it — "Red Mick
and His Relations", "A Mountain Station", "In No Man's Land",
"The Finding of Considine", and so on . . . I fear the love-making is
very flat and there is too much fight and drink all through it. Still I
hope to please a large section of the public and if we do that the
critics won't break our hearts.
                                        Yours truly,
                                        A. B. PATERSON.

A few days later (8 August) Paterson asked for the manuscript to be
returned:

    . . . Please give bearer my ms. I think I will let Farrell have a look at
    it, before I start on altering it. I was working at a new scheme last
    night — I am afraid to put any reliance on Jose's opinion as he is
    a hopelessly bad judge where humour is concerned — at least that is
    my opinion. A lot of the stuff that he wants isn't exactly the stuff that
    will appeal to the same public who bought *Snowy River*. Anyhow
    it will be more satisfactory to get another reader's opinion as I am
    very frightened that a lot of weak points have been overlooked by
    Jose . . .

An undated note, presumably written a short time after this, says:

    . . . Farrell is not inclined to advise much alteration except in the
    way of condensing and making the plot more probable. He seems to
    like it pretty well . . .

In September Paterson wrote to Robertson and returned the manuscript,
saying that he had re-written a good part of it "on the lines suggested by
Jose"; also that he had shortened it. He asked for an advance: ". . . if I
go to South Africa I will want the money . . ."
    On the way to South Africa Paterson still had the novel (and its title!)
on his mind. He wrote "c/- Troopship Kent, off Albany, W.A." on
5 November 1899:

    I think a good name for my book would be "An Heiress from the
    Never Never". It is rather like Bret Harte but not a bad fault I
    think, and gives an idea of locality, etc. . . . This is written in a very
    heavy sea with horses all over the deck . . .

Back from his overseas travels, Paterson has a note during 1902 that he wanted to include "a war part" in the novel. There does not appear to have been further action about it (presumably George Robertson told him to re-write it again) until, in a note to Robertson dated 25 May 1905, Paterson said he would "take a week's holiday and finish the novel". This he must have done, because in 1906 he wrote on 29 May to say he had finished it (still, incidentally, referring to the title as "In No Man's Land"), and finally on 19 June he wrote to Robertson from Woollahra:

> . . . I send at last the long-promised novel. I am very frightened about it and if you think it will be a frost for goodness sake say so and I will try the racing yarn . . .*

Early in 1906 Paterson gave up the editorship of the *Evening News* and was appointed editor of the *Town and Country Journal*, a weekly journal in the same stable, which, like the Adelaide *Chronicle* and other publications of its type, was designed specially for a country readership. In addition to a summary of the week's news and sporting results, its sixty pages were heavily loaded with features likely to interest the man (and woman) on the land. Thus there were sections on rural industry, markets, agricultural shows and competitions, and a pictorial supplement spotlighting a different country town each week. There was also a "Ladies' Page", a section on cookery and the usual magazine features. It sold for sixpence — with slogans such as "Circulation three times that of any other weekly journal in Australia", "The best illustrated weekly", and so on. The process of its editing was largely automatic, and the leisurely pace of its production resulted in an atmosphere much more congenial to Paterson. He did not appear ever to have written for it under his own name, but occasional articles, such as "The Control of Horse Racing", are obviously his in style.

Towards the end of 1908 Paterson sold up in Sydney, and, with his wife and two young children, went back to the land. He had written to George Robertson[30] from the Australian Club on 15 June of that year:

> . . . I am going in for a sheep station and I want to raise as much cash as I can. Will you make me an offer for my copyright in *Snowy River* and my other books with you. *Snowy River* has been returning a pretty steady sale for some years so I suppose it has a value for a few years more . . .
>
> If I get into the bush again I hope to get some decent work done. Am always seedy down here.
>
> I have about £100 worth of books and pictures I might also put in with the rest; won't want them up there . . .

Many years afterwards, in his reminiscences, Paterson implied that this move had been made as a step towards ". . . curing some sort of nervous breakdown", but this was undoubtedly his sense of ironical humour at

*Presumably *The Shearer's Colt*, published in 1936.

work. What he meant was that the city had got on his nerves; as his letter to Robertson implied, he needed a change of air; and there was that hankering to get back to the bush life. But not anywhere in the bush. The country he loved most of all was the Upper Murrumbidgee — the Illalong country of his boyhood — and he had watched and waited for over a year for a suitable property in that area to come his way. Perhaps it would realize the dream expressed in the ballad, "A Mountain Station", he had written many years before:

> I bought a run a while ago
>   On country rough and ridgy,
> Where wallaroos and wombats grow —
>   The Upper Murrumbidgee.
> The grass is rather scant, it's true,
>   But this a fair exchange is,
> The sheep can see a lovely view
>   By climbing up the ranges.

The opportunity came through an advertisement in the *Town and Country Journal* with Coodravale (sometimes called Coodra) in the magnificently rugged country of the Wee Jasper district, approximately midway between, and to the west of, what are now Canberra and Yass. The station itself comprised 40,000 acres of mountainous country with good narrow flats.* Paterson took the property over as a member of a syndicate comprising two of his friends, Andrew Moore (managing director of Goldsbrough, Mort & Co.) and Charles Chapman, a brother-in-law to the fourth member, Charles Lindeman. Paterson and Lindeman bought the syndicate out; and in the records of the Yass Pastures Protection Board there is an entry of the registration of Paterson's and Lindeman's brand, dated 20 October 1908. It is "P" and "L" conjoined.

Coodravale was just what Paterson had been waiting for. "I want my children to grow up loving the country and the horses like I did . . . and Alice is only too happy about it," he said.[31] And then it was closer to Melbourne too: "easier to get to the Cup." Above all, it was magnificent bush country: ". . . one could ride for miles and miles in the ranges, seeing nothing but wild horses, wild cattle, wombats and wallaroos, and hearing at night the chatter of the flying squirrels playing among the gum tree blossoms."[32]

---

* Coodravale, as advertised for auction in 1965 (*Bulletin*, 9 October) now is a homestead block of but 1,694 acres described as a property ". . . splendidly watered in all paddocks with a frontage of about three miles to the Goodrabidgee or Little River, one of the best minor rivers in N.S.W. and a renowned trout stream. The river flows into Burrinjuck Dam and affords an abundant and personal supply of running water . . . Coodravale is a most attractive property situated in one of the State's most favoured districts and close to the rapidly expanding city of Canberra. It is a property of many purposes, and, with its wide expanse of rich river flats, is capable of fattening every class of stock and growing all crops. It has produced heavy crops of maize, lucerne, sorghum, potatoes, and would grow vegetables in abundance if required. It would be difficult to imagine a better setting for a stud for horses or cattle or both . . ."

In the earlier days, the mountain country abounded in "unbranded cleanskins" — wild stock, some of it with the good blood lines of recently escaped breeding cattle from adjoining stations, the rest "pike-horned scrubbers" which had been roaming the bush for years. Paterson claimed that one of the previous owners of Coodra, John McDonald, "a hardy and determined Scot . . . who became a big financial magnate and breeder of three Derby winners",[33] spent years with a branding-iron, cattle-dogs and a stockwhip and little else but his courage, working from dawn to dusk and sometimes by moonlight rounding up these wild cattle in their thousands and driving them into trap-yards he had built, to be branded as his property and become the foundation of his later wealth. This recollection of a single-minded pioneer was, alas, as inaccurate as it was inspiring, since McDonald had owned not Coodravale, but Wee Jasper station which adjoined it.

In any case, there were no "cleanskins" left on the ranges by the time Paterson took over the property — and in later life, forgetting the enthusiasm which had taken him to the station, he recalled his two years on the property in sardonic strain, seeing himself as a "hill billy" on country "left over after the rest of the world was made". Yet in his account, despite a disparaging humour, he could not control his nostalgia for this, the very country of the Man from Snowy River:

As a station proposition it was best avoided; as a homestead there was nothing better. We had eight miles of a trout river, which ran all the year round, clear and cold in summer, a fierce snow-fed torrent in winter. As the sun was setting, the lyre-birds came out of their fastnesses and called to each other across the valley, imitating everything that they had ever heard. Gorgeous lories came and sat in rows on the spouting that ran round the verandah, protesting shrilly when their tails were pulled by the children. Bower birds with an uncanny scent for fruit would come hurrying up from the end of the garden when the housewife started to peel apples, and would sit on the window-sill of the kitchen, looking expectantly into the room.

Part of the run was enclosed by a dingo-proof fence of thirteen wires, with a strand of barbed wire at top and bottom; and outside of this there were about ten thousand acres of unfenced country, where one could put sheep when there was any water, and chance the dingoes coming in from Lobb's Hole.

One winter they came in when there were a couple of inches of snow on the ground, and the fiery cross was sent round to the neighboring stations; for the presence of a "dorg" will make the hill people leave all other work and go after him. We mustered some eight or ten armed men, and as I rode in front on a cream-coloured mountain pony I happened to look round at the overcoated and armed figures following me through the snow.

"Where," I thought, "have I seen that picture before?" And then I remembered it. Napoleon's retreat from Moscow! I, too, retreated from the mountain Moscow, fortunately with less loss than Napoleon . . .[34]

His mention of the trout river adds an interesting postscript to his recollections. This was, as has been previously noted, the Goodrabidgee, one of the rivers of the upper waters of the Murrumbidgee into which trout fry were liberated, and it was not long before the area became the Mecca of the dry-fly fishermen. But indirectly this situation was of great advantage to the owners of the relatively inaccessible mountain stations, who hitherto had always found it difficult to get good shearers. For the shearers themselves became trout-fishing enthusiasts, and even the crack shearers willingly came to these remote places for the sake of the fishing offered.

Although his spells of verse-writing were few and far between in these years, Paterson commemorated his Coodravale experiences in at least two ballads, eventually published in *Saltbush Bill J.P. and Other Verses*: "The Road to Hogan's Gap" —

> They like to make it pretty strong
>   Whenever there's a chance;
> So when a stranger comes along
>   They always hold a dance.
>
> There's recitations, songs, and fights —
>   A willin' lot you'll meet.
> There's one long bloke up there recites;
>   I tell you he's a treat.

— and "The Mountain Squatter", one of his best ballads, in which he sang of his ". . . mountain home / On rugged hills and steep . . .", and, perhaps with thoughts of the Man from Snowy River, made particular reference to the expert horsemanship that the terrain demanded:

> These Riverina cracks,
>   They do not care to ride
> The half-inch hanging tracks
>   Along the mountain side.
>
> Their horses shake with fear
>   When loosened boulders go
> With leaps, like startled deer,
>   Down the gulfs below.

In 1911 Paterson and his family left Coodravale and took up a smaller but better-established property, "Glen Esk", near the township of Bimbi, about twenty-five miles south-west of Grenfell in central New South Wales. Not far to the north was Molong and the district where his grandmother had lived at Boree Nyrang. Mrs Barton had died at Gladesville in August 1909 at the age of ninety-two, and Paterson's most affectionate link with the past was thereby severed. His new property was some 150 miles to the north of Coodravale, in surroundings which, though hilly, lacked the grandeur and ruggedness of the Murrumbidgee country. There is little record of his stay here except that it was brief; he settled back in Sydney (at The Grove, Woollahra) at the end of 1912, and only his verses "Song of the Wheat" remain as a reminder of his brief association with the arable and pastoral country stretching down from Grenfell across the northern plains of the Riverina to Temora and Junee. But even in the opening lines of this ballad Paterson seemed, with marked overtones of Kipling, to be making quite clear that not only the outback days were over, but his career as a bush bard too:

> We have sung the song of the droving days,
>   Of the march of the travelling sheep —
> How by silent stages and lonely ways
>   Thin, white battalions creep.
> But the man who now by the land would thrive
>   Must his spurs to a ploughshare beat;
> And the bush bard, changing his tune, may strive
>   To sing the song of the Wheat!

Until he left in 1914 for the First World War, Paterson was occupied with freelance journalism, and he also devoted much of his time to completing a book on Australian horse-racing begun while he was at Coodra — covering every aspect of it from breeding to betting, although as it turned out it was never published.[35]

Paterson was by now famous not only in Australia; his reputation had extended even to the United States, for it was in 1913, in a letter to Newton Wanliss,[36] that Theodore Roosevelt, writing that he was an "old admirer" of Gordon's poems, said also: ". . . By the way we also admire a more recent poet of yours, Paterson, very much." Roosevelt some years before had written to Claude McKay too telling him how much he enjoyed the "speed and gusto" of Paterson's ballads.*

*McKay recalled this in his autobiography *This is the Life* (1961). He had met Roosevelt in San Francisco in 1908, and when he discovered that the President was interested in the "frontier life" of Australia, had presented him with books of verse by Paterson and Lawson.

NOTES

1 In an A.B.C. radio script, "News", written in 1935.
2 In the George Robertson papers, Mitchell Library, Sydney.
3 9 April 1903.
4 In *Bohemians of the Bulletin* (1965).
5 Ibid.
6 In an A.B.C. radio commentary on A. B. Paterson compiled by Peter Macgregor.
7 In his *Sydney Morning Herald* reminiscences.
8 In *The Evening News 1867-1931* (1926).
9 Ibid.
10 In *The Press in Australia* (1964).
11 *Evening News*, 13 January 1903.
12 *Evening News*, 23 March 1903.
13 *Evening News*, 21 January 1903.
14 *Sydney Morning Herald*, 11 November 1952.
15 Ibid.

[16] 24 May 1903.
[17] 29 November 1903.
[18] Ibid.
[19] *Evening News,* 23 February 1905.
[20] In his *Sydney Morning Herald* reminiscences.
[21] *Evening News,* 23 February 1905.
[22] In the George Robertson papers, Mitchell Library, Sydney.
[23] Ibid.
[24] Ibid.
[25] 2 February 1906.
[26] 17 January 1906.
[27] *Yass Tribune-Courier,* 11 July 1949.
[28] In *The Romantic Nineties* (1933).
[29] In the Mitchell Library.
[30] Ibid.
[31] Recalled by Mrs MacSmith of Orange in reminiscences made available to the author.
[32] In his *Sydney Morning Herald* reminiscences.
[33] Ibid.
[34] Ibid.
[35] See Chapter XVI.
[36] The letter which is dated 28 August 1913 now hangs on the wall of the Adam Lindsay Gordon cottage in Ballarat.

CHAPTER XIII

At the Great War

In this war we're always moving, moving on,
When we make a friend, another friend has gone.
  Should a woman's kindly face
  Make us welcome for a space
Then it's boot and saddle, boys, we're moving on.

— A. B. PATERSON.*

IN NOVEMBER 1914, at the age of fifty, Paterson was off to London, hoping to get to the Front as a war correspondent. He travelled with two battalions of infantry commanded by Brigadier MacLaurin; the ranks, he recalled, were "full of English ex-Service men wearing as many ribbons as prize-bulls . . ."[1] They had volunteered in the hope of joining their own regiments when they got back to England — Yorkshiremen, Cockneys and Cornishmen — but as it turned out these battalions were ordered to disembark when the ship reached Egypt, and were put into training camps for the Gallipoli campaign, where MacLaurin was killed at the landing.

On the way to Colombo, Paterson became friendly with a tall, strapping lieutenant named Massie, ". . . an international cricketer, strong and rugged as an ironbark tree",[2] a man of considerable resourcefulness and acumen, who had been made adjutant of his battalion. Paterson admired him enormously for making a success, despite any previous experience, of this difficult and frustrating post aboard a disorganized troopship — simply by applying sheer personality and common sense, qualities always esteemed by Paterson. When they reached Colombo they found the population in a state of enthusiastic excitement because of the sinking of the *Emden* by the Australian cruiser *Sydney*. The latter ship, now in Colombo Harbour among Japanese, Russian and British warships and merchantmen, aroused the Australian troops to a fever-pitch of patriotic fervour — so much so that they were not allowed ashore in case they should, as Paterson put it, take Colombo to pieces.

But it was through Massie that Paterson achieved one of the most memorable journalistic scoops of the War. For Massie, whose family were people of substance and importance in Sydney social circles, had often entertained Captain Glossop of the *Sydney*. Massie offered to take Pater-

---

*These lines are from "We're Always Moving", which, according to Florence Earle Hooper, was written by Paterson as a farewell to Major Weir of Yass, who visited him at Moascar, in Egypt, during World War I.

son ashore and introduce him privately to Glossop so he would "get some stuff that the other correspondents wouldn't get". They found Glossop in mufti having a quiet drink on his own, quite calm about his achievement, having rationalized the whole affair as a combination of range of guns, weight of metal, speed of ship and a good deal of luck. Paterson's account[3] of the interview is now a part of World War I naval history. He recorded Glossop's story as follows:

. . . Fancy her coming to Cocos just when we were right on the spot, and fancy just having the luck to be on that side of the convoy. If I'd been on the other side, then I wouldn't have got the job. Of course I had the speed of her and the guns of her, but if our people hadn't served the guns properly or if she'd dropped a shell into our engine-room, we might have been sent to the bottom instead of her. You can work out a fight on paper, and one shell will upset the whole calculation.

She had no idea that there was any vessel of her own power in that part of the Pacific, and she came out looking for a fight — and she got it. She must have got a surprise when she found she had to fight the *Sydney*; and I got a surprise, too, I can tell you. When we were about ten thousand five hundred yards apart I turned nearly due north so as to run parallel with her, and I said to the gunnery lieutenant that we had better get a thousand yards closer before we fired. I knew the *Emden*'s four-point-one guns would be at their extreme limit at ten thousand yards, and I got a shock when she fired a salvo at ten thousand five hundred and two of the shells came aboard us. That's modern gunnery for you. Fancy one ship, rolling about in the sea, hitting another ship — also rolling about in the sea — six miles away! She must have elevated her guns and fired in the air, for we were technically out of range; but it was great gunnery.

Her first salvo was five guns, of which two shells came aboard us. One shell burst and carried away the after-control, wounding all the men, including Lieutenant Hampden, but no one was killed. The other shell passed within six inches of the gunnery lieutenant and killed a man working a range-finder, but it never burst. There was luck again for me — I was in that control and if the shell had burst I suppose I would have been a goner.

There was a boy of about sixteen in the control working a telescope. When the shell landed he was stunned by the concussion and was lying under the body of the man that was killed. As soon as he came to himself he threw the man's body off him and started looking for his telescope. "Where's my bloody telescope?" was all he said. That's the Australian Navy for you.

The whole thing didn't last forty minutes, but it was a busy forty minutes. She tried to get near enough to torpedo us, but she could only do seventeen knots and we could do twenty-seven, so we scuttled out of range. The *Emden* had a captured collier called the *Buresk* hanging about, and trying to get near enough to ram us, and I had to keep a couple of guns trained on this collier all the time. We hit the

Emden about a hundred times in forty minutes, and fourteen of her shells struck us, but most of them were fired beyond her range, and the shells hit the side and dropped into the water without exploding.

When the *Emden* made for the beach we went after the collier, but we found the Germans had taken the sea-cocks out of her, so we had to let her sink. They were game men, I'll say that for them.

Then we went back to the *Emden* lying in the shallow water and signalled her "do you surrender?" She answered by flag-wagging in Morse "we have no signal book and do not understand your signal". I asked several times, but could get no answer, and her flag was still flying; so I fired two salvos into her and then they hauled their flag down. I was sorry afterwards that I gave her those two salvos, but what was I to do? If they were able to flag-wag in Morse, they were surely able to haul a flag down. We understood there was another German warship about and I couldn't have the *Emden* firing at me from the beach while I was fighting her mate.

We waited off all night with lights out for this other vessel, but she never showed up, and then we sent boats ashore to the *Emden*. My God, what a sight! Her captain had been out of action ten minutes after the fight started from lyddite fumes, and everybody on board was demented — that's all you could call it, just fairly demented — by shock, and fumes, and the roar of shells bursting among them. She was a shambles. Blood, guts, flesh, and uniforms were all scattered about. One of our shells had landed behind a gun shield, and had blown the whole gun-crew into one pulp. You couldn't even tell how many men there had been. They must have had forty minutes of hell on that ship, for out of four hundred men a hundred and forty were killed and eighty wounded and the survivors were practically madmen. They crawled up to the beach and they had one doctor fit for action; but he had nothing to treat them with — they hadn't even got any water. A lot of them drank salt water and killed themselves. They were not ashore twenty-four hours, but their wounds were flyblown and the stench was awful — it's hanging about the *Sydney* yet. I took them on board and got four doctors to work on them and brought them up here.

I've seen my first naval engagement, Massie; and all I can say is, thank God we didn't start the war.

In London in December, which he described as a stricken city cut off from all reliable news, Paterson immediately set about the job of getting to the Front as a correspondent. He soon found that this was almost an impossibility. One of his South African fellow-correspondents, now chief leader-writer for the *Daily Mail*, told him that he should try the War Office, but that he had little hope of success. Paterson found the War Office a place of utter confusion, crowded with old army officers from generals down, and civilians of all ages, all with the same object: to get to the Front. There was a waiting-list of from ten to thirty days for interviews; there were people prepared to donate equipment and money, entertainers who wanted to sing to the troops in France — every type of excuse was put forward. It took Paterson little time to realize that he would have to try other avenues. He went therefore to Sir Timothy Coghlan, whom he had known in Sydney and who was at the time Agent-General for New South Wales in London. Coghlan told him he could get him over to France, but not as a newspaperman; indeed, that was the one thing that would disqualify him. Coghlan's idea was rather that, if Paterson could get to France on some pretext or other, correspondents might be allowed to enter later on, at which point Paterson could make contact with them. The pretext was that Paterson should go to France as an ambulance-driver attached to Lady Dudley's Australian Hospital at Wimereux.

Now, here was for Paterson an unexpected stroke of luck. For it so happened that he knew Lady Dudley quite well. She was the wife of the Earl of Dudley, who had been Governor-General of Australia from 1908 to 1911 (he later commanded the Worcester yeomanry in the Gallipoli campaign). In 1909, after travelling in various parts of the Australian outback, Lady Dudley, a Quaker by birth, conceived the idea of establishing all over Australia a chain of bush nurses. It seemed as if the scheme would appeal to wealthy Australians, who could be expected to subscribe to it for reasons of social status as well as of philanthropy, but opposition came from the medical profession which saw this as likely to reduce both its reputation and income. Various compromises were offered, but Lady Dudley refused to budge. It was at this point that Paterson, at Coodravale, was summoned to Sydney and Government House. He was mystified about it all, and wondered if, for instance, he might not be required to write an ode on bush nursing:

> I went down and was shown into a private parlour. Lady Dudley came in; a singularly beautiful woman, graceful, and with a voice that had the range of an organ and had been carefully trained by professors of elocution. Portraits of deceased governors looked down from the walls; menials in uniform moved noiselessly about, and there was nothing in the world to show that a fight was on.
>
> "You have heard of my scheme, Mr Paterson," she said, "and of the opposition there is to it. You are well known among the bush people, and I want you to organize a trip for me through all the backblocks towns. I will live in the Governor-General's train, and I will address meetings and ask for subscriptions in every centre, even in the small places. I will get twenty thousand pounds without any trouble. Will you help me to do it?"[4]

Paterson greatly admired the courage of Lady Dudley, but he had to decline the offer because of the continuing responsibilities of running his property. Although the scheme gradually wilted away, Lady Dudley did manage to establish nurses in a few centres.

Apparently she had carried the same enthusiasm and determination into the setting-up of a hospital behind the front lines near Boulogne. She formed a committee of women in London (hence the Agent-General's reference to it to Paterson as a "petticoat-ridden outfit"), which canvassed

subscriptions from rich Australians resident there; it did not take long
to raise the money needed, nor to recruit the hospital staff, since many
of the Australian doctors and nurses in London readily volunteered for
duty. Paterson was delighted to learn that a Colonel Eames, whom he
had known in South Africa, where he had been in charge of a military
hospital, was the head of Lady Dudley's hospital (the War Office had
refused to accept any hospital unless it was run by a man who had held a
hospital command in war-time).

While Sir Timothy Coghlan went about making passport arrangements,
Paterson went over to Ireland. A keen student of race-horse breeding and
a great admirer of Irish bloodstock breeding, he had arranged to visit
Edward Kennedy's Straffan Stud near Dublin — where one of the fastest
racehorses the world has known was bred, The Tetrarch. "A land of
trouble," wrote Paterson, "and yet would anyone wish to live anywhere
else if he could live here?" He was entranced by the green grass of the
"paddocks", the hedges used as "boundaries", the old stone houses with
their wide entrance-halls and double stairways of polished oak, and the
lawns, carriage-drives and gardens, that made up their grounds. He got
on famously with Kennedy himself, a sturdy, energetic Irishman who
maintained a firm but affectionate control on his Irish peasants, and
with whom Paterson discussed every aspect of thoroughbred breeding and
handling. His most memorable experience during this visit was his
participation in an Irish hunt — "a thing to be remembered, with the soft
turf underneath, the grey skies overhead, the dewdrops on the grass and
the flakes of mist drifting over the blue hills in the distance . . .".[5] He
managed accidentally to knock one of his fellow-huntsmen into a ditch
and was given a tongue-lashing by the master, but when he got back to
the stables, the head groom consoled him. "Ye done well," he said.
"They'd have felt hurted if an Australian hadn't done something quare
for 'em."[6]

On 23 December 1915 Paterson arrived at the Australian hospital to
start his duties as an ambulance driver. In addition to Colonel Eames, he
found there an old friend and fellow-Boer War campaigner, Dr Alexander
McCormick, and Dr Thring, a Sydney surgeon whom he also knew. He
was intrigued by the fact that another Sydney surgeon, Herschell Harris,
had a "private X-ray outfit", reputed to be the only one at the Front at
this time. Many of the junior staff were young doctors from Sydney and
Melbourne who had been taking post-graduate courses in England when
the war broke out. The hospital was a converted château and golf-club,
and whenever there was a lull in the proceedings, the staff was able to
improve its golf on the Wimereux links. But the wounded soon started
to pour into the hospital as a result of the fighting at Mons: Paterson and
his fellow drivers used to meet the hospital trains at the railway station
and drive the stretcher cases ". . . over those infernal cobbled roads,
bumping and jolting their wounds and shattered bones, but there was
never a whine out of the Tommies . . .".[7] But since the hospital was not
part of the war machine, and could, because of its private endowment,
buy whatever supplies it wanted, the Tommies passed the word back that
the Australian hospital was a home from home. The reputation of the

surgeons there caused it to have many of the most difficult cases sent to it — and Lady Dudley had at last come into her own, since her hospital became one of the most important along the Front. But while Paterson was kept very busy, he saw his hopes of being a correspondent gradually dissipating, and he decided to "ship" back to Australia to seek some other way of getting into the war. In any case, he had heard rumours of the formation of a special remount unit there. He recorded his admiration for Lady Dudley as ". . . a wonderful woman. She should have been a general, for no doubts assailed her and no difficulties appalled her . . ."[8]

It was quite true that a remount unit was being organized in Australia. Known as the First Australian Remount Unit, the express purpose of its formation was to take charge of horses of the Light-Horse Regiments whose soldiers were fighting as infantry at Gallipoli. In this way it was planned to release for the fighting front a number of trained officers, N.C.O.'s and rankers who had been left in Egypt in charge of the horses of their respective regiments. The establishment of the unit comprised headquarters and four squadrons: a total of twenty-one officers and 816 other ranks, including three veterinary officers and one medical officer. Men were selected for the unit for their knowledge of horses, and for related trades and activities, since blacksmiths, saddlers and wagon-drivers were also needed. Men with a knowledge of horses and a potential for leadership were especially sought after as officers, and Paterson, who, according to official military records enlisted in the A.I.F. in Sydney on 13 October 1915, was commissioned immediately as a lieutenant. He was soon transferred to Maribyrnong in Victoria (where the unit had begun training during September 1915) and was assigned to one of the squadrons of a second unit, with the rank of captain.

There were four squadrons in the first unit and six in the second, and in each squadron there were forty or more rough-riders whom Paterson dubbed "Australia's last hope". They included jackaroos, horse-breakers from the backblocks, ex-jockeys, buckjumping riders from country shows (nowadays we would call them rodeo-riders) — "the best lot of men that were ever got together to deal with rough horses," Paterson wrote. Many of them had hesitated to enlist because they thought they could never cope with army drill; some of them were illiterate; some would never have wished to join up unless they could be with horses. They were a motley crowd; many of them small, wiry men in uniforms that were far too large for them. All the officers were over-age or medically rejected for active duty. Most of them "did not even know a sergeant-major from any other major". The men, in the manner of their kind, called themselves the "Horsedung Hussars".

On 12 November 1915 the units embarked on the transport ship *Orsova* arriving at Suez on 8 December, disembarking then and travelling by train to Zeitoun. At the end of December the units moved on to Maadi to form a Depot there. In the meantime, however, the evacuation of Gallipoli had begun, and consequently the original purpose for which the units had been formed, no longer existed. It was decided therefore that the units should become part of the Remount Service in Egypt, under the general command of Brigadier-General C. L. Bates, Director of

Remounts. Bates decided in March 1916 that the two Australian units should be reduced to one, the rough-riders however being retained. Captain A. B. Paterson was appointed as Officer Commanding Squadron in the combined Remount Unit, and assigned with his men to a depot in Moascar.

Here he set about organizing his squadron with an efficiency and a personal enthusiasm and involvement that earned him the respect of the Australian fighting men all over Egypt. His work here included the control of horses bought by the army buyers all over the world, and, in whatever state they were, to break them in or subdue them, condition them and eventually bring them to the stage of training and docility where they could be mounted at will by a heavily armed trooper. During the time he was in charge of the depot, Paterson had 50,000 horses and 10,000 mules put through in groups of a thousand or two at a time. These animals had to be fed three times a day and watered twice a day, groomed properly, and exercised every day, including Saturdays and Sundays. Stables had to be kept clean, manure carted away and burned. It was, as he described it, a "perpetual motion job".

The rough-riders were in their element; they were headed by Sergeant-Major Dempsey, whom Paterson affectionately recalled as "a six foot two Australian, straight as a stringybark sapling and equally as tough . . .".[9] Their uniforms comprised shirt and riding breeches, with no leggings or puttees; their socks were pulled up outside the ends of their breeches and their elastic-sided boots had smooth tops so that the rider's foot did not catch in the stirrups. The saddles, specially made, had high pommels and cantles with big knee- and thigh-pads. Sir Edward Knox recalls that Paterson coined the description "patent self-emptier" for them. The depot at the edge of the desert, with the Nile just behind it, was dominated by the Pyramids on the skyline; as Brigadier-General Royston (whom Paterson had known in South Africa when he commanded "Royston's Horse") remarked once, "I don't think the Pyramids ever saw anything like this. What an outfit!" Paterson has described a commonplace scene at the depot:

> A waspish little bay mare refused to move at all when mounted, and crouched right down till her chest nearly touched the ground. It appeared that she was going to roll over, and her rider kicked his feet out of the stirrups. As he did so, she unleashed a terrific spring that shot him out of the saddle and sent him soaring in the air, high enough to see over the Pyramids — or at any rate so he said. Some unmouthed brutes bolted back into the compound and fell over the ropes, while others set sail out into the desert as though they were going back to Australia.[10]

Paterson was disdainful about the aggregation of generals in Shepheard's Hotel in Cairo; probably he exaggerated when he wrote there were ninety or so making themselves busy "about such jobs as reporting upon the waste of jam tins". There was hardly room for junior officers. So he welcomed the arrival of Allenby.

It was a changed Allenby who came to take command in Egypt fourteen years after the South African war. He had been through the
shambles of Mons, where he had dismounted his cavalry and thrown
them into the fighting line in a vain effort to stop the German rush.
He had lost his son in the war; and being a full-fleshed man, the heat
of Egypt tried him severely, and made him harder than ever. Where
he had been granite before he was steel now.

He came to inspect our horse depot — a great lonely figure of a
man, riding silently in front of an obviously terrified staff. He seemed
quite glad to recognize a friend in me. For a Remount officer is like
a Field-Marshal, he has no hope of promotion and no friends whatever in the army . . .[11]

They chatted about the old South African days; Allenby thought the
Australian horses a "common hairy-legged" lot after the Lancers' horses
in South Africa, but Paterson explained that the latter had been police
horses, hand-picked and in superb condition.

Allenby soon dispersed the Shepheard's Hotel generals by a weeding-
out process; according to Paterson "he tried general after general as a man
would try hat after hat in a hat shop before he bought one". Army H.Q.
was moved 150 miles nearer the enemy, and the Remounts were moved
up to an advanced depot near the Front. Paterson and his men had no
fear of being cut down to size — they were not "tall poppies" — but more
than one general earned a "tin hat" instead of a brass hat (the former
expression from the tin extinguisher once used to snuff out a candle).
"When Allenby issued a tin hat to a man," recalled Paterson ,"that man
was forthwith extinguished."[12] He saw how Allenby organized his engi-
neers and did wonders keeping the water-supply abreast of the troops;
he also noted the interest Allenby took in the flying-school near the
camp. The pressure was on for pilots; as many as eighteen planes were in
the air all day long, and Paterson marvelled that the horses became so
used to the din that they scarcely looked up. But Paterson noted the
"pitifully short" life of a pilot, since so many of them were killed during
training. His wife had come out to Egypt early in 1916 and was working
as a voluntary nurse in a hospital at Ismailia: Paterson recorded the grim
fact that she and her fellow-helpers were "constantly making shrouds" for
the young men that were killed, often on their first solo flights.

It was about this time that an American war correspondent, Kermit
Roosevelt, visited Moascar, and left a memorable account of Paterson:

When I left Mesopotamia I made up my mind that there was one
man in Palestine whom I would use every effort to see if I were
held over waiting for a sailing. As soon as I landed I asked every
Australian officer that I met where Major Paterson was, for locating
an individual member of an expeditionary force, no matter how well
known he may be, is not always easy. Everyone knew him. I remember well I enquired at the Australian headquarters in Cairo how the
man I asked turned to a comrade and said, "Say, where's Banjo now?
He's at Moascar, isn't he?" Whether they had ever met him personally

or not, he was "Banjo" to one and all. . . . At Moascar . . . I found him. He was a man of about 60 with long moustaches and strong aquiline features very like the type of American plainsman that Frederic Remington so well portrayed. He has lived everything that he has written. At different periods of his life he has dived for pearls in the islands, herded sheep, broken broncos and known every chance and change of Australian station life. The Australians told me that when he was at his prime he was regarded as the best rider in Australia. A recent feat about which I heard much mention was when he drove 300 mules straight through Cairo without losing a single animal, conclusively proving his argument against those who had contested that such a thing could not be done. He told me that among American writers he cared most for the works of Joel Chandler Harris and O. Henry . . .[13]

Paterson had been promoted to the rank of major on 21 October 1916. By this time, some of the Light-Horse contingents were being put in charge of the horses again, and by early 1917 his group was substantially reduced — most of the rough-riders being sent back to Australia or (those that were assimilable) assigned to other units. But then Paterson got the idea of giving rough-riding displays, and his dwindling unit became suddenly famous. Egyptian notables, wandering English celebrities, aristocratic ladies — all tried to secure invitations to the "displays", and even the Commander-in-Chief, Murray, sat through an entire show — an achievement, since he had never been known as Paterson wrote, in a jubilant letter[14] to George Robertson, of Angus & Robertson, "to stick out more than half an hour of any other regiment's sports or entertainments". The rest of his letter is a striking picture of his work and impressions, couched in the easy-going irreverence of a typical Australian:

All joking apart, the work is hard, monotonous, and dangerous, and the men deserve every credit, I don't think the world ever saw such a lot of horsemen got together as I have in my squadron — Queensland horsebreakers and buckjumping-show riders from New South Wales. It is queer to note the difference in the various States — the other squadron are Victorian, Tasmanian and South Australian farmers and they are quite a different type from my lot — far easier to handle not having had the real rough horses to deal with they can not touch my men at horse work. We (my squadron) won five out of seven events open to all troops in Egypt at a show the other day. In the wrestling on horseback one of my Queenslanders, a big half caste named Nev Kelly, pulled the English tommies off their horses like picking apples off a tree. You say what does this do towards winning the war? Well, it shows that we are up in our work and are doing it and it is not too easy. At the present moment I have two men with broken legs, one with a fractured shoulder blade, two with badly crushed ankles, and about seven others more or less disabled, in hospital at one time out of about 100 riders; so it is not altogether a "cold-footed" job, and I have never had to tell a man twice to get on a horse no matter how hostile the animal appeared; in fact they dearly like to do a bit of "grandstand" work even though they risk their necks by it.

Well, that is enough of "shop" — I have done a few odd jingles over here but nothing very satisfactory; reveille at daylight, horse exercise, varied by orderly room and settling difficulties and disputes all day, and a cinema show at night make up life as I see it at present. This country is the queerest I ever was in — one sees vast estates belonging to wealthy and well educated Egyptians and yet they are farmed with the same implements (and even worse) are stocked with the same stocks that comprised Jacob's outfit when he first took up some fresh country alongside his father-in-law. I can't understand why the English people interested in Egypt don't put some decent stock on. I suppose there is some reason. One sees a flock on the move here and everything is exactly reversed from what it is in Australia. For example first of all comes the shepherd, usually a black girl locally known as a "bint". Then come the dogs. Then usually a couple of donkeys loose with possibly a fat Egyptian asleep on one of them. Then last of all come the sheep — or what pass for sheep here — mixed up with goats all trotting along so as not to be left behind. The favourite grazing ground is a garbage tip outside a hospital. As they near this the pace is put on, the bint in the lead waving a stick to keep the dogs and sheep off until she gets first lick of the jam tins. Then the whole lot turns in and scoff up cabbage stalks, broken biscuits, bones, fowls' legs and heads, and decayed oranges; they eat anything they can bite; and then the whole outfit lies down in the dirt — sheep, goats, dogs, donkeys, and bint under the blazing Egyptian sun until it is time to go home. When they get down on the irrigated land their behaviour is even stranger to our eyes for all the lot — sheep, goats and donkeys and even camels and buffalo — are trained not to go on to the crop but they feed ravenously along the edge of the paths and gobble up weeds and dust and never think of going on to the beautifully green crop just ahead of them. The bint certainly watches with her stick to crack any of them over the nose that try it on, but with our animals they would be all over the paddocks in two shakes. What beats me is why, if they are going to keep sheep at all, why don't they get good sheep, and why if they are going to raise water all, they don't get a decent pump. They can distribute water all right having the same natural eye for levels that the Javanese have. I am fed up of them anyhow and we live in daily hope of a move to Jerusalem. That would be something to look forward to. I have quite a lot of devout R.C.'s in my lot and they have got the holy tree at Matariah very nearly niggled down with pocket knives when the custodian was after backsheesh from tourists and took his eyes off them. If they get to Jerusalem they will send most of the Jordan home in bottles, and will fill their bully-beef tins with hunks of the Holy Sepulchre. It will be no good putting it out of bounds, they will get anywhere.

In the latter part of 1917 Paterson was assigned to duties involving the transfer of horses and mules from one centre to another — arduous and exacting work in desert conditions — and the following entries are recorded in the Official War Diary:[15]

> *19/10/17:* Major A. B. Paterson and 40 other ranks were despatched to Kantara on the above date, conducting 130 horses and 20 mules, the party to take the draft on to Rafa by similar stages as the other two already sent forward.
>
> *29/10/17:* Major A. B. Paterson with conducting party and animals reached Rafa on the above date, animals arrived in a very satisfactory condition. The above particulars of the conducting of animals to Rafa are entered in the Diary to show that the distance and heavy nature of the route really did no harm whatever to them rather the reverse as the animals actually improved.

During 1918 Paterson continued his work superintending the movement of horses, acting often in command of the unit, and moving between Cairo, Moascar and Belbeis. By the beginning of 1919, as a result of the Armistice and the defeat of the Turks in Palestine and Syria, there was little work left to be done in these depots and eventually on 1 April 1919 Paterson with his wife left Egypt for Australia by the *Kildonan Castle.*

NOTES

[1] In *Happy Dispatches* (1935).
[2] Ibid.
[3] Ibid.
[4] Ibid.
[5] Ibid.
[6] Ibid.
[7] Ibid.
[8] Ibid.
[9] Ibid.
[10] Ibid.
[11] Ibid.
[12] Ibid.
[13] In *War in the Garden of Eden* (1919).
[14] From Heliopolis, Egypt, dated 26 March 1917. The letter is in the possession of Angus & Robertson, Sydney.
[15] In the Australian War Memorial, Canberra.

CHAPTER XIV

Full Harvest

For the rain and drought and sunshine make no changes
in the street,
In the sullen line of buildings and the ceaseless tramp of
feet.

— A. B. PATERSON.

. . . My heart went back to the droving days
Back to the road, and I crossed again
Over the miles of the saltbush plain —

— A. B. PATERSON.

PATERSON AND HIS family set up house in the eastern suburbs of Sydney (where they remained for the rest of their lives), living first of all in New South Head Road, Woollahra and Edgecliff, then at Darling Point, moving eventually to South Street, Double Bay.

Paterson was immediately in touch with his publishers, Angus & Robertson. While he was in Egypt, they had published a number of his short stories and sketches under the title of *Three Elephant Power and Other Stories* and the third volume of his ballads, *Saltbush Bill J.P. and Other Verses*. George Robertson of Angus & Robertson had written to Paterson in Egypt suggesting this further volume of verse, and had asked for the use of a number of ballads of which Paterson still owned the copyright. Robertson subsequently wrote: ". . . When your cable asking £150 for them came to hand I thanked God you were only a Major. Another step in rank and *Saltbush Bill* had never been born. . . ."[1]

This volume included some of his earlier work, and as with the other collections, was uneven in quality, largely because of Paterson's easy-going tendency to pass in what he termed "jingles" and "junk" rustled out of discarded early work, once he realized that, strange as it seemed to him, people wanted to read his verse. It is hard therefore to detect a progressive chronological development in the three collections; on the other hand, one can discern in the best ballads of the last two volumes a greater confidence and craftsmanship. The narrative dexterity of "A Ballad of Ducks", "Mulligan's Mare" and "The Gundaroo Bullock" (all from his third book, *Saltbush Bill J.P. and Other Verses*) is hardly equalled by even the best of his early verse in that style; there are more and more phrases of poetic mastery:

   . . . the wild ducks cry
   Their long-drawn note of revelry.

And in "The Road to Hogan's Gap", "The Mountain Squatter" —

   My little collie pup
     Works silently and wide;
   You'll see her climbing up
     Along the mountain side . . .

— and "The Road to Gundagai" —

   The mountain road goes up and down
   From Gundagai to Tumut Town.

   And branching off, there runs a track
   Across the foothills grim and black.

   Across the plains and ranges grey
   To Sydney city far away.

Paterson has also learned the priceless (especially in the ballad) lesson of simplicity.

Coming back on the ship, Paterson had written a short novel called *The Cook's Dog*.* He sent it immediately to George Roberston, with an accompanying letter:[2]

                      Rockwell,
                      New South Head Road,
                      15 December, 1919.

Dear Robertson,

   I wish you would read this yarn and see what you think of it. I meant to try the *Saturday Evening Post* with it. They pay well, but I am very dissatisfied with the thing; and am afraid I will have to do it over again to make it readable. The style is so stiff. I thought it might appeal to the *Post* Editor on the ground of being new Australian stuff but I don't feel at all satisfied with it. Let me know what you think and is it worth rewriting?

                      Yours truly,
                      A. B. PATERSON.

Paterson's forebodings were not unjustified. Robertson wrote back to him at the Australian Club a letter[3] dated 6 January 1920, in which, making no bones about it, he said *inter alia*:

   . . . I am sure you will never make anything of the ms. you left with me ten days ago. It has hardly a redeeming feature and probably will

---

* The MS. is in the Mitchell Library, Sydney.

do no better if you rewrite it till hell's blue. You lack the ability to *construct* a novel. . . . Your forte is verse — descriptive, humorous, pathetic. But just because it's your forte, you want to do something else. . . .

That was the end of *The Cook's Dog*, and reading the story one agrees that it was just as well. It was a rambling story centred about the ownership of a clever and valuable sheep-dog. The heroine was an Australian girl, Ellen Macalister, who wanted to return to her own country: she was tired of being a governess to Lady Grizel Muckleston and the Mountsnuffinghams. (Paterson, writing of the English aristocracy, seemed often lost between over-emphasized satire and a weird and wonderful assessment of their virtues and vices.) The hero was one Farquharson — a "tall, looselimbed good-natured young Hercules with a strong hawk-like face, very dark and sunburned". He had been a Rhodes Scholar, and won his blue for "rowing or putting the shot or something like that . . .". Somehow, in his descriptions of these young Englishmen coming to Australia, there seemed more than a little projection of Paterson himself. At any rate, the plot hinged on Farquharson, with sheep-dog especially imported, working on the property of Hungry Duncan Macalister — related, of course, to Ellen — and the escape and adventures of the dog itself. Robertson was undoubtedly right. The novel was a long way short of *An Outback Marriage*: in style and plot it was much more stilted and cliché-ridden, and most times it read like an amateurly told children's story.

With *The Cook's Dog* fallen by the wayside, Paterson concentrated his energies on assisting Robertson to bring out the first collected edition of his verse, which was published in 1921. Not a great deal was discarded from the three volumes previously published; there seems to have been cordial agreement between Paterson and Robertson on the selection. Curiously, their only argument was about "The Travelling Post Office"; Robertson wanted to substitute

And Curban and Gulargambone have marked it "Further down"

for the familiar

And Conroy's Gap and Conroy's Creek have marked it "Further down"

since he thought the word "Conroy's" a "blemish". But Paterson dug his heels in and wrote (9 August 1921):

I wouldn't alter the Conroy's Gap and Conroy's Creek line. There is some sense in it and it has at any rate stood the test of time.[4]

The other point of interest in their publishing relationship at this time was that, in collaboration with Angus & Robertson, Paterson sold the film rights of "The Man from Snowy River" for £100. (He commented, in the following year, ". . . What a pity they murdered the picture as they did.")

In 1921, too, Paterson launched into jounalism again, this time as editor of the *Sportsman*, a publication of the John Norton Estate.* (Its publicity line was "The Most Authoritative Sporting Newspaper in Australia".) Paterson held this post till 1930, and such was his love of thoroughbred racing and sporting journalism that those who knew him at the time recall that these were years that he enjoyed to the full. In addition to editing the *Sportsman*, he covered the races each week for the Sydney *Truth*, published by the same interests. (Back in the turbulent days of the Sydney press of the 1890s, not the least turbulent of its characters was John Norton, who in the latter part of that decade assumed control of the Sydney *Truth*, and in 1900 founded the *Sportsman*.)

Paterson brought much colour to the *Sportsman*, and, in the first few years of his editorship especially, this weekly newspaper was clearly imbued with his personality and interests. In the days of intense competition from other established sporting journals such as the *Referee* and the *Judge*, the *Sportsman* of this period was as vital and readable as any similar publication in Australian newspaper history. In addition to horseracing, it covered remarkably well other major sports such as athletics, cricket, football, tennis and boxing — internationally as well as locally — and yet with suitable and interesting attention to minor sports and pastimes such as surfing, sailing, swimming and billiards. It was an intensely lively newspaper, no less in its presentation than in its reading matter: the photographs were full of action; cartoons, including those by Arthur Mailey, the cricketer, were a feature; and any controversial sporting stories were hard-hitting and direct.

Paterson's hand, in the early days of his editorship at least, was quite apparent. Buried in the pages of the *Sportsman* of 1922[5] is one of his best humorous ballads. I do not know that it has ever been re-printed or even referred to in the years that have followed; and yet, so excellent an example of Paterson's mature balladry (and, incidentally, of his ironic irreverence for religious institutions) is it that it deserves quotation in full:

That Harp Crown Sweep

A Tale of The Territory — by The Banjo

The run of Billabong-go-dry
  Is just beyond Lime Burner's Gap:
Its waterhole and tank supply
  Is excellent — upon the map.
But, lacking Nature's liquid drench,
  The station staff are wont to try
With "Bob-in Sweeps" their thirst to quench,
  Or nearly quench, at Bong-go-dry.

---

* Paterson was for several years at this time a director of the company which until 1923 conducted the Estate's newspaper affairs.

The parson made five yearly rounds
    That soil of arid souls to delve,
He wrote, "I'll come for seven pounds
    Or I could stop away for twelve."
But lack of lucre brought about
    The pusillanimous reply:
"Our luxuries are all cut out,
    You'll have to come to Bong-go-dry."

There'd been a kind of rabbit rush —
And what with traps and sticks they'd shy
Now rabbit skins were very high —
    The station blacks were very flush,
And each was taught his churchman's job,
    "When that one parson's plate come roun'
No good you put in sprat or bob,
    Too quick you put in harp-a-crown!"

The parson's word was duly kept,
    He came and did his bit of speak;
The boss remarked he hadn't slept
    So sound and well for many a week.
But Gilgai Jack and Monkey Jaw
    Regarded preaching as a crime
Against good taste; they said, "What for
    That one chap yabber all the time?"

Proceedings ceased: the boss's hat
    Was raked from underneath his chair;
The coloured congregation sat
    And waited with expectant air.
At last from one far-distant seat
    Where Gilgai's Mary'd been asleep,
There came a kind of plaintive bleat,
    "Say, Boss! Who won the harp-crown sweep?"

Again, Paterson did not hesitate to use the columns of the *Sportsman* to record his tribute[6] to J. F. Archibald on the latter's death. It was a brilliant piece of biographical journalism that could have distinguished the columns of any newspaper in the land. Paterson elaborated on his first meeting with Archibald in the *Bulletin* office, ". . . the small shabby brick building hidden away among ship-chandleries, fish shops and wool stores . . ."; in a few lines he gave a striking impression of the man:

Racially, Archibald looked like a Jew. He had the hawk nose, the open eye and the quick movements of that Oriental people; physically he was a fairly strong and well set-up man of medium size, long in the arms, untidy in dress, wearing a moustache and a pointed beard . . .

And (after nearly thirty-five years) he released the text of the letter Archibald had written him, after their first meeting, confirming his advice to Paterson for his future writing; Archibald's *Bulletin* credo is implicit:

> . . . 1 want you to remember that Australia is a big place and I want you to write stuff that will appeal not only to Sydney people, but that will be of interest to the pearler up at Thursday Island and the farmer down in Victoria. On all public questions the press are apt to sing in chorus. If you go to a concert you may hear a man sing a discord which is put there by the composer, and that discord catches the ear over the voices of the chorus. Well, don't be afraid to sing the discord. Even if you are wrong, you will have drawn attention to what you want to say, and you may be right. . . .

Paterson made it clear in his article that he admired Archibald for "singing the discord" — and for being the first Australian to "call the English bluff". In a time, recalls Paterson, when "we were patronized by imported Governors, insulted by imported globe-trotting snobs, exploited by imported actors and singers, mostly worn out and incompetent", it was Archibald who maintained loudly and strongly that an Australian lawyer, doctor, singer or actor was every bit as good as any importation. And it was Archibald who had dared to portray in a cartoon a Governor of his day, a "worn-out diplomat with a hobby for fowls", as "a broken-down swell leading a Muscovy drake by a string and carrying a hat full of eggs" That was singing the discord on the top note! Paterson concluded:

> Even after his death he has done something to carry on the advancement of Australia, as he has left a fairly large sum of money to provide for the purchase each year of the best portrait painted in Australia of any Australian distinguished in art, literature, or research, and this in itself speaks the character of the man's mind. Cynic and pessimist as he was, he never lost faith in the ultimate success of Australians, and when in the process of time his name is forgotten and people ask "Who was this Archibald who left this bequest?" the question can be answered by saying ". . . he was the first man who believed in the home-made Australian article".

It is easy to see that Paterson himself shared these convictions, and that they were an essential part of his own brand of Australianism.

Paterson also ran an entertaining assessment[7] of Adam Lindsay Gordon's rhyming "Racing Tips in Verse" — Tim Whiffler and The Barb in the Melbourne Cup, and "The Fields of Coleraine" as "a tip for the Great Western Steeplechase". More specifically, in his paper's concern with matters of current horse-racing, Paterson conducted a column of "General Turf Notes", and wrote topical articles on subjects such as "Tick-tackers: Getting the Oil from Paddock to Leger" and "Racing Systems" (". . . it is a deplorable fact," he wrote in the best Patersonian manner,[8] "that in spite of our civilization, education and scientific knowledge, there are still hundreds of thousands of people who believe in fortune tellers, the divining rod, the rich uncle in Fiji, the philosopher's stone, perpetual motion and betting systems. . . .") . And he was in his element when the annual Yearling Sales came round, where all his knowledge of the thoroughbred and its breeding was crystallized in his reports of the sales. For instance:

> . . . a big plain filly by the new sire Gadabout is a wonderfully long-strider when walking; and this one seems likely to go a distance . . .

Or, writing of a "fine big gelding" whose owner seemed likely to race it only at bush picnic-meetings:

> . . . it would be a pity to "picnic" this horse as he is a big-framed, heavy, long-striding fellow that would not shine on iron-hard tracks or dodging rabbit holes . . .

Much of the interest in Paterson's sporting journalism over these years, however, rests in the laconic wit and edge he gave to his "stories" of the Sydney racing scene for the *Truth*, which, in the fashion of the racing press of the day, brought to a fine art the epigrammatic and alliterative headlines of its paragraphs: "Pike's Polish not Potent"; "Royal Tea is Too Weak"; "Pericles Full of Pep". He shared the reporting of each Satur day race-meeting with two fellow-journalists, Harry Frank and George Palmer; but there is no doubt, in reading through Paterson's hundreds of reports and "side" (i.e., human interest) stories of the Turf over these years, that for his humour, knowledge of what he was writing about, and conscious or unconscious literariness of style, he must share with C. J. Graves ("Iroquois") of *Smith's Weekly* — who contributed that splendid series "Diary of a Punter" in the Pepysian manner — the distinction of being the outstanding racing journalist of the time.

Veteran newspaper men still recall Paterson's memorable stories and sallies. C. H. Bateson of the Sydney *Daily Mirror* has told me of the time when a young apprentice who clearly had the race in his keeping allowed his horse to veer aside in the shadow of the judges' box, and "presented" the race to the eager jockey slipping through on the inside rail. Paterson next day in the *Truth* sympathized with the lad: of course, he had the race won, but then it was Boy Scout Week and the kid was obviously determined to do his good deed!

Then there was the time when, in a startling reversal of form, a race-horse named Dreblah, owned by a controversial Turf identity of those years, one "Grafter" Kingsley, won the main race of the afternoon to "the great discontent" (as C. J. Graves, à la Pepys, would have written) of the crowd. Paterson's droll and sardonic account[9] ran:

> They gave "Grafter" such a hooting yesterday as falls to the lot of a few men in a racing lifetime. "Grafter" like the villain in the play acknowledged the shouts of the audience by bowing repeatedly to the crowd. Then he took an apple out of his pocket and Dreblah ate it to the frenzied howls of "Rub him out!", "Give him two years", etc., etc. ad lib. . . .

A few weeks later, as a postscript to the incident, Paterson wrote,[10] no less characteristically, and with the bushman's instinctive sympathy for the horse itself:

> "Grafter" Kingsley has kept Dreblah at it till the bay horse about answers to Kipling's description "a rag, a bone and a hank of hair". Poor old Dreblah looked about half his usual size when he went out to run in the Welter yesterday and he soon put his backers out of their misery for he refused to start. Even when the others were well on their journey, he stuck at his post and would not go for a yard.
>
> If Dreblah is drawn any finer, the turf scribes will miss him in describing the races, for it will be impossible to see him end on, and if he comes home first the judge will be apt to look right through him and place some horse on the inside as the winner.

Bateson recalls, too, the occasion when the Associated Racing Clubs, which controlled the "pony" races around Sydney, fell out with the *Truth*'s racing journalists and refused them admittance to their racecourses. Paterson one day handed in a piece of "copy" which read:

> ### Gatekeepers' Oath
> I swear to keep out the *Truth*
> The whole of the *Truth*
> And nothing but the *Truth* and *Sportsman*,
>   So help me, A.R.C.

At a time when the racing game was no less afflicted with disreputable and dishonest practices than it is at present, Paterson's involvement in it — since he was a man of such probity and integrity as well as of literary and social standing — might well be questioned. He gave the answer in his usual forthright fashion in a letter[11] in 1924 to George Robertson, who had invited him to write the introduction to a racing book called *Piebald* which Angus & Robertson were about to publish:

> Many thanks for your offer to pay me for an introduction to *Piebald* but the book does not appeal to me at all so I will have to decline. You will remember O. Henry's yarn about the man who went to a South American Republic that was rotten with graft and he decided that his own "graft" was to be honest. Well, I made the same resolution when I went into sporting journalism with the result that the horsey men look on me with respect and contempt, and I would not like to forfeit the one or deserve the other by publishing an appreciation of this book. I will be sixty years old in a few days and I don't want to forfeit my self-respect by writing against my convictions and I know you would be the last man to ask me to do so. . . .

Indeed, Paterson's bearing and demeanour were no less dignified on the racecourse than off it. Vince Kelly recalls that, as a celebrity in his time, Paterson moved with ease and composure among those eminent men of Sydney whom he met in the Members' enclosure at Randwick: he was tranquil, slow in walk and movement, as unflurried in his conversation as he was quick in mind. Yet his head was never in the clouds. He had what Kelly calls that "bullock-driver's assessment" of men and situations, enlivened by a mischievous humour. Once, at Randwick, Kelly asked Paterson what he thought would win the next race. "Banjo" pointed to an obvious racecourse "urger" and his woman friend talking on the grass below, and then to a horse entered for the race called Hum and Haw.* Paterson and Kelly used to watch hurdle races together; whenever a horse fell at a jump, Paterson would murmur to himself the title of one of his ballads, "There's another blessed horse fell down!"

Around the newspaper office, as his contemporaries recall, Paterson was held in great affection. He had a quick smile for everyone, even the copy-boys who used to buy second-hand copies of his poems for the great "Banjo" to autograph; invariably Paterson would ask, with his pen in hand, "Now, what's your name, Sonny?"

He was, according to Kelly, most reticent about his private life, as he was about references to his friends. He was a member of the Australian Club, and had a passion for playing bridge there at all hours of the day. His greatest pleasure was a quiet drink, a pipe and a yarn with club members. One of his particular friends at the time was A. B. Piddington, then President of the Industrial Commission of New South Wales and one of the most eminent jurists in Australian legal history, who was drawn to Paterson by a great admiration for his work; this was not un-connected with the fact that Piddington was for a time President of the Fellowship of Australian Writers.

Nor did Paterson talk very much about his writing past. Vince Kelly recalls that only once, in his memory, did Paterson make any particular reference to the old days, and that was that he regretted that Daley, Ogilvie, Lawson and his fellow-writers of the 1890s had had no head for business: they had sold out their copyrights for "a few bob", not visualiz-ing the days of mass publication and broadcasting when royalties assumed a much greater financial significance.

Paterson resigned the editorship of the *Sportsman* in 1930 to concen-trate on the writing of several books that were to follow. He restricted his journalism to free-lance work for *Smith's Weekly*, a publication unique in Australian press history because of its polemical approach to politics and social events of the day, its hard-hitting personal attacks which frequently involved it in legal actions, and its curious dependence for readership, in the manner of the Sydney *Truth*, on the exposure of the scandalous doings of Sydney society, both high-life and low-life. Paterson contributed odd articles, mainly for the excellent sporting pages which *Smith's Weekly* maintained. It is a matter of some interest, nevertheless, that throughout these years Paterson, while he always had one leg in, as it were, with the upper crust of Sydney life (he was *persona grata* at Government House and in the area of government and business affairs), had a knowledge of the happenings in what might these days be termed

---

* Hum and Haw was beautifully named: by Absurd out of Impediment!

the "underworld" that never failed to intrigue his journalistic confrères. Perhaps this stemmed in part from his contacts with the Turf; but he knew more of the activities of "crooks" and "lurk men" in the difficult years of the early 1930s than most. Charles Bateson recalls that he once tipped off his fellow-reporters to a "scoop" story about a well-known confidence man's activities in a leading city hotel. Word had come to Paterson that a certain gentleman had put out at night a half-dozen pairs of shoes to be cleaned; this said Paterson was a sure indication of the confidence man at work, since this was the oldest ploy in the game whereby hotel employees might be impressed with the suggestion of unlimited means.

It has been said that Paterson was in some way connected with the New Guard movement of the early 1930s. This was a somewhat notorious association described by its supporters as a force for maintaining constitutional law and order against Communism, but denounced by others as a fascist or neo-fascist body. At all events, Eric Campbell, one of the founders of the New Guard, relates in his reminiscences of the movement:

> One morning A. B. Paterson called to see me. I was delighted to make his acquaintance and to listen to his shrewd summing up of the situation. His trim, well-dressed figure and his alert crisp manner was quite unlike what I imagined any poet could be . . .[12]

But those who knew Paterson well at the time have assured me that he had no active association with the New Guard, and that nothing significant can be read into this somewhat ambiguous reference.

It was about this time (1932) that Paterson became interested in broadcasting, and he contributed to programmes of the Australian Broadcasting Commission with talks and scripts for the next few years.[13] He was also busily engaged in bringing three books to publication: *The Animals That Noah Forgot, Happy Dispatches* and *The Shearer's Colt*.

It would be not an exaggeration to say that whatever elegances of simplicity and explicitness and graces of poetic expression Paterson had developed in the writing of his verses down the years came most felicitously to fruition in this last volume of verse, *The Animals That Noah Forgot*, which was published by the Endeavour Press, an offshoot of the *Bulletin*, in 1933. The volume was gloriously illustrated by Norman Lindsay. Written as poetry for children, like all the classic examples of this genre in our literature, it reaches out to all ages. For here Paterson has written the most charming verses imaginable about Australian animals (which, sadly one must say, his poems may well outlast — the platypus, the wombat, the flying squirrel, the white cockatoo, the buffalo, the bandicoot), not forgetting that unusual ballad, "The Billygoat Overland":

> And never a dog had pluck or gall in front of the mob to stand
> And face the charge of a thousand goats on the billygoat overland.

There has not been better children's poetry about animals written before or since — for, somehow, here best of all, Paterson's love for the bush,

his poetic sense, his innate humour and his accurate observation combine
to give his writing the most delicate touch:

> Far from the trouble and toil of town
> Where the reed-beds sweep and shiver
> Look at a fragment of velvet brown —
> Old Man Platypus drifting down,
> Drifting along the river . . .
>
>   ("Old Man Platypus")

> The chorus frogs in the big lagoon
> Would sing their songs to the silvery moon.
> Tenor singers were out of place
> For every frog was a double bass.
>
>   ("Frogs in Chorus")

> Each little dormouse sleeps
> In the spout of a gumtree old,
> A ball of fur with a silver coat;
> Each with his tail around his throat
> For fear of his catching cold.

> These are the things he eats,
> Asking his friends to dine:
> Moths and beetles and new-born shoots,
> Honey and snacks of the native fruits,
> And a glass of dew for wine.
>
>   ("Flying Squirrels")

Happy the child who numbered these poems in his literary education!

As for *Happy Dispatches*, there is evidence that Paterson had turned
over in his mind for many years the idea of a semi-autobiographical work
combining recollections of his various activities and travels and reminiscences of famous people he had met. Even as far back as 1901 he had
written as a footnote to a letter[14] to George Robertson, from London:
"I have kept very full diaries and think I can give you a rather amusing
book of travel — something new in that line — will talk it over with you."
It was not, however, until he had got free of his many involvements, not
least those journalistic, that he began, early in the 1930s, seriously to collate
the jottings and accounts he had obviously kept in diaries and notebooks.
He used to talk to Norman Lindsay, when they met in the *Bulletin*
office from time to time, about his experiences as a war correspondent
and elsewhere. Lindsay writes:[15]

> . . . I said, "This stuff is too good to throw away in talk. Why don't
> you write it?"
>
> "The nuisance is to know how far to go," he said. "Not so much
> in what to say as in what to leave out. Tell the whole truth or only
> half of it?"

I gave him the advice I have always given to biographers or auto-
biographers. Write everything in and then sub it out for publication,
if you must. Let the record remain for a future generation to read,
and to value for what light it throws on the era in which it was
written. I wonder if the rough journals "Banjo" wrote during the
action of affairs are still extant. They should be preserved, for there
must be much in them revealing the man who jotted them down,
often under fire, and some good stories of the hazards of an adven-
turous life.

At any rate, Paterson set to work in earnest, having interested Angus &
Robertson in the book. As it neared publication, Paterson's correspondence with his publishers show his usual vacillation about titles — and
indeed his monumental inability to distinguish between a good title and
a bad one (*All Nurses Swear; Giants I Have Met!*), and as well as the
curious dichotomy of his attitude to Royalty. How different the Paterson
of these letters[16] hanging on to the idea of royal patronage, from the
Paterson who applauded Archibald's almost republican enthusiasms!

19 South Street,
Double Bay.
Thursday 8 Feb. 1934.

Dear Mr Cousins,
    I am sending three more chapters of the book which ought to make
it long enough with the addition of the chapter on Allenby which I
am re-writing.
    I would like to know what you think of it as soon as possible, as
if it could be got out while the Prince is here he and his entourage
might take it home with them and spread the gospel of Australian
literature in England. You have got enough of it now to know
whether it appeals to you or not.

Yours truly,
(Signed)   A. B. PATERSON.

If I played up the Teck princes and called it "Princes
and Potentates" we might get Royalty interested.

19 South Street,
Double Bay.
21 February 1934. Tel. 2877.

Dear Mr Cousins,
    I send a couple more chapters which should nearly be enough but I
would like, if there is time to do a couple of humorous chapters
away altogether from the military men. I want to make it as English
as possible in hopes of catching an English sale.
    I understand you want to get the title out. The best title I can
think of is "Happy Despatches".
    It is easily remembered and conveys the idea that there is some
humour in the book. Others that might do are "Famous Folk at
Close Range" — "All Nurses Swear" with a subtitle explaining what

the book is about, "Princes in Private" or "Princes and Privates", "Notes on the Notables", "From Prince to Puppet — I met 'em all".

Of these I think "Happy Despatches" is the best — you may have some suggestions. I leave Lambert's sketch. I will go on with two extra chapters and come in on Friday at two if that will suit.

Yours truly,
(Signed)   A. B. PATERSON.

How would "Strictly Private" go as a name?

22nd February, 1934.

ANGUS & ROBERTSON LTD.

A. B. Paterson, Esq.,
19 South Street,
DOUBLE BAY.

Dear Mr Paterson,

We have received the two extra chapters of "Happy Despatches" which on first sight is a good title. Carry on with the two additional chapters. We will get the book out in plenty of time.

Lambert sketch. We do not think this is good enough for publicity purposes. Your photograph is far better.

Yours faithfully,
ANGUS & ROBERTSON LTD.
(Signed)   W. C. Cousins.

14th March, 1934.

Dear Mr Cousins,

How would this go for a title and subtitle —

GIANTS IN OUR DAY or GIANTS I HAVE MET

(and as a subtitle)

RACY RECOLLECTIONS OF WORLD FAMOUS PEOPLE.

Then we might add in quotation marks

"Some were so big and some were so small; but it was every man for himself as the elephant said when he danced among the chickens."

I don't like either "Happy Despatches" or "Bye-paths and Bridle-ways". They might mean anything and not many people will bother themselves to find out. The above title might make even the English people want to know what is inside the book. The quotation would assure them that the book is humorous and most historical. I tried the idea on various people — Claude Reading of the Commonwealth Bank, Consett Stephen, etc. — and they all said they would like to read a book of outspoken opinion about the big people: so we may as well let them know what the book is about. "Giants I have met" seems to me the best as it gives the idea of the personal touch. Let it go at that.

Yours truly,
[Signed]   A. B. PATERSON.

19 South Street,
Double Bay.
27 July 1934.

Dear Mr Cousins,

I am worried because I cannot remember whether I cut a sentence out of the galley referring to the Duke of Teck. I meant to cut it out. I said that it was reported that he had laid ten thousand to a thousand on a horse, and that the Royal Family had to pay pay pay. This potentate may be alive and while one can hardly imagine a Royal Duke coming out and suing Angus and Robertson for libel, more curious things have happened: and in any event we don't want to get in bad odor with the visiting Prince. See that it is cut out. This should be the last of our troubles. It is in one of the early galleys.

Yours truly,

(Signed)   A. B. PATERSON.

Happy Dispatches was not a success, and to his dying day Paterson was aggrieved at this. And yet, the reasons are not hard to see. The book suffers from a chronological untidiness as he dodges about the years — and it is hard for the reader to get the hang of it; there was a surfeit of travel books at this time, most of them much more exotically and lavishly presented, with photographs to boot (*Happy Dispatches* was not illustrated) ; and in any case the book dealt with a period of time long past and hardly likely to interest readers coping with the Depression. Despite its many fine vignettes of characterization, it fell between the stools of autobiography, travel book and history: clearly Paterson would have done better had he written a straight autobiography capitalizing on the legend of himself as simultaneously Man from Snowy River and bushman-of-the-present, and using much of the material of *Happy Dispatches* as incidental colour. The fact is that the book is much more valuable in 1966 as a source-book of Paterson, his times and his experiences than it was in 1934 when it was published.

The Shearer's Colt, Paterson's last published work, appeared in 1936. As I say in a later chapter, it was his challenge to the racing "novelettes" of Nat Gould; it did not sell very well and is now buried in the anonymity of the ephemeral fiction of the time. Yet its writing was to Paterson an enthusiastic exercise for his knowledge of the world of horse-racing and he held it in as great an affection as any of his published works.

Despite the heavy load of his writing activities during the 1930s, Paterson took an active and intelligent interest in the rapidly changing times of a new generation, keeping pace with it, yet injecting occasional notes of nostalgia for an era now past. He spoke or lectured frequently to clubs and associations, often about his adventures as a war correspondent in two campaigns, sometimes about Australian writing or the problem of the writer generally. Thus we find him reported in 1932[17] expounding to the Fellowship of Australian Writers his own particular theory about the current vogue for stories of mystery and detection: "The popularity of this type of book is attributable to an inherited instinct. In cave-man days the murder of a member of the tribe would get everybody wild with excitement and if the cause of the murder was a mystery no member of the tribe would sleep soundly at night till the mystery was cleared up. . . ." As guest of honour at the weekly luncheon of the Kooroora Club during 1934, he talked on writing too. The ordinary bread-and-butter writer, he said,[18] must consider his public; on the other hand, "if you are a genius your writing will make its own living, if not while you live, then after you are dead . . .".

Any problem of the country or the outback excited his immediate attention, and invariably resulted in a letter to the newspapers. Thus, for instance, in January 1932, when the State was suffering a savage rash of bushfires, Paterson wrote[19] to the *Sydney Morning Herald* to explain that bushfires always connoted good seasons; no grass meant no bushfires, and it was the irony of fate that the far-western country then being swept by bushfires had rarely grass enough to keep a fire going. Then came the sage old bushman's advice on fighting bushfires especially in mountainous country:

> There is a great deal more strategy about fighting a mountain fire, for a fire always burns slowly down a hill and there are always a good many creeks and gullies that can be used as natural firebreaks. On the other hand if a piece of burning cinder gets a start from a dead tree on top of a mountain, the wind will sometimes carry it a mile and a half across a valley and a fresh fire at once is started on a distant mountain-side. Sometimes too a barrage of logs is formed in a dry gully on the side of a steep hill and when these logs are burnt through, an avalanche of red hot stones kept in place by the logs will roll down the hill setting fire to the long grass on the flats below. . . .

He wrote other letters about irrigation and water conservation, the short-sightedness of using fertile coastal districts for sheep-raising when intensive cultivation could be practised and dairy herds developed, the need for statesmanlike action in appropriating large areas of Australia for wild life protection.

Nor did his interest in people flag in his last years — especially in those whose love of adventure and experience of it matched his own. He was stimulated by his meeting in 1934 with an Englishman, J. H. Curle, whom Paterson described as "author, mining-engineer and world wanderer". Curle had written several books on his travels which Paterson admired; Curle told him that years before he had met in Western Australia a young American mining-engineer who had risked buying on his own judgement a gold-mine "The Sons of Gwalior", which turned out to be one of the richest in the area. The young mining-engineer was Herbert Hoover, later President of the United States, and Paterson was fond of telling this story to prove that the world could never "become flat stale and unprofitable when these things happened . . ." — what might have been Hoover's story if the mine "had turned out a duffer"! Paterson left a lively portrait of Curle:

. . . After a life spent mainly in steamers, railway trains, hotels, clubs, and hospitals, Curle is still a massive figure, well over six feet high, clean-shaven, except for a grizzled moustache, and with the face of a French savant. His conversation is bewildering; for one cannot mention any place but what he has been there, nor any name but what he has met the owner of it. . . .[20]

The following year Paterson renewed associations with Reuter's, when one of its overseas representatives, William Wearne, visited Australia. Since Wearne had worked with "Chinese" Morrison in China, he excited Paterson's special interest, and they spent many hours in the Australian Club exchanging stories about Morrison. Paterson has recorded[21] that it was from Wearne that he heard for the first time how Morrison got his great scoop about the Russian demand on the Japanese for Port Arthur to link it with the trans-Siberian railway. Sensing that this was likely to happen, Morrison wrote six columns of copy in advance and posted it to *The Times*, telling the editor to run the story when he cabled him. Sure enough, in a few weeks' time General Paratiloff, the Russian spokesman, sent for the news correspondents to say he had an important announcement to make. Morrison, acting on his hunch, cabled *The Times* to use the story. When Paratiloff sprang his surprise, Morrison laughed in his face, and told him he had already sent the story. So he scooped the world press, and so, said Paterson, "newsgetting, after all, is a trade like any other: and the man who wants to see the big things happen must set to work and learn his business".

It was in 1935, too, that Paterson had his portrait painted by Sir John Longstaff, and in the course of his sittings became a firm friend of the artist. Longstaff was almost the same age as Paterson; Paterson warmed to him because Longstaff too had been born in the bush (in a very small mining township near Ballarat) and loved the outback, and Paterson admired especially his painting "Bush Fires in Gippsland", which Longstaff had painted at the turn of the century. Paterson has left a vivid and amusing description[22] of Longstaff at work:

And now, how is a portrait painted? Does the artist sit down, sucking at a pipe, and remaining immobile till the day's sitting is done? Not a bit of it, or at any rate not in Longstaff's case. Wiry and energetic in spite of his years, he requires one of those big rooms in which to do himself full justice. He never sits down while painting, not for a moment. Having posed his sitter, he goes back to the far corner of the room and studies his subject. Then he dashes at the easel and paints feverishly for a moment. Then he dashes back again to the end of the room, compares the sitter with the work on the easel, and then makes another dash at the picture. All told, he must walk miles while painting a portrait, the distance being added to by a few false starts when he changes his mind half way to the easel and goes back to have another look. At the end of a two hours' sitting he suggested that I, as the sitter, must be tired, but I replied: "Well, if you can stand running a footrace for two hours, I can stand sitting here watching you. . . ."

Longstaff told Paterson that he thought Australian landscape-painters had great opportunities in the inland country. He did not believe that a picture had to have a mountain or a river or a glimpse of the sea in it. "There is good material in the flat country," he said, "and perhaps the great Australian picture of the future will be painted far out on the Western Plains." With this remark, needless to say, he especially endeared himself to Paterson.

On 1 January 1939 Paterson was awarded the C.B.E. for his services to Australian literature (along with similar honours to Professor Walter Murdoch and Mrs Aeneas Gunn). "The Commonwealth does well," wrote the *Sydney Morning Herald* in its leading article on that day, "to recommend royal recognition of the writers who interpret the life and spirit of this land."

It was in this year, too, that his last published work appeared: a series of five articles in the *Sydney Morning Herald*, which were published weekly from 4 February, in which he reminisced about various events and happenings in his life, and of various celebrities, such as Lawson, Morant, Sir Henry Parkes and others he had known in his lifetime. The articles were uneven in quality and rambling in style, even if they do fill in some of the gaps in his life-history.

Early in 1941 Paterson was treated in hospital for a short illness. He died on 5 February, twelve days short of his seventy-seventh birthday, sitting in a chair at the hospital waiting for his wife to take him home Both his son, Hugh, and his son-in-law were away at the War.

One is left with a feeling of amazement (since Paterson was fifty-five when he returned from the Great War) at the enthusiastic activity of his last twenty-two years, normally, for the most part, years of retirement. Yet Paterson had published three books of original work, had written thousands of columns of newspaper articles and reports, and had engaged extensively in broadcasting and lecturing. Right up to his death he had impressed everyone who knew him with his energy and the complete exercise of his faculties. If his was a full life, as indeed it was, it was fullest in its ripeness.

Paterson "was one of those fortunate men who, dying, are never dead," wrote an obituarist,[23] "since the work they have done in life, the forces they have been instrumental in inspiring and releasing, continue after they have gone as part of the national life. Posterity will pass its own judgment on Paterson's works, but the judges themselves, whether they realize it or not, will be men and women whose temperament, outlook, and national spirit will have been conditioned to no inconsiderable extent by the writings of this bush balladist of a literary era we have already left behind us."

NOTES

[1]   The letter is among the George Robertson papers in the Mitchell Library, Sydney.
[2]   Ibid.
[3]   Ibid.
[4]   Ibid.

[5] In the issue of 11 January 1922.
[6] In the *Sportsman*, 25 January 1922.
[7] Ibid., 31 January 1922.
[8] Ibid., 8 August 1922.
[9] In the Sydney *Truth*, 24 August 1924.
[10] Ibid., 9 September 1924.
[11] Dated 2 February 1924. The letter is among the George Robertson papers in the Mitchell Library.
[12] *The Rallying Point* (1965).
[13] See Chapter XVI.
[14] Dated 12 December 1901.
[15] In *Bohemians of the Bulletin* (1965).
[16] Among the George Robertson papers in the Mitchell Library.
[17] *Sydney Morning Herald*, 30 April 1932.
[18] Ibid., 14 February 1934.
[19] Ibid., 9 January 1932.
[20] In a hitherto unpublished broadcast script "An English View" for his A.B.C. series *The Land of Adventure* (see Chapter XVI).
[21] In a script called "News" in the above series.
[22] In a script called "An Interview" in the above series.
[23] In the *Sydney Morning Herald*, 6 February 1941.

CHAPTER XV

The Sport of Kings

Paterson always had a warm spot in his heart for the horse.
If Shakespeare had not put the words "A horse! A horse!
My kingdom for a horse!" into Richard III's mouth, it is
more than likely that Paterson would have uttered them.
He dearly loved a horse, a good horse, and to have deprived
him of his "horsey" talk would have deprived him of one of
the pleasures of speech. Whether it was the most famous
colt of the day: whether it was the slickest polo pony ever
bred; or one of the wilder horses of which he sings in his
verse — was all one to "The Banjo".

— G. A. KING.[1]

Before the North Pole was discovered, some cynic said that
it would be discovered easily enough by advertising a race
meeting there, when a couple of dozen Australians would
infallibly turn up with their horses . . .

— A. B. PATERSON.[2]

IN A PREDOMINANTLY pastoral country it is not to be wondered at that
horse-racing has become Australia's national sport. Apart from the capital
cities where there are in most cases at least three established racecourses
conducting Saturday and mid-week race-meetings, every country town of
any size has its racecourse — from Gosford to Geraldton, from Mount
Gambier to Townsville. And even in the small outback townships and on
remote stations, picnic race-meetings are regularly held, which can and do
attract people from outlying areas up to three and four hundred miles
away. Some of the larger towns, especially those nearer the cities, have
become centres of provincial racing, rivalling city race-clubs — like
Gawler, near Adelaide, or Werribee, near Melbourne; some picnic race-
meetings have become annual holiday events attracting tens of thousands
of visitors, like Onkaparinga in the Adelaide Hills, where the Great
Eastern Steeplechase is run; others are the occasions for fashionable social
activity, like the Bong Bong Picnic Races in the Bowral, New South
Wales, area.

Altogether, there are upwards of 4,000 race meetings held each year.
Racing, indeed, has become a major industry employing 50,000 people in
full-time occupations: breeders, trainers, jockeys, stable-hands, bookmakers, racing officials, racing journalists and commentators and so on.

A racing jargon has developed; the activities, personal or public, of a jockey will often attract more attention in his local press than important international happenings, and a successful racehorse more adulation than a Prime Minister.

Racing was almost certainly an unofficial pastime in New South Wales, in the Hawkesbury River settlements and in the Parramatta district, even before 1800. By the time Lachlan Macquarie landed in Sydney to take over as Captain-General and Governor on 1 January, 1810, there were nearly 1,200 horses in the colony. In Parramatta on 30 April of the same year, the first officially recorded race-meeting was held; the principal race was a match between two horses, Parramatta and Belfast, won, appropriately enough, by the former. Officers of Governor Macquarie's regiment, the 73rd, who were much addicted to racing, laid out a track in Hyde Park and began regular meetings in October 1810.

In 1842 the Australian Jockey Club, now the headquarters of racing in the Commonwealth, was formed in Sydney, conducting race-meetings first at Homebush, and, from 1860 onwards, at Randwick. In Victoria, where race-meetings were held as early as the 1830s, the Victoria Racing Club was founded in 1864, under whose auspices the Melbourne Cup (first run in 1861 — then organized by the Melbourne Racing Club — and won by Archer) has become the most famous event in the Australian racing calendar, and, indeed, an event of world-wide importance. With this race have been associated some of the great thoroughbreds of Australian racing whose breeding lines have been carried forward into the present generation.

When the extent of racing as a sport — "The Turf" — is considered in Australian life, its huge ramifications as a gambling medium, its hold on the national consciousness, its patronage by the ruling classes of the nation — princes, peers and politicians, industrialists, merchants and pastoralists — it is the more surprising that it has made such a slight impact on our literature. It is safe to say that Banjo Paterson alone of any Australian writer has made it a considerable and enduring subject of his attention; he is at once its historian and commentator, in his ballads as well as in his stories and sketches. Adam Lindsay Gordon essayed a number of racing ballads, it is true, and occasional writers have contributed odd stories and sketches around this theme. Contemporary writers, such as Frank Hardy (especially in his powerful novel *The Four-legged Lottery*), deal with the "race game" as one of the diversions of the working-classes, and Cecil Mann wrote a short story "Stiff Luck for the Colonel" which is a classic of its kind — but Paterson alone consistently and unashamedly wrote of racehorses, jockeys and the racing fraternity: punters, bookmakers, and "battlers".

For Paterson accepted the importance of the horse in the average Australian's consciousness of his traditions, taking in, as it does, the drover, the cattleman, the boundary-rider, the bush picnic meeting, the Royal Agricultural Show, the Man from Snowy River, the Australian Light Horse, the Mounted Police, and Phar Lap. And Paterson was proud of his associations, as he recorded in his *Sydney Morning Herald* reminiscences.

One of my father's forebears was John Paterson of Lochlyoch who founded the breed of Clydesdale horses by importing a black Flemish stallion called Robin. Robin was to the Clydesdale breed what Eclipse was to the thoroughbred, as may be seen in the Clydesdale stud book. There was also a further connection with horses in that my grandfather, going out to India to seek his fortune, joined up with John Company's army, in which his original rank was that of a roughrider. He rode the rough horses so well that he afterwards obtained his commission; and it is something of a coincidence that in the Great War more than a hundred years afterwards I, his grandson, was given a commission as Major in a rough riding unit. This, and my early experiences as a small shepherd, may account for whatever of accuracy there may be in my versified descriptions of bush life and of horses.

His characteristic modesty is not likely ever to dim the admiration and excitement his ballads of horses and horsemanship will always generate in his readers, especially those who can sense his appreciation that the horse is a method of expression for the horseman and that poetry can be woven into that fact. Paterson, from the time he rode miles to and from school as a small boy, knew, just as did the horsemen he wrote about, the joy and certainty of having a good horse under him way out in the bush: Rio Grande, "the big horse running free", or the Snowy Mountain horse whose "flank was still undaunted, and his courage fiery hot". But he was not a horse-*lover* in the sentimental sense. Like a true bushman, he saw the horse (like the dog) as an animal trained or useful for certain purposes — for rounding up cattle, for buffalo-hunting, for racing — and to be admired accordingly for its excellence therein.

Into this picture, of course, Nat Gould must be fitted, but his position is unique; in a sense he is to the Turf what Edgar Wallace was to the detective story or Marie Corelli to the popular romantic novel of her day — in output, and weight of contemporary impact, and yet ephemerality. Gould was born in England in 1857, and came to Australia in 1884, where he worked for eleven years as a journalist, beginning on the Brisbane *Telegraph* and then moving to Sydney, where he wrote for the *Sunday Times, Referee* and *Evening News,* and later for eighteen months he was editor of the *Bathurst Times.* It was there that he conceived the idea of the racing novel and wrote his first one, *With the Tide,* which ran serially in the *Referee* and was then published in London as *Double Event* in 1891. This was to be the first of one hundred and twenty-five novels, all of them published in London, all selling millions of copies and earning him a fortune. They invariably followed the same pattern: hero, heroine, villain from the racing fraternity; the horse the centre of the plot; virtue and good horse triumphant. His titles, epigrammatic and often alliterative, virtually explained the plot: *A Chestnut Champion, Jockey Jack, The Rajah's Race, The Roar of the Ring.* Some of his material was drawn from the Australian racing scene, and several of his novels, *Bred in the Bush, The Miner's Cup, A Coolgardie Romance,* etc., had an Australian setting.

Paterson met Nat Gould in Sydney. He was not impressed with Gould either as a man or a writer. Paterson, a genuine lover of the thoroughbred horse, took the racing game much more seriously than Gould, and regarded the latter's novels as caricatures and stereotyped, artificial conceptions of what went on at a racecourse. Paterson seldom resorted to parody, but he did this successfully, savagely and sarcastically in a short "story" *"Done for the Double* by Knott Gold, Author of *Flogged for A Furlong, Won by a Winker,* etc., etc."*. The plot went that Algernon de Montgomery Smythers, a merchant, "wealthy beyond the dreams of avarice", had bought for his son, Algy, a champion racing pony, Sausage II, sold with a sad heart by its owner, Blinky Bill, who was heavily in debt. The pony, with Algy aboard galloped straight back to Blinky Bill's stable, who decided to keep the one and kidnap the other. In vain the distraught parents sought the child; the mother even consulted a clairvoyant who prognosticated, "What went by the ponies will come by the ponies". Paterson's finale to the story — "Chapter V — The Tricks of the Turf" — was a superb piece of satirical parody:

It was race day at Pulling'em Park, and the ponies were doing their usual performances.

Among the throng the heaviest punter is a fat lady with diamond earrings. Does the reader recognize her? It is little Algy's mother. Her husband is dead, leaving her the whole of his colossal fortune, and, having developed a taste for gambling, she is now engaged in "doing it in on the ponies". She is one of the biggest bettors in the game.

When women take to betting they are worse than men.

But it is not for betting alone that she attends the meetings. She remembers the clairvoyant's "What went by the ponies will come by the ponies". And always she searches in the ranks of the talent for her lost Algy.

Here enters another of our dramatis personae — Blinky Bill, prosperous once more. He has got a string of ponies and punters together. The first are not much use to a man without the second; but, in spite of all temptations, Bill has always declined to number among his punters the mother of the child he stole. But the poor lady regularly punts on his ponies, and just as regularly is "sent up" — in other words, loses her money.

To-day she has backed Blinky's pair, Nostrils and Tin Can, for the double. Nostrils has won his race, and Tin Can, if on the job, can win the second half of the double. Is he on the job? The prices are lengthening against him, and the poor lady recognizes that once more she is "in the cart".

Just then she meets Tin Can's jockey, Dodger Smith, face to face. A piercing scream rends the atmosphere, as if a thousand school children drew a thousand slate pencils down a thousand slates simultaneously. "Me cheild! Me cheild! Me long-lost Algy!"

It did not take long to convince Algy that he would be better off as a son to a wealthy lady than as a jockey, subject to the fiendish

198 BANJO OF THE BUSH

caprices of Blinky Bill.

"All right, mother," he said. "Put all you can raise on Tin Can. I'm going to send Blinky up. It's time I had a cut on me own, anyway."

The horses went to the post. Tons of money were at the last moment hurled on to Tin Can. The books, knowing he was "dead", responded gamely, and wrote his name till their wrists gave out. Blinky Bill had a half-share in all the bookies' winnings, so he chuckled grimly as he went to the rails to watch the race.

They're off. And what is this that flashes to the front, while the howls of the bookies rise like the yelping of fiends in torment? It is Dodger Smith on Tin Can, and from the grandstand there is a shrill feminine yell of triumph as the gallant pony sails past the post.

The bookies thought that Blinky Bill had sold them, and they discarded him for ever.

Algy and his mother were united, and backed horses together happily ever after; and sometimes from the backyard of their palatial mansion they hand out the empty bottles, free of charge, to a poor old broken-down bottle-O, called Blinky Bill.

Paterson's introduction to the Turf was as a small boy when a station-hand took him to the Bogolong races, and the Snowy River mountaineer borrowed his saddle so that his horse Pardon, could win the main race of the day. Probably from that day, nurtured by his own love of riding, the excitement of horses racing against each other entered his veins.

Certainly he never forgot Pardon's race and it was the subject of one of his first, and best known, racing ballads:

> Then right through the ruck he was sailing —
> I knew that the battle was won —
> The son of Haphazard was failing,
> The Yattendon filly was done;
> He cut down The Don and The Dancer,
> He raced clean away from the mare —
> He's in front! Catch him now if you can, sir!
> And up went my hat in the air!

It was not, however, his first racing ballad: this was "A Dream of the Melbourne Cup", the second set of verses signed by "The Banjo" to appear in the *Bulletin*. (Paterson, by the way, set Sydney honour to rest by writing "The Sydney Cup, 1899" in the *Bulletin* in March of that year.)

In the 1890s, as a young man about Sydney and amateur race rider, Paterson indulged his interest in horse-racing to the full. He regularly attended race-meetings, and at the turn of the century, according to some of his contemporaries, including Norman Lindsay, owned racehorses, though without great success; indeed, Lindsay remembered an occasion[3] when he attended a race-meeting at Randwick where Paterson had a horse running in one of the events: Lindsay had a "quid on it" with him. and lost his money.

Paterson's son, Hugh, has recalled[4] that "he trained jumpers of his own earlier on, and won races with them".* By the time, Paterson was at the Boer War, he was recognized as an astute judge of racehorses; soon after he arrived in Capetown he achieved instant fame by "putting a cavalry regiment on to back the Australian horse, The Grafter, in the City and Suburban".[5] On his Far-Eastern visit soon after the Boer War, he went to race-meetings in Manila and was fascinated by the varieties of breeds of the horses there: tiny Manila ponies, sturdy China ponies "of much the same shape as hogs", American and Australian horses from nondescripts to thoroughbreds — all ridden by dwarf-like natives who clung like monkeys to the horses' necks. Paterson spoke to Filipino trainers and owners: he found that the English or Australian thoroughbred did not thrive in that country; the climate was too hot and steamy.

But the highlight of Paterson's trip to the East was his experience at race-meetings on the Chinese mainland, where at Chefoo he was persuaded by a doubtful trio, a Russian banker, a French importer and an Italian, to ride their pony in one of the races (the horse had allegedly won the Peking Derby). As Paterson wrote to the *Bulletin*,[6] at the time, the pony was an evil-tempered brute that kicked sideways as well as backwards, struck with either front foot and bit savagely. The "marfoo" (Chinese trainer) was afraid to mount him, so instead "stuffed him with food all day, and let him eat his bedding at night so he wasn't exactly fit". The pony led by four lengths to the turn; then he went into "low gear" and was out of the race. Paterson refused to ride him again; he found later that the pony was a "ring-in", a "green Manchurian pony" substituted by the wily Chinese. In another race for ponies ridden by their Chinese grooms, the European punters backed the "certainty" only to find that the riders "had put their heads together and backed the biggest outsider on the totalizator". Paterson concluded that the wily Chinese had very little to learn from their European brethren.

In his numerous ballads and short stories and sketches on racing, and in his novel *The Shearer's Colt*, Paterson drew on his varied turf experiences, exploited many of the situations and characters of the racecourse, and time and time again, notwithstanding his appreciation of the less salubrious aspects of the sport, demonstrated that it was one of his chief pleasures and enthusiasms. To contend with each other, to race, he maintained, was a natural and joy-giving instinct in all creatures:

> Why, everything races, no matter
>   Whatever its method may be:
> The waterfowl hold a regatta;
>   The possums run heats up a tree;
> The emus are constantly sprinting
>   A handicap out on the plain;
> It seems that all nature is hinting
>   'Tis time to be at it again.

* However, in a letter to me dated 7 June 1965, the Secretary of the Australian Jockey Club, D. D. Glasgow, says that a search of the Club's records gives no evidence of this. Probably Paterson owned and raced horses only at unregistered and amateur meetings.

>   The cockatoo parrots are talking
>   Of races to far-away lands;
>   The native companions are walking
>   A go-as-you-please on the sands;
>   The little foals gallop for pastime;
>   The wallabies race down the gap;
>   Let's try it once more for the last time —
>   Bring out the old jacket and cap.

And when such instincts were translated to horse-racing as a popular sport, even with the added complications of commercialization and betting, Paterson still defended the Turf as an institution and saw what he regarded as its positive virtues. As he wrote:

> Absolute purity is not obtainable on the Turf any more than in any other walk of life. Milkmen water their milk and some are occasionally caught at it and fined and yet we do not hear any cry for the abolition of dairies. A certain number of wild cat mines are put on the market every year but what if that were put forward as a reason for doing away with mining? In every British community the Turf is for thousands and thousands their chosen form of amusement and so long as that amusement is carried on as fairly as possible, it has as much right to live as any business or trade undertaking.
>
> One great factor in keeping the Turf clean is the publicity of racing. Every man who goes on the Turf is in the same position as an ordinary citizen would be whose every act was watched by 10,000 skilled detectives. Happy indeed would be the man whose daily life would stand such scrutiny. The fierce light that beats upon a throne is twilight compared to the illumination that throws every step of the racehorse owner into high relief. . . . A few years on the Turf would be an invaluable training for some of the thin-skinned public men who are for ever afraid to take any direct course for fear of losing popularity, and who are ever complaining about being misunderstood or misrepresented by newspapers.[7]

As a lover of the thoroughbred, a bushman at heart, and one who had a sympathetic, if at times sardonic understanding of his fellow-men with their follies and foibles, Paterson knew every trick of the trade, every stratagem and ploy of the vast fraternity of the Turf — from the august race official and the wealthiest racehorse owner to the most humble camp-follower of the lowliest trainer. As already outlined, he was able to put his knowledge to practical use when in the 1920s and 1930s he was a sporting and racing journalist with Sydney newspapers and rarely missed a Saturday race-meeting.

A number of his ballads had as their themes racecourse charlatanry. There was the story of the biter bit in his ballad, "Our New Horse", where the smart bush boys decided to palm off their failed racehorse on to some unsuspecting cityite —

> Let's send him to Sydney and sell him
> There's plenty of Jugginses there . . .

only, in the course of time, to be themselves outsmarted when, deciding to buy another racehorse in the city, they found the same horse back on their hands. Then again there was just plain bush roguery, as in "An Idyll of Dandaloo":

> He won the race by half a length —
>   *Quite* half a length, it seemed to me —
> But Dandaloo, with all its strength,
>   Roared out "Dead heat!" most fervently;
> And, after hesitation meet,
> The judge's verdict was "Dead heat!"
>
> And many men there were could tell
>   What gave the verdict extra force.
> The stewards — and the judge as well —
>   They all had backed the second horse.
> For things like this they sometimes do
> In larger towns than Dandaloo.

But these were the hazards of the game: Paterson became a much more exciting balladist when he was in the saddle as it were, riding with The Ace in "The Open Steeplechase" — with the honour of ". . . old Monaro and the mountain boys . . ." at stake, or following the fortunes of the English "toff" with "the pants and the eyeglass and all" in "The Amateur Rider", who won the race to the astonishment of the regulars. The thrill of jumping races attracted Paterson, as they had Adam Lindsay Gordon; Paterson's verse achieved incredible momentum in his descriptions of these, and never more memorably than in "Rio Grande", the ghostly story of the death-dream of Jack Macpherson, the only man "with hands to hold" this great, black horse:

> But on his ribs the whalebone stung —
>   A madness, sure, it seemed —
> And soon it rose on every tongue
> That Jack Macpherson rode among
>   The creatures he had dreamed.
>
> He looked to left, and looked to right,
>   As though men rode beside;
> And Rio Grande, with foam-flecks white,
> Raced at his jumps in headlong flight
>   And cleared them in his stride.
>
> But when they reached the big stone wall,
>   Down went the bridle-hand,
> And loud we heard Macpherson call

"Make room, or half the field will fall!
Make room for Rio Grande!"

"He's down! he's down!" And horse and man
    Lay quiet side by side!
No need the pallid face to scan,
We knew with Rio Grande he ran
    The race the dead men ride.

Paterson never failed to emphasize the dangers of steeplechase riding
and his prose sketch "Concerning a Steeplechase Rider" is a hard-hitting
piece of writing about "the worst profession in the world": the life and
death of "a small, wiry hard-featured fellow, the son of a stockman on a
big cattle station . . . naturally a horseman, able and willing to ride
anything that could carry him" who rode to his death for £2 10. Perhaps
he was commemorating in that sketch also, as he did in his ballad
"Tommy Corrigan", the jockey of that name who was killed in a steeplechase at Flemington:

But now we'll keep his memory green while horsemen come and go:
We may not see his like again where silks and satins glow.

It is probable that Paterson's contempt for the romanticized and exaggerated string of novelettes turned out by Nat Gould like sausages from
a machine, as much as his passion for the thoroughbred racehorse,
prompted him in his last tranquil years, when racing was his main recrea-
tion, to settle down and write as a pleasant exercise his own racing novel,
The Shearer's Colt. His knowledge of every aspect of his subject, and a
much easier and more colloquial prose style, made this novel demon-
strably superior to any of the Nat Gould stories, even though it is buried,
unnoticed, in the ephemeral fiction of an earlier period of Australian
life. Paterson, indeed, with his dry sense of humour, would have been
quietly amused at the rather desperate efforts of some of his present-day
admirers to cover up the fact that it was ever written.

Yet it is an interesting novel for a number of reasons. The plot is much
more ingenious than the average Nat Gould equivalent: Paterson works
in Australian bush characters, typical and recognizable as such, and the
novel gains considerably from his descriptions of the outback.

The story runs as follows: Hilton Fitzroy, a son of an English county
family, gets into trouble at Oxford, is sent down, and packed off to
Australia so that the new country can make a man of him. (There is more
than a suspicion that Paterson had "Breaker" Morant in mind here.) He
is given a thousand pounds to make a start. He joins the Queensland
Mounted Police. At a bush race-meeting he makes the mistake of arresting
a wealthy squatter, Fred Carstairs, on a stolen-money charge and is
dismissed for making this false arrest. Carstairs is an ex-shearer who made
a fortune from a gold strike, and is not by any means the conventional
squatter type; indeed he is known as Red Fred. He takes a liking to
Fitzroy and employs him as his aide and companion. Carstairs buys a

couple of racehorses from a station-owner, Delahunty, and Carstairs and Fitzroy then travel round various bush race-meetings with their jockey, Bill the Gunner. At one of these meetings they make an enemy of a Chinese bookmaker called Jimmy the Pat, who swears to get even with them. Fitzroy during his travels meets Moira who is Delahunty's daughter and also owns racehorses.

After a fairly successful tour, Red Fred and Fitzroy now decide to descend on Sydney, and naturally they attend a meeting at Randwick. Here Red Fred is attracted by the appearance of a magnificent colt called Sensation, which he buys for the then unbelievable price of ten thousand guineas. After he wins the A.J.C. St Leger with Sensation, Red Fred decides to take the horse to England. The party sails in the *Oronia*, where we now meet a new character called Lady Seawood, a music-hall star who married an English earl and is now widowed. (Paterson could have had Marie Lloyd as his model here.) She has a companion named Miss Fysshe (a distant relative of the late Earl), who incidentally is a racing addict. Paterson's impressions of London and the English aristocracy, as conveyed in the novel, are as amusing as they are exaggerated. Sensation is entered in a Grand International Stakes, a race created for the champions of four countries; as well as Sensation, there is an American horse, Clean Sweep; a French Horse, Edouard; and an English horse, Crusader.

Visitors come from all over the world for this great race, including a gang of American criminals, members of the "International League of Dopers", in which inevitably we find Jimmy the Pat figuring, obviously bent on revenge. He puts up £10,000 for the gang to use to bet on the horse which the gang plan to make win the race after all the others have been doped. There follows then the drama of the preparation for the race and the English racecourse scene (Bill the Gunner of course will ride Sensation), and in the course of this Red Fred and Lady Seawood (Connie) become engaged.

The race is decided in three heats: the first one is over six furlongs, the second over a mile and a quarter and the third over a mile and a half, and there are graphic descriptions of each race. The six furlongs is won by the American horse by half a length from Crusader. Fitzroy, by the way, puts his thousand pounds on a double at twelve to one on Crusader and Sensation in the second-last and last heats of the International Stakes. The second heat, after an exciting finish, is won by Crusader from Sensation. Fitzroy, inspecting the stables one night, disturbs the doping gang at work and is struck down by Jimmy the Pat with an iron bar, in the course of which the stallion Crusader kicks out and kills Jimmy the Pat. There is great excitement about this, and Fitzroy, taken to hospital, lies for the next few days critically ill. Then, of course, comes the last day's racing, and after a desperate struggle Sensation wins by a half head and Fitzroy has won his double. Red Fred's love affair with Connie does not seem to be going very smoothly, and eventually Connie gets a note of apology from Red Fred to say he has gone off with Miss Fysshe and married her in a Registry Office. He is very happy with his wife, who shares with equal enthusiasm his racing and betting interests. Fitzroy, of course, recovers, and now with enough money to justify himself, is able to marry Moira. So all ends happily.

Put as baldly as this, the novel sounds less interesting than it is. But it amply repays reading by anyone who has more than a superficial knowledge of racing — and this is all the audience Paterson sought.

There was a shrewd prognostication in his fancy about an International Race: indeed such races have now, since World War II, become a part of world racing; events of this type have been held both in Australia and the U.S.A. There is plenty of humour in the book, some of it the laconic variety of the racecourse — as when Paterson invents or includes such Turf saws as "If you back favourites you'll have no laces in your boots, but if you back outsiders you'll have no boots", and ". . . a man's first winner makes him a critic; his second winner makes him an expert; and the third winner makes him a candidate for the bankruptcy court". On the score of humour Miss Fysshe is something of a "character" too. She doubts the abilities of Sensation, even when she is told about the records he has run. "That was out in the sticks," she says, "out in Australia where they time 'em with a kitchen clock. I'll bet even money he don't win any of the three races over here." And then there is Lady Seawood, ". . . a peroxide blonde with the face of a Roman emperor", who sometimes goes to the board meetings of the directors of her late husband's company ". . . just to see their beaks hangin' over the table like pelicans at feeding time . . .". One does not find these diversions in the novels of Nat Gould; nor did Gould see the bush as Paterson did — and there are many passages where Paterson writes from a deeply felt experience — as when Fitzroy and Red Fred on the way to Delahunty's Cockatoo Creek Station pass through the "West in a good season":

> . . . In the intensely dry inland air, colours are intensified and sizes are magnified. Silver grey and bright green trees such as the myall, belah, krui-bush and emu-bush gleam in the bright light and a clump of Old Man Saltbush in the distance looks like a dome of silver. The breeze brings sweet scents of ripening herbage. Looking out over that immensity a whole thunder-storm looks like a wandering patch of black against the blue of the sky, sometimes two or three such thunder-storms can be seen moving in stately fashion along the horizon, like wrestlers manoeuvring for a hold.

And when it came to descriptions of the racehorses themselves, all Paterson's years of observation and his experience and study of horses were immediately apparent — as in this picture of the colt Sensation, with Paterson, the student of the thoroughbred, making his odd expert asides:

> Dark chestnut in colour, with a long, narrow blaze down his face, Sensation strode out on to the grass with the easy stride of a panther. It seemed strange that so massive a creature could move so daintily. His silky tapering ears and his steel-like legs, told of a throwback to his Arab ancestry while his size was evidently an inheritance from the other blood — possibly Spanish — that goes to make up the

thoroughbred. His head was set on at an obtuse angle, throwing his
nostrils forward, and the width of his gullet left room, as his trainer
said, for a bird to build its nest between his jaws. His neck was only
slightly arched and appeared light for so big a horse, but the arch
and the solidity would come later on in life. He presented a sort of
streamline effect, for his neck ran back into his shoulders, and his
shoulders ran back into his ribs, with a smoothness that made it hard
to say where the one ended and the other began. A deep, but by
no means broad, chest was another streamline feature. And he had
no suspicion of a "waist", for his ribs ran back to a slightly arched
loin which gave the impression of the strength and suppleness of a
steel spring. His hips were broad and his rump was carried back for
an appreciable distance without any droop — much as one sees it
in the old picture of Stockwell taken in the days when the thoroughbreds were closer to the Arab type than they are today.

The merit of the book, indeed, as befits a racing story, is in the narrative and action of it; most of the characters, lacking depth, are unconvincing, but then Paterson does not allow himself the opportunity to
develop them. But just as in his racing ballads, when "the hoof-strokes
roar like a mighty drum", the tension and turmoil of the crowds on the
racecourse build to a climax as the horses sweep down the straight to the
winning post. So Paterson in this novel has left his most memorable
passages in his race descriptions, nowhere better than in the final heat of
the International Race:

It was time now for the French and Australian riders to go after him,
and for the first time Bill the Gunner let Sensation have the whip in
earnest. Just one cut awoke his fighting spirit and he bounded away
from the Frenchman and went after the leader. But the Frenchman
did not mean to be left behind and at five furlongs from home he
was again up alongside Sensation, and the two of them were closing
on Crusader. The latter's rider had managed to steady his horse again
and was trying to save up a run for the finish. As they swung into
the straight the three of them were practically level, with the Frenchman forcing the pace. He could stay for ever, but was just a little
bit short of speed and his rider knew that if it came to a short dash
home he would be beaten. The English rider knew that if he could
steady his horse even for a few strides, he could beat the others for
speed, but Crusader's temper was so thoroughly aroused that he
would not let a horse pass him while he had a breath in his body.
Seeing the position, Bill the Gunner let his horse drop back a length,
trusting to get the last run at the Frenchman and beat him for speed,
and hoping that Crusader's early contest with his rider might have
left him without a finishing run. The English horse was feeling the
strain, but he fought on and kept the Frenchman at top pace to live
with him. A hundred yards from the post Bill the Gunner called on
the staying power that his lazy horse had kept in reserve. With whip
and spur he drove him up to the leaders and the three of them

battled it out without flinching. They flashed past the post locked
together, with whips going, and until the numbers went up no-one
could say what had won. The judge's verdict was Sensation first,
Crusader second, and the Frenchman third, with only half heads
between them. The American was tailed off.

There is good reason for Paterson's son, Hugh, to recall that his father
was

> . . . a tremendous racing enthusiast. He had a very good knowledge
> of breeding and of everything to do with racing and he was a very,
> very good judge of horses. He actually purchased yearlings for a lot
> of his friends. They would ask him to select yearlings for them at
> the yearling sales and with fairly cheap purchases he had quite a lot
> of success for some of his friends. They won quite a lot of races.[8]

For there is extant the manuscript of a book, *Racehorses and Racing in
Australia*,* which, in 257 pages of foolscap typescript, covers almost every
aspect of racing in this country and has also much reference to racing
overseas. Paterson wrote it in his leisure time while he was at Coodravale
(it was completed in 1914, up to which year its statistics and records
refer), as an interesting (and characteristic) letter[9] to George Robertson
reveals:

Coodra Station,
Wee Jasper. via Yass.
7 Jan. 1910.

Dear Robertson,
    I got a circular letter from your firm about a book on horsebreed-
ing issued by a German. I am writing a small book on racing and
would like to get hold of the German's book for reference. Will you
lend it to me — I take great interest in the matter and would do an
article for Herald on the book which I think they would accept as it
could not offend any advertisers. Would mention your firm as
supplying it.
    I can't afford luxuries like £2. 10. for a book or would buy it right
out.
    My health is quite restored now. I used not to be able to sleep,
now I can't keep awake.
    The lines I am going on in my book are that of all the thousands
who attend races very few have any idea of "the game". People who
go to cricket and football mostly know a bit about the games and
have played them themselves. But thousands on thousands go racing
and bet their money cheerfully on mysterious whispers imparted to
them by men without any seat to their pants. It struck me that if

---

*This MS. was made available to me through the courtesy of Angus & Robertson Ltd.
in Sydney, in whose possession it now is. It was never published, probably because it
would have appealed only to a relatively small readership interested in the history of
thoroughbred breeding in Australia as in the sport itself. However, the historian and
biographer M. H. Ellis, who knew Paterson at the time, believes that negotiations for
publication broke down because of a disagreement over terms.

one wrote a book on the practical side of racing it ought to sell well.
Nothing heavy, but a sort of Royal Road to Racing. Do you think
they would stand a humorous book on racing? People seem to me
to take racing so gloomily. One could make it very funny without
much effort and it would point a good moral as I could show the
folly of betting. We might get it into the schools in course of time.

I think the verse market over supplied and since the majestic
failure of The Outback Marriage I don't intend to try fiction again.

I hope your health is better. I may be down at Easter & will look
in & see you. Anyhow lend me the German's book & I will keep it for
you when I sell you mine if you like. I know all about him and his
stud and he should be one of the greatest authorities in the world
on the subject.

With best wishes,

Yours sincerely,

[Signed]   A. B. PATERSON.

Paterson has gone into astonishing detail in this book. He had studied
the work of world authorities on the modern thoroughbred racehorse:
Baron Burchau von Oettingen, Bruce Lowe and his theory of breeding,
and Admiral Rous. His researches had extended to the history of horse-
racing in England from the time of the Emperor Severus when in A.D. 206
the Roman soldiers arranged races with Arabian horses near York, and
Paterson believed that the most important stage in the development of
the thoroughbred racehorse in England was reached when Charles II
imported thirty or forty Arabian mares — the Barbary Arabs.

But it was when Paterson turned to subjects like "Buying a Yearling",
"Trainers and Training", "Handicap Racing", "Jockeys", "The System
of Book-Making", "Punters and Professional Backers" and similar aspects
of Australian racing, that he seemed most likely to justify the object of
his writing, as stated in his modestly worded Introduction:

> . . . The book is written with the idea of giving a little simple infor-
> mation on turf matters to some of the hundreds of thousands of the
> public who go to races for amusement. . . . One can buy books on
> bridge, books on racing, books on cricket, books on football, why not
> a book on the nobler science of racing? . . .

Why not indeed? Certainly it can be said that Paterson, with a rare
enthusiasm and an admirably colloquial lucidity, set out to give the race-
goer, rich or poor, every possible advantage from his years of experience.

His chapter on buying a yearling, for instance, could almost be a
standard manual for a would-be racehorse-owner. No wonder Paterson
was sought after by his friends as their agent at the yearling sales!*

---

* C. H. Bateson, who edited the Sydney *Truth* at the time, recalls that one evening,
after he had attended the yearling sales in the early 1920s, Paterson said he had been
most impressed with a yearling for which a very low price had been bid. He felt sure it
had the conformation of a champion. The horse, as it turned out, was Windbag which
became famous in Australian racing.

He described aspects of pedigree, soundness, temperament, appearance (". . .a good head, a long rein, well sloped shoulders, deep ribs, a broad and firm loin, wide hips, sound and wiry legs — all these are things to look out for . . ."), constitution, price — all in knowledgeable and indeed professional detail. The characteristic Paterson humour was always near the surface: when talking of temptation to buy a yearling of doubtful soundness at a bargain price, he quoted the Arabian proverb, "He is a ruined man and a son of a ruined man who buys horses to cure them"; and again, to illustrate the hard road of experience, "One must buy all faults before one is fit to buy horses in the market place". And Paterson's love for the sport is never more in evidence than when he described the lot of the lucky owner:

> . . . Non-racing people do not understand what it means to own a good horse. But yesterday the buyer was a nobody, a mere merchant or landholder or brewer or peer: he was not exactly like Wolsey, "none so poor as do him reverence", but all the reverence he got he had to pay for, and then most of it was of a spurious brand. But let his colt become favourite for the Derby! He drives up to a railway station and the cabman whispers to the porter "Do you know who that is?" "No," says the porter vaguely and not interested. "Dook of Nonesuch is it?" "Dook of Nonesuch be blowed!" says the cabman. "That's the owner of Mortimer, me lad! That's who that is!" Off goes the porter with the luggage, and he will break all the regulations to get the owner of Mortimer the best seat; he tells the sleeping-car attendant whose luggage it is, and the sleeping-car attendant treats the owner of Mortimer better than he would treat a royal Prince. When he goes anywhere for a meal, the waiters — there are no more persistent pointers in the world than waiters — will see that he gets the best of everything, and gets it quicker than anybody else. His own friends and acquaintances, who but lately thought him rather a dull dog, now cluster round him. Women, lovely women, just besiege him for tips and opinions. A great politician, a great lawyer, a great surgeon, a great general, when he goes abroad, is known to but a few. But there is a vast silent army without generals or colonels or captains, an army that is camped everywhere on ceaseless picket duty — the army of those who back horses. To them the owner of a really first-class horse is a greater hero than your politician or your lawyer or your singer or you yourself . . .

When it came to the training and racing of the young horse, Paterson again wrote from a vast experience of horses and horsemanship. He knew that most owners tended to suffer from "horse delusion", tending to see their horses "in the same golden light in which a young mother sees her children". Yet when it came to the quality of racehorses, the margin between a mediocre and a good horse was small — and Paterson went into detailed calculations of performances and times down to tenths of a second to demonstrate his point; the owner therefore who succeeded in getting an out-and-out champion racehorse could count himself most

fortunate indeed. First of all, however, there was all the complicated
procedure of breaking in the youngster, its early training and trialing —
and here again Paterson wrote from the heart:

> . . . Nothing in racing is more pleasant than these quiet after-
> breakfast trials. The course is sweet with the scent of newly-cut grass;
> the gaunt empty stands seem to sleep in the sun; all the early workers
> have gone home and left the world to sunlight and to us. There is
> something restful about the morning sun on an empty racecourse,
> something so tranquil and pastoral . . .

Paterson wrote of the gift of race-riding, of the attributes of a champion
jockey (balance, determination and especially nerve), of good training
and bad training practices. But where he was really in his element was
when he described the racecourse scene:

> . . . Let us venture, then, into the wild and whirling maelstrom that
> makes up a modern race-course. Owners, backers, bookmakers,
> trainers, jockeys, battlers, hard-heads, touts, and whisperers: princes,
> potentates, and prawn-merchants: actresses, society leaders, ladies,
> wives and daughters of the populace: horses that are worth fortunes,
> and horses that are going to cost ditto: stayers, sprinters, and middle
> distance horses: horses that begin badly and finish well, horses that
> dash to the front and do not finish at all, horses that plod at the one
> pace from end to end of a face all in full condition, all thoroughbred,
> and with only a couple of seconds in the mile between the best and
> worst of them. What a kaleidoscope of humanity, what a fascinating
> gamble . . .

He analysed systems of bookmaking and betting in the minutest detail
and worked out pages of arithmetical calculations to prove his points. He
offered advice (over fifty years ago) on a subject that racing administra-
tors in Australia even today have not as yet solved: the role of book
makers and totalizators in the best interests of racing. He felt there was
likely to be less dishonesty with bookmakers, since a dishonest owner
planning a coup was more likely than not to be anticipated by well-
informed bookmakers. He also considered that totalizator betting as a
monopoly would make for "secrecy and mutual distrust", since a betting
owner could not, as he could do with a bookmaking system, tell his
friends and acquaintances to back his horse once he had "got his money"
on — otherwise the odds would shorten. Finally, Paterson was of the
opinion that a totalizator system freely available, both off course and on
course, was more likely, from a national point of view, to encourage
betting, than a system of bookmakers on the racecourse, which would
keep the volume of betting in check. Present-day experience has probably
proved him correct.

On the denizens of the race-course he was superb. He described the
"knowledge boxes" and "whisperers", the men who made a living by
"telling the tale" — to separate a trusting punter from his money. ("It

was once said of a really great whisperer," wrote Paterson, "that he could talk a punter off a battleship into a canvas dinghy in mid-ocean.") These gentry ranged from the sophisticated confidence-men to what are known as "urgers". Then there were the "battlers" and the "tipsters"; and higher up the scale of the racing hierarchy, the professional backers and punters. No wonder, with this rich knowledge of the fraternity of the Turf, Paterson was able to write one of the best short stories of the racecourse in our literature, "The Oracle"[10] — as authentic in dialogue, atmosphere and character as any such story could possibly be.

No tram ever goes to Randwick races without him; he is always fat, hairy and assertive; he is generally one of a party, and takes the centre of the stage all the time. . . . He knows all the trainers and owners, or takes care to give the impression that he does. He slowly and pompously hauls out his race book, and one of his satellites opens the ball by saying, in a deferential way:

"What do you like for the 'urdles, Charley?"

The Oracle looks at the book and breathes heavily; no one else ventures to speak.

"Well," he says, at last, "of course there's only one in it — if he's wanted. But that's it — will they spin him? I don't think they will. They's only a lot o' cuddies, any 'ow."

No one likes to expose his own ignorance by asking which horse he refers to as the "only one in it"; and the Oracle goes on to deal out some more wisdom in a loud voice.

"Billy K—— told me" (he probably hardly knows Billy K—— by sight) "Billy K—— told me that that bay 'orse ran the best mile-an'-a-half ever done on Randwick yesterday; but I don't give him a chance, for all that; that's the worst of these trainers. They don't know when their horses are well — half of 'em."

Then a voice comes from behind him. It is that of the thin man, who is crushed out of sight by the bulk of the Oracle.

"I think," says the thin man, "that that horse of Flannery's ought to run well in the Handicap."

The Oracle can't stand this sort of thing at all. He gives a snort, wheels half-round and looks at the speaker. Then he turns back to the compartment full of people, and says: "No 'ope."

The thin man makes a last effort. "Well, they backed him last night, anyhow."

"Who backed 'im?" says the Oracle.

"In Tattersall's," says the thin man.

"I'm sure," says the Oracle, and the thin man collapses.

Paterson in the final chapters of his book went to great pains, with details of breeding and performance, to compare English and Australian horses. Apart from his statistical analyses and research, he wrote from first-hand experience, too;* in 1914, as he recalled in *Happy Dispatches*,

---

* Sydney journalists who worked with Paterson in the 1920s have told me that Paterson's knowledge of racehorse breeding was phenomenal. He could give the breeding of any horse nominated, up to three removes back.

he had spent several of the most memorable days of his life at Straffan
Station stud in Ireland, where The Tetrarch, one of the fastest racehorses
in history, was bred. He saw the famous sires Roi Herode and Symington
and The Tetrarch's dam, ". . . a big, coarse mare, with harpoon shoulders, just the sort that anyone would select to ride in a cattle camp. The
idea of her breeding the world's greatest sprinter seemed ridiculous." He
discussed breeding with Irish stud-masters and was convinced that Irish
and English horses were superior to any in the world because of the soil
and the climate and "the green grass all the year round to keep their
insides clean . . .".

Paterson came to the conclusion that, in his time at any rate, no great
sire of racehorses had ever been bred whose parents and grandparents
were all born in Australia. Carbine, he noted, "whom all Australians
proudly claim . . ." was bred and reared in New Zealand from an imported
sire, and not even such a horse as Trafalgar qualified, since, although his
sire Wallace, by Carbine, was to that extent Australian-bred, Trafalgar's
sire on his dam side, was an imported horse. He examined closely horse-
breeding in Australia and saw its future not in the stallions bred in this
country, but in the mares with the qualities that this hotter and drier
country had inevitably had born into them: "soundness of wind, good
constitution, pluck and above all a hardness of type approximating
almost to the Arab." He forecast that the greatest Australian horses in
the future would come by the mating of Australian mares, with their
characteristic soundness and endurance, with the English sires who would
give the quality and speed. Most of all, he hoped that Australia would
breed great stayers rather than sprinters — a conservative and traditional
view he had held ever since he wrote those lines in the late 1880s about
"Old Pardon, The Son of Reprieve".

Three miles in three heats: — Ah, my sonny,
  The horses in those days were stout,
They had to run well to win money;
  I don't see such horses about.
Your six-furlong vermin that scamper
  Half-a-mile with their feather-weight up,
They wouldn't earn much of their damper
  In a race like the President's Cup.

Paterson completed his book with a magnificent piece of sustained
fiction in three chapters where he described, in all its details and activity,
a day at the races — to illustrate most of the points and observations he
had made in the previous eighteen chapters. And probably nothing of its
type has been done as well, if at all, in our literature before or since, than
in his description of the main race of the day — a weight-for-age race in
which he drew together an imaginary field of champions and near-
champions and poured into the telling of it all his love, understanding
and enthusiasm for a sport he knew so well:

It is a sight not to be forgotten when the six turn out to parade —
the grand swinging walk, heads held high and confidently, manners
sober and determined, their frames laced and braced with bands of
muscle, coats shining like glass. No other animal in the world reaches
the same level of excellence as the thoroughbred horse. And this
field now going to the post has been arrived at by centuries of breeding, feeding, selection, judgment, and constant weeding out of the
inferior and the unfit. Turf history rises before us as we look at
them. It was to produce such horses that the Darley Arabian was
brought from the desert, that the Byerley Turk was taken from his
work as an officer's charger, and that the Godolphin Barb was
rescued from drawing a water-cart in France to be the founder of
a long line of courageous and determined horses. As they canter past,
the mind goes back to the old-time races, and we almost seem to see
a race meeting of a hundred years ago — the noble owners on their
hacks cantering up to watch the start, and galloping back across the
course to see the finish; the bookmakers congregated at the betting
post; royalty in its chariot looking on; and the common people, not
so educated as now, stubbornly supporting their local champions
irrespective of favour or weight or distance. Where the great grand-
stands are now, we seem to see the little booths strictly reserved for
the quality — for a gentleman was a gentleman in those pre-demo-
cratic days. In that fiery chestnut rushing down the running with his
head in his chest, his great stride sweeping the ground behind him,
we seem to see again the mighty Eclipse — that evil-tempered nerve-
beaten equine phenomenon going out to battle once more to make
mincemeat of the opposition. In the brown colt lazily lobbing past
we see again the Flying Dutchman, to whom distance and weight
were as nothing, while the little wiry excited bay mare, reefing at her
bit and gliding along like a snake — is that Beeswing come back on
earth again? Not a horse starting in this race to-day but has its
pedigree as carefully kept as that of any aristocrat in the land.

At its worst racing may have many faults, but at its best it has
always been the one sport that gripped the mind of the English; for
the grim pluck and fiery dash of the blood horse have always
appealed to something deep down in the breast of every Englishman.

And so our field goes to the post to show themselves worthy of their
sires. And even as the horses are good, so are the owners; for not an
owner in the race is racing for money or for the excitement of
betting, but simply for the pleasure of seeing his colors carried by a
really good horse in really good company.

Though we have decided not to bet on this race, still we must try
to pick it; so let us see how they have run. Oligarch is a good horse
in every sense of the word. He won his Derby by sheer grit against a
much faster animal; he is neither sad nor sorry; he does not pull or
fight in a race; hard going or soft makes no difference to him; he has
raced at two three and four years old and has never run a bad race.
He has a jockey on his back who has ridden him half-a-dozen times
already, and he is up to the mark in the matter of condition; but

he has something to beat to-day, and, though he is favourite and the
public money is going on him in bushels, the ring are prepared to bet
even money till the cows come home. In these weight-for-age races
the price of the favourite is always short, as there is no need to ask
owners' intentions. One horse usually stands out as a likely winner,
but at short prices the ring will take a lot of silencing. So it is even
money Oligarch, and still even money though the fivers, and the
tenners, and the hundreds and the thousands pour steadily in on
him.

Second favourite at three to one is Dragoon, a fine three-year-old
who was not too lucky in the running of the Derby and is said to
have improved since. The Derby winner having gone wrong,
Dragoon may be considered the best three-year-old of this year, but
he has not yet met any really first-class older horses at this distance,
and it is not too certain that he can see the mile-and-a-half right out,
if pace is on all the way; but if the pace is slow in the early part,
then Dragoon's great burst of speed may just land him a winner.
We should see some good riding in this race, since it will be a matter
for rare judgement how much pace to set and when to make the
final dash. Here comes Pleasantry, a beautiful graceful gazelle-like
creature; she hardly seems to touch the ground as she moves past.
But she has speed enough, and is bred to stay for ever, though her
fiery temperament will be all against her in a race like this; she will
probably fret in the race, and not be able to do herself justice at the
finish.

Now here comes the old one, Flint Arrow, hard as flint too. An
indifferent two-year-old and three-year-old, he suddenly showed form
as a four-year-old, and now at five — so it is whispered — is a far
better horse than he ever was before in his life. There are families
in the racehorse aristocracy whose characteristic it is to develop late,
and these are nearly always the best-constitutioned and best-fibred
animals in the world. But the craze for early racing — for large
profits and quick returns — has driven these families out of fashion,
and Flint Arrow represents what is an almost unfashionable family
on the sire's side, while on the mother's side he has a strong cross of
Herod blood. He looks hard enough and tough enough for any trial,
but the race will need to be run at a full pace all the way, if he is
to do any good; and there is nothing in the race to make the pace
for him. The books are therefore offering sixes about him, and he
too has a host of followers.

Moonlighter, the handicap champion, has never met this class of
field before, and the general notion is that he will find himself
outclassed. With him, at outside prices, is Tornado, a tough-looking
game-headed sleepy customer who looks like staying all day, but who
has done nothing to warrant any one thinking he can see out a mile
and a half with this lot. And so they go to the post.

A little delay, and the barrier goes up. The two stayers, Tornado
and Flint Arrow, move off at once, settling down to the long journey
with easy wolf-like strides, heads stretched out, and just a nice easy

pull on their bridles; the two fliers, Oligarch and Dragoon, are running behind them, each a bit inclined to pull and to resent being steadied; but the superb hands of their riders calm them down and humour them, and after a hundred yards or so they settle to it contentedly enough. The handicap king Moonlighter bounds along, a ball of muscle, in last place; he is so used to carrying top weight in big handicaps that he is accustomed to run all his races behind, and he only wonders why there are so few horses in front of him. So far, nothing looks like setting an extra fast pace, though the whole lot, easily as they seem to be going, are cutting up the ground at a great rate. But suddenly the fiery little mare Pleasantry, who has failed to get a place on the rails and is running alongside the two colts, begins to show very plain symptoms that she does not think she is going fast enough. She is fighting at the bit, and her rider, to hold her, has to pull till her mouth is wide open and her neck bent so that the free current of air to her lungs, so important in long distance racing, is sadly interfered with. She throws her head from side to side and gets out of her stride, while her rider recognises that it is better to let her go than to let her beat herself pulling; so all at once she flashes to the front, and away she goes with a three lengths lead, and what looks like a slow-run race gives every promise of being a remarkably fast one.

As soon as she goes out to the lead, the whole field quickens, and before long it is not much trouble to hold anything. They run the first half-mile in 52 seconds, and all the time the little mare draws further away; the two stayers are getting all the pace they want, and, when the mile is reached in one minute forty-one-and-a-half seconds, it looks as if the fliers may not have a run left to finish with. As they begin the last half-mile, the rear division imperceptibly quicken. They are "going out after the mare", since it is time now to get within striking distance in order to get into position for the final run. Flint Arrow, hugging the rails and saving every inch of ground, begins to draw up on her, but his mate Tornado cannot go on with him. The company is a shade too good for him, and in a flash he has dropped back, and the two fliers, Oligarch and Dragoon, are past him. The boy on the handicap king Moonlighter asks him to go on after them; but it is one thing to come with a burst of speed through a lot of inferior horses, and quite another to last out a mile and a half with this lot; and he soon shows that, if the field are going to improve the pace, they will have to improve it without him, and he and Tornado drop to the rear and are no more thought of. Three furlongs from home Flint Arrow has caught the little mare, while just at their heels the other two are thundering, the riders watching each other and waiting to make a drive in the straight. They are fairly flying now, and the little mare, game as she is, has taken too much out of herself to be able to finish. Rounding the turn, she drops back beaten, leaving Flint Arrow in the lead. The two colts have to come round outside the mare. She rolls a little with distress, and Dragoon gets a bump — the slightest thing in the world, but a very slight thing is going to make a very great difference in this race. It throws him off his balance for an instant, and when he gets into his stride again, Oligarch has got a clear length from him. Dragoon, owning a high-strung nervous system, refuses to make the supreme effort necessary to get in line again, and in an instant he is out of the race. This leaves Oligarch the favourite, to chase Flint Arrow down the straight, and, running straight as a gun barrel, he swoops down on the tiring leader.

How the crowd yells! Foot by foot he draws up on him, to his quarters, to his girth, to his shoulder. Can he maintain the effort? If he had been just a little bit nearer the leader at the entrance to the straight: if he had had time to get just one long breath to fill his lungs before the final dash, then his pace would be sure to prevail. But he has been racing at his very top for the whole of the last half-mile, and though he draws level with the leader, he seems unable to pass him. Out come the whips, and, while the crowd yell themselves hoarse, Flint Arrow calls on the reserve force and determination which all really great horses seem to carry packed in their system somewhere, and, with whip and spur cutting him to pieces, he draws away again from the favourite and wins a desperate race by half a neck. As he comes back to weigh, blood is on his sides and weals are on his ribs. But the horse knows he has won, and holds his head high, and one old-time sportsman points at him a hand shaking with excitement and says, "Look at that! You don't see many nowadays would stand a question like that put to them. He's one of the old sort!" And so they come in through cheering thousands, and before the saddles are off the news is flashed to all parts of the world that Flint Arrow, who never won a really big race in his life, has beaten the best in the land and at weight for age. We have seen a race that will make turf history. . . .

A contemporary of Paterson wrote, when Paterson died, that up to within a few weeks of his death ". . . he was a conspicuous figure on the principal racecourses of Sydney with his outsize in field-glasses".[11] Another recalls him at Randwick as one of the "regulars", with his tall, lean figure and lined saturnine face — not communicative, but obviously known to most sporting pressmen, trainers and owners with whom he sometimes yarned quietly between races. "After the races were over he would put his old glasses carefully away, stand up, look round, and depart leisurely."[12]

Yet, from this environment and just as unostentatiously, this modest and unassuming man gave a welcome flash of new colour to the spectrum of our popular literature.

NOTES

[1] In a letter in the *Sydney Morning Herald*, 8 February, 1941.
[2] In an A.B.C. script "News" written in a series "The Land of Adventure" (1935).
[3] In *Bohemians of the Bulletin* (1965).

[4] In Peter Macgregor's A.B.C. radio documentary previously referred to.
[5] In *Happy Dispatches* (1935).
[6] 16 November 1901.
[7] In his unpublished MS. *Racehorses and Racing.*
[8] See Note 3.
[9] In the Mitchell Library, Sydney.
[10] Included in the collection *Three Elephant Power.*
[11] G. A. King. See Note 1.
[12] Quoted by Sydney May in the *Story of Waltzing Matilda* (1944).

CHAPTER XVI

Interlude for Broadcasting

*He enjoyed writing very much and he'd get an idea to write
a thing and then he'd write it off very quickly, and a lot of
it was for his own amusement : . .*

— HUGH PATERSON.[1]

IT IS NOT generally known that Paterson became very interested in broadcasting in the early 1930s — as soon as its potential as a communications
medium became apparent to thinking Australians. Indeed, along with
Vance Palmer,* and later H. M. Green,* Paterson was something of a
pioneer of established authors taking part in radio broadcasting.

His interest began when he was invited in 1932 by the newly constituted Australian Broadcasting Commission to give a talk on Australian
literature.[2] In this talk he referred especially to David Scott Mitchell's
collection of Australian works, which he had recently been invited to
inspect; he was "astounded at the number of books written by Australians on or about Australia". He continued:

> . . . While Australian literature has failed to make a lasting impres-
> sion overseas, Australian writers have done at least as well as the
> writers of Canada and South Africa. The time is nearly ripe for a
> great Australian historical novel on the lines of the stories of Winston
> Churchill and Mary Johnston, who wrote of Virginian life . . .

It was a coincidence that two years later Brian Penton's *Landtakers* was
published.

In 1933, W. H. Ifould, a member of the Australian Broadcasting Commission's Adult Education Committee, had written to Paterson suggesting
that he talk on his own work in relation to Australian literature generally.
Paterson, as a potential performer in the medium, replied[3] with observations that reflected a good deal of common sense:

> I received your letter suggesting that I should talk for twenty minutes
> about myself. I think a man would need the "robur et aes triplex"
> of the classical writer to undertake any such task.

---

* Vance Palmer was a radio personality during the 1930s with his literary talks and
book reviews. H. M. Green broadcast in 1942 a series of short talks on Australian writers
for the A.B.C.; some of these were later published as *Fourteen Minutes* (1944).

I could give a talk on Australian verse in general including Henry
Lawson's, my own, etc. and I submit a list of other subjects on which
I think I could interest and instruct my fellow-Australians.

I would like to be one of the team for this series but unless I got
at least three appearances I would not care to undertake the considerable labour of preparing one talk.

During the rest of that year Paterson submitted and broadcast several
scripts on Australian subjects on the A.B.C.; Sir Charles Moses, General
Manager of the A.B.C. from 1935 to 1965, but at that time in charge of
spoken word programmes, recalls from correspondence with Paterson that
two of these subjects were "The South Coast" and "Australian Men and
Horses".

Paterson continued his occasional contributions during 1934. (He is
remembered as a clear rather than a good speaker, tending always to be
nervous on the air, and rather nasal in tone.) Some of the material he
used, as can be seen from correspondence with Moses, was clearly derived
from diaries he had maintained over the years — certainly as far back as
the late 1890s. What Paterson had in mind, however, was a series of
engagements from the A.B.C. which would give him the opportunity for
a period of concentrated writing. During November 1934 he met the then
General Manager of the A.B.C., Major W. T. Conder, at an official
luncheon in the city, and the following correspondence[4] ensued:

> 19, South Street,
> Double Bay, Edgecliffe.
> 17 Nov. 1934.

Dear Major Conder,
Following our conversation of yesterday, would you let me try to
do some work for you on the following lines?

I meet all sorts of people from Field Marshals to buffalo shooters
and I would like to try getting interviews with them and working in
as much information as possible about their lives, the people they
meet, and so on. If I saw a good prospect I could get the stuff and a
trial or two would show if it caught on. I used to get more letters
about this sort of stuff than about anything else. Of course it all
depends on how it is done.

> Yours truly,
> [signed]   A. B. PATERSON.

> 26th November, 1934.

Dear Mr Paterson,
Thank you for your letter of 17th instant. Your suggestions interest
me a good deal and I trust that we may be able to reach some satisfactory arrangement.

Interviews of the sort you suggest could probably be worked out
very well — as in your "Happy Dispatches". Any people from field-
marshals to buffalo-shooters (to use your own words) would do very
well, so long as they were interesting people; and I have no doubt

that we could leave it to you to select them and to write the interviews in an entertaining way.

I am, however, a little uncertain about the best use to make of
things of this sort. It may seem to you a curious sort of contradiction,
but there can be little doubt that matter which is put on the air as
literary matter is more widely appreciated than even the best of
"talks", lectures, addresses, interviews in person and all the other
things which would naturally appear to be better suited for radio
presentation. That, at least, is our experience — possibly because
people in the mass associate the written word with stories that have
amused them and the spoken word with classes which have bored
them — and so what I should like you to consider would be to write
us a series of these interviews and let us read them in the different
States, not as "talks" by you but as your "literary" work.

I trust that this idea will appeal to one who understands public
psychology as well as you obviously do.

Yours truly,
AUSTRALIAN BROADCASTING COMMISSION.
[signed]   W. T. CONDER

(Major Conder's diplomacy was an astute translation of the opinion of
his senior A.B.C. officers concerned that Paterson's voice was not well
suited to broadcasting.)

19 South Street,
Double Bay.
12 Decr. 1934.

Dear Major Conder,

Re your suggestion that I should write literary matter to be read
in the various States.

This appeals to me very much, the only trouble being to write the
stuff well enough. As an experiment I have written the enclosed
matter, and would like you to consider it.

Yours truly,
[signed]   A. B. PATERSON.

A. B. Paterson, Esq.,
19 South Street,
DOUBLE BAY.
Dear Sir,

In Major Conder's absence from Sydney, I am acknowledging
receipt of your letter of 12th instant, enclosing with it suggested
article for broadcasting on "Australian Local Colour".

Major Conder will return to Sydney at the week-end, and will no
doubt write to you concerning it without delay.

Yours faithfully,
[signed]   E. K. SHOLL
(General Manager's Secretary)

The script referred to was written around the theme of the unwilling-ness (at the time) of Australian readers to buy books of "local colour. . . . by this I mean books descriptive of Australian life". "Admittedly," wrote Paterson, "in a literary sense, we are at the bullock-dray stage of development while older nations are, or should be flying literary aero-planes: still there is good copy in a bullock-dray if properly handled . . ." He then set out to show how in fact Australian writers used ". . . our box of new paints, some of them our own exclusive property" — and in so doing he wrote a worthwhile, if unorthodox, piece of literary criticism.

Marcus Clarke, he said, in *For the Term of His Natural Life* had used local colour lavishly, daubing it on in great lumps, pouring the misery of the convict system, "out of a bucket". Then there were Gordon's poems (here was one balladist about another) — no song of gladness here, but of melancholy, a note followed by others: ". . . where Shelley wrote the song of the skylark our poets have written the wail of the curlew." In what followed, Paterson wrote in a prim aside, the Australian public was to blame, since it manifestly preferred ". . . murders, mysteries and companionate marriages . . .". Nor did we have the required "sort of crimson colour on our local palette" — no Indians, feuds or civil war. All we had was "mostly sheep and cattle, and our life may be described as a little space between a sheep and a sheep" (an original and diverting piece of Patersonian satire). Yet Jeannie Gunn was able "to paint a great picture of Australian life without over-colouring anything, and without straining after effect . . .". Paterson was vastly amused at the "over-colouring" of Jules Verne who in one of his novels had described an overland journey of a thousand cattle travelling at "full gallop", with stockmen dressed in red shirts racing alongside and cracking their whips. Paterson concluded in characteristic style:

Apart from the flaming reds and sombre blacks of mystery, murder and melancholia, what colors have we on our palette? Here are a few subjects which suggest themselves, a few little odds and ends like the hurried scrawls which the painter makes in his sketch book. The pearling fleets in the Torres Straits where the lugger just wets her gunwale as the trade wind tips the blue of each wave with a feather of white: the still dark night on a new selection where the little points of light, flashing through the trees, show where the settler and his wife are hard at it, burning off, glorying in the chance to make a home for their children: the little coastal trading boats of the Pig and Whistle line dipping their noses into the big seas as they slip quietly out of the harbor at dawn and lay their course, not by compass, but by reef and headland, for the coastal rivers where every man is their mate and every dog is their friend: the slow majestic march of the cattle down the Overland in a good season, with every bullock keeping his place beside his accustomed mate and with the sun shining on their strawberry-roan and snow-white hides. The late Frank Mahony once painted a picture of a mob of cattle on the road, with one big bullock head up staring over the backs of his mates at something in the distance. All my life I have wanted to possess that picture . . .

A.B.C. programme officers to whom this "trial" script was referred were quite impressed with it. One commented that it was "an intelligent criticism of Australian writing methods"; it was something of an ironic sidelight on the supposed fame of Paterson in his own country that the suggestion was made, however, that if the series was undertaken ". . . a little judicious publicity over the air, a reading of extracts from 'The Man from Snowy River', etc. would be a good idea: most people in other States, I think, believe that he is dead, along with Milton, Keats and all the rest of them." But then perhaps the suggestion was not as odd as it seemed: Paterson's great triumphs had been at the turn of the century and most Australians knew him as a balladist;* *Happy Dispatches* had only just been published, and anyhow it referred to the past and not the present; and *The Shearer's Colt* was published two years later.

Major Conder wrote to Paterson accepting the idea of a series, emphasizing the matter of continuity, ". . . so that we should be able to advertise a series of regular articles to be broadcast at the same time on the same day each week, or at similar regular intervals. . . ." Paterson replied:

19 South Street, Double Bay.
31 Dec. 1934.

Dear Major Conder,

In reply to yours of 18th inst. as to a title for a series of articles. After much consideration and experiment I think I could do what you want on the following lines.

Run a series called "Through Many Gates" the basic idea being to tell them something informative and interesting about such matters as Hubert Murray's work in Papua (the Gate of the Far North): Prell's work at Crookwell where he is carrying three sheep to the acre on poor country and opening a new avenue for Australia (The Sheep-Yard Gate): the big scheme for the Northern Territory where a Chartered Company is to chill beef (The Cattle-Paddock Gate): Australian Press in town and country (The Gate of the Inky Way): and similar topics of National rather than of State interest.

Some years ago I visited various districts for the Herald and was surprised to find how much interest people took in hearing of places where there was some chance of getting a living.

This first-mentioned scheme would entail an awful lot of work interviewing people who know things, etc.; but it would be worth while if you thought you might see your way to giving me some small weekly assignment later on where my knowledge of Australia would be useful.

Yours truly,

[signed]   A. B. PATERSON.

There was also a suggestion at this time that an arrangement should be made to have *Happy Dispatches* read over the air, but Paterson

---

* Vince Kelly told me once that when Paterson joined the staff of the Sydney *Truth*, where he (Kelly) was a junior reporter, he was startled to realize that Paterson was still alive, having thought of him up to that point as a legendary figure long since dead.

hesitated on this, saying he preferred to wait until he had heard from his English publishers. In the event, nothing further happened about the idea.

Paterson, as usual, changed his mind about the title of his broadcasting series, and when he submitted the first script suggested the new title of *The Land of Adventure*. This the A.B.C. accepted. There was some bargaining over the amount to be paid Paterson for the scripts, since it had been agreed that his voice was not suitable for a "national" (i.e., a relayed) series, and that the scripts, as Charles Moses correctly said at the time, "would be of a higher broadcasting value if given by the author than by one of our announcing staff".[5] Eventually, however, it was agreed that he should write this series of fifteen, but not broadcast them person-ally: they would be read independently in each State. It is interesting to note, too, the views of some (but not all) of the A.B.C. officers assessing the material at the time that Paterson "was probably as well known throughout the world as any other Australian writer".[6]

Naturally, in view of the title, Paterson in writing this series relied very much on his past experiences and travels, and in a number of cases clearly quoted from diary material. In some of his scripts, too, he adopted a viewpoint demonstrated in previous writings. For instance, his intro-ductory article, "The Land of Adventure", which gave the title to the series, maintained, as did his sketch, "The Cycloon, Paddy Cahill and the G.R.", written forty years before, that although the Northern Territory offered an enormous potential for settlement, trade and industry, it still baffled would-be investors and settlers. (Perhaps he would have seen little reason to alter his point of view had he been alive in 1965.) "Capital has been poured like water into the Territory in the past," wrote Paterson, "and, like water it has sunk into the sand." The pioneers who had gone north had passed on; their homesteads were abandoned; the only traces ". . . here and there a few coffee or cotton plants that are still fighting an uphill battle against the prolific growth of grass and weed." Yet Paterson nevertheless saw a future for the Territory by the use of motor transport, provided roads were built to permit the development of a "chilled-beef" industry. Here again one sees Paterson, as a far-seeing Australian, con-cerned with his country's future, recognizing its dependence on primary industry and the need for the settlement of its great open areas. But, he wrote,

It may be only what Adam Lindsay Gordon called a "vision in smoke" but at any rate there is pleasure in the contemplation; for many of us have grown old and grey waiting for something to be done with the Territory.

Continuing his theme of a "great enchanted land", Paterson dealt in succeeding scripts with the romance of gold discovery in New Guinea, and the air-lift of machinery to develop these fields; with the trading industry in the islands to the north of Australia and the pearl fishing in these waters — a description of the latter remarkable for its detail and observation. He recounted his experience with the New Hebrides settlers in 1902 (much more fully than in his later reminiscences in the *Sydney Morning Herald*) : it was a venture, he concluded, ". . . that failed but which deserved a better fate . . .". He also wrote about incidents in his earlier life, including his enthusiasm for rowing and sailing on the Parramatta River; about horses, sheep and cattle, but most notably about the bush. For the best of these scripts is one entitled "Bush Life", some of the incidents of which, Paterson wrote, ". . . were roughly sketched in a notebook on a trip to Brewarrina". Here once again he was on his much-loved Western plains:

> And who shall describe the eerie loneliness of this country? A few sheep, a few galahs, and a few magpies; these are the only living things, other than human, seen in two hundred miles. Travelling through a station of a hundred thousand sheep, one hardly sees any of them. At little dusty wayside stations the people get in and out — long-legged, thin men, sunburnt to a mahogany colour. Women almost as sunburnt, with quick and earnest faces. The lounge lizard and the baby doll have no place in this life. Two women meet on the platform, get into the carriage, and start a conversation. Of what will they speak? Will they talk about trips to Sydney, about fashions, or about their families? Not a bit of it. One says to the other, "Have you had the mice yet?" And there we get the key-note of bush life. Nature, resenting human invasion, keeps up a sort of guerilla warfare, using such weapons as plagues of mice, grasshoppers, caterpillars, and in some places even kangaroos and emus. The bushman and his wife can never go to sleep on the job.

And Paterson sketched his own vision of the future:

> A couple of hundred years hence, perhaps, someone will write the history of these early days, a lot of it incredible, or, at the least, difficult of understanding. But when that date arrives, time will have mellowed the past. The man who carted away the Gongolon hotel, brick by brick, will be as romantic as a Highland raider; the hard-bitten Captain and deck-hand of the "Wandering Jew" will rank with the early Vanderbilts who ran a ferry in New York; and there will be a terrific demand for samples of old colonial curios — beds with strips of green-hide in the place of springs, and crudely-carved stockwhip handles made of the scented myall wood. Then, and then only, will the bush people come into their own.

Paterson did no more work for broadcasting after this series in 1935. After all, he was seventy-one at his point. But it is clear that the stimulus of writing these scripts prompted him a few years later to undertake a series of reminiscences which were published in the *Sydney Morning Herald* in 1939 — his last published work before his death.

NOTES

[1] In the A.B.C. radio documentary referred to previously.
[2] Broadcast on 2FC, 15 May 1932.
[3] 16 August 1933 — original letter in Mitchell Library, Sydney.
[4] These letters are in A.B.C. archives.
[5] In a note attached to these letters.
[6] Ibid.

CHAPTER XVII

Paterson as Poet

There can't be too many men in this world singing about what they know and love . . .

— RUDYARD KIPLING (1895).*

Paterson is the bush rhymester raised to his highest power, humoursome and human . . .

— A. G. STEPHENS.[1]

IT HAS ALWAYS seemed to me unfair that Paterson should be regarded merely as a stringer-together of popular verses, the assumption being that ballads and poetry do not mix. Probably his predilection for the horse (translated more often than not into "the Turf") has been partly responsible for this, since literary criticism (especially of the academic type) and horse-racing are indifferent bedfellows. It is customary therefore to discuss Paterson as a balladist (". . . he was really only at home in the robust, masculine world of action, where men played uproarious practical jokes or raced heroically down the perilous mountainside . . .", wrote Vance Palmer,[2] for instance), and thus be spared the necessity of justifying him as a poet. The banner "Balladists Shall Not Pass" is too readily displayed.

But the poet, I think, stems from the balladist. As a balladist Paterson in his best work is superb, ranking with any in English literature, for after all as Quiller Couch said in his introduction to the *Oxford Book of Ballads*, the way to define a ballad is to quote lines that have the ring of balladry. Paterson qualifies with distinction: he rings truest in his lines that tell of action and adventure. Leaving aside his horse-racing verses which are discussed in another chapter, and which are in a peculiar category, there are sufficient of his ballads remaining, equestrian and other, to allow them to be seen as "a minstrelsy of action":[3] to remind us of that particular Australia of his time — the vigorous, sprawling, challenging Australia of the outback.

The landscape of action and the action itself combined, as never before or since, most tellingly in "The Man from Snowy River":

> Then fast the horseman followed, where the gorges deep and black
> Resounded to the thunder of their tread,

---

* In a letter of congratulation to Angus & Robertson Ltd. (dated 10 December) about Paterson's *The Man from Snowy River and Other Verses* (Mitchell Library).

And the stockwhips woke. the echoes and they fiercely answered back
    From cliffs and crags that beetled overhead,
And upward, ever upward, the wild horses held their way,
    Where mountain ash and kurrajong grew wide;

Often the action seems effortless, like a finely engined motor-car, tuned to perfection, silently and swiftly eating up the miles of a smoothly surfaced highway, so magnificently geared is rhythm to context in such lines as these from "Conroy's Gap":

He left the camp by the sundown light,
    And the settlers out on the Marthaguy
Awoke and heard, in the dead of night,
    A single horseman hurrying by.
He crossed the Bogan at Dandaloo,
    And many a mile of the silent plain
That lonely rider behind him threw
    Before they settled to sleep again.

He rode all night, and he steered his course
    By the shining stars with a bushman's skill,
And every time that he pressed his horse
    The Swagman answered him gamely still.

But it is not always the action of the saddle, though Paterson has left us in little doubt that this is the finest evocation possible of the adventure and challenge of the outback. There is, too, the everyday excitement of station life: the dust and swirl and confusion of mustering and yarding, the exhilaration of the shearing-shed —

The youngsters picking up the fleece enjoy the merry din,
They throw the classer up the fleece, he throws it to the bin;
The pressers standing by the rack are waiting for the wool,
There's room for just a couple more, the press is nearly full;
Now jump upon the lever, lads, and heave and heave away,
Another bale of golden fleece is branded "Castlereagh".

— and the urgency of "The Flying Gang", the pioneer railwaymen patrolling the country tracks:

By the uplands bright and the homesteads white
    With the rush of the western gale —
And the pilot swayed with the pace we made
    As she rocked on the ringing rail.

This facility to translate experience and imagination into action — with a still-tingling pulse, as A. G. Stephens put it, to sit down and convey the tingle to the pulse of his readers — never deserted Paterson. whether he was retracing in his mind's eye the chase of the bushrangers as they "wheeled their tracks with a wild beast's skill" or setting down on the spot his account of General French's drive to Kimberley, although with an idiom much less natural to him:

The gunners plied their guns amain; the hail of shrapnel flew;
With rifle fire and lancer charge their squadrons back we threw;
And through the pass between the hills we swept in furious fray,
And French was through to Kimberley to drive the Boers away.

But next to their expression of action, the most abiding and attractive feature of Paterson's ballads is their humour. And the many facets of Paterson's understanding of the day-by-day humour of bush life (and, for that matter, some aspects of urban life, as for instance in his "Wreck of the Golfer",* unaccountably never included in his collections) enlighten as they gleam through his ballads, since, after all, as Chaucer has shown from the beginning (and he was a minstrel too), the life and

* Published in the *Sydney Mail* of 14 September 1897 and never subsequently reprinted, it is worth quoting in full as an example of Paterson's skill in parody and comic improvisation:

It was the Bondi golfing man
    Drove off from the golf-house tee,
And he had taken his little daughter
    To bear him company.

"Oh, Father, why do you swing the club
    And flourish it such a lot?"
"You watch it fly o'er the fences high!"
    And he tried with a brassey shot.

"Oh, Father, why did you hit the fence
    Just there where the brambles twine?"
And the father he answered never a word,
    But he got on the green in nine.

"Oh, Father, back from behind those trees,
    What dismal yells arrive!"
" 'Tis a man I ween on the second green,
    And I've landed him with my drive."

"Oh, Father, why does the poor Chinee
    Fall down on his knees and cry!"
"He taketh me for his Excellency,
    And he thinks once hit twice shy."

So on they fared to the waterhole,
    And he drove with a lot of dash,
But the balls full soon in the dread lagoon
    Fell down with a woeful splash.

"Oh, Father, why do you beat the sand
    Till it flies like the carded wool?"
And the father he answered never a word,
    For his heart was much too full.

"Oh, Father, why are they shouting fore!
    And screaming so lustily."
But the father he answered never a word,
    A pallid corpse was he.

For a well-swung drive on the back of his head
    Had landed and laid him low.
Lord save us all from a fate like this
    When next to the links we go.

manners of an age can be the no less effectively set down in the romps
and jokes of its people. But in the Australian bush there was humour to
be extracted, too, from the sardonically endured disasters of its people.
And certainly drought, dust, heat and ruin were part of the scheme of
things that Paterson laconically contemplated. Yet, since his was a
homely, hearty humour, open as daylight, he looked more often than not
for its kindlier manifestations in the outback, as in the explanation of
the elements by the Aboriginal "Frying Pan" —

>   Him drive 'im bullock dray
>   Then thunder go;
>   Him shake 'im flour bag —
>   Tumble down snow!

— or in the genial Saltbush Bill's Christmas Day version, to his "little
rouseabouts", of the story of Isaac and Jacob:

> But when the stock were strong and fat with grass and lots of rain
> Then Jacob felt the call to take the homeward track again.
> It's strange in every creed and clime, no matter where you roam,
> There comes a day when every man would like to make for home.
>
> So off he set with sheep and goats, a mighty roving band,
> To battle down the dusty road along the Overland —
> It's droving mixed-up mobs like that that makes men cut their throats,
> I've travelled rams, which Lord forget, but never travelled goats.
>
> But Jacob knew the ways of stock, for (so the story goes)
> When battling through the Philistines — selectors, I suppose —
> He thought he'd have to fight his way, an awkward sort of job;
> So what did Old Man Jacob do? Of course, he split the mob.
>
> He sent the strong stock on ahead to battle out the way;
> He couldn't hurry lambing ewes — no more you could today —
> And down the road from run to run, his hand 'gainst every hand,
> He moved that mighty mob of stock across the Overland.

Saltbush Bill of course was probably Paterson's best comic creation in a
ballad genre that Douglas Stewart once defined as a new variety, the
Australian Comic. Here Saltbush Bill was in his kingdom — on the great
tracts of land that he claimed were for all, irrespective of boundaries,
surveyors and the like:

> For the name and fame of Saltbush Bill were over the countryside
> For the wonderful way that he fed his sheep, and the dodges and
>   tricks he tried.
>
> He would lose his way on a Main Stock Route, and stray to the
>   squatters' grass;
> He would come to a run with the boss away, and swear he had leave
>   to pass;

Outback custom triumphed over lawyers' law, though in "Saltbush Bill J.P." our hero did not hesitate to use this same law to claim his justice's fee for inquests on fires that he contrived to have lit. But then this is one of the brands of Paterson's humour — the tricks and simple villainies of his bush citizens. There is, for instance, the stranger in Walgett "taken down" with the local joke of wagering to ride what turns out to be a clothes horse and in turn selling the still-laughing citizens a batch of kangaroo skins still on the kangaroo. Or again there is the unwary mining man in Coolgardie who hires a camel in return for "shouting" it a drink — which turns out to be unlimited buckets of water at half-a-crown a time. This is the rudimentary humour of the unsophisticated bushman, who in turn is permitted by Paterson, in probably his best-known comic ballad, to have the last laugh on the city slicker, the barber "small and flash" who pretended to cut the throat of the Man from Ironbark and was upended for his pains.

> And now while round the shearing-floor the listening shearers gape,
> He tells the story o'er and o'er, and brags of his escape.
> "Them barber chaps what keeps a tote, by George, I've had enough.
> One tried to cut my bloomin' throat, but thank the Lord it's tough."
> And whether he's believed or no, there's one thing to remark,
> That flowing beards are all the go way up in Ironbark.

Inevitably Paterson tends towards the humour of the larger-than-life, which anyhow is the stock-in-trade of the bush humourist, as with the outback Ananias telling his far-fetched yarns to gaping and gullible audiences in bush pubs and in drovers' camps. They are the same listeners and *Bulletin* readers, who, Norman Lindsay recalls, stood drinks for many a bogus Lawson and Paterson. And it is a short step from the larger-than-life to what becomes bush legend — Mulga Bill's epic bicycle ride, Saltbush Bill's immortal deed of producing an Australian emu to fight an English gamecock, and William Johnson down on Snakebite River seeking his snakebite antidote with the single-mindedness and dedication of a mediaeval alchemist in search of the philosopher's stone.

> Here it is, the Great Elixir, greatest blessing ever known
> — Twenty thousand men in India die each year of snakes alone;
> Think of all the foreign nations, negro, chow, and blackamoor,
> Saved from sudden expiration by my wondrous snakebite cure.
> It will bring me fame and fortune! In the happy days to be
> Men of every clime and nation will be round to gaze on me —
> Scientific men in thousands, men of mark and men of note,
> Rushing down the Mooki River, after Johnson's antidote.
> It will cure *delirium tremens* when the patient's eyeballs stare
> At imaginary spiders, snakes which really are not there.
> When he thinks he sees them wiggle, when he thinks he sees them
>   bloat,
> It will cure him just to think of Johnson's Snakebite Antidote.

For Paterson is, in his ballads, myth-maker too, and if we do not know his ingenious ballad about Driver Smith who with his ambulance on the Transvaal veldt captured Kruger and "ended the blooming war", at least we all know "The Man from Snowy River". And it was the magic of this poem that gave the excitement to his first collection of verse: it was not just a book that had been written; it was as if a word had been uttered that was to awaken a dumb country, giving it a language of its own, a laughter of its own, and spreading a sense of fellowship between one man and another. *The Man from Snowy River and Other Verses* travelled over Australia as no other book had done before or has done since, and soon its verses were being recited at every bush gathering and around every campfire; and The Man from Snowy River himself had become a legend like Till Eulenspiegel or William Tell.

And in all this Paterson had the instinct of the folk-singer to make sure of the material at hand, to shape it in more telling fashion and give it a national vogue. In words that soon seemed as natural as breathing, he made a balladry of the scattered lives of back-country Australians who thought nobody noticed them and who until then had hardly noticed one another. He discovered the simple tunes of these lives; tunes that mostly had the easy, obvious rhythm of an exhilarating barn-dance. (And indeed "Waltzing Matilda" is the best of barn-dances with everyone joining in and roaring the famous, pseudo-melancholy choruses.)

It was a varied, interesting and, above all, lovable country that he revealed to the people of his day and has left as a legacy to his readers in our and future generations: a country where Nature was not merely a bitch-goddess, as some soured immigrants had painted her, but had her own beauty and even her moments of gentleness. And though we recognize the action and adventure, the humour and the myth-making as essential parts of his balladry, it is in these inspired moments when he takes up the lyre instead of the banjo, when he opens those "occasional windows . . . into the heart of the bush's own music . . .",[4] that Paterson becomes poet — the poet of the western plains, the Australian Plainsman of our literature. Geographically this area might be thought of as the great hinterland lying between the upper reaches of the Lachlan to the north and the Eumerella to the south; alternatively we might think of it, as Paterson probably did, as the whole of the illimitable outback of the Australia he knew and loved from his own travels: western New South Wales, the Snowy country, the Queensland downs (where he wrote "Waltzing Matilda") and the Northern Territory ("If you've heard the East a-callin' you don't never heed naught else", he wrote. "And the man who once goes to the Territory always has a hankering to get back there.")[5] Or then again, it might well be bounded by the familiar sign-posts recurring in his ballads: "the land of lots o' time" along the sleeping, loitering Castlereagh, stretching up to Kiley's Hill and Conroy's Gap, dropping away to Dandaloo and "the black soil flats across by Waddi-wong".

At all events, this is Paterson's country: where "the plains are all awave with grass, the skies are deepest blue", but where, too, there is the "fiery dust-storm drifting, and the mocking mirage shifting", where there is "waving grass and forest trees on sunlit plains as wide as seas", but where there is the "drought fiend", too, and the cattle are left lying "with the crows to watch them dying — / Grim sextons of the Overland that fasten on their prey"; where there is "the dry sweet scent on the salt bush plain", but where, too, "fierce hot winds have set the pine and myall boughs asweep" — so vast a country indeed that the lonely rider is seen as "a speck upon the waste of plain".

And in this setting Paterson opened his heart and his talent to the outback he loved. There was the smell of it in "The Wind's Message" —

> It brought a breath of mountain air from off the hills of pine,
> A scent of eucalyptus trees in honey-laden bloom;
> And drifting, drifting far away along the southern line
> It caught from leaf and grass and fern a subtle strange perfume.

and in "In the Droving Days":

> At dawn of day we could feel the breeze
> That stirred the boughs of the sleeping trees,
> And brought a breath of the fragrance rare
> That comes and goes in that scented air;
> For the trees and grass and the shrubs contain
> A dry sweet scent on the saltbush plain.
> For those that love it and understand
> The saltbush plain is a wonderland.

There was the magic of the bush —

> The waving of grasses,
>   The song of the river
> That sings as it passes
>   For ever and ever,
> The hobble-chains' rattle,
>   The calling of birds,
> The lowing of cattle
>   Must blend with the words.

— which often would seem to have been absorbed into his very verse:

> By the winding Wollondilly where the weeping willows weep,
> And the shepherd with his billy, half-awake and half-asleep.

And especially there were its characteristic sights evoking lines of true landscape poetry, as in "Brumby's Run" —

> The traveller by the mountain-track
>   May hear their hoof-beats pass,
> And catch a glimpse of brown and black
>   Dim shadows on the grass.

— and, in "White Cockatoos" —

> Over the mountain peaks outlying
> Clear, against the blue
> Comes a scout in silence flying
> One white cockatoo

— climaxed in his "Black Swans", where, as Douglas Stewart has remarked (and he seems to me to have read Paterson's verse with more affection and understanding than most critics), only a man who was truly a poet at heart could have soared into such stanzas as these:

> O ye wild black swans, 'twere a world of wonder
> For a while to join in your westward flight,
> With the stars above and the dim earth under,
> Through the cooling air of the glorious night.
> As we swept along on our pinions winging,
> We should catch the chime of a church-bell ringing,
> Or the distant note of a torrent singing,
> Or the far-off flash of a station light.
> From the northern lakes with the reeds and rushes,
> Where the hills are clothed with a.purple haze,
> Where the bell-birds chime and the songs of thrushes
> Make music sweet in the jungle maze,
> They will hold their course to the westward ever,
> Till they reach the banks of the old grey river,
> Where the waters wash, and the reed-beds quiver
> In the burning heat of the summer days.

And it is when the balladist and the poet come together that Paterson is at his most memorable — never more so than in the concluding lines of "The Travelling Post Office":*

> Where fierce hot winds have set the pine and myall boughs asweep
> He hails the shearers passing by for news of Conroy's sheep.
> By big lagoons where wildfowl play and crested pigeons flock,
> By camp-fires where the drovers ride around their restless stock,
> And past the teamster toiling down to fetch the wool away
> My letter chases Conroy's sheep along the Castlereagh.

It was part of Paterson's art, as of his sheer love of the country he wrote about, that people and places became recurring symbols. "Along the Castlereagh" is a key phrase in a half-dozen of his ballads, so is "Conroy's Gap", the Bland ("It's homeward down the Bland we'll go, and never

---

* "In 'The Travelling Post Office'," wrote Paterson in "Looking Backward", "I took the risk of describing how a letter was sent c/- Conroy's Sheep rather than the P.O. I argued that letters must have been sent this way in the past. Years afterwards I was travelling down the Diamantina in a coach. Across the waste of plain there came a lonely horseman to interrupt us and as he rode up he said 'Have you got any letters on board for J. Riley care of the Carrandotta cattle?', and sure enough the driver had one."

more we'll roam . . ."), the Marthaguy and Walgett Town. These are the signposts of his verse. As for the people, Conroy is the average home-steader; Clancy, cropping up here and there, the overlander; Carew, the remittance man — ne'er-do-well; and Tyson the landlord of the outback — "I've got the cash / I'm T.Y.S.O.N." — or as in ". . . not old Tyson himself could pay / The purchase money of Mongrel Grey."

This fascination with the names of the bush was converted by Paterson into a technique. Thus, when he came across a small town called Come-By-Chance he could not get it out of his head; he wrote a ballad about it:

> I shall leave my home, and forthward wander stoutly to the
>   northward
> Till I come by chance across it, and I'll straightway settle down;

He rolled round his pen Puckawidgee, Booleroi and Bumble; and found the material for another ballad "Those Names",* where, as the shearers sat in the firelight telling their stories, "to give these stories flavour they threw in some local names" until

> . . . a man from the bleak Monaro, away on the tableland,
> He fixed his eyes on the ceiling, and he started to play his hand.
> He told them of Adjintoothbong, where the pine-clad mountains
>   freeze,
> And the weight of the snow in summer breaks branches off the trees,
> And, as he warmed to the business, he let them have it strong —
> Nimitybelle, Conargo, Wheeo, Bongongolong;
> He lingered over them fondly, because they recalled to mind
> A thought of the old bush homestead, and the girl that he left behind.

And it is this very nostalgia for the outback that is unforgettable in Paterson too, whether he fixes for posterity such a long-gone bush sight as ". . . the pack-horse running after; for he follows like a dog . . .", or frankly confesses the feeling itself:

> But, as one half-hearing
>   An old-time refrain,
> With memory clearing,
>   Recalls it again,
> These tales roughly wrought of
>   The Bush and its ways,
> May call back a thought of
>   The wandering days.

These qualities of Paterson's verses have led a recent critic to conclude that "the desire to push experience into an idealized land-that-never-was . . . plays in and about practically every good line Paterson ever wrote. He did not, in effect, write about the Australian bush: he re-created Arcadia 'down under'."[6] This is, of couse, a misinterpretation of Pater-

---

* Paterson had in fact "been everywhere" sixty or seventy years before the popular singer of the 1960s who became famous with a song of similar theme.

son's attitudes and motives. Kendall perhaps, but Paterson never. Who
could be further from Arcadia than he

> . . . away on the far Barcoo
> Watching his cattle the long year through
> Watching them starve in the droughts and die . . .

than the teamsters

> . . . out on the Castlereagh, when they meet with a week of rain,
> And the waggon sings to its axle-tree, deep down in the black-soil
> plain,
> When the bullocks wade in a sea of mud, and strain at the load of
> wool,
> And the cattle-dogs at the bullocks' heels are biting to make them
> pull,

than those characters born of Paterson's ironic contemplation of some
most un-Arcadian facts of outback existence:

> It's grand to be a Western man,
> With a shovel in your hand,
> To dig your little homestead out
> From underneath the sand.

> It's grand to be a shearer
> Along the Darling-side,
> And pluck the wool from stinking sheep
> That some days since have died.

> It's grand to be a rabbit
> And breed till all is blue,
> And then to die in heaps because
> There's nothing left to chew.

It is true, of course, that Paterson wrote some very bad verse, mainly
when his reputation had been made, and he felt it now and then incum-
bent on him to "produce" verse, usually for national or patriotic reasons
or occasions. When it came to contrived emotion or sentiment, Paterson's
muse wholly left him, just as it has deserted many a poet laureate. Most
of his really atrocious verse, and there was not much of it, stemmed from
these circumstances. There was, as has been noted previously, "The
Reveille", for instance, included in *Saltbush Bill, J.P.*, but dropped, and
rightly so, from his *Collected Verse*, and the doggerel of "That V.C.".

Yet it would be unfair to judge Paterson by standards he never set
himself. The fact is that in most of his verse he caught and set down
something that sounds, and always will sound, the authentic Australian
note. I have heard of a nurse in a lonely bush hospital who, when she
was exhausted or depressed, locked herself in her room and recited

Paterson to herself till "she felt better";* I have travelled with a Sydney
taxi-driver who recited the whole of "The Man from Snowy River"
without a mistake from beginning to end as he wove in and out of the
traffic through the city and across the Harbour Bridge. "I have often been
intrigued in the classroom to find," Russel Ward has written, "the
Reimersmas or Komorofskies riding on with 'The Man from Snowy
River' even more wholeheartedly than their Old Australian classmates
. . ." And as far back as 1927 a school teacher wrote in the *Sydney Morning
Herald*[7] a moving tribute to the capacity of Paterson in his verse to give
his readers, as artlessly as effectively, the quiet pleasure that is akin to the
pleasure of possession, the pleasure, as one writer has put it, of "a non-
professional patriotism". This school teacher explained his difficulties
with a class of boys who regarded poetry as piffle: ". . . the combination of
mechanical accuracy and absolute apathy with which the works of the
masters were rendered made me despair of ever convincing them that
poetry was not the unenvied monopoly of a few unathletic madmen, but
the proud heritage of a nation". One day, in a history lesson, he read by
chance a few lines from Paterson's "Song of Freedom". Polite indifference
gave way to interest: Who was the poet? What had he written? Soon, an
enthusiastic reception to "The Geebung Polo Club" and "The Man from
Ironbark" led to a complete and genuine interest in all of Paterson's
poetry. The teacher concluded his account:

> This enthusiasm may be attributed to his humour, to his lack of
> ambiguity, to the spirit of adventure which is manifested in many of
> his poems or it may be the fact of his being a fellow countryman who
> writes of familiar things and places. Be that as it may, I have found
> him an ideal poet for the classroom. Paterson himself, speaking of his
> poems, tells us that
>> They are just the rude stories one hears
>> In sadness and mirth
>> The records of wandering years —
>> And scant is their worth . . .
> But a poet who can amuse and inspire the unimaginative, intensely
> practical, ruthlessly logical boy of 14 or 15 must possess elements of
> greatness . . .

Nor can there be any question about it. Though Paterson is a balladist
of balladists and in such stanzas as this from "A Bushman's Song" —

> I'm travelling down the Castlereagh, and I'm a station-hand,
> I'm handy with the ropin' pole, I'm handy with the brand,
> And I can ride a rowdy colt, or swing the axe all day,
> But there's no demand for a station-hand along the Castlereagh.

*cf. ". . . Take Irene, our tea-lady, for instance. She was brought up by a Danish
sailor father and an English seamstress mother who settled here in 1896. In the pub on
a Saturday 'arvo Irene will recite Banjo Paterson till everyone else is black in the
face . . ." (David Beard in "Take My Old Dad", *Nation*, 24 July 1965) .

— he becomes part of our folk-song (since these lines but translate into words the familiar rhythms of our national life and temperament), yet as frequently and as felicitously* as any poet in our literature who has written of our great hinterland, he has caught its sunlight and colour, hinted at its mystery and magic:

> Land of plenty or land of want, where the grey Companions dance,
> Feast or famine, or hope or fear, and in all things land of chance,
> Where Nature pampers or Nature slaps, in her ruthless, red romance,
> And we catch a sound of a fairy's song, as the wind goes whipping by,
> Or a scent like incense drifts along from the herbage ripe and dry
> — Or the dust-storms dance on their ballroom floor, where the bones
>   of the cattle lie.

And especially, as in these lines from "Sunrise on the Coast" —

> Like mariners calling the roll of their number
> The sea-fowl put out to the infinite deep.
> And far overhead — singing softly to slumber —
> Worn out by their watching the stars fall asleep,

— he justified H. M. Green's observation that "the quality that in the end he stands by is after all a poetic quality"[9] and John Manifold's contention that "Paterson is a far richer, more subtle and more versatile poet than people appear to believe to-day".[10]

---

* Even as far back as 1907, a Madalen Edgar had written to Paterson from Edinburgh, Scotland:
> . . . I am preparing a book of English verse for use in schools and would venture to ask your kind permission to include in it your verses "By the Grey Gulf Water". Their beauty is so distinctive that I would be exceedingly pleased could you permit me to place them in the collection . . .[8]

NOTES

[1] In "Australian Literature" (*The Commonwealth*, 1901/2).
[2] In *The Legend of the Nineties* (1954).
[3] The phrase is Douglas Stewart's.
[4] Brian Elliott in "Australian Paterson" (*Singin' to the Cattle*, 1947).
[5] In "The Cycloon, Paddy Cahill and the G.R." (*Bulletin*, 31 December 1898).
[6] H. P. Heseltine in "Banjo Paterson: A Poet Nearly Anonymous" (*Meanjin*, 4/1964).
[7] *Sydney Morning Herald*, 12 December, 1927. The writer was D. A. Riddell, under the heading of "A Schoolboy's Poet — The Lure of Paterson".
[8] The letter dated 20 February 1907, written from 36 Fountainhall Road, is in the Mitchell Library.
[9] In *A History of Australian Literature* (1961).
[10] In *Who Wrote the Ballads?* (1964).

CHAPTER XVIII

Novels, Sketches and Stories

*Good or bad, serious or trivial, Paterson's style is always
Australian. . . . His compass is narrow, but within it he
savours his experience richly . . .*

— BRIAN ELLIOTT.[1]

*Paterson is vigorous, fresh, breezy, racy of the soil, and the
land to him is not barren and sterile, not melancholy, its
people not sorrowful dreamers, but men and women of
stalwart frame, looking forward from a bright to-day to a
bright to-morrow.*

— W. FARMER WHYTE.[2]

I HAVE ALREADY remarked on the appearance of Paterson's first prose
sketch ("How I Shot the Policeman") in the *Bulletin* in 1890. Archibald
reminded him again of his earlier advice to write about his experiences
and knowledge of the bush and its characters, as a result of which in the
next year or so Paterson submitted and had accepted four or five sketches
and stories of this type. The most interesting of these was "The History
of a Jackaroo in Five Letters",[3] where not only did he essay an epistolary
approach unusual for the period, but in so doing showed a developing
capacity for ironic commentary — in this case on contemporary station
practices. As with his ballad writing, his characters began to appear as
larger-than-life exaggerations, though not caricatures. The unfortunate
young remittance-man-jackaroo was named Jocelyn de Greene (". . . of
course it's not quite the same as going to India; but some really decent
people do go out to Australia, sometimes, I'm told, and I expect it won't
be so bad . . .") ; the station to which he was sent was called "Drybone",
and Paterson's satirical contempt and indignation were implicit in Letter
No. 2, from Moneygrub and Co. (the parent company in London) to
the Manager of Drybone (Mr Robert Saltbush) :

> Dear Sir — We beg to advise you of having made arrangements to
> take a young gentleman named Greene as colonial-experiencer, and
> he will be consigned to you by the next boat. His premium is £500,
> and you will please deal with him in the usual way. Let us know
> when you have vacancies for any more colonial-experiencers, as
> several are now asking about it, and the premiums are forthcoming.

You are on no account to employ Union shearers this year; and you
must cut expenses as low as you can. Would it not be feasible to work
the station with the colonial-experience men and Chinese labour?

&c, &c, &c.

For, as Paterson developed in the rest of his "Letters", Moneygrub,
with his £500 premium for each raw jackaroo, instructed his manager to
give the unfortunates the usual treatment: that they be sent out riding
the boundaries with a week's rations, so that eventually, crazed with
loneliness, they attempted to run away, and were skilfully led by one of
the stockmen to the nearest township, where they drank themselves to
death, or became shiftless wanderers in the outback; ". . . old Moneygrub
collars the £500 and sends out another jackaroo". In such a sketch as
this, as in "Concerning a Steeplechase Rider", Paterson's social conscience
was much in evidence. There are parallels in his ballads, and again in
one of his two novels, *An Outback Marriage*, where he stressed that no
Land Act could restrain the Moneygrubs of the vast areas of the interior:

> . . . Before Bully Grant had been in the firm long he had secured all
> the good land, and the industrious yeomanry that the Land Act was
> supposed to create were hiding away up the gullies on miserable little
> patches of bad land, stealing sheep for a living . . .

But for all that, Paterson was not cast in the role of a social reformer.
The world of the outback offered wider and more rewarding scope for his
shrewd observations, and for his sense of kinship with the bush folk. Nor
was it merely the fact of a subject-matter at hand: Paterson's own writing
style was developing — a journalistic style it is true, but attractive,
immensely readable and always colloquially literate. He displayed quite
early in his writing career the capacity to salt description with details of
human interest. Reporting, after all, as A. J. Liebling once said, is being
interested in everyone you meet; the most casual meetings can turn up
fascinating material, the off-beat events can create curiosity about people.
As early as 1892 Paterson had described for the *Bulletin*[4] a tug-of-war
held at Darlinghurst Hall, Sydney:

> . . . Then came what was supposed to be the tug of the evening,
> Australia v. Ireland. As the teams took their places you could feel the
> electricity rising in the atmosphere. The Irish were a splendid team,
> a stone a man heavier than their opponents all round, but the latter
> looked, if anything, harder and closer knit. As they took their places
> the warning yells rang out all over the building: "Now boys, sunny
> N.S.W. for it!", "Go it, Australia!". And from the Irish side came a
> babel of broad, soft, buttery brogue: "Git some chark on yer hands,
> Dinny!", "Mick, if yez don't win, never come to the wharf no more!",
> "For the love of God and my fiver, bhoys, pull together!" It was a
> national Irish team right through — regular Donegal and Tipperary
> bhoys. They were genuine; every other man answered to the name of
> Mick. They wore orange and green colours, to give the Pope and

Protestants equal show. They spat on their enormous hands, planted their brogues against the battens, and at the sound of the pistol, while every Australian heart beat high with hope, the Mickies simply gave one enormous drayhorse drag and fetched our countrymen clean away . . .

Any present-day sporting journalist would be proud to sign his name to this; it is actuality reporting at its best, rich in atmosphere and with a rare touch of style, as in "babel of broad, soft, buttery brogue" and "one enormous drayhorse drag".

This reporting instinct never left him; sixteen years later, with much more poise as a journalist, Paterson covered for the *Evening News*, as already recorded, the first motor reliability trial from Sydney to Melbourne. He still had the reporter's unerring eye for the detail to catch immediately the reader's attention:

> The road from Goulburn to Yass is in splendid order. We got away badly and ran over a calf. The animal was either purposely left there or wished to commit suicide. . . . Friedman in trouble near Gunning; Harry Skinner who is in a Darracq, hit a gully and bent an axle like a hoop . . . He starts later to-day. We expect to reach Jugiong safely unless we meet more calves . . .[5]

And, like any good journalist with a literary imagination, Paterson relied on his very experience with people and places to give life and colour to his creative pieces. Undoubtedly his adventures on this trial prompted his motoring short story "Three Elephant Power", as delightfully and ironically amusing as any story Paterson has written.

Many parts of *Happy Dispatches* illustrate Paterson's literary journalism at its best. In his modest foreword he described himself as a looker-on seeing most of the game, a "not very proficient" writer in the game, able to say something about the players. Yet his descriptions, at first hand, were superb, whether of the Modder River engagement during the Boer War, the pony races at Chefoo, the roughriders at work in Egypt, or his entertainingly evocative account of the scene at the races at Marseilles:

> . . . Motor cars fly past, each with a French poodle sitting on the front seat with the wind blowing through his whiskers. We pass a Frenchman and his wife in a little donkey-cart drawn by an infinitesimal donkey . . . The air is crisp and clear, and filled with the aromatic smell of dead leaves as we drive through an avenue of sycamores. About half the crowd gets in free; or rather, they sit just outside the course on a grassy slope where they have a splendid view; for it is only divided from the running by a deep ditch. Here they smoke cigarettes and drink light wines and eat things out of baskets, while their children, in hundreds, roll and play on the grass. . . .

His bushman's eye for the tell-tale detail gave particular sharpness to his thumbnail sketches of many great men whom he met, as he put it, "stripped of their official panoply, and sitting as one might say, in their pyjamas"; certainly his portraits have stood the test of over thirty years, and by present-day journalistic standards, when the cult of the personality has been so zealously and indeed ruthlessly exploited, they read entertainingly and vividly in their own right. Churchill, Kipling, "Chinese" Morrison, Haig, French, Allenby, Marie Lloyd, Phil May — his descriptions are all vignettes, their etching the more remarkable since they were by an easy-natured and unassuming colonial who had "started on his travels unencumbered by any knowledge of the world other than what could be gleaned from life in the Australian bush and in a solicitor's office in Sydney". Yet in these pieces there are flashes of quite unusual insight and epigrammatic assessments that convey more than long passages of descriptive prose — as in his observation of Lord Derby: ". . . a man who stood four-square in a world peopled largely by weather-cocks"; of a local Sussex magnate whom he met on his ramblings with Kipling: ". . . as stodgy as a bale of hay"; and of Captain Towse, v.c., as one of those men who ". . . in a regiment, a ship, or a shearing shed . . . unobtrusively exerts the same sort of influence that lubricating oil exerts in a motor car". Then again there was Paterson's skill — that of a first-class journalist—in recording items of memorable detail: the Chinese trader in his tiny shop in a Manila bazaar, with a gamecock tied by the leg to a counter watching for an opponent to come along; a little brown Malay carrying a sword trotting behind a corpulent Dutchman with spectacles and silk umbrella in a small port in the Celebes. Quite apart from its wealth of biographical detail about Paterson himself, *Happy Dispatches* can be read with much pleasure for Paterson's prose style at its casual and unpretentious best.

The abiding characteristic of most of Paterson's prose, as it is of his ballads, is his humour: laconic, tinged with the sardonic. As Brian Elliott has said, "every nation has its own characteristic humour, maybe this is ours".[6] For the essence of Paterson's humour lies not in contrived situations, nor in any form of wit, but simply and purely in the everyday occurrences and manifestations of the environment that he frequented. It is invariably near-the-knuckle humour; as in his essay on "The Merino Sheep":[7]

> The cross-bred drives his owner out of his mind, but the merino ruins his man with greater celerity. Nothing on earth will kill cross-breds, while nothing will keep merinoes alive. If they are put on dry saltbush country they die of drought. If they are put on damp, well-watered country they die of worms, fluke, and foot-rot. They die in the wet seasons and they die in the dry ones. The hard, resentful look which you may notice on the faces of all bushmen comes from a long course of dealing with the merino sheep. It is the merino sheep which dominates the bush, and which gives to Australian literature its melancholy tinge, and its despairing pathos. The poems about dying boundary-riders, and lonely graves under mournful she-oaks, are the direct outcome of the authors' too close association with that soul-destroying animal, the merino sheep. A man who could write

anything cheerful after a day in the drafting yards would be a freak of nature.

Paterson had studied animals as closely as he had human beings. In another of his "animal" pieces, "The Bullock", he wrote of the idiosyncrasies of individual bullocks: ". . . the one-eyed bullock that always pokes away out to the side of the mob, the inquisitive bullock that is always walking over to the drover as if he were going to speak to him, the agitator-bullock who is always trying to get up a stampede and prodding the others with his horns". (Paterson was convinced that any man who worked cattle for sport "would wheel bricks for amusement".) When it came to dogs, he saw them, especially working dogs, as similar to musicians whose art was sacred to them — Art before everything; cats, on the other hand, he felt had the most many-sided characters of the animal kingdom.

A dog is the central character in one of his most farcical stories, "Hughey's Dog"; but Paterson's finest achievement in the rollicking comedy of the absurd is "The Cast-Iron Canvasser"[8] about the activities of Sloper and Dodge, the firm of publishers and printers who sold books on time-payment through the agency of canvassers:

> Reports appeared in the country press about strange, gigantic birds that appeared at remote selections and frightened the inhabitants to death — these were Sloper and Dodge's sober and reliable agents, wearing neat, close-fitting suits of tar and feathers.

Facing ruin, Sloper, "a long sanctimonious individual, very religious and very bald", and Dodge, "a little fat American with bristly black hair and beard, and quick beady eyes", who smoked a reeking pipe "puffing the smoke through his nose in great whiffs like a locomotive on a steep grade", hired an inventor to make them "a patent cast-iron canvasser — a figure which, when wound up, would walk, talk, collect orders and stand any amount of ill usage and wear and tear". From then on the story develops to an almost unbelievable point of hilariousness. The remarkable thing is that the story stands up just as well in 1966 as it did in 1897: the term "robot" had not been invented then, and the high-pressure door-to-door book salesman seems a phenomenon of the mid-twentieth century. Certainly, as a classic short story of Australian humour, "The Cast-Iron Canvasser" ranks with Lawson's "The Loaded Dog", and Paterson's piece is richer in characterization.

Paterson, indeed, should long ago have invited comparison with Lawson as a writer of the short bush sketch, since this was part of the means by which both directed the attitudes and values of the nomadic bush-workers towards the framing of a national ethos. Of course, in output there is no comparison: Paterson's quota is minimal against Lawson's. But there is a quality in most of Paterson's work likely to be just as enduring as Lawson's even though the vogue of the latter has dimmed the appreciation of the former — just as, by an ironical tit-for-tat, the popularity of Paterson's verse has damped down an appreciation which should justly extend to Lawson's. Admittedly Paterson wrote nothing that, as a short story, could be compared with the bush pathos of "The Drover's Wife" or the intense characterization of the Spicers in "Water Them Geraniums"; but then he did not, like Lawson, see life as a mixture of humour and tragedy: the whites of bush humour and blacks of misfortune were more clearly dissociated. But where the bush sketch of Paterson seems to me to ring truer than that of Lawson is in the cheerful and uninhibited approach to the scenes and people concerned — what H. M. Green calls Paterson's "lyrical glimpses". Lawson, despite what some have said to the contrary, knew the bush, but his knowledge of it was restricted to certain parts of New South Wales; Paterson's love of it and familiarity with it was wide-ranging, from Darwin and the Gulf Country to the Snowy country — and went as far as most men had pushed out. Therefore there is a greater authenticity in his descriptions. Lawson loved the bush in his fashion, a love-hate relationship, at best, as in "His Country — After All", where one sees a nostalgic patriotism. But in Paterson's affection for his country there are no reservations at all — a sardonic appraisal, yes, but this has always been the Australian's privilege. From this standpoint, the two or three of Paterson's best stories seem to me superior to any of Lawson's—especially "White-When-He's-Wanted", where Paterson's knowledge and understanding of a good horse coalesces with a glorious sense of environment and action:

> He ran the mob from hill to hill, from range to range, across open country and back again to the hills, over flats and gullies, through hop-scrub and stringybark ridges; and all the time White-when-he's-wanted was on the wing of the mob, pulling double. The mares and foals dropped out, the colts and young stock pulled up dead beat, and only the seasoned veterans were left. Most of our horses caved in altogether; one or two were kept in the hunt by judicious nursing and shirking the work; but White-when-he's-wanted was with the quarry from end to end of the run, doing double his share; and at the finish, when a chance offered to wheel them into the trapyard. he simply smothered them for pace, and slewed them into the wings before they knew where they were. . . .

Even where there is a more than usual feeling of movement in Lawson's stories — as in "Gettin' Back on Dave Rogan" and "A Rough Shed" — there is not the same excitement as in this story by Paterson.

When it came to bush "spielers", Paterson's "The Downfall of Mulligan's" and "Bill and Jim Nearly Get Taken Down" certainly invited comparison with Lawson's "Steelman" stories; on the other hand, nothing in Lawson, since he was not particularly interested in the Turf, approached "The Oracle", which as I have already said, I believe to be an Australian classic of its kind.

As for humour, one can take little away from Lawson because throughout his stories humour is woven into their substance, no matter what the theme; even in sadness there is a tinge of it. But at least one can say for Paterson that his dry, quiet humour, as in "His Masterpiece", is often like Lawson's, even though it is more prone to veer away towards the sardonic. When Paterson chooses, however, to be genuinely funny, as in 'Hughey's Dog" (and "The Cast-Iron Canvasser" and "Three Elephant Power"), the result is a broader, more open sort of humour verging on the farcical — and here he is as successful and as memorable as Lawson in "Bill, the Ventriloquial Rooster" or "The Loaded Dog". And certainly, because geographically he ranged far more widely than Lawson, Paterson is pre-eminent in such satirically humorous sketches of the Australian scene as "The Cycloon, Paddy Cahill and the G.R." and "Thirsty Island".

There is one other thing that remains to be said about Paterson's stories and sketches, and that is that his style, generally consistent if sometimes journalistically over-seasoned, now and then captivates altogether with its ease and elegance. Take these lines from his sketch "The Cat":

> He saunters down his own backyard, springs to the top of the fence with one easy bound, drops lightly down on the other side, trots across the right-of-way to a vacant allotment, and skips to the roof of an empty shed . . .
>
> Arrived on the top of the shed, the cat arches his back, rakes his claws once or twice through the soft bark of the old roof, wheels round and stretches himself a few times; just to see that every muscle is in full working order; then, dropping his head nearly to his paws, he sends across a league of backyards his call to his kindred — a call to love, or war, or sport.

Undoubtedly Paterson's wide reading as a youth and young man gave poise and gloss to his prose style. In his stimulating study of Paterson's verse, H. P. Heseltine[9] referred to Paterson's latinisms as they occur in his ballads as ". . . more than humorously remembered scraps from an inert bump of learning he had brushed against in pursuit of the pound. . . . they were the relics of that rich cultural matrix which might have given his work a more ample life". I would suggest that this matrix did just that in the case of Paterson's prose, where literary allusions fall sweetly into place and give, sometimes because of their very unexpectedness, a freshness to his writing. "Virtue herself 'scapes not calumnious strokes", he quoted in his racing manuscript when writing of the race-horse-owner whose horses, sent out as favourites, were beaten; and he used a line from Hamlet, "I speak by the card", as the heading for his chapter on bookmakers. A punter, like the witness in Dickens, he wrote, had to be "prepared in a general way for anythink"; often his lot in the end was that of "Marius sitting among the ruins of Carthage". In his general writing he drew often on Byron and Swinburne; "had Kipling been a spectacular person like Gabriel d'Annunzio", he wrote in *Happy Dispatches*, "he might have led a great Imperialist movement"; he compared Kipling, in another passage, to Goethe's hero who "toiled without haste and without rest". He referred back to Carlyle's *Sartor Resartus* for the word "hinterschlag" in describing his school-days, and throughout his prose sketches quoted from Tennyson, Swift and Shakespeare and made it clear that his reading had ranged from Horace to Conan Doyle. Yet there was never a suspicion of conscious literariness in his work: on the contrary his idiom was invariably that of the bush-workers and "battlers" he wrote about.

Most of the characteristics of his prose style can be found in his novels *An Outback Marriage* and *The Shearer's Colt*. The latter is limited in plot and atmosphere because it deals entirely with horse-racing. *An Outback Marriage* allows Paterson much more scope: he is able to roam through the Australia he knew and to draw on the characters he met. Yet Paterson as a prose writer was much better served by his short pieces than by his novels: he did not have the patience to develop his characterization, and while the shorter sketch came as naturally to him as the writing of a ballad, he had not studied sufficiently the form and structure of the novel to master it effectively. It is all the more credit to him then that those parts of his novel where he was on his most familiar ground, the mountain country and the plains of the outback, remain in the memory, and the people he writes about there are eminently recognizable as bush types.

Yet, as a pioneer novel of its type, *An Outback Marriage* would have made a lively and indigenous film thirty years ago, when Australian film-makers were showing some activity, much more so than the stereotyped "Dad and Dave" productions with which they eventually came to light. It is a healthy story of bush station life (the realistic scenes of which are its chief virtue), with most of the places and events recognizable as part of Paterson's own experience and can be outlined as follows:

William Grant, a wealthy outback station-owner who married during a visit to England — his wife died there — eventually brings his daughter aged twenty-four out from England to get accustomed to his main property, "Kuryong", of about 60,000 acres, situated near Kiley's Crossing. On this station lives Hugh Gordon, the son of Grant's former partner and station manager, and the latter's widow, Mrs Gordon, who acts as the general mistress of the household. This is the main romantic plot, i.e., between Mary Grant and Hugh.

Surrounding this station are the families of the Doyles and the Donohoes and all their bush clans. One of the sub-plots is that a rather aggressive female member of the Donohoe clan, Peggy, claims she married the elder Grant, and when the latter dies during the story she makes a claim on his estate. Much of the story is devoted to the efforts of Hugh and Mary to disprove this claim, which is being fought on behalf of the Donohoes by a local lawyer, Gavan Blake, who, as a relative of the Doyles and the Donohoes, is looked up to by them and has their confidence. Blake rescues Mary Grant from near-drowning when she first arrives at the station, is invited to the homestead, and falls in love with her. Prior to this he had been conducting an affair (harmless flirtation type — Paterson was much too moral for anything worse) with the governess at the station, Ellen Harriott, with whom he now breaks off. Another sub-plot is related to a visiting Englishman, Carew (an Oxonian and Triple Blue), who is seeking a certain Patrick Considine who has come into an inheritance in England and is believed to be in Australia. By a coincidence Considine turns out to be a man named Keogh who is running one of Grant's distant outback stations and comes into the story early in the piece. Considine, however, claims that he married Peggy Donohoe and left her, and because he does not wish to share his possible inheritance with her, he "clears out" when he learns that she is very much in circulation, and takes refuge with some buffalo-hunters in Northern Territory. Hugh Gordon is sent up to bring him back, since it is felt that he can clear up the mystery of Peggy Donohoe's alleged marriage to Grant. Blake learns eventually that Peggy had in fact married Considine, but had forged the marriage papers to make it appear that she had married Grant — aided and abetted in this enterprise by "Red" Mick Donohoe, the leader of the Donohoe-Doyle faction. Eventually of course the case is disproved in court (Blake having decided to try to bluff it out), and, faced with disgrace then, Blake commits suicide. All ends happily otherwise with Mary Grant marrying Hugh and presumably the Englishman Carew marrying Ellen Harriott.

The weakness and strength of Paterson's characterization can be seen immediately in his treatment of Carew and the bushman Charles Gordon. Paterson had only a vague idea of the English University man:

> . . . his face was square and rather stolid, clean-shaven, brown-complexioned, with honest eyes and a firm-set mouth. As he stood at the door he adopted the wooden expression that a University man always wears in the presence of strangers. He said nothing on being introduced to Pinnock; and when the globe-trotter came up and claimed acquaintance, defining himself as "Gillespie of Balliol", the stranger said he didn't remember him, and regarded him with an aspect of armed neutrality. After a sherry and bitters he thawed a little . . .

This is Paterson's idea of his speech:

> "Ah! yes; awf'lly rough, I believe. Quite frightened me, what I heard of it, don't you know. Still, I suppose one must expect to rough it a bit. Eh, what!"

But there is, on the other hand, depth and understanding when Paterson writes of the bushman:

> . . . the eyes were . . . very keen and piercing . . . deep-set in the head; even when he was looking straight at anyone he seemed to be peering into endless space through the man in front of him. Such eyes men get from many years of staring over great stretches of sunlight plain where no colour relieves the blinding glare — nothing but dull grey clumps of saltbush and the dull green Mitchell grass . . . when he spoke he used the curious nasal drawl of the far-out bushman, the

slow deliberate speech that comes to men who are used to passing
months with the same companions in the unhurried Australian bush.
Occasionally he lapsed into reveries, out of which he would come
with a start and break in on other people's conversation, talking
them down with a serene indifference to their feelings.

Somehow the names of Carew and Considine must have haunted Paterson; he wrote a ballad called "Jim Carew" about the "ne'er-do-well"
Englishman, who "gained at his college a triple blue" but eventually
"came to grief" and became "Jimmy the Boozer all down at heel". His
ballad "Anthony Considine" was of a man who exiled himself on the
western plains, and

> . . . counted the world well lost
> For the love of his neighbour's wife . . .

In his novel, Paterson drew heavily on his own associations, environment and experience. Kuryong is of course Narambla-Illalong, and the
homestead descriptions match those in "On Kiley's Run". The situation
of the elder Paterson becoming manager instead of owner is repeated
here, Banjo Paterson giving the name of his son, Hugh, to the story's
hero. The Doyles and the Donohoes·are the bushranger progeny and outback nomads he knew in his childhood youth:

> . . . the headquarters of the clans was at Donohoe's "Shamrock
> Hotel", at Kiley's Crossing. Here they used to rendezvous when they
> went away down to the plains country each year for the shearing; for
> they added to their resources by travelling about the country shear-
> ing, droving, fencing, tank-sinking, or doing any other job that
> offered itself, but always returned to their mountain fastnesses ready
> for any bit of work "on the cross" (i.e., unlawful) that might turn
> up. When times got hard they had a handy knack of finding horses
> that nobody had lost, shearing sheep they did not own, and branding
> and selling other people's calves.

In the legal arguments and court scene, A. B. Paterson the lawyer is
writing from that experience, although if he has identified himself with
Blake it is sardonically so. Nor can Paterson the traveller forbear to introduce an episode taking in the exciting experiences he always treasured of
a buffalo-hunt in the Northern Territory, and this he does superlatively.
But the best parts of the book are in the bush and station descriptions,
and it would be difficult to imagine that Paterson's accurately drawn
picture of a station office at the turn of this century is much different from
its present day equivalent:

> The office looked like a blend of stationer's shop, tobacconist's store,
> and saddlery warehouse. A row of pigeon-holes along the walls was
> filled with letters and papers; the rafters were hung with saddles and
> harness; a tobacco-cutter and a jar of tobacco stood on the table, side
> by side with some formidable-looking knives, used for cutting the

sheep's feet when they became diseased; whips and guns stood in every corner; nails and saws filled up a lot of boxes on the table, and a few samples of wool hung from a rope that was stretched across the room. The mantelpiece was occupied by bottles of horse-medicine and boxes of cartridges; an elderly white cockatoo, chained by the leg to a galvanised iron perch, sunned himself by the door, and at intervals gave an exhibition of his latest accomplishment, in which he imitated the yowl of a trodden-on cat much better than the cat could have done it himself.

And finally there is continually and superbly illustrated throughout the novel Paterson's unerring handling of outback dialogues, and the quiet humour of his certain knowledge of the foibles of his bush characters. As for the former, there is the cameo of the drover's horse — a sketch that, brief as it is, could stand on its own in any anthology of bush anecdotes:

> Just as the coach was about to start a drover came out of the bar of the hotel, wiping his lips with the back of his hand. He stared vacantly about him, first up the street and then down, looked hard at a post in front of the hotel, then stared up and down the street again. At last he walked over, and, addressing the passengers in a body, said, "Did any of yous see e'er a horse anywheres? I left my prad here, and he's gorn."
>
> A bystander, languidly cutting up a pipeful of tobacco, jerked his elbow down the road.
>
> "That old bloke took 'im," he said. "Old bloke that come in the coach. While yous was all talking in the pub, he sneaks out here and nabs that 'orse, and away like a rabbit. See that dust on the plain? That's 'im!"
>
> The drover looked helplessly out over the stretch of plain. He seemed quite incapable of grappling with the problem.
>
> "Took my horse, did he? Well, I'm blowed! By Cripes!"
>
> He had another good stare over the plain, and back at the party.
>
> "My oath!" he added.
>
> Then the natural stoicism of the bushman came to his aid, and he said, in a resigned tone,
>
> "Oh, well, anyways, I s'pose — s'pose he must have been in a hurry to go somewheres. I s'pose he'll fetch him back some time or other."

And nothing is so true of the manner of news dissemination in the bush as when Mary Grant, en route to Kuryong, introduces herself to the garrulous hotel-owner, Mrs Connellan; the latter immediately tells the cook, who tells the landlord's son:

> Dan told the stationmaster when he went back for the next load, and when he had finished carting the luggage he got on a horse and went round telling everybody in the little town. The stationmaster told the ganger of the four navvies who went by on their trolley down the line to work. At the end of their four mile length they told the

ration-carrier of Eubindal station, who happened to call in at their
camp for a drink of tea. He hurried off to the head station with the
news, and on his way told three teamsters, an inspector of selections,
and a black boy belonging to Mylong station, whom he happened to
meet on the road. Each of them told everybody that they met, pulling
up and standing in their stirrups to discuss the matter in all its
bearings, in the leisurely style of the bush. . . .

Of those who have written on Paterson, only Brian Elliott[10] has effectively
made the point of the wider aspects of Paterson's talents shown in his
prose, and that here "out of his singing robes, he appears in strength",
most himself, as it were, and "best of all in short passages of digressive
reflection". This, combined with his humour, made him, as Elliott
describes him, "tantalizingly Australian", because, no matter how or
what he wrote, his style was always Australian, made up of a sort of
indolent cynicism and above all of his intimate knowledge of his country
and his people and of the moods of which they were blended. This
"happy intimacy with all sorts of queer people", as Elliott notes too, gave
him an unrivalled capacity to translate Australian dialogue to the printed
word. Indeed, I think this was the strongest, and, as in the case of Steele
Rudd, likely to be the most enduring quality of Paterson's prose —
reflected not so much in "queer" characters as in outback characters, in
the articles of mateship, in bush talk:

> Billy paused in his narrative. He knew that some suggestions would
> be made by way of compromise, to tone down the awful strength of
> the yarn, and he prepared himself accordingly. His motto was "no
> surrender" . . .
>   "That was a wonderful bit of ridin' you done, Billy," said one of
> the men at last, admiringly. "It's a wonder you wasn't killed. I
> suppose your clothes was pretty well tore off your back with the
> scrub?"
>   "Never touched a twig," said Billy.
>   "Ah!" faltered the inquirer, "then no doubt you had a real
> ringin' good stock horse that could take you through a scrub like
> that full-split in the dark, and not hit you against anything."
>   "No, wasn't a good un," said Billy decisively, "he was the worst
> horse in the camp. Terrible awkward in the scrub he was, always
> fallin' down on his knees; and his neck was so short you could sit far
> back on him and pull his ears."
>   Here that interrogator retired hurt; he gave Billy best. After a
> pause another took up the running.
>   "How did your mate get on, Billy? I s'pose he was trampled to a
> mummy!"
>   "No," said Billy, "he wasn't hurt a bit. I told you he was sleepin'
> under the shelter of a log. Well, when those cattle rested they swept
> over that log a thousand strong; and every beast of that herd took
> the log in his stride and just missed landing on Barcoo Jimmy by
> about four inches."

The men waited a while and smoked, to let this statement soak well into their systems; at last one rallied and had a final try.

"It's a wonder then, Billy," he said, "that your mate didn't come after you and give you a hand to steady the cattle."

"Well, perhaps it was," said Billy, "only that there was a bigger wonder than that at the back of it."

"What was that?"

"My mate never woke up all through it."

Then the men knocked the ashes out of their pipes and went to bed.[11]

NOTES

[1]   In *Singin' to the Cattle* (1947).
[2]   *Daily Telegraph*, 6 January 1906.
[3]   *Bulletin*, 5 September 1891.
[4]   *Bulletin*, 20 February 1892.
[5]   *Evening News*, 22 February 1905.
[6]   Op. cit.
[7]   *Bulletin*, 14 December 1895.
[8]   Included in his collection, *Three Elephant Power* (1917).
[9]   "'Banjo' Paterson: A Poet Nearly Anonymous", *Meanjin*, No. 4, 1964.
[10] Op. cit.
[11] "His Masterpiece" (*Bulletin*, 22 April 1891)

CHAPTER XIX

A Portrait from Memory

*. . . he was terribly fond of Australia, naturally, but he did
not make a very great parade of that. But you could sense
it the whole time — that he loved Australia and he loved the
bush of Australia, and anything to do with the Australian
way of life.*

— HUGH PATERSON.[1]

*He laid hold both of our affections and imaginations; he
had made himself a vital part of the country we all know
and love, and it would have been not only a poorer country
but one far less united in bonds of intimate feeling, if he
had never lived and written . . .*

— VANCE PALMER.[2]

PATERSON, BY THE VERDICT of his fellow-men, and by his own conduct and
precept, was, in every sense, a great Australian. Ballad-writer, horseman,
bushman, overlander, squatter, he helped make the Australian Legend
and yet in his lifetime was a living part of that legend, simply because he
had more than a touch of that very rare thing, the folk-poet: that he
could give body and outline to the ideas in the popular imagination.

Then, Paterson, again, was adventurer, traveller, man of two wars,
venturer into whatever unknown was possible for him — in the days
when distant travel, even within Australia, was an achievement. And even
before the thing became a cult of everyday Australian immortality,
Paterson was sportsman too: polo-player, cricketer, tennis-player, race-
rider, and in his off moments an enthusiastic fisherman. And finally, he
was a celebrity of the city, at the city's own values: newspaperman and
editor, novelist and essayist, man about town, clubman, lecturer, broadcaster, settling back in his sere years with the revived image of the
town-lawyer of his salad days.

And he was a man of singular personality in all this — even in the days
when he was launching himself on Sydney literary society. Take Norman
Lindsay's recollection of him at the turn of the century:

It is rare also that a superior spirit is given a superior casing, but
Paterson had it. A tall man with a finely built, muscular body,
moving with the ease of perfectly co-ordinated reflexes. Black hair,
dark eyes, a long, finely articulated nose, an ironic mouth, a dark

pigmentation of skin. . . . His eyes, as eyes must be, were his most distinctive feature, slightly hooded, with a glance that looked beyond one as he talked. If he focussed it on you, it could be tolerant or completely ruthless, as he accepted or rejected you as a human being . . .[3]

Lindsay has elaborated on this. In a radio interview[4] at one time, he called Paterson an aristocrat: ". . . there'll always be superior men who are aristocrats of the mind. On these men civilization exists — well, Banjo was one of them." He talked about Paterson's slight austereness and aloofness, not an offensive unsociability by any means, rather the habit of a man who kept just that certain distance between you and himself. Lindsay always remembered his eyes:

His eyes held you. When he looked at you, you dashed well looked at him, you know what I mean. And he had a rather — well he did not make any elocutionary way of speaking, he spoke simply and directly and with a slightly sardonic air — there was always that accent in Banjo. It's the typical Australian accent, you can't kid the Australian, you see. Banjo was that way.

His personality, unchanged in its elements, was mellowed by the years as it passed into the ken of those, younger than Lindsay, who remember him in the days after World War I. Sir Edward Knox recalls him[5] as a pleasant if taciturn neighbour and family man who loved his week-end tennis, partnered by his wife, "a most intelligent and well-read woman who must have been a great help to her husband in every way"; Peter Macgregor adds his recollection[6] of Alice Paterson, "a sweet gentle person".

Malcolm Ellis and Vince Kelly[7] join in their memory of Paterson as they met him from day to day or week to week around Sydney. There was his mode of dress: he always affected the style of the countryman in the city — broad-rimmed hat, tweedy suit.* He looked the part, too, Kelly remembers, because he never seemed to have lost "that outback tan — it was burned into his face, round his eyes, the lines of the bushman engraved on his face". His was (as his portraits of the time reveal) the classic bushman's head: a strong crop of iron-grey hair, always with the characteristic grizzled look. He was until his death wiry and limber in figure, despite his seventies. Vance Palmer recalled[8] meeting him in Sydney shortly before his death: ". . . a modest, grizzled, tough-looking old man, not very ready to talk about himself; knowing little, it seemed to me, of the great place he had in his country's affection. But he still kept his lively eye and his sardonic humour . . .". Vince Kelly has that particular recollection of his conversations with Paterson that he often referred to himself as the underdog — a harking back to his admiration for Archibald of the *Bulletin*. I asked Ellis if he remembered Paterson as a par-

---

* ". . . He always looker sartorially like a colonel of cavalry who had just left Tattersall's Sale Ring with a field-marshal after having bought a steeplechaser . . ." (M. H. Ellis in "Lindsay's Bohemia", *Bulletin*, 28 August 1965).

simonious man (since this might be inferred from Paterson's frequent
concern with royalties and advances in his correspondence with his
publishers). "Not parsimonious," replied Ellis, "but cautious, yes."

But caution in financial matters never masked his generosity of spirit.
In the same publishers' correspondence is letter after letter in which he
willingly agreed to the re-printing, free of charge, of his verses in antholo-
gies and text books. Even when irate friends brought forward examples of
the pirating of his ballads (country newspapers were the worst offenders,
in some cases even inventing a fictitious author), Paterson shrugged his
shoulders, as it were, and thought the most he could except would be an
"advertisement" (i.e., acknowledgement). C. H. Bateson remembers[9] the
times when Paterson, with his own copy to write up for the Sunday
Truth, sometimes worked extra hours (always uncomplainingly and
philosophically) to help out a fellow-reporter, who, through illness or
absence, could not come up to scratch.

Added to this was his sense of humour, of which instances have already
been given in his writings and in his ordinary life. Humour all his life
was his great stand-by: a homely, hearty humour, open as daylight. And
he spoke not merely for one class, but for all who were battling along in
the face of flood, drought, and disaster. Now he saw life through the eyes
of old Kiley who had to watch the country he had pioneered turned over
to the mortgagees; now through the eyes of Saltbush Bill fighting a well-
paid overseer for grass for his starving sheep; again through the eyes of
Clancy of The Overflow, riding happily through the smiling western
plains:

> While the stock are slowly stringing, Clancy rides behind them
>   singing,
> For the drover's life has pleasures that the townsfolk never know.

He lifted the settled gloom from our literature of the bush, as Douglas
Stewart once put it, and in so doing he let in the happy sunshine and
the fresh breezes of the plains.

The example I like best to illustrate Paterson's comfortable philosophy
came in his own words[10] when once he described an incident earlier on,
at the hey-day of his ballad-writing days. It was "up near the Diamantina", when "a bronze and bearded bushman about seven feet high nearly
wrung my hand off saying he had ridden thirty miles that day to shake
hands with the man who wrote 'When Your Pants Begin to Go'. Lawson
wrote that, but I didn't undeceive the giant, not knowing how he might
take it . . .".

And finally there was his modesty — a quality which endured all his
life. There are the many instances recorded in previous pages, beginning
from the days when he first began to have his verse published — "jingles"
which he could never quite understand should have been as popular as
they became. "I never aimed very high," he once said,[11] "in fact I never
aimed anywhere, but just wrote of the little things I knew about." His
son, Hugh, confirms[12] this endearing trait of his father — as an un-
emotional fact of family life:

No, he didn't like us children to write anything or say anything of his at all. He was very much against it and felt very embarrassed if people asked you to do it and always shut up if you did. He was very reticent about his writings.

. . . He enjoyed writing very much and he'd get an idea to write a thing and then he'd write it off, I imagine very quicky, and a lot of it was for his own amusement particularly some of the more amusing verses and then when he was frustrated with them he'd laugh about it himself. He never had any idea that they would become so important — these verses when he wrote them . . . He never valued them highly. He said he was just a bit of a jingle man . . .

". . . Dead men meet on the lips of living men," wrote Samuel Butler, but Paterson, long after the living who remember him have passed on, will continue to live on in the affections and the traditions of Australians. And this will be not only for what he wrote, but for what he will always mean to his people as the greatest of the literary pioneers of the outback as it once was, and as it will for ever exist in our imaginative life.

All this was based on experience, right into the very core of the heart of the land he sang about, and his own modest words enshrine his accomplishment:

Such was the material and such the work, rough and unpolished like its subject; and looking back on a long life I suppose I can account myself fortunate to have seen so much of the changes and developments in a new country. The "covered wagons" and the "nesters" of America had their counterparts in our bullock drays and our free selectors: the main difference being that in early American days individuals shot out their quarrels with revolvers, and the States shot out their quarrels in a Civil War. Luckily Australia was spared these experiences. Swinburne wrote in his "Triumph of Time"

It is not much that a man can save
  On the sands of life, in the straits of time,
Who swims in sight of the great third wave
  That never a swimmer shall cross or climb.

Some waif washed up with the strays and spars
  That ebb-tide shows to the shore and the stars,
Weed from the water, grass from a grave,
  A broken bloom, a ruined rhyme.

Our ruined rhymes are not likely to last long, but if there is any hope at all of survival it comes from the fact that such writers as Lawson and myself had the advantage of writing in a new country. In all museums throughout the world one may see plaster casts of the footprints of weird animals, footprints preserved for posterity; not because the animals were particularly good of their sort, but because they had the luck to walk on the lava while it was cooling. There is just a faint hope that something of the same sort may happen to us. . . .[13]

NOTES

[1] Spoken in an A.B.C. radio documentary, broadcast in 1964.
[2] In an A.B.C. broadcast tribute on the night of Paterson's death, 5 February 1941.
[3] In *Bohemians of the Bulletin* (1965).
[4] In the A.B.C. documentary referred to.
[5] In conversations with the author.
[6] Ibid.
[7] Ibid.
[8] In the radio broadcast referred to.
[9] In conversations with the author.
[10] In "Looking Backward".
[11] Ibid.
[12] In the A.B.C. documentary referred to.
[13] In "Looking Backward".

Bibliography

BOOKS BY A. B. PATERSON

The Man from Snowy River and Other Verses: Angus & Robertson: Sydney: 1895.

Rio Grande's Last Race and Other Verses: Angus & Robertson: Sydney: 1902.

The Old Bush Songs (Collected and Edited with an Introduction): Angus & Robertson: Sydney: 1905.

An Outback Marriage: Angus & Robertson: Sydney: 1906.

Saltbush Bill J.P. and Other Verses: Angus & Robertson: Sydney: 1917.

Three Elephant Power and Other Stories: Angus & Robertson: Sydney: 1917.

Collected Verse (The Man from Snowy River: Rio Grande: Saltbush Bill J.P.) : Angus & Robertson: Sydney: 1923.

The Animals Noah Forgot (verse) : Endeavour Press: Sydney: 1933.

Happy Dispatches: Angus & Robertson: Sydney: 1934.

The Shearer's Colt: Angus & Robertson: Sydney: 1936.

UNPUBLISHED MSS, ETC.

The Cook's Dog: 1919 (Mitchell Library, Sydney).

Racehorses and Racing in Australia: 1914 (Angus & Robertson Ltd., Sydney).

The Land of Adventure — Radio Scripts: 1935 (Australian Broadcasting Commission, Sydney).

Letters (included in George Robertson papers) : (Mitchell Library, Sydney).

MISCELLANEOUS UNCOLLECTED PROSE SKETCHES, ESSAYS, ETC.

"Australia for the Australians" Sydney: 1888.

"How I Shot the Policeman": *Bulletin*: 4 January 1890.

"My Various Schools", "More Reminiscences": *Sydneian*: May, August, 1890.

"The History of a Jackaroo": *Bulletin*: 5 September 1891.

"The Tug-of-War": *Bulletin*: 20 February 1892.

"Our Ambassador; or Sharp Practice on the Darling": *Bulletin*, 4 February 1893.

"Hughey's Dog: *Bulletin*: 17 February 1894.

"Bill and Jim Nearly Got Taken Down": *Bulletin*: 3 April 1897.

Review of "Where the Dead Men Lie and Other Poems" by Barcroft Boake: *Review of Reviews*: September, 1897.

"The Cycloon, Paddy Cahill and the G.R.": *Bulletin*: 31 December 1898.
"Polo": *The Australian Magazine*: 6 July 1899.
"Port Darwin, North Australia, Buffalo Shooting, etc.": *Eastern and Australian Steamship Co. Tourist Guide*: Dymocks: Sydney: 1899.
"A War Office in Trouble": *Bulletin*: 4 November 1899.
"The Offer of Troops", "Horses in Warfare", "The Mounted Infantry Horse": *The Story of South Africa* Vol. II: World Publishing Co.: Sydney: Undated (probably 1901 or 1902).
Preface to *For the Term of His Natural Life* by Marcus Clarke: Angus & Robertson: Sydney: 1899.
Boer War Despatches: *Sydney Morning Herald*: December, 1899, to September, 1900.
"J. F. Archibald — Great Australian Journalist": *Sportsman*, 25 January 1922.
"Dr Morrison: a Notable Australian: *Evening News*: 21 January 1903.
"Banjo Paterson Tells His Own Story", I-V: *Sydney Morning Herald*: 4 February to 4 March 1939.

ESSAYS AND STUDIES, ETC. ON A. B. PATERSON

Coombes, A. J.: "A. B. Paterson" *Some Australian Poets*: Angus & Robertson: Sydney: 1938.
Elliott, Brian: "Australian Paterson": *Australian Quarterly*: June, 1941.
Glasson, W. R.: "Famous Australian Poet": *Queensland Geographical Journal,* 1960/61.
Green, H. M.: "Banjo Paterson": *Fourteen Minutes*: Angus & Robertson: Sydney: 1944.
Green, H. M.: *A History of Australian Literature* Vol I, pp 360-370: Angus & Robertson: 1961.
Heseltine, H. P.: "Banjo Paterson: A Poet Nearly Anonymous": *Meanjin*, No. 4, 1964.
Hooper, Florence Earle: "Andrew Barton Paterson, A Memoir": *Yass Tribune-Courier*, I-VI, June-July, 1949.
Hooper, Florence Earle: "A. B. Paterson, Some Adjustments": *Southerly*, October 1949.
Howard, Donald: "So the Man from Snowy River is a Myth": *Riverlander*, September 1956.
Jose, A. W.: "Paterson and Lawson": *The Romantic Nineties*: Angus & Robertson: 1933.
Long, Gavin: "Young Paterson and Young Lawson": *Meanjin*, No. 4, 1964.
Macartney, F. T.: *Introduction* to *The Collected Verse of A. B. Paterson*: Angus & Robertson: 1965.
Macartney, F. T.: "Jostling Matilda": *Meanjin*, No. 3, 1965.
Manifold, John: "The Banjo": *Overland*: Spring/Summer, 1954/5.
Manifold, John: "The Australian Literary Balladists, etc.": *Who Wrote the Ballads?*: Australasian Book Society: Sydney: 1964.
May, Sydney: *The Story of Waltzing Matilda*: Smith & Paterson: Brisbane: 1944.

Mendelsohn, O.: *A Waltz with Matilda*: Lansdowne Press: Melbourne: 1966.

Palmer, Vance: "Literature Emerges": *The Legend of the Nineties*: Melbourne University Press: 1954.

Semmler, Clement: *A. B. "Banjo" Paterson*: Lansdowne Press, Melbourne: 1965.

Semmler, Clement: "Banjo Paterson and the Nineties": *Southerly*: Spring, 1964.

Sheridan, R. C.: "Banjo Paterson — A Biographical Note": *Biblioneus*, May 1951.

Stewart, Douglas: "Banjo, the Minstrel": *Bulletin*, Red Page (date unknown).

Stone, W. W.: "Materials Towards a Checklist of *Bulletin* Contributions by A. B. Paterson to 1902": *Biblionews*, December 1957.

Thomas, Elizabeth S.: *Banjo and His Grandmother* — a Play-reading in Three Scenes (Unpublished).

Ward, Russel: "The Man from Snowy River": *Hemisphere*, December 1957.

Ward, Russel: "Waltzing Matilda": *Australian Signpost*: Cheshire: Melbourne: 1956.

Unsigned: "The Banjo of the Bush": *Salt*, April 1945.

Unsigned: "Whose Matilda?": *Nation*, 27 November 1965.

Index

JUP